ADVANCE ACCLAIM FOR *THE CHURCH BUILDER*

"*The Church Builder* has it all. I love this book. Bethany is my kind of super hero. Smart, compassionate, and oh so wise."

—Lis Wiehl, best-selling author
of the Triple Threat series

"Don't miss this provocative tale by a craftsman at the top of his game. Besides being riveted and entertained, you will be challenged by *The Church Builder* to think in new ways."

—Jerry Jenkins, #1 *New York Times* best-selling
author of The Left Behind series and *I, Saul*

"Outstanding. Riveting and disturbing in equal measure, *The Church Builder* illuminates the battle between church and cult with gripping force. Highly recommended."

—Davis Bunn, best-selling
author of *Prayers of a Stranger*

THE CHURCH BUILDER

A NOVEL

A.L. SHIELDS

ZONDERVAN

The Church Builder

This title is also available as a Zondervan ebook. Visit www.zondervan.com/ebooks.

Requests for information should be addressed to:

Zondervan, *Grand Rapids, Michigan 49530*

ISBN 978-0-310-33861-1 (ITPE)

Library of Congress Cataloging-in-Publication Data

Shields, A. L.
The church builder : a novel / A.L. Shields.
pages cm. -- (The Church Builder Series ; 1)
ISBN 978-0-310-33211-4 (trade paper)
1. Hit-and-run drivers--Fiction. 2. Murder--Investigation--Fiction. I. Title.
PS3619.H535C45 2013
813'.6--dc23
2013015621

Printed in the United States of America

13 14 15 16 17 18 19 20 /RRD/ 20 19 18 17 16 15 14 13 12 11 10 9 8 7 6 5 4 3 2 1

To the people of St. Luke's Episcopal Church

PROLOGUE

Annabelle Seaver saw the inside of five different churches on the rainy March day the car ran her down, and people said later that she must have been very pious or in a great deal of pain, and her family insisted that she was both. To be sure, none of her relatives had heard from her in months, but as they admitted to the police, this was not unusual. Although Annabelle had been a quiet, reflective child, she had grown into a decisively flighty adult, loosely tethered to the world of convention, and prone to vanish for weeks or more. And, no, nobody had any idea what she was doing in Washington, D.C. The family had sort of lost track. The police quickly dug up the business about rehab, and of course, a couple of years back, the ninety days in a suburban Chicago jail for possession. Friends said her family had disowned her at that point, although her sister Polly insisted that Annabelle had disowned herself. But Polly, from the same painful beginnings, had made something of herself, whereas Annabelle manifestly had not.

The car came streaking toward the alley behind U Street Christian Church, after the Wednesday night Bible study group had barred the back door to keep Annabelle from sneaking back in. Not that they knew her name. They had asked, of course, but she hadn't answered. She had barged into the meeting, noisily and showily, just as Brother Everson was discoursing on what his boyhood pastor down in Tennessee had said was the right understanding of the phrase "armor of God" in Ephesians 6, and although some of the members admitted to police later that they had been suspicious from the moment of her arrival, they were under a general injunction to welcome the stranger. Sister Murray took one look at the wild eyes and scuffed jeans and the way she clutched at her battered knapsack and made sure that this particular stranger knew where the coffee was.

What happened next was unclear. The press accounts, copied from the police reports, simply referred to the stranger as "disruptive." At some point the disruption became intolerable, and they put her forcibly out. Later on, when the bombings began in earnest, it would turn out to matter a great deal what Annabelle had been shouting as they assisted her into the alley, but the good people of U Street Christian could be pardoned for thinking that they were listening to the ravings of a madwoman.

The stranger—said witnesses—seemed disoriented to find herself outdoors once more. She kept frowning at the door, as if hoping to open it by force of will. At last she began to walk, still clutching the bag. There was no way out of the alley but toward U Street, and U Street was where the car was waiting, dark and muddy, something foreign, the witnesses agreed, unless of course it was American, which they also thought was possible. There was a driver inside, male or possibly not, and there were also two other men, or one, or none. But the car was waiting: on that everybody concurred. The car was waiting on the street for Annabelle Seaver to emerge from U Street Christian, and, come to think of it, might have followed her there to begin with.

As soon as Annabelle stepped from the alley, the car turned up its lights and streaked toward her. She stood, eyes wide but still addled, holding one palm out as if to stop the car via supernatural means.

The car struck.

The young woman flipped up and back, like a circus acrobat, landing in a heap several feet down the alley. The car backed up and roared forward again, evidently meaning to run her over, and it would have done so very easily—on this, too, the witnesses agreed, as did the forensics team, later that night—but somehow the bumper clipped a light pole that it should have cleared by a good two feet, knocking the car off course, and it only crushed her legs instead of smashing her to bits. By now a crowd had gathered, and there was no time for a third try. The car backed up, bumper dragging, and shuddered off down the street.

The car was found within hours, abandoned in a fast food parking lot half a mile away. It turned out to have been stolen. No prints. No clues. No suspects. On the way to the hospital, Annabelle opened her eyes long enough to grab the arm of one of the paramedics and ask him a single quite lucid question: "Where's my backpack?" But she was dead before he could tell her that he knew nothing about it. The police, overwhelmed with work as always, never even bothered to look.

Big mistake.

PART ONE

PERCEPTION

God sometimes expresses his wrath towards wicked men in this world not only outwardly but also in the inward expressions of it on their consciences.

—Jonathan Edwards, preaching
on 1 Thessalonians 2:16

ONE

As lawyers go, Bethany Barclay was nobody, especially in the District of Columbia and its environs, where every attorney who matters is in a big firm or in government service or shuttling between the two. Bethany had a small practice way out in Virginia, and therefore counted less than zero in legal circles. But the nightmare swept her up all the same.

The beginning was deceptively normal: a May afternoon crisp with sunshine, the first fair day after what seemed a month of rain. Bethany was in her office, behind her desk, massaging her temples and trying to work out the cause of her lingering migraine. The candidates were—one—that it was less than a week until Mother's Day, an occasion Bethany would observe as usual in North Carolina with Aunt Claudia, whom she loved and dreaded. Or—two—that before leaving on Friday for the six-hour drive, she would likely be laying off Will, her paralegal, whom she had kept on well past the point where she could afford him, the solo practice of law being what it was. Bethany adored Will, and his wife, and their baby, and cringed at the thought of wrecking their already shaky fisc, but her accountant had laid the figures before her, and she knew she had no choice. Unless of course she dipped into her mad money, the several thousand dollars she kept in cash and inviolate, because her mad father had taught her always to have ready to hand the means for getting out of town in a hurry.

Candidate number three involved the lingering effects of her lunch with

Thelma McKittrick, who sought to enlist Bethany in her doomed campaign to bring liturgical dance to their church, an Episcopal congregation dating to before the Revolution.

"We're so old-fashioned," said Thelma.

"I think people like it that way," said Bethany, remembering how the senior warden had recently sent out a note reminding the members of the impropriety of applause during Sunday services.

The fourth possible cause of the searing migraine was the failure of Bethany's most recent foray into the world of self-discipline, an effort that had ended two nights ago, her nemesis the package of Oreo Minis in the cabinet above the refrigerator. No doubt Aunt Claudia would spend half the weekend tut-tutting, but then would reassure Bethany in her gently devastating way that there were men (a few men, Claudia would say) who preferred their women a little stout. The fifth candidate was tonight's dinner at her cousin Eva's, over in Warrenton, an event almost certain to be heralded by the presence of yet another unsuitable man. Bethany knew she would be required to feign a degree of interest, the better to fortify herself against the barrage of sweet reminders she would soon be suffering from Aunt Claudia, who was bound to point out that Bethany would be thirty in three months, which in her aunt's cosmology was the magical age at which eligible bachelors vanished from the face of the earth.

But perhaps the most likely cause of Bethany's migraine was candidate number six, the fact that at this moment, here in her inner office, a furious client was threatening a malpractice suit—or, more precisely, the only son of a former client, Mrs. Kirkland, who had died last week. Ken Kirkland, the son in question, had been all but written out of his mother's will, as had his two sisters, so of course they blamed the lawyer who had done the writing, and that lawyer was Bethany.

"Did you really think I'd let you get away with this?" He pounded a fist into a palm. "We're going to sue you for everything you've got!"

"I'm not sure what I'm supposed to have gotten away with," said Bethany, fingers digging into her palms to keep her voice calm as the headache grew bright and sharp. She was the sort of churchgoer who was more familiar with the Book of Common Prayer than the Bible, but her Aunt

Claudia had taught her to recite Proverbs 3:5–6 in her head whenever the stress threatened to become unbearable. She recited it now, and felt her breathing slow.

Her serenity was like a goad to him. "I'm serious, Bethany. You make this right or you're finished in this town."

Ken was now pacing her office, the back room on the first floor of a period Victorian cottage on Route 522, now converted to professional space. A dentist had the suite upstairs, and the whine of his drill was buzzing through the ceiling, as it did several times each day.

"I did what my client asked me to," she said. "Your dispute is with your late mother, not me."

Ken spun around, brown eyes wild, and for a mad moment she thought he was going to slap her. Payback. After all, Bethany had slapped his face twelve years ago almost to the day, when he had attempted to take certain untoward liberties after the senior prom at Pennville High. Kenny, as he was known in those days, captained the Pennville football team, and considered the girls in the school his natural property. A fair number were complaisant, but Bethany had been raised otherwise. Her college roommate used to tease her about wanting to save herself for her husband, but Aunt Claudia, who raised her, liked to say that being exactly unlike everybody else was what made a woman attractive.

"Come on, Beth." Ken had to know she hated the nickname, but at least his voice had dropped a few decibels. She reminded herself that the Kirklands were a power out here. His grandfather had built a local empire in real estate, and in rural Virginia, land was everything. Ken now controlled a piece of the empire, but his mother had controlled a much bigger piece; and had left very little of her fortune to her children.

"Your client was non compos mentis," Ken was saying. "Seriously." He had slipped over to the charming, syrupy tone that was supposed to make her melt. Ken was the sort who could switch moods in an instant, because none of them were real. His spit-shined black boots with side buckles, eight hundred dollars a pair, winked at her as they caught the sunlight. "My mother was declining for years. She wasn't in any shape to make decisions about her legal affairs."

"She seemed fine to me," Bethany said, or started to, but her cell phone beeped. "Wait," she said, lifting a finger. A text message, from an unknown sender:

don't listen to him

Bethany stared at the screen. The throbbing in her temple continued to bloom. She rubbed the spot. A coincidence, she decided. A joke. The message pertained to something else entirely, not the self-important small-town pooh-bah looming over her desk. She snapped the phone closed. Her hand trembled. Ken noticed. He noticed everything, especially where women were concerned.

"Are you okay?" he asked, voice rich with sympathy. He gestured toward the phone. "Bad news?"

A coincidence, she reminded herself. Nothing to do with Kenneth Kirkland. Because the alternative was to put the text message in the same mental box with a lot of other odd things that had happened over the past few weeks, like the woman in the mirrored sunglasses who kept showing up in the aisle next to hers at the supermarket and the CVS, and the silver Jeep she had noticed parked outside her house a couple of times, and all the other peculiar little distractions she had endured in the two months since the car ran Annabelle down—and if Bethany started thinking along those lines, she would have to concede not only that she was getting paranoid at the ripe old age of twenty-nine, but that she had something to be paranoid about.

The thought of Annabelle brought a cascade of memories she had managed, with difficulty, to keep at bay. They had called each other running buddies, and had been best friends since rooming together freshman year at Barnard. True, Bethany had been a follower of the rules, a hard worker, a bit of a loner, and Annabelle quite the opposite on every count; but both had been raised by powerful, pious aunts, and they turned out to have commonalities galore. They had traveled the world together, shared stories of bad employers and bad dates, and the last time they had laid eyes on each other, when Annabelle visited last November, they had quarreled—

Tears were suddenly very close. Bethany stood up, fighting the pain of the pounding migraine; and of her best friend's passing. In her mind, she switched to Psalm 16, another of Aunt Claudia's favorites, and forced a smile onto her round face. "I'm sorry, Ken. I have to be at the other end of town.

If you have a complaint about the will, you should file your objection in the probate court."

He leaned closer. "This is personal, isn't it?" he said, with the executioner's gentleness. "You're still mad at me after all these years." He lifted a hand, and likely would have touched her face had she not stepped hastily back. "My mother was nuts, but you changed her will anyway. It was to get back at me, wasn't it?"

Naturally. In the world of Kenneth Kirkland, everything that happened was about him. Bethany said, "This has nothing to do with—"

Her phone beeped.

She looked down, grew queasy. "Gotta go," she said.

Five minutes later, Bethany was in her sensible Volvo XC90, eggshell blue, cruising along the county highway toward her cousin's house, trying to summon a little optimism about the matchmaking to be endured, determined not to worry about Ken's silly threats, and refusing absolutely to think about the last text message:

tell him his mother was sane

I'm nobody, Bethany kept telling herself as she drove far too fast through the sun-dappled meadows of her changing county: miles of grazing cattle broken here and there by the rising weekend mansions of the Washington rich. I'm nobody, she repeated, and things like this don't happen to nobodies, it's all my imagination, none of this is real. On and on she whispered her comforting mantra, unaware that she would never be nobody again.

TWO

The tricky part of building a bomb is surviving the experience," the specialist was saying. "The science is trivial. A ten-year-old could do it. There are parts of the world where ten-year-olds *do* do it. Those"—sweeping a hand toward the shelves—"are made with plastique. A little easier to mold, a lot safer to build with, but harder to obtain, and illegal to possess. Whereas this one"—indicating the work table, where he had been grinding metal into shavings—"is going to be thermite."

"It looks like tinfoil," said the woman sitting beside him. The room was cramped and shadowy, the only illumination the halogen lamp mounted on a pole beside the table. She felt uneasy, alone like this with this peculiar little man and the implements of his deadly trade, but he knew what he was doing, and she had to learn.

The specialist nodded. He wore thin sterile surgical gloves, and a metal smock. His fingers moved with delicate authority. "Aluminum foil, actually. We're going to use iron oxide to excite the oxidation process in the aluminum. This will produce a reaction that generates something like 2,000 degrees Celsius." He was pouring a mixture of metallic powders, silver and brown, into a metal cigar case. "That's twice as hot as, say, napalm." He looked at her. "Do you believe in God?"

"No."

"The afterlife?"

"No."

"In that case you might want to back off a little. If the thermite should ignite accidentally, it will burn through me and you in milliseconds. It will incinerate the table and the chairs. Then it will burn a hole in the floor."

Her stomach somersaulted. "The floor is concrete."

"Precisely."

She slid several feet away, watched while he measured magnesium for the fuse. She wished he hadn't made her join him in this creepy room. She didn't understand why he couldn't have met her somewhere and handed over the bomb. But she had been instructed not to upset his aplomb for any reason.

"There's some disagreement about the proper ratio." He shined a penlight into the tube, tamped down the contents, added more powder. "Some people say four-to-one, some will tell you three-to-two. I myself have found that two-to-one is ideal if the ignition is enclosed."

"If thermite is so dangerous," she asked, too loudly, "why don't we use plastic explosive? You have plenty."

"Number one, plastique is too sophisticated. This one has to look like anyone could have made it." He cut the magnesium panel with a pair of clippers, leaving the edge ragged. He twisted it into the cigar case, and left the end hanging out. "Number two, the plastique is easier for the authorities to trace."

"I thought we wanted it traced."

"In time. Not yet. Later. Hand me the cap."

She picked up the freshly machined plug for the case, also made of magnesium. It occurred to her that she wasn't wearing gloves, and it evidently occurred to him, too, because he polished the surface with a silk cloth, rubbing away her prints. Then he held the plug beneath a magnifier, turning it this way and that, inspecting it for she knew not what.

"Are you almost done?" she asked. The thought of her body incinerating still had her nerves tingling.

"This is the last one." Apparently satisfied, the specialist screwed the cap onto the cigar case. He laid it beside three others in its own specially cut groove in a metal cylinder. "The thermite isn't an explosive in the strict sense. But when you burn it in the tight cylinder, the gases and heat have nowhere to go, so the cylinder explodes. Do you understand?"

"Yes."

"Does dying frighten you?"

"Of course it does."

"Do you wish to die gloriously? To etch your name in history?"

"Not particularly."

"Then perhaps you are not suited for this work. The best bombers accept that their own deaths might be required." He held the cylinder toward her. "Here. Come closer. Look. You open the bottom. Like so. Coiled inside the bottom is the fuse, a filament wire, also magnesium. You extend it. Be careful. The wire is fragile. Don't break it, or the bomb will fail. You light it—here—with an igniter."

"Then what?"

"Then you run. Fast. You will have perhaps two minutes to get clear."

She swallowed. "That isn't much time."

"You wanted portable, I built portable."

The woman stiffened. "Why can't I use a timer? Or a remote control?"

"They add weight and they are not reliable. Also, you want to make her out a fanatic. This is the sort of risk a fanatic would take." He laid the box aside. "Also, you wanted crude. This is crude. You say she has a workshop."

"A shed in the backyard."

He handed her a plastic bag. "These are filings from when I machined the magnesium. Scatter a few. Not many. And only in corners or under furniture. It must look as if she tried very hard to clean up."

"Maybe I should leave a few in plain sight. To make sure they're found."

"No. Do exactly as I say, and don't improvise. You must not make matters too easy, or the authorities may grow suspicious. This way, not only will the forensic people find the filings, but they will be proud of themselves for their cleverness."

She turned the bag in her hands, watching in fascination as the dull gray filings tumbled. He was right. Two or three, no more, piled in with other dust and debris. Add it to the other carefully planted evidence, all of it showing signs of attempted concealment, and their target would soon be the sole suspect. She almost felt sorry for the poor woman.

Almost.

THREE

I don't think you're crazy at all," says Judge Harrigan with a sardonic grin. "No crazier than I am, anyway. You're worried about a couple of text messages. I once had a pro se litigant leave a poisonous snake in my mailbox after I dismissed his case. I had a terrible time getting anybody to believe me."

Bethany Barclay is curled on the sofa, facing the mammoth fireplace, two stories high and of cut fieldstone. She is wearing a business suit. Her shoeless feet are tucked beneath her. Her fingers are wrapped around a mug of cocoa. She takes a sip, savors the warmth, and the slightly smoky aftertaste. Edna Harrigan has never disclosed her secret recipe, even to her closest friends, or those who, like Bethany, she has mentored along.

"Everybody else thinks I'm crazy," Bethany says. It is the Monday after Mother's Day and she is just back from North Carolina. "My friends. My cousins. My aunt."

Judge Harrigan's smile fades. She is sitting primly in an armchair, this tiny dynamo of eighty-three years, wearing her daily uniform of jeans and sweater and sneakers, silvered hair in an unruly bun. Glasses hang on a gold chain. Pale eyes are narrowed and reflective. Once upon a time she was the first woman to serve on the Supreme Court of Virginia, as she was the first to do many other things. Twice she was a finalist for elevation to the Supreme Court of the United States. Rumor said she twice removed herself from consideration. She never wed. She never bore children. She values her solitude. She seems to take a secret enjoyment in knowing that those few who remember her seem to assume that she is dead.

"Don't tell anybody else," Judge Harrigan commands, sternly.

Bethany yawns. "Because they'll put me in the booby hatch."

The judge's tone of correction never slackens. "Because somebody might start believing you. That's the danger."

The younger woman sits up sharply. "What are you talking about?"

Judge Harrigan stands, leaning on her ornately colored cane. The tip is stainless steel, and makes a clopping sound when she walks. When Bethany begins to rise, the older woman waves her still, then strides toward the window. She does not lean on the cane exactly: she thrusts it into the period hardwood floor, which everywhere bears the nicks and scrapes of her passing. It is Bethany's secret theory that the cane is an affectation, even a bit of misdirection. Edna Harrigan wants the world to think her less able than she is.

"Let's go over the facts," says the judge. The telephone begins to ring, an aging wall unit in the open kitchen, but she ignores it. Bethany, trained as all lawyers are to respond instantly to the sound, sits up and looks around nervously. Edna Harrigan never budges. The ringing stops, and Bethany subsides. The judge is still at the window, which, like the room itself, is two stories high. She is gazing out at the lazy spring sun settling along the horizon of her sixty private acres, grassy near the house, woods in the distance. Beyond the trees are unseen fields, where she lets local farmers graze cattle. The woods are posted against trespassers. A few years ago, Judge Harrigan took a shot at a hunter, and nobody has bothered her since. "Let's work out a solution to your problem."

"That's why I'm here," says Bethany. She sips her cocoa.

The judge glances over her shoulder as if suspecting her protégé of insolence, then turns back to the glass. "Very well. The facts. Sylvia Kirkland was pretty much the wealthiest woman in two counties, not counting the ones who drive out from Washington on the weekends. She comes to you to rewrite her will. Now, this should have struck you as odd from the beginning. The Kirklands have always handled their family business through a firm down in Charlottesville. I assume you knew that."

"I knew that," the younger woman concedes.

"So, what did she do? Walk in off the street? Tell you she was unhappy with her current representation?"

"She made an appointment."

"And you asked how she got your name?"

Bethany nods, but answers slowly, picking her way through the minefield of ethics. "She was referred by a mutual friend. She didn't say who."

Judge Harrigan makes her wait. The faint distant rumble of thunder rides the wind. "It would have been interesting to find out, don't you think?" *Don't you think*: the way the judge has always given orders, including back when Bethany served as her law clerk. "Number two. She tells you she wants to leave everything—almost everything—to a man you've never heard of. Martin Potus his name is, correct?"

"Correct."

"I assume you Googled him at least. Mr. Potus."

Bethany lets out a long breath. She is guessing what tone the judge wants. "He runs some silly outfit in Chicago telling people how to get rich quick."

"He runs a religious cult," says the judge, coldly. "There's nothing else to call it." She does not wait to be told whether she is right or wrong. "Number three. Mrs. Kirkland dies, the family turns out to have no idea that Mommy redrew her will, they threaten to sue—"

The telephone rings again. Judge Harrigan's eyes swivel toward it in distaste. Perhaps a dozen people in the world have the number, and half of them reside in nursing homes. The ringing continues. The judge clenches her fists. Bethany is too savvy to offer to answer. "One moment, my dear," the older woman finally says, and strides angrily across the foyer, ferrule stabbing the floor. She picks up the phone, which hangs on the tiles beside the refrigerator. She says nothing, just listens. Bethany watches her, this woman who has accomplished nearly everything in life, yet sits alone in her converted farmhouse, without family or companion or even maid, for Edna Harrigan does all the cleaning and cooking herself.

"I see," says the judge finally, and "I will"—and then, without any pleasantries, she hangs up. Although Judge Harrigan's expression never changes, Bethany has a shrewd intuition that her mentor has received bad news. Perhaps it is the way she hesitates briefly, glaring at the silent phone as she might at a betrayer. Perhaps it is the way she stabs her cane into the wooden planks even more aggressively as she returns to her place by the window.

Either way, the judge resumes the conversation as if it was never interrupted. "Tell me more, my dear," she says. "Mrs. Kirkland comes along, tells you she wants to leave her money to a cult. So you took her measure, of course? Satisfied yourself that she was compos mentis?"

"That isn't my job."

"Of course it is," says the judge, blandly. "Rule 1.14(b)."

"Which doesn't require me to make an assessment. It only says I shouldn't act if I have a reasonable belief—"

"Morality requires the assessment." A moment for this to sink in. "And so does the rule. If her impairment was obvious, you could face sanctions. Reprimand. Maybe even suspension." Another pause. "Never mind, dear. Let's deal with the problem of the moment. You get these funny text messages while you're with Kenny Kirkland. You also think people are following you. At first you think these are his friends, giving you a hard time, but now you're not so sure. Fair?"

Bethany swallows. Stated so baldly, her story sounds absurd. "Yes."

"And it's gotten worse over the past week?"

"I told you, I had a break-in at my house—"

"In which you told the sheriff nothing was taken."

"Yes, but I know it was them."

The cane beats a tattoo on the floor. "*How* do you know, my dear?"

Bethany shakes her head, feeling smaller by the second. "I just know," she says miserably.

"You hired people to sweep your office. Check your phones. Your house. No bugs. Correct?"

A moment. "Yes."

"But you think somebody's listening." A pause. "You just don't know who they are. Correct?"

"Yes." Bethany is hunched now, knees drawn up to her chest, head down, eyes shut. "There are ways to intercept cell phone signals. I looked it up. With the right equipment, you can fool the phone into thinking it's in contact with the carrier when it's not, even where there's no service. Once you fool the phone, sending text messages is easy. But I don't know who it is."

"What about the people Mrs. Kirkland left the money to?"

"That was my guess. But why would they be bugging me? I'm defending their right to the money!"

"Perhaps they didn't know that when they started," says Judge Harrigan. "Perhaps they weren't sure what you would do. They are strange people, my dear. Paranoid. Possibly violent. You should have done more checking." Her tone never changes, even as she finally voices the one question that mattered. "And how much is it, Bethany? The residuum after the family gets their share, after taxes and claims and so forth?"

"Eleven million dollars and change."

"Well, my dear, for eleven million dollars, you should learn a little more about the recipient. Wouldn't you agree?"

"Yes, but—"

"You should go to Chicago," says the judge, and Bethany knows at once that her mentor has been working around to this advice for some time. "You should take a look. See for yourself."

Bethany licks her lips. Even after all these years, disagreeing with the judge costs her something. "I don't think there's anything I can learn there that I can't learn here." She hesitates. "Even assuming you're right. I still don't think I'm in any trouble."

Edna Harrigan's eyes are half lidded. "Except for one small detail, my dear."

"What detail is that?"

"If you exercised undue influence over a sick woman—if you caused Mrs. Kirkland to change her will for your own benefit—then you might be disbarred. Even prosecuted."

This brings Bethany at last to her feet. "What undue influence? I'm not benefitting!"

"Martin Potus is."

"So?"

"So, Potus isn't his real name." The sardonic grin is back. "It's well buried, dear, but he seems to have stolen someone's identity. The real Martin Potus died years ago. And that's not the worst of it."

Bethany was afraid to ask. "What's the worst of it?"

"I'm afraid you know him."

The old woman watches her protégé steering down the winding gravel drive, the eggshell blue of her Volvo seeming to wink as it reflects the westering sun. When the car disappears, the judge picks up the phone and dials a number.

"Hello, Edna," says the man at the other end. "Please make this brief. I'm in Beijing. On my way to a meeting."

"She didn't go for it."

"I see."

"I thought the text messages would be enough to get her moving. She was scared, naturally, but she has considerable internal resources." The judge gazes out at her property, pondering the costs of betrayal. "She's an impressive young woman. You should meet her."

"Let's hope that never becomes necessary." The voice from Beijing is stiff. "Are you sure you're covered? Technologically, I mean?"

"Lillian says there's no way for Bethany to know. The device works by spoofing the chip in her phone so she thinks she's in touch with her carrier, but really—"

"And you're still confident that Lillian is secure?"

"We've been friends for thirty years."

"Who operated the device?"

"My nephew. He's a good boy. You have to trust me." The man at the other end makes no response. The ball is in Edna's court. "It's not over," she insists. "The plan can still work. There are things we can still do. Ways to get Bethany to change her mind."

A beat.

"That's entirely your call, Edna."

"I just wanted to bring you up-to-date."

"Consider me updated. Now, if you'll excuse me, I have to get over to the Ministry."

"I'll call you if anything changes."

"No hurry."

He hangs up.

FOUR

Bethany lived in a two-family house at the north edge of town. A gaggle of ever-changing, ever-sullen teenaged girls drifted through the other half, some of them students at the community college, some of them clerks at the shopping mall, some of them both. All the way home, she fumed. *Martin McAdams.* Martin Potus was Martin McAdams.

How could she not have known?

Martin McAdams, the college sweetheart who long ago had broken her heart. Martin McAdams, spellbinding but lazy. Martin McAdams, whom she hadn't seen since graduation. Martin McAdams who three years ago changed his name, returned to his hometown of Chicago, and founded the World Foundation for the Fulfillment of God's Personal Plan.

God's Planners, they called themselves; and here she was, helping a client turn over eleven million dollars to him.

Judge Harrigan was right. Bethany was in trouble. But she had no idea what to do about it. She had made the sort of mistake that could not only end her career but lead to personal liability. Slowed by a lumbering dump truck, she wanted to scream. She gritted her teeth instead. She had excelled in college, spent time at Oxford, then attended Harvard Law School. She had joined a mammoth law firm in Washington, only to quit the next year and hang out her shingle back here in Flint Hill. She had wanted to be close to her dying father, and to find a slower pace of life.

That was three years ago. Her father was two years in the ground, but Bethany had stayed on.

She had not expected anything like this.

There was no way she could have known. She had Googled Martin Potus, of course, and spent a couple of hours studying his group. No hint of the identity theft had come up. Because of the work she did, she subscribed to a variety of websites that did criminal background checks and the like. None of them had so much as hinted—

She slowed; almost turned around.

How had Judge Harrigan known?

If Google didn't know that Martin Potus and Martin McAdams were the same person, if none of her usual sources knew, then how could her beloved mentor possibly know?

If only she could talk to Annabelle. Her running buddy would have seen the comic side of the predicament. She would have taken the text messages and Sylvia Kirkland's will and Martin and all the rest, and rolled them into a story that would have had Bethany splitting her sides. It had been a good while since she had laughed like that.

But Annabelle was in the ground, too.

Well, fine. She would make up her own mind. She would find out the easy way. As soon as she got home, she would call Judge Harrigan and ask.

When Bethany pulled into the driveway, another car was blocking her garage. The girls must be having a party. They entertained constantly, and they mostly invited the kind of friends who did not much care whether they blocked your egress. Bethany went over to knock on their door, but there was no music or laughter from behind it, and it occurred to her that late afternoon this early in the week was a funny time to have a party. She knocked anyway but nobody seemed to be home. Turning, she noticed that her own door was ajar.

Bethany hesitated.

She had a gun. Her late father had insisted on it once she went out into the world—meaning, once she started dating—and so on his rare visits to Aunt Claudia's he had taught her to shoot, finally buying her a 9 mm Smith & Wesson Sigma because, he said, those tiny guns most ladies carried wouldn't stop the crack-crazed escaped prisoner whom Everett Barclay was certain lurked behind every tree. Bethany couldn't remember when she had last held it in her hands. For a while she used to go target shooting with old Sam DeMarco, an occasional client who lived way out on the county road. Sam, if you believed half his tales, had done a thing or two in his day, but six or eight months ago he had decamped to the Midwest. Besides, the gun was safely in its lockbox, and the lockbox was in her bedroom, which was a long way to run when an intruder might be waiting inside.

Bethany backed toward her car, then fished out her cell phone, figuring that she would rather be the fool who called the police when she didn't need to than the other way around.

That was when she noticed the shoe.

The shiny black boot with side buckles that she saw around town constantly, and in her office yesterday. There it was, propping the door open. This was just more of Ken Kirkland's shenanigans. She might owe him an apology—if Judge Harrigan was right, she might wind up owing him more than that—but he still had no business barging into her house.

Bethany marched through the door, calling Ken's name, and almost stumbled over him. He was on the kitchen floor. His eyes were wide open, but would never see again. There was blood everywhere, and lying beside him was her gun, and, now, her footprints and fingerprints too, because she was cradling him.

And arose covered with blood.

The staging was perfect.

Her gun, from her lockbox, and she alone knew the combination.

Her gun, which now had her prints all over it.

Everybody knew that Bethany and Ken had been feuding for years, and everybody would soon think they knew that he had caught her funneling his mother's millions to an ex-boyfriend.

In her mind's eye the cell door was already slamming shut.

Bethany backed down the hall on trembling legs. Her father had always made her keep emergency cash in the car, and lots more around the house, just as he had made her keep the gun, but when she peeked into the spare room she used as a study the safe was standing open and there was more blood.

And not just blood.

Daubed on the wall, in what she hoped was red paint, was an odd squiggly line, like a stylized letter S. It was only three or four inches high but it was right beside the safe, where she couldn't miss it. The top of the S was split at the end, with what looked like an arrow protruding from it. It took Bethany a moment to understand what she was seeing.

She was looking at a snake.

The police were pointedly polite, the way they behave when they expect you to confess on the spot. As the technicians photographed and swabbed and bagged, the detectives kept suggesting that she might want to talk in more comfortable surroundings. But Bethany was a lawyer, and knew she had no obligation to go with them anywhere, and the last thing she wanted was to face those cajolingly unfriendly smiles across a rickety table in an interrogation room.

Especially given that they obviously thought she did it.

A female detective named Florio told her she might consider staying somewhere else tonight, and Bethany assured her that she would never sleep in her house again.

"Do you have a friend we can call?"

"Thank you. I'll be fine."

"Boyfriend, maybe?" the detective asked pointedly. She was a small woman but confident. She wore a tailored pinstriped suit, and had a habit, when asking a question, of hitching back the tails of the jacket aggressively to show the sidearm on her hip.

"No."

"Family?"

"I can take care of myself."

"You wouldn't be thinking of leaving town, would you?"

"Are you asking me to stay, Detective Florio?" Because Bethany also knew that although everyone is required to follow all lawful orders of the police, the police possess no actual authority to make you stay where you don't want to be.

Not unless they place you under arrest.

Bethany thought the interview was done. She gathered some things from the bathroom but wanted nothing else from the house. She always kept a packed overnight bag in the trunk of her Volvo, along with some extra cash: two more of her father's crazy ideas that had rubbed off, because Everett Barclay had made a lifelong specialty of getting out of places fast.

Florio was standing right outside the bathroom door. "This is your gun, isn't it?" she asked, indicating an evidence bag of thick, clear plastic, already tagged.

"It certainly looks like mine."

"Did you touch it?"

"I told you. My prints are all over it."

"Because you picked it up when you found the body. Right." Florio's narrowed eyes announced what she thought of this story. "By the way, that's red paint on the wall, not blood."

"I see."

"And, Bethany, I have to confess. To me, it just looks like a smear. Not an S."

"Ms. Barclay."

"I'm sorry?"

"I'm an officer of the court, Detective Florio. I'd prefer to keep this formal."

"Ms. Barclay." The voice was correct, yet faintly mocking. The dark eyes were growing larger and more insistent. "We found a can of red paint next to the shed out back."

Bethany rubbed the bridge of her nose. "Look at the shed. It's red. I repainted it."

"Recently?"

"Two weeks ago." She let out a long breath. "I left the can inside. On a shelf. Whoever did this must have moved it."

The detective's gaze never wavered. "Possibly."

"As opposed to what?" Bethany was growing angrier by the second, as probably she was intended to. "Have you found the car? The one that was in my driveway when I got home?"

"You mean the one that nobody else saw and you can't describe?"

"I told you, it was red."

"I remember." The detective made a note. "Anybody else have a grudge against Mr. Kirkland that you know of?"

"I don't know what 'else' means."

Detective Florio smiled, and repeated the request that Bethany not leave the county. The smile never reached those searching eyes.

"Does that mean I can go now?"

"Of course."

"Thank you."

"One more thing," said the detective as they descended the steps together: just like in the movies.

"Yes?"

"Didn't I read somewhere that your father did time in prison for fraud?"

"Eighteen months. I was three years old."

"And three years for assault when you were ten, isn't that right?"

She drove off thinking not of Ken's body but of Detective Florio's dark, intelligent eyes: like father, like daughter, they accused.

Bethany should have called Judge Harrigan. She knew that, of course. She should have contacted her mentor and curled up with another cup of that marvelous hot chocolate and let the judge's warmth and wisdom relax and reassure her. But crisis had always brought out a certain stubbornness in Bethany, a determination to go it alone—a legacy, no doubt, of the years of growing up with Aunt Claudia's fierce children, for whom every challenge you faced was an opportunity for endless teasing about your intelligence and fortitude. And there were other reasons . . .

Like that business about Judge Harrigan knowing Martin McAdams had become Martin Potus.

Maybe she would call the judge tomorrow.

In the event, Bethany took a room at a bed-and-breakfast a few miles away in the village of Washington, denoted Little Washington by the locals, to distinguish it from the tax-funded behemoth ninety minutes away—and, since the fame of its restaurant, by others as well. She dutifully called Detective Florio and told her where she could be found if they needed her. The owner was an old friend, and gave Bethany the Captain's Suite on the second floor, in the back, with its wide view of the meadow. The walls were knotty pine, more New England than Virginia, but then the house had been built by an actual ship's captain. The lamps were done up to look like oil lanterns. Bethany read a couple of Psalms from the Gideon's Bible she found in the nightstand drawer. She could not remember when she had felt so lonely. She even considered calling her aunt, except that she wasn't sure how the conversation would go:

"Hi, Aunt Claudia. It's me. I wanted to thank you for a lovely weekend. No, no, everything's fine. Well, not really. It seems that somebody shot Ken Kirkland—right, Kenny, he took me to the prom—and, anyway, they used my gun and they did it in my kitchen and they painted this snake on the wall, and, anyway, I wanted you to know that I'm the prime suspect, so it might be a while before I can get down there again—"

Bethany frowned. Something about that snake on the wall—but she was too dozy to catch up with the thought. She lay in bed half awake, waiting for sleep and instead listened to toilets flushing and latecomers tiptoeing and, when she shut her eyes, saw poor Kenneth Kirkland sprawled on her kitchen floor, shot with her gun after likely telling half the town that she had stolen his inheritance.

She shivered in the bed, feeling more than hearing the cell door clang shut. Closed spaces were her worst thing. Ever since that time that Aunt Claudia's sons had locked her inside the closet—

Her cell phone beeped.

Impossible. There was no service out here. Everybody knew that. The town fought furiously to keep it that way, defeating every effort to build a convenient cell tower. Bethany was a prominent signatory on every petition.

It beeped again.

She sat up, grabbed it from the bedside table.

The first message:

florio has orders to arrest you

And the second:

she will be there in ten minutes

Bethany shut her eyes, and tried to pray. Whoever was sending these messages had an agenda. But so did whoever was framing her.

It took her no more than ninety seconds to decide to run.

FIVE

There was a particular student who kept getting on Stuart Van Der Staal's nerves, probably because of the insistent drumbeat of her disagreement with his theories—theories he has proved correct with a brilliance that left his colleagues in the field breathless. Now here was another paper of hers, this time taking on his well-supported view, popular these days in his corner of the literary theory world, that the inchoate subtext of the Declaration of Independence demonstrated conclusively that the dead white males who founded the United States would willingly have endorsed the ideology of the Nazi Party. He remembered the day, years ago now, when he presented *that* paper at the annual meeting of the Modern Language Association. What a stir! And old Margolis had stood up and called him unprofessional, just because he hadn't read many writings of any of the men he spoke about, other than the Declaration itself! But look who'd wound up on top! True, it was death and not the force of Stuart's argument that had got Margolis two years later, but still: Margolis and people like that were troglodytes. They didn't understand the first rule of the modern academy, to wit: Evidence was nothing. Theory was everything. Stuart Van Der Staal had a clever theory; he needed no more. What the troglodytes called evidence was really just a selective interpretation of perception, chosen precisely to support a theory: nothing was true unless it was useful.

The professor leaned back in his chair. He was an oddly proportioned man, with very thin legs and very broad shoulders that he did his best to disguise with shapeless tweed jackets, lest his students mistake muscle for flab. Behind his glasses with their trademark steel frames, his eyes were of an icy blue. Dark hair was split in the middle by a startling shock of white. He was probably fifty. After a quarter century, he had lost interest in the struggle up the academic ladder. His third wife—like the first two, a former student—bored him immensely. Fortunately, he had other pursuits to keep him occupied; and happy.

That was why he was looking forward to tonight's call. Too bad it wasn't yet time.

With a sigh of resignation, Stuart Van Der Staal returned to the silly paper: silly by definition, because it rejected his conclusions. He was surprised that people could still miss a connection so brutally obvious, but then—he reminded himself charitably—not everyone was as intelligent or learned as he. Lesser minds could be forgiven for overlooking what came to him so easily, that the Framers whom America worshiped were no better than fascists. And while Stuart was no historian or legal scholar—his field, to be precise, was literary theory, and his dissertation had been a marvelous deconstruction of the poetry of Clemens Brentano—he should have won the Capote prize for the book that grew out of it, and he had always suspected old Margolis of fixing the vote—he was quite certain that he knew enough history and law to attack the great legal and political texts, just as he was certain he knew enough philosophy to attack theology, and enough theology to attack the Bible. He glanced at the girl's silly essay but didn't bother to read it through. It differed from his own conclusions and thus by definition had to be sub-par work. He graded it accordingly, shoved it rudely aside, drew the next paper from the stack. Much better. One of his acolytes, whose glowing endorsements of Stuart's own views were intelligently crafted.

Obviously an A. Well, no. Toward the end of the paper, the writer took issue with a tiny corner of one of Stuart's earlier works. A-minus, then.

His cell phone rang.

At last.

He picked it up, didn't say anything.

"She's in or near Pittsburgh," said the voice on the other end. "The competition thinks she's heading west, but I don't think they'll have the Pittsburgh connection for another six hours or so."

Stuart waited.

"We need her met."

He punched a key in acknowledgment, then ended the call. At last.

Seized by a marvelous excitement, he locked the papers away in his desk, then called his fool of a wife to say he had to go out of town unexpectedly and, no, he didn't have time to discuss it. There was a mirror on the inside door of his closet, and he peered into it now, adjusting the jacket so it hung just so, combing the dark hair with that remarkable streak of white, adjusting the steel glasses. Image was everything. Odd how few supposedly smart people understood that. We were masses of perception, nothing else: the world comprised entirely of observers and observations.

That, at least, was the view of Professor Stuart Van Der Staal, and it helped explained why he was so good at his secret career.

He left the building, climbed into his black Lexus, drove to a storage room he rented under another name on the far side of the little academic town where he lived. He pulled on gloves, then shoved up the door and went inside. Behind the stacks of unwanted books he had bought by the pound was a battered old piano he had picked up a yard sale. More books were heaped on the piano bench. All camouflage. He swept them aside. Inside the bench were reams of yellowed sheet music with curling edges. He moved the music, too, uncovering the heavy felt pouch. Inside was a box, and in the box was ammunition.

The guns were stored separately.

The professor made two more stops at two more storage facilities, but by noon he was on the road. Not to Pittsburgh. The quarry was no fool, and would not long stay in one place. Pittsburgh was a path to someplace else. He was fairly certain he knew where she was going; and that was where they would meet.

The Virginia operation had not worked out as designed, but the fault was hardly Stuart's: that end had not even been his assignment. He had warned them of the holes, but they had gone ahead anyway. The plan to set her in motion had worked perfectly; but nobody had expected the target to be quite so levelheaded. She was supposed to panic, because a subject in panic is easier to track. Had she not fled—had she been arrested—well, his employers could have lived with that result. Bethany Barclay in custody was better than Bethany Barclay dead at the scene: again, perception was everything. There were other ways to reach their goal. But, in the event, those silly text messages had goaded her into the action most useful for their purposes: flight.

Too bad the fools tasked with watching had been unable to carry out their assignment. They had followed her to Front Royal, fifteen miles north of her home, and had lost her in a welter of confusing side streets.

After that it was his employers' turn to panic.

And to call in Professor Stuart Van Der Staal, who never failed, and whose services were priced accordingly.

He smiled, pleased to be recalled to the field. He enjoyed his secret work, and it fit his philosophy. What lesser humans called existence was in any case only a matter of observation: the good professor had demonstrated this many times over. We were not actual selves, but only the sums of our perceptions, and the perceptions of others.

It would soon be time for Bethany Barclay to cease being perceived.

Actually, Bethany wasn't in Pittsburgh at all. She'd been there—she'd even abandoned her beloved Volvo at the airport, after four and a half hours of hard driving from Little Washington. She had no idea how one avoided being caught, but intended to do her best. Her father used to say that the police aren't ten feet tall, and for a while Bethany consoled herself with that knowledge.

On the other hand, the police had been plenty tall enough to put Everett Barclay in prison, twice.

At the airport Bethany dragged her bag to the shuttle bus, rode into town, and alighted at a hotel, where she took a room in her own name, made a fuss so she'd be remembered, then went out the back without bothering to head upstairs. At another hotel two blocks away, she grabbed a taxi and rode to the ritzy northern suburbs. She shut her eyes and sent a silent apology to a law school classmate who lived out here and whom she had visited twice in recent years, a woman she had no intention of visiting today, although the authorities would presumably think she had.

"Please don't let anything happen to her," Bethany whispered, only half aware that she was praying.

She had the driver leave her at a low-rise office plaza. When he was gone she dragged her overnight bag two blocks to a shopping mall. She bought a backpack. In the ladies room she transferred what she needed, then chopped her hair. She donned a head scarf and caught the bus into the city. By now it was early afternoon. She walked to the nearby terminal and caught the bus for Philadelphia, where she had intended to go all along, hoping that by showing her face in Pittsburgh, she would persuade the authorities that she was heading north into New York State or west, where they would certainly expect her to go.

But she had business back on the East Coast first.

Having used the drive to calm herself and work through the facts—what Judge Harrigan called doing her sums—Bethany had developed two premises that were guiding her actions.

First, whoever was framing her wanted her to run. The same person had to have sent the text messages to the cell phone she had discarded in a dumpster along Route 522. Otherwise the coincidence was too much to be borne. One would have to imagine two elaborate conspiracies that just happened to collide in the unknown and unimportant Bethany Barclay.

Second, whatever was happening to her was related to Martin Potus and his God's Planners. Again, the coincidence would otherwise be too absurd. Sylvia Kirkland walks in off the street and asks a lawyer she has never met before to write a new will that just happens to favor Bethany's former fiancé, the text messages begin when Sylvia's son, Kenneth, raises the possibility of challenging the bequest, and Ken is shot dead with her gun two days later.

Why, then, Ms. Barclay—the voice of Professor Delavan, who had tortured her contracts section for an entire year at Harvard Law—*why, then, are you headed for Philadelphia? Was I dreaming, Ms. Barclay, or do I remember you saying that these Planners are located in Chicago?*

"Because both the FBI and whoever is manipulating me will expect me to go to Chicago," she had answered, driving north and then west through West Virginia, carefully watching her speed to avoid being pulled over. "I'm nobody's puppet."

Then why not Tallahassee or Timbuktu?—a favorite Delavan mot—*Why Philadelphia?*

"Because of the snake."

Snake, Ms. Barclay? What snake? I don't believe that your recitation of the facts thus far has included a snake.

"The snake on the wall. The one they painted after they killed Ken Kirkland."

And what, pray, does the snake tell you?

"First, that Annabelle may not have been so paranoid after all. Second, that the people who are after me are the same people who were after her." She almost smiled. "And, third, that they don't know I know that."

Last November—again, she imagined herself telling the story in Delavan's classroom, reciting the facts of the case before being skewered by her professor—last November, Annabelle called and said she planned to come down and visit for a few days. She never asked if it was convenient, she simply announced her intentions. She sounded nervous but she always sounded nervous. Lots of different Annabelles, she often said, chased each other around in her head; and lots of different therapists over the years had confirmed it.

Tell us about her, said Delavan. *Give us her background if you please, Ms. Barclay.*

Annabelle was clever, jittery, and entirely charming, the product of a short-lived union between a pair of domestic servants at a mansion in the Hamptons: Russian on her father's side, and, on her mother's, West Indian by way of Panama. She had a half sister, Polly, two years older, and Delores, their mother, had dumped both daughters on her aunt, Tia Christina, when they were still quite small. Polly had made a great success of her career; Annabelle was bright enough to have excelled in school, but found being out from under her stern aunt's roof far too thrilling. Over the years she traveled a bit, held jobs when she had to, studied here and there, usually winding up on Bethany's doorstep, even when Bethany was at Oxford and Annabelle was, supposedly, working in Atlanta as a paralegal.

"It wasn't right for me," Annabelle explained. "I'm still finding myself."

Which was what she always said.

When she called Bethany last fall to say she was coming down, Annabelle was in New York, visiting family, but living in Chicago. She worked for some sort of food co-op, but had taken to going off by herself for weeks at a time, and for months Bethany had been able to reach nothing but her voicemail. So of course she was delighted that her running buddy planned to visit. Annabelle arrived on a Saturday night, red-eyed and jumpy, although not on the train she had asked Bethany to meet. When they got to Flint Hill, Annabelle went straight to bed. In the morning Bethany tried to get Annabelle to go to church, and Annabelle tried to get Bethany to stay home.

"I didn't sleep last night," Annabelle said. "Bad dreams."

"All the more reason."

"They're after me. They're probably watching us."

But in Annabelle's mind somebody was always after her; and so Bethany went on to church alone. She got home to find both doors on the chain and had to bang on the window to get her running buddy's attention, because Annabelle had a pillow over her head.

"I have to go away for a while," she said when Bethany made her dress and took her out to brunch.

"Where?"

"I can't tell you."

"Where have you been?"

"I can't tell you."

"Everybody's worried about you."

This at least brought a smile, and it was, briefly, like old times. "With this economy and the world going to pieces, you'd think people could find something else to worry about."

They drove around on back roads for a bit, the farmland rolling on in the crisp autumn sunlight, because Bethany had always found that the sleepy countryside of Rappahannock County helped her running buddy to relax; besides, Annabelle thought they had a better chance of losing surveillance this way. Back at the house, the girls in the other apartment were having a party, but when Bethany started shouting to be heard over the pounding music, Annabelle said they should whisper instead, just in case.

"In case what?"

"I made you something," Annabelle said. She was already packing. "A parting gift."

"That's sweet."

The gift turned out to be a charcoal rendering of two crossed arrows beneath some sort of flat cylinder.

"What is it?"

"Something to remember me by." Annabelle smiled sweetly. "I did it while I was locked up. Sort of like therapy."

"When were you locked up?"

But she would say no more.

That evening Bethany drove to Fredericksburg to put her running buddy aboard the Amtrak sleeper train, heading south.

"I wish you'd stay longer."

"I can't. I just wanted to say good-bye." A long hug like a final farewell; and a warning whisper in her ear.

"I don't know what that means either," said Bethany as Annabelle climbed aboard.

"That's probably best."

Bethany stood on the platform hoping to wave but couldn't find Annabelle's window. For weeks she waited for an email or a card or a telephone call. In January she was in New York on business and stopped in to visit Tia Christina, the formidable Panamanian aunt who had raised Annabelle and her sister, but Tia hadn't heard a word either. Bethany refused to worry: her running buddy had vanished before. Yet even before the bad news, she sensed that this time was different. Maybe it was those last whispered words:

"The serpents are after me. They'll probably be after you now."

Annabelle had worried about the serpents; Ken Kirkland's killer had painted a snake. It couldn't be coincidence.

Still on the bus for Philly, satisfied that she'd done her sums correctly, Bethany decided to catch up on sleep. But first she snuck a peek at the iPad on which the woman sitting beside her was checking the headlines. No mention of the murder. Good. As her seatmate scrolled, the only Virginia news Bethany noticed was something about a bombing at a university laboratory. Nothing to do with her.

She slept.

Stuart Van Der Staal stood in the sunlit park, watching youngsters playing soccer. He had sniffed the air, as he called it, and was pretty sure he had found her scent. He had not bothered with Pittsburgh; Pittsburgh was a feint. Bethany was cleverer than they thought. Stuart could make a shrewd guess about the target's destination: one of two places. He could not stake out both, and he was not about to give someone else the satisfaction. So he waited in one town, knowing that if he was wrong she would certainly turn up in the other—and that Bethany's decision to choose the other town would in any event yield further information about her plan.

That she was planning at all was impressive. And although the Virginia operation had been a fiasco, at least she was running. Now if they could only get her to run in the right direction.

They could do it by nudges, slowly pointing Bethany Barclay where they wanted to go, but Stuart was familiar with Zeno's Paradox—he had read William James on Zeno's Paradox, and Jorge Luis Borges on William James on Zeno's Paradox—and what it all added up to was that you could sweep away all the philosophical mishmash about the distance between two points with bold, dramatic action.

Something bold, then, to get the target to change course *now*.

Others might be unsure how to proceed, or, worse, might choose a course that led to destruction. But this was what Stuart Van Der Staal did; nobody was better. He had already worked out his course of action—violent, to be sure, but violence was how you marked the world, showing it to be yours to mold rather than the other way around.

Violence, boldness, audacity, all without leaving a trace to mark his passage: this was his element.

The professor smiled, enjoying the sunlight, and the company of the lesser humans around him, going blithely about their little lives unaware of the talents and intentions of the kindly man chatting with a couple of parents along the sideline. He enjoyed fooling people because the act provided further evidence for his fervent belief that we are bundles of perception. They perceived him as a friend and would never mention him to the police, because everybody would take him for somebody's father.

Nobody would have guessed that there was a gun in his jacket, and other necessities of the trade in his car.

Stuart shut his eyes, letting a small frisson of pleasure glide through his strong body. He did not believe in a Creator, but could not help thinking that this work he did so well was what he was made for.

SIX

The house was a spanking new Tudor, massive and oddly alert on its six-acre lot. It stood near the crest of a pretty avenue of multimillion-dollar homes in Haverford Township, not far from Coopertown Elementary, one of the finest primary schools in the nation. The train ride from Philadelphia had been only about fifteen minutes, and Bethany had sat with her head down as if dozing, a knit cap pulled over her hair. Whenever she closed her eyes she saw Ken's body; whenever she opened them they filled with tears. She spent so much time with her face in her hands that one of her fellow passengers, a kindly woman who was everybody's grandmother or everybody's head of surveillance, touched her shoulder and asked if she was okay. The look on Bethany's face as she tried to smile caused her would-be friend not only to withdraw her hand but to change her seat. Perhaps she took Bethany's expression of despair for one of derision. With her backpack and scuffed jacket, Bethany supposed that her fellow passengers must take her for a bag lady, although when she alighted at Haverford Station, they might have decided she was a student instead.

From the station Bethany walked.

The distance was no more than a mile, and a passing shower had cooled the evening, so the perspiration must have been due to her constant fear that one of the passing cyclists or joggers would pull out the cuffs and order her onto the ground.

But nobody did.

She had not rung Polly to say she was dropping by. One reason was her own ambiguous legal position. Another was the bleak possibility that Annabelle's sister would refuse to help. The siblings had been raised by the same remarkable Panamanian woman, Tia Christina, after their mother—Tia's niece—decided to go home, leaving her daughters behind. Although not twins, the two girls were similar in voice, and affect, and personality. The difference was that Bethany and Annabelle were the best of friends; whereas Bethany and Polly were quite the other thing.

Bethany stood beneath a tree across the street, wondering. She had strolled past the house three times before admitting to herself that she would have no way of identifying surveillance. Still, at least Polly was evidently at home: the two cars in the forecourt, both sprinkled with droplets, reassured her.

Bethany murmured a prayer, took a deep breath, and strode boldly up the curving drive, proclaiming through her body language that she dropped in every day, and rang the bell.

The door was opened by a sad-faced, worn-out man in his early forties, in jeans and bare feet: Polly's husband, David Hollins. Bethany had met him for the first time when she and Annabelle attended the wedding six years ago. David, a good decade older than his wife, was a history professor at Bryn Mawr, and, on the side, wrote polarizing books about popular culture. He stood before her, pale toes curling into the intricate tilework, staring in astonishment at the visitor, who offered her friendliest smile. She was not really surprised: in the twenty-four hours since the murder, her photograph had been everywhere.

An instant later, tiny Polly joined him, still wearing her pinstriped skirt from work although her creamy blouse was untucked. In her stocking feet she was all of five-foot-two. She was two years older than her late sister. Although the slighter of the two, Polly had the same smooth sepia skin, and the same questioning intensity in her hazel eyes. Bethany smiled at her too.

"Look at this, David," said Polly. "It's not every day a wanted felon shows up on your doorstep."

Bethany could not keep the tremor from her voice. "A felon is someone who's committed a crime."

Polly's expression became wolfish. "That's right."

Nevertheless she stepped aside to let Bethany in, then closed the heavy door with bony hands that looked too weak. She possessed a surprising vitality. David, at his wife's swift command, had their guest's jacket in her hands almost before Bethany could remember to remove it. By now his eyes were mainly on the floor. Up the floating central staircase the television was barking some nonsense about the latest Washington scandal, loud enough to drown conversation. Bethany had the sense that they had been fighting.

"You shouldn't be here," said Polly, scarcely above a murmur, fists balled on her slim hips. She had clever eyes that could be playful or accusing, and a short, prim Afro. "Are you out of your mind?"

"I'm sorry. I wouldn't have come if I had a choice. I only need a couple of minutes."

"We have children, Bethany. You know we can't help you."

Floppy-eared David followed the byplay between the two women with big sad eyes. He was of German and Irish extraction, and his academic field was nineteenth-century America. At the funeral he had sobbed helplessly, to his wife's patent fury.

"I didn't kill that man. I think whoever did might have been involved with what happened to your sister. The same people." Bethany waited, but Polly waited better. She tried again. "All I'm asking is that you help me solve your sister's murder."

The smaller woman's smile was chilly. "I don't want to hear anything you have to say. I'm not going to be an accessory."

"Listening to me isn't a crime."

"Just go, Bethany. Please."

A different tack, as anger and frustration rose: "Maybe you should hear what I have to say first. You're the one who's broken immigration laws. Maybe fraud. Abetted other crimes, too."

"Get real." Folding thin, confident arms.

"You know what I'm talking about. And you know who."

"Maybe I should wait upstairs," said David, unsmiling. "I'll check on the baby."

"The baby is sleeping. She's fine," said Polly.

"Actually, I think that would be a good idea," said Bethany.

"Well," said David, followed by, "uh," and he stood there, bare white ankles crossed like a child's, needy eyes still hopping back and forth.

"I don't have any secrets from my husband."

"Yes, you do," said Bethany.

Another grim silence.

"Go," said Polly at last. "Make sure the kids don't come down." She looked the enemy in the eye. "I don't think our guest will be here very long."

Alone together.

For a long moment they fought without speaking. Although just a couple of years older than Annabelle, Polly stood inestimably higher in the hierarchy of people who ran the institutions that ran the world. She was a molecular biochemist by training, and had been a rising Merck executive, until snatched away by a private equity firm in Philadelphia, advising on tech investments—half-time, to free up her afternoons for the children—and possessed a well-earned reputation for standing no nonsense.

"Two minutes after you leave," said Polly, "I'll be calling the police."

"I understand."

"I won't put my family in danger for your sake, Bethany."

"I wouldn't ask you to."

Because there were no pleasantries to share, Polly invited her unwanted guest to get straight to the point. They were seated in the living room, the windows open just a crack to bring in cool air from outside. A Spode service stood on a trolley, but Polly had offered no tea; or even a glass of water.

Bethany held only one card; and played it. "When I said you could go to prison, I meant it. Immigration fraud is a very serious charge, even more so these days, and, when it comes to border offenses, the country is not in an acquitting mood." Polly sat unbudging in her skirt, slim legs crossed as she listened, weighing the words with her eyes. "You know what I'm talking about, Polly. You lent Annabelle your passport. You're not twins, but in a photograph the likeness is close enough."

Polly crinkled her stern nose in disapproval. Her pout was worth writing home about. The electric fire in the grate created the illusion of warmth. The wallpaper was a chilly blue. She said nothing.

"Annabelle visited me last October," Bethany continued. "She left her purse on the counter while she used the bathroom. I knocked it down by accident, and everything fell out, including your passport. I know it was yours because it opened while I was putting it back. I was going to ask Annabelle about it, but when she started talking about"—

—serpents—

—"something else, and, well, I never got the chance to bring it up again. After that, I sort of forgot about it until now."

Upstairs, David was walking heavily back and forth, a sullen child needing to be noticed by the grown-ups who had excluded him. On the mantel, photos of the proud parents and their two small children, and of David, avid fisherman, holding a large and impressive catch.

There was no picture of his first wife.

"Her bag fell by *accident*." Polly's sarcasm was scathing. "My passport *happened* to fall out. And you *forgot* to ask." She crossed her legs the other way and leaned back. "You're quite the little snoop, aren't you? But you're wrong, Bethany. I didn't loan Annabelle my passport. Like you said, that's against the law. I lost it. I reported it lost, oh—well, probably January, when I needed it for a cruise and couldn't find it. So now it turns out that my sister had it. I'm not really surprised. She stole everything else to support her habit—money, jewelry, you name it—so why not a passport, too?"

Bethany was undeterred. "Form DS-64 requires a signature certifying under penalty of perjury that all your statements are truthful. If you lied on the form about losing your passport, you could go to prison." She saw the thunder gathering on Polly's face. "I don't want to get you in trouble. I just want to know why Annabelle needed the passport. That's all. I have to find out where she went."

Polly's smoky beauty, roused to anger, was scary yet exquisite, like a spring thunderstorm. Annabelle, who possessed a not-insignificant temper of her own, used to tell awestruck stories about her half sister's tantrums. Polly hunched forward on the love seat yet seemed to be receding and, at the same time, expanding, like clouds building along the horizon. "I want you to go."

"Tell me where she went, and I'm out of here."

"Why is it so important? I'd have thought you'd be more worried about your own skin."

Bethany told the truth: "I think what I'm mixed up in is connected to what she was mixed up in. If I can find out what she was up to, maybe I can prove I'm innocent."

"Why am I not surprised?" Polly smirked. "That's what she did. Whenever Annabelle got in trouble, she'd drag everybody else in after her. I loved my sister to death, but the truth is, she couldn't be happy until everybody else was as miserable as she was."

"She had problems, Polly. She was an addict."

"And you think that explained her behavior? Her addiction? You met her in college, Bethany. I knew her a lot longer. And I can assure you that Annabelle was just the same as a little girl. And as a teenager. 'I need to borrow some money.' 'I need a ride.' 'I need that dress.' I-I-I, always I. Our mom used to call her 'Little Miss Do-For-Me.' She had Tia wrapped around her little finger. From what I can tell, she had you, too. I bet she never picked up a check when you guys went out." Contempt, mockery, banked flames, fanned by the furious heat of a painful childhood. "If you didn't give her what she wanted? She just took it when your back was turned. Sometimes she didn't even give you the chance to say no, because she didn't bother to ask first. And she—well, let's just say my dear sister never cared who she hurt." The catch in her confident voice came as a surprise—what else had Annabelle taken from her?—but Polly suppressed the emotion, even turning it to anger. "And don't you go telling me how her father hated her and Dolores abandoned her and the Russian side of the family wouldn't have anything to do with her. I had the same challenges. I overcame them."

Still Bethany refused to match Polly's fire. "Fine. You were stronger than she was. You made it further than she did. God doesn't love her any less, and He doesn't love you any more." Her voice remained low and even. "And now, unless you have any more calumny to heap on your dead sister's image, why don't you tell me about the passport?"

———

For the next while, they waited each other out, neither wanting to be first to challenge the hard, shiny silence that had fallen between them like a blade. Bethany sat like a stone. Polly cast a couple of long glances at her cell phone lying on the coffee table, wanting her guest to notice where she was looking. Bethany never wavered, even though deep inside she wanted to scream, and to flee, possibly pausing to strangle Polly on her way out. David was stalking around upstairs, still upset at the intrusion. Bethany remembered the stare-down contests she used to have with her cousin Eva when they were small, and how she always won because she mastered the trick of transporting the self away and leaving only the eyes behind—eyes that only seemed to watch the instant reality, but in truth were focused inward, yet at nothing nearby. She used it now.

"I don't know where she went," Polly finally said, flicking her fingers to show that she had not really lost, because she did not really care. "Congratulations. You're right. I loaned her my passport. She dropped in last fall—uninvited, like you—and stayed a couple of hours, then just asked for it out of the blue. 'I need, I need, I need.'"

This time Polly's bitter laughter was directed at herself. Until this moment it had never occurred to Bethany that it was not she but Annabelle whom the smaller woman despised.

"I told her no. She said it was only for a quick trip, she'd be back in a week. I told her to use her own. She said hers was compromised, which probably meant it was out of date, and she hadn't bothered to renew it. I asked her what was so important that she had to go now. She said she couldn't tell me, but I'd be proud of her. I kept asking for more, but all she'd say was that when she found what she was looking for there'd be headlines all over the world." Polly gazed longingly at the phone. "I still said no. I could tell she was running some scam. She denied it. She insisted she was clean. She said she'd joined a church. She was getting ready to go back to grad school, but she had to do this one thing first. Her mission, she called it."

Bethany waited for more, but realized this was all there was. Faced with her sister's flimsy argument, Polly had said yes; the way people always said yes to Annabelle's wheedling. Suddenly the point of the anger was clarified: Polly had been waiting six months for a knock at the door, and the accusations, and the trial. She had spent that half year working up a story.

"And that was the last time you saw her," Bethany prompted.

"She never gave it back. Little Miss Do-For-Me." A beat. "I couldn't tell the police, obviously. After she died, I mean. I couldn't tell the police, I didn't tell Tia, I didn't even tell David. The cell phone number she'd given me went dead the next day. I asked around. Nobody had seen her. She'd disappeared."

"You can't blame yourself."

Something in her tone irritated Polly afresh. "I don't blame myself. There wasn't any time to think. She came by while I was feeding the kids. David had a faculty meeting. Frankly, I wanted her out of my house before he got back."

Again that mysterious shadow of pain in Polly's voice, and on her face. She scratched nervously at a thin wrist.

"And no hint of where she went?" asked Bethany, just to keep the conversation going. "What she was after?"

Another shake of the head. "Except when she needed something, my little sister was never the confiding type. Of course, when she was in trouble, she'd talk your ear off about how much she loved you." That harsh laugh again. "The only other thing she said was that the people who'd hidden whatever it was had been very clever. They had everybody thinking it had already been found."

Bethany considered. "And that it would make headlines all over the world."

"And that she could hardly wait to tell you all about it. You, Bethany. Not me or Tia. You." Polly was on her feet. "She said only you would understand the path she took. You."

Bethany took a wild chance. "Is it possible she said something to David?"

Polly went, if anything, stiffer. "I told you. He wasn't home."

"It's just that Annabelle didn't know that many people. Maybe she called, or dropped in when you weren't here—"

Polly cut her off, voice icy. "I've answered your questions, Bethany. I've endured your threats. I won't put my family in any more danger. So now, if it's all the same to you, I would very much like to see you to the door."

"I didn't mean to—"

But Polly was already in the foyer, calling out to her husband, elsewhere in the pricey house. "David? Is that the baby?"

An unnatural pause. "Yes, honey. I'll get her."

"Nonsense. You were up with her all night. It's my turn." Polly turned to her uninvited guest. "Now, you'll have to excuse me. Duty calls, as you can see."

"Polly—"

"It's time you left, Bethany." Talking over her shoulder. "You haven't asked my advice, but I'm going to offer it anyway. You're a fugitive. I think it's time to turn yourself in to the proper authorities and make a deal."

And she was gone, clomping furiously up the stairs.

David came downstairs, smiling. Bethany flinched. If he touched her she would scream. But he was a kind man, a little weak, said Annabelle, but he loved his wife and family with a dreadful devotion. That was her word: *dreadful*. David apologized nervously for the baby, who had the colic: they had to take turns walking her around at night until she brought her bubble up. Bethany said she understood. David held the door open, and seemed to hesitate. She sensed in his manner the burden of tragedy. She looked into his unhappy, questioning eyes, and knew that this instant, with Polly upstairs, would be her only chance to ask. And although it might have been her imagination, Bethany sensed, even, that he wanted to tell her. But when she opened her mouth, all that came out was an apology for disturbing their evening. Aunt Claudia's patient lessons held: something inside Bethany would not let her dredge up a past that might spoil what peace they had found—even to save her own life.

Besides, she was out of time.

So she said good night, and he said good night, and Bethany felt his moist gaze on her back as she hurried down the driveway. She turned at the corner, making hard for the station, wondering whether it was safe to take the train back to Philadelphia. For all she knew, Polly was already on the telephone. A mother's ear for her baby's cry is perfect, but Bethany's ears were better still, and she had heard no whisper of a whimper.

SEVEN

The Church Builder sat in his favorite alcove, an undecorated gray brick outcropping in a dusty corner of the library. He was working his way through the crumbling pages of a thick diary kept in the nineteenth century by a vice president of the United States who held the position to which the Builder had succeeded. The chandelier gave the paper a yellowy tinge. There was no natural light because there were no windows. There were no computers in the room; nothing in the archive was digitized; an affectation, to be sure, but these days a kind of protection as well. What was not in a computer could not be hacked. There was an index, but it would have been gobbledygook to anyone not trained in its arcana. The very location of the archive was a secret known only to a few: certainly the neighbors had no idea.

In his other life, the Builder was an architect, a specialist in the harmonizing of the modern with the classical. He enjoyed an international reputation. He was a partner in Miller, Stean, and McCabe, one of the most prestigious architectural firms in the world. He had built hotels in Paris, performing arts centers in Scandinavia, university buildings in the Ivy League, office towers in Abu Dhabi, and churches and cathedrals in every corner of the globe. He liked designing structures balanced between the traditional and the contemporary, or, as he preferred to say, the old and the new.

For two decades he had been trying to rebuild the group he led on much the same model. If they had a name, they were the Garden, and for five centuries, the members had labored in the shadows to hold off the determined assault of its increasingly powerful adversary. The society they protected could know nothing of their activities, or they would turn on the Garden in a secular frenzy.

And the adversary would have its victory.

The Builder turned a page. He had read the diary before, but took solace in knowing that the problems he confronted today were different only in degree, not in kind, from those faced by his predecessors. He was a balding, pudgy little man, who had a way of puffing hard when forced to walk at anything but the most leisured pace. If you saw his face in a crowd you'd forget it immediately, and anonymity was what he liked.

"Fascinating," he murmured, studying the perfect copperplate in which the vice president had recorded the cat-and-mouse battle with the opposition during the era before the Civil War, when both sides despised slavery, but the opposition believed that the preachers whipping up Northern sentiment against it were dangerous, and should be stopped.

As the Builder turned the pages, it occurred to him that much of history might be rewritten, were these archives ever opened.

He had often expressed to the Mathematician the hope that one day they could share what had been so carefully stored here.

"Maybe one day," the Mathematician always said. "But not until long after you and I have left this world behind."

"You don't want to see the end of this conflict?"

"Only if we win."

The Mathematician was a dear friend and a good man; perhaps he would even succeed to this chair when the Builder passed from the scene.

An event likely not far off.

The Church Builder shut his eyes and rubbed the bridge of his nose. In the artificial daylight of the archive it was impossible to tell the time, but he did not need to look at his watch to know that it was the middle of the night. His doctors said it was a myth that the old need less sleep than the young, but the Builder found himself increasingly wakeful in the hours when the world slumbered.

The world he fervently prayed he was helping to protect.

He stood and stretched, waiting for news. He shut the file and turned to the heavy volume lying on a side table: a Bible that once adorned the study of Jonathan Edwards. He opened it and ran his hands along the smooth leaves. He was touching pages that the greatest preacher of the eighteenth century had touched. He shivered with pleasure, bewildered that anyone could believe that placing the image of a book like this on a hard drive somewhere could ever yield the same experience as laying hands on it. Reading was not just an intellectual experience but a tactile one. Why was it so hard for the world to see—

The Builder stopped, shut the Edwards Bible, and scolded himself for his vanity and covetousness. He wished his wife were alive and at his side, to help keep him grounded, as she used to put it; but if what the doctors said was true, he would likely be seeing her soon.

The door opened and an attendant stepped in. There were only six, carefully chosen, for intellect and faith, not for brawn. The archive was mostly unguarded.

Mostly.

The attendant moved silently along the rows of shelves bursting with books and cabinets bursting with files. Speech inside the reading room was kept to a minimum. Nobody knew why; it was a tradition. The two of them were alone. The attendant could have shouted his business down the room and nobody would have been the wiser. But the tradition held.

The Builder waited.

He hated the rigmarole and secrecy that accompanied the work he did. He saw their necessity, but hated what they symbolized. To the Builder, it all smacked of the sort of high-church-bells-and-smells frippery that always seemed to him a distraction from true Christianity. Yet he also saw the logic of what the Christian tradition used to call the *adiaphora*, literally "the things of indifference," the notion that one ought not to condemn another believer for using as part of worship things neither required nor forbidden by Scripture, as long as nobody pretended that they were mandated by Christ.

"What is it?" the Builder demanded when the man drew within earshot. He was not usually so impatient; more evidence that the stress was wearing him down.

"Sir, a message from the Mathematician. Ms. Barclay went to see Ms.

Seaver's sister. I gather this was unanticipated." The attendant spoke dryly. All the attendants were like this, cultivating a tone so diffident and bemused that one would suppose them to exist on a higher plane.

"Are we certain?"

"Sir, the Mathematician says yes."

"Do we know what was said?"

"Sir, the Mathematician says we're working on it."

The Builder hesitated. "Does anyone else know?"

"Sir, the Mathematician says the authorities know. Ms. Seaver's sister called the police. Apparently her husband tried to dissuade her—"

"I didn't mean the authorities." But he was only musing aloud, and the attendant, sensitive to his mood, did not interrupt. If the authorities knew, then the opposition knew. Poor woman. Her troubles were about to multiply, and there was nothing the Builder could do for her but watch and wait. He felt sullied by what they were doing. Their goals were just and moral; he only hoped the Lord would forgive the means forced upon them by the nature of the struggle against evil.

"Please inform the Mathematician that I will meet him tomorrow for dinner. The usual place."

Alone again, the Builder knelt beside the table in prayer. Kneeling was out of fashion these days, and it was increasingly hard on his aging legs, but he was persuaded by C. S. Lewis, who argued, following Aristotle, that there was a posture proper to every activity.

He prayed, as so often, for wisdom and guidance; and that their side, if right, would be victorious; and that his health would hold out long enough for him to complete the work set before him. But mostly he prayed that Bethany Barclay would live long enough for him to make amends to her for the terrible risks she was being forced to run.

EIGHT

Bethany did not return to Philadelphia, but went up to Newark, where she had no trouble finding a dingy hotel near the train station that took cash and asked no questions. She slept a few hours, then tried to catch up on the news. CNN pulsed a peculiar neon on the ancient television set in her room, but as far as she could make out from the jagged sound, no search had been launched in the Haverford area, so perhaps Polly hadn't called the police after all; or maybe the authorities were keeping the tip quiet; or maybe they just had bigger fish to fry.

Like that bombing in Virginia yesterday.

A small bomb, concealed in a cigar case, had gone off in the foyer of a biology laboratory at George Mason University. Nobody was hurt. The explosion was meant as a warning, or so said the email sent to the college president's office minutes before the blast: no more human embryo research, or the attacks would get worse. This was the second college science building to be bombed. The first was in North Carolina a month ago. There, too, research using human embryos was under way. An instant expert was already placing the blame proudly on "Christian extremists," and Bethany supposed that anything was possible, although the experts on whom the media nowadays relied seemed to consider an extremist anybody who had the smallest of moral qualms about, say, abortion. The extremists, the expert predicted, wouldn't stop. But the part that really interested her was the video from a security camera near the lab. The image was grainy, and black-and-white, but it showed a Volvo very much like hers speeding away shortly before the explosion.

A blue Volvo, witnesses said; with Virginia plates.

"Police declined to speculate on whether the bombing might be connected to Tuesday's brutal slaying of a prominent George Mason alum just a few miles down the road in the little town of Flint Hill," the grave announcer was saying. "Sources tell CNN that the suspect in that crime, the ex-fiancée of the victim, drives a car fitting that description. Sources say the car was found at the subway station near the campus."

Then it was on to the latest from Wall Street.

Bethany sprinted around the room, gathering her things. Despite her rising panic, she was impressed by the precision of what was happening: The murder. The video of a car like hers at George Mason. The other bombing, in North Carolina, which happened, she now recalled, not far from where Aunt Claudia lived.

And Bethany was willing to bet a witness would soon come forward who'd seen her down there, too.

They were *flushing* her, she told herself. That was the purpose of the bombing, and of the clues linking her to it: whoever killed Ken wanted her to burst from cover and run, like the frightened deer whose pelt makes her invisible as long as she stands still, but whose flashing tail renders her a target the instant she turns to flee. Her father had taught her. On his rare visits to Aunt Claudia's, he had forced his daughter to join him at deer hunting. Patience would win the day, Everett Barclay insisted: you waited your quarry out. If that didn't work, you made sure the deer heard enough noise to know you were coming. The idea was to get the poor creature to run away from the sound, toward a line of hunters hidden up ahead. It was called deer driving.

Good plan.

The FBI arrived at breakfast. Bethany was in a booth at the diner across the street, trying to come up with a new plan while munching eggs and home fries, murderous on her waistline, but a treat she allowed herself, seeing that she was on the lam. Nearby a clutch of what Aunt Claudia would have called "ladies of the evening" sat chattering about other possible lines of work. It occurred to Bethany that if she spent much more time underground she would need to find work, too. Her mad money was only a few thousand dollars, and she suspected that she had a great deal of traveling ahead of her. Fighting off the bedbugs last night at the hotel, she had even considered taking Polly's advice and turning herself in—except for the fact that most courts nowadays allowed the prosecution to introduce evidence of flight to show consciousness of guilt. The innocent, according to the judges, never fled.

Right.

Bethany was finishing up her coffee and waiting for her change when the car pulled up in front of the hotel, and she knew at once that it was official, not only because it was dark and nondescript but also because of the carelessness with which it was double-parked and the easy manner of the two suited men who climbed out. And then there was the way that one of the ladies of the evening at the next table whispered "Cops" and another, reading some secret sign, shook her head and said "Feds" and the first one said "Oh, right."

The women sounded like experts.

For a mad instant Bethany was frozen, too panicked to act. Then she was fighting the urge to leap from the table and run, because she remembered how deer driving worked. So she sat and ogled with everyone else, forcing upon herself the calm her father had preached in times of crisis. Again she did her sums. One car, two men. No SWAT, no helicopters. Meaning, this was routine. They were searching the hotels in the area, meaning that she had been spotted, probably at the train station.

"Keep the change," she said. The restaurant had a back door—Bethany had marked it down on a trip to the ladies' room—and she used it now. Everything she had was in her backpack, other than a couple of items she had washed in the sink and left over the shower to dry. The FBI was welcome to apply to them all the mighty forces of forensic technology. None of that would help predict where she was going next, not least because the plan she had hatched last night was still only half-formed.

People who run too fast get caught. Sam DeMarco had told her that one day when they went for ice cream after the shooting range, and Sam, whichever version of himself you believed, knew what he was talking about. And so Bethany forced legs that longed to spring, to walk instead, down an alley and out on a side street.

Nobody followed.

Rutgers University was three blocks away, and nothing was easier than going unnoticed on a modern college campus, where students paid attention, only and always, to themselves.

Stuart Van Der Staal was proud of himself. He had made two correct guesses. He had reasoned, first, that Bethany showed her face so fussily in Pittsburgh only to persuade her pursuers that she was heading west; ergo, she was heading east. Second, if she was heading east, she could only have two destinations in mind. She was going to talk to either Annabelle's aunt in Harlem or Annabelle's sister in Haverford.

Stuart, who preferred to work alone, could not possibly cover both places. The FBI, he suspected, was at neither, because it would be some time before they saw the Annabelle connection, if indeed they ever did. But Bethany was too intelligent not to have winkled it out.

Thus his second guess.

Whichever she chose would likely lead her to the other. She was exhausted and would need a place to go to ground in between the two stops. Manhattan was big but too well policed. She wouldn't risk her friends, and she couldn't trust even the tiniest hotels. But New Jersey—New Jersey was midway between the two people Bethany needed to see.

Where in New Jersey?

A city, and one with a train or bus station, and with the sort of hotels where they didn't care who you were—and in walking distance of the station—and—

And there were several candidates, but his instincts said Newark. Trains to everywhere, buses, an airport, and suffering people who would sell you their cars for a thousand dollars cash. And if he was wrong, well, there were other ways.

In Newark, he hung around in the crescent between the station and the Rutgers campus. This is where she would be comfortable. She could walk to the station, but the campus would reassure her: like most educated people, she perceived colleges as safe. And Rutgers was indeed very safe.

Although not today.

Stuart spotted Bethany when she crossed the street toward the campus, and for a weak moment wished he had a God to thank.

She had changed her hair, and that was good, but the baseball cap made her conspicuous, and she had yet to master the true arts of deception, because the greater disguise was not appearance but behavior. Simply walking as if you belonged and hadn't a care in the world could help you avoid a great deal of trouble.

He gave her a head start, using the time to check the athletic bag again, to be sure that all the components of his Springfield M1A with its EBR Tactical Chassis system were ready at hand. He slid the mount along the rail, and it moved freely.

He zipped up the bag and followed her onto the campus.

On the far side of the Rutgers campus, Bethany found a cab rank. She had decided that she needed to see David, but with the FBI in the area she could no longer trust the Newark train station, so she told the driver to head for Manhattan. She would buy a ticket on Amtrak. Now that she had cut her hair—

Glass shattered around her.

Twice.

Stuart was already on the move, fleeing the high ground he had chosen to catch the taxi at the long traffic light where it would cross the boulevard. In the movies people shot at moving cars all the time and, if they were the good guys, mostly hit them; in real life that was a fantasy. Distance, wind, leaves, gravity, the flutter of a bird's wings—anything could spoil the rotation that kept a bullet on its straight course. So could the target's motion: even with a rifle spitting out a projectile at a speed faster than sound, you had to estimate where the target would be when the bullet arrived, and, as a rule, had only one chance.

If you were aiming for a precise spot, better to wait until your target was still.

And Stuart had fired a precise shot. Two, actually: one to break the glass and one to do the damage.

Not to Bethany—he wanted her alive—and not to the driver—that would lead to a more serious investigation.

Stuart had aimed at the empty seat beside hers, a good two feet away, and from the overpass had no trouble hitting it. He had not waited around to see the response, but he could easily envision it. The driver would call the police, supposing the attack to be the work of kids playing with guns. Because nobody was killed, there would be no forensic team, and nobody would ever realize that the steel-jacketed slug had come out of a specialty sniper rifle.

Bethany Barclay would flee the scene long before the police arrived. The driver would let her go, even though he would misunderstand the reason for her panic—again, perception would define reality—and the authorities would never connect the missing passenger in a mindless urban shooting to the woman the feds were looking for.

Or imagine that she could have been the target of the shots.

But Bethany would know. Bethany would believe—incorrectly, but here truth hardly mattered—that the shots had been intended to kill her. Being the stubborn individual that she was, she would not collapse and turn herself in. But being the compassionate soul that she also was, she would also turn away from any further involvement with people who knew her, not wanting to put anyone else's life at risk.

Thus she would be left with one option only.

She would head west after all, which was what his employers wanted.

Back in his car, confident that he would reach Chicago ahead of her, Stuart Van Der Staal congratulated himself on a job well done.

NINE

By the time Bethany's terror had settled into mere panic, she was deep inside a residential neighborhood. She was still carrying her backpack, and she knew that she must be terribly conspicuous.

She wondered whether she should just turn herself in. The police might not be ten feet tall, but Bethany was starting to believe that whoever was manipulating her was taller still. What kept her moving was her refusal to let them win. She didn't know who they were; she didn't know what they wanted; but she knew they had killed Annabelle, and that nobody would believe her if she tried to explain.

If Annabelle's murder was going to be solved, Bethany would have to do it herself.

Bethany had always been a loner, and self-reliant: the effect, she knew, of growing up with the mockery of Aunt Claudia's children, who had never let her forget that her father had dropped her on the doorstep on his way to prison; or that he had never said who her mother was. When she wasn't doing chores, saying prayers, or going to school, Bethany had sat around the tidy house reading, and reading, and reading. She had created a life in her books, and learned to be reserved in the presence of others who—

She saw a church.

It was not the first one she had passed on her quick march away from the site of the shooting. She was not looking for a church; she was not looking for anything in particular; but for some reason the church drew her.

The church was narrow and whitewashed, its crumbling spires squeezed between two larger buildings, and it occurred to Bethany that it had been here a very long time, and had probably housed congregations from several different denominations in the course of its existence. Now the message board proclaimed it to be non-denominational, and she realized what had drawn her attention. Beneath the name of the church was a slogan, in black moveable letters under glass:

Are You Running Forward or Just Running Away?

Bethany smiled in spite of her predicament; and before she could quite make up her mind, found herself climbing the steps. The doors were old, and of heavy wood, but were well-oiled, and gave easily. Inside was cool. She stepped into what an Episcopalian would call the nave. A black man of some years was sitting at the piano, leafing through sheet music.

"Excuse me," she said, her voice not yet level.

He looked up in surprise, then stood, walked down the aisle toward her. "May I help you?"

"I . . . I'd like to see the priest."

"I take it you mean the pastor."

She colored. "Yes. I'm sorry."

"Not at all." He brushed off his hands, then offered one. "I'm Pastor Perryman. How can I help?"

They sat down on a wooden pew. Bethany cried a little, and Pastor Perryman, being old school, summoned a church sister to comfort her rather than touching her himself. When they were alone again, Bethany began to talk. She had not realized until this instant how desperately she needed to. She didn't tell him everything; not even close; and he didn't press her to say more. But she made clear that she was wanted by the police in Virginia for a terrible crime she hadn't committed, and that a friend of hers had been killed, and that she thought the two crimes were related.

The pastor, having heard her out, reminded her that Moses, too, had run off, after killing the Egyptian who was beating one of the Hebrews. God had delivered Moses, and made him a great leader.

"I'm no Moses," said Bethany.

"That's not the point of the story."

"You're saying God will still deliver me."

The pastor shook his head. "I don't purport to know the mind of God or what plans He has for you. You shouldn't listen to anybody who claims to know either one. But I am saying you should put your faith in Him, and nowhere else."

Here Bethany ran up against the blank wall that had always stymied her. "I don't have any way of knowing if I'm doing what God wants me to do."

"But you do. You study Scripture, you pray for guidance, you spend time with your fellow believers, and beyond that, you do the best you can." His voice was gentle. "I suppose there's no point in urging you to turn yourself in."

"I can't. Not yet."

"Scripture teaches us that the authorities are constituted by God."

She shut her eyes briefly. "But they're mortal. They're capable of error."

"You can't run forever."

"I was just thinking that."

"You'll need your faith to sustain you in your flight, but you'll need it even more when they catch you."

They prayed together. He never asked her name. He never questioned her tale. She left the church with a pocket New Testament, and a fresh determination to succeed in her quest.

Pastor Perryman also gave her some practical parting advice.

"If they're driving you in a particular direction, it must be because there's something they want you to do when you get there. You might ask yourself what it is that you can do that they can't do for themselves."

The pastor had told her where she could catch the commuter bus. Riding toward New York City, Bethany pondered his question. Why her? What could she do that nobody else could?

She saw only one possibility: Annabelle. She knew Annabelle better than anyone. Whatever they wanted likely involved her running buddy.

Bethany huddled in her seat. The forces arrayed against her were titanic. She was only one person. She opened her bag to hunt for a granola bar and found the pocket New Testament instead. She started on the first page of Matthew's Gospel and began to read. By the time she was through the tunnel and into Manhattan, Stuart Van Der Staal had driven over a hundred miles in the wrong direction.

"Ms. Barclay was definitely in Newark," says the Mathematician. "I have it from the Senator, and she has it directly from the Bureau."

The Church Builder picks listlessly at his food. He is, ordinarily, a man of large appetites; but not tonight "I take it we don't know where she is now."

"No."

"Or if she was the one in the taxicab that got shot up."

"No. But it would make sense." The Mathematician shoots his elegant cuffs, twirls his wineglass, doesn't drink. "They want her to do the same thing we want her to do."

The Builder cannot shake his uneasy mood. They are seated in a quiet corner of one of the finest restaurants in Boston. "The difference is, they're willing to be violent, and we're not."

"We can't use the devil's methods to do the Lord's work."

"In time of war, according to Augustine, it is licit to—never mind. You're right. Morality for us is found in method, not merely in result." He sits back, looks around the crowded dining room. Nobody looks back. They are just two old friends of a certain age, the sort who would never be remembered or even noticed. Anonymity is their best protection. "But, George, if anything happens to her, it's on our heads."

The Mathematician shrugs. "We can't protect her if we don't know where she is. I wish she'd get to Chicago where she's supposed to be."

"I suspect she has a plan of her own. I'm beginning to get a sense about this Bethany Barclay." The Builder finally allows himself a small bite of the duck confit. Absolutely delicious, but he is in no mood to appreciate it. "She won't be kept in line."

"You mean Annabelle all over again? That's the last thing we need."

"Let's just concentrate on keeping her alive."

"We have to find her first."

The Builder looks at his old friend. "There's something else on your mind."

The Mathematician toys with his water goblet. "We're still not sure why Bethany ran. After the murder, I mean. She was settled at the bed-and-breakfast, then she suddenly up and fled. Why?"

"Nerves."

"Maybe. But the Senator says the working theory is that she was warned." He leans in. "The trouble is, they don't know how. There were no calls to the inn that night after she was settled. No visitors. No calls to her cell phone, other than the two texts Edna's nephew sent on Monday. The phone was under our control at that time, so the feds don't know about those. There's no cell service at the bed-and-breakfast. So the only way she could have been warned was if someone else had the same idea. Get control of her phone."

"How likely is that?"

"Edna's nephew swears he only sent two texts."

"You obviously have a counter-theory."

"Maybe when we hacked her phone, someone else was already in. Someone who read our texts and sent his own to put her in motion."

The Builder is thoughtful. "I'll be leaving the country tomorrow. Work to do overseas. Unavoidable, I'm afraid. I'm going to have to leave matters in your hands."

TEN

There's a science to running," says the federal agent. His name is Carraway, and, like his literary namesake, he covers deep wells of intelligence and self-regard with a smiling Midwestern boyishness. "We see it all the time, Judge Harrigan. There are guilty fugitives and there are innocent fugitives, but all of them face the same choices. Either they run to the people and places they know, or they run away from them. The trouble is, both paths lead to disaster. Running is never the right thing to do."

Edna Harrigan sits solemnly, occasionally sipping at her tea. She requested this briefing on the search for Bethany Barclay, and, knowing the people she knows, swiftly prevailed. She is perfectly aware that the two men sitting in the great room of her secluded house are spending as much time assessing her as she was assessing them. The county sheriff would never dare ask the great judge whether she had anything to do with Bethany's escape. Probably these men won't either; but they will prod her for information all the same. It is Wednesday morning, and Bethany has been on the run since Monday night.

"That doesn't sound very scientific, Agent Carraway." The smile Edna offers is bland and disapproving. "That sounds rather more like a cliché."

Carraway's smile is considerably more ingenuous. His straw-colored hair is flat and well-ordered. "Maybe you're right, Judge. But, just for a minute, let's pretend that I'm right. Which path do you think Ms. Barclay would choose? To whom would she go for help? Friends or strangers?"

"Let me turn the question around, Agent Carraway. I assume you have reconstructed Bethany's movements. Which does it seem to you she is doing?"

"I'm afraid we lost the trail in Pittsburgh. But there are people—my partner here for one—who think she's on her way to Ohio."

The partner in question is a Samoan named Pulu. He is broad shouldered and thick through the hips, but his delicacy of movement suggests training in something cautious and conceptual, like classical dance. Until now he has been sitting quietly, studying the woods beyond the two-story windows. Twice he has responded to text messages, even though service out here is horrendous for ordinary mortals. He has also made occasional notes on his leather-bound pad. Now he speaks, mostly toward the window:

"She used to have a friend. A Mr. Sam DeMarco. I'm sure you remember him."

Edna nods. "He used to live over toward Little Washington. A rather angry-looking man. Always looking for an argument. People used to say he was in the witness protection program, because there was no record of him anywhere before he showed up. We thought he was a Mafia hit man or something. He disappeared, oh, a year ago. We assumed you people moved him."

The senior agent shakes his head. "We didn't move Mr. DeMarco, ma'am, and neither did the Marshals Service. He wasn't in witness protection. He was an executive who moved out here when his business went belly up. That's all. The reason you folks couldn't find him on Google was that he changed his name." He continues gazing at the view. "The reason Ms. Barclay is likely headed for Ohio is that Mr. DeMarco now lives there."

This is news to the judge, but she covers her surprise well. "Do you have reason to believe that Bethany knows that he lives there?"

Pulu finally shifts his eyes her way. "Do you?"

When Edna does not dignify the question with an answer, boyish Carraway deftly takes back the ball. "The point is, your friend Bethany Barclay was very close to Mr. DeMarco. They went hunting together, they went to the shooting range, they rode horses. Sort of a surrogate father for her. The leading theory is that if she knows where he is, that's where she'll go."

He is asking the same question as Pulu, but more politely. And Edna answers in kind. "I'm afraid that I have no information that can help you, Agent Carraway. I had no idea that Mr. DeMarco was in Ohio, and I certainly have no knowledge of any contacts between the two of them subsequent to his disappearance."

Pulu again: "We're open to alternative theories."

"I really have none to offer."

"There must be somebody."

"Not really. Bethany wasn't close to many people. I assume you know her history." She waits but nobody tells her to stop. "Her father is from what they still call white trash down here. Nobody knows who her mother was. The father—Everett, his name was—just showed up one day with this little girl, not a year old, and dumped her in the lap of his older sister, Claudia. Claudia was married, and had five of her own, but she took in Bethany because she was a Christian woman and could do no other. Her husband worked construction. He had his welder's card, but they had to move around to follow the boom. They lived down toward Newport News back in the eighties when the Navy was building ships hand over fist, and when the shipping boom dried up the housing boom went with it they headed down to North Carolina, where Claudia had people. Later on, they came back up here and settled over in Pennville, which, if you don't know, is a working-class town twenty miles west of Front Royal, right at the foot of the mountains. Bethany was smart, she did well in school, her teachers adored her, but she rarely put down roots deep enough to make best friends. She went to Barnard on a scholarship, went to Oxford, did Harvard Law—I'm sure you know all that—and in all that time, the only close friend I've ever heard her speak of was Annabelle, and of course she's dead. So's Claudia's husband, which is why Claudia moved back down to North Carolina, to be near her people."

"But you don't think Bethany would go to her aunt," says Pulu, stating a fact. "She wouldn't go to any of the cousins she grew up with, either, would she? She wasn't close to her family. She wouldn't be able to count on them to keep their mouths shut."

Edna knows he is provoking her intentionally; but she allows it. "I suspect, Agent Pulu, that the reason she wouldn't go to her family is that she would not want to place them at risk."

Pulu is unimpressed. His scowl is impressively intimidating. "But she'd put her friend Annabelle's sister at risk?"

"I don't know. I take your word that Bethany visited her. I have no idea why. She wasn't close to Annabelle's family. They didn't like her very much." She stirs her tea but doesn't drop her eyes. "I believe that they blame her for not keeping Annabelle clean."

"So you think she's running alone? Not asking for help?"

"I wouldn't hazard a guess, Agent Pulu. She certainly is a strong-willed and independent young woman. Whatever she is doing, she is perfectly capable of doing without help."

"Or so she believes," says Pulu, unsatisfied.

Carraway's turn: "You were her mentor, Judge Harrigan. The biggest influence on her. Her model. You knew her better than anyone else out here."

"And based on that knowledge, Agent Carraway, I can tell you only that Bethany is smarter than you seem to think. She won't fall into some familiar pattern that you studied on the course. She won't endanger those close to her by relying on them. She won't do anything predictable." She presses her cane into the floor and forces herself to her feet. The agents also stand. "It has been a long afternoon, gentlemen. I want to thank you for your time."

They all shake hands.

On the front porch the judge offers parting advice.

"One more thing, gentlemen. Bethany Barclay is not only intelligent. She is also an individual of enormous dedication and purpose. I very much doubt that she is running in the sense that you mean it. Oh, I'm sure she would prefer not to risk prison for a crime I am confident she did not commit. But she is not the sort simply to run away. If she's running, she's running toward something."

Pulu catches her drift an instant before his partner did. "You think she's trying to find out who did it."

"You're the ones who say that she has modeled herself on me. Well, that is what I would do."

"Ohio?" says Pulu as they drive off along Route 647.

Carraway offers the boyish smile. "Best I could come up with under the circumstances."

"DeMarco's not in Ohio," his partner persists.

"But the cover story the Marshals spread around town when they moved him says he is. Ashland, Ohio. I'm sure Bethany Barclay would have heard the gossip."

Pulu thinks this over. "What if she knows where DeMarco really is?"

"We have that contingency covered."

"This is not going well," says Edna later. She has driven fifteen miles north to Front Royal, where the mobile reception is clearer, and is speaking on a disposable cell phone: her house line is now out of bounds. The Garden as an entity is not as technologically advanced as its adversary; the Builder's greatest weakness, Edna sometimes thinks, is his dogged determination to keep them old-fashioned.

"It was never a perfect plan," says the voice at the other end. "The trouble is, we don't have a better one."

"I'm worried about her, Builder. They're not fools. What if she gets caught?"

"That would be a true tragedy. But the decision to put her in motion was unanimous."

Edna shuts her eyes. She is a loner, and close to few people, but she loves Bethany Barclay – loves her as friend and protégé and surrogate daughter. When the Church Builder recruited the judge, he warned her that the task would require great sacrifices. He never mentioned that the sacrifices would be of other people.

"We're supposed to be different," she finally says. "We're supposed to be the good guys."

"We are different." A beat. "Try to remember what's at stake."

She rubs tired eyes. "It's just that the poor girl has suffered so much."

"I wish matters were otherwise." The Builder's voice is sad. "But I'm afraid she's going to have to suffer a little more."

ELEVEN

The restaurant was the sort of cosmopolitan masterpiece that you will find nowhere on earth except Brooklyn: to enjoy the Russian cuisine, you are seated by a voluble maitre d' who speaks mostly Spanish, and served by a stolid, watchful Korean whose knowledge of the menu is phonetic. And the owners, Bethany suspected, lived neither in Moscow nor Brighton Beach but would turn out instead to be Lebanese or French or Australian, living happily out in Montclair. Whatever the true answer, she was wary of meeting Peter Zhukov on his home turf of Little Odessa, because he was always frenetic here, and therefore dangerous, whereas in Manhattan—where she had seen him last, at his sister's apartment a couple of years ago—he seemed in some peculiar way smaller and even calmer, as though the experience of venturing beyond his neighborhood served as tranquilizer, or perhaps intimidator.

But that option was not available. Peter had designated the meeting ground, and Bethany was not about to question his choice. She was the supplicant, and she would have only one chance to talk to him, after which he would perform his calculations: so much value if he turned her in, so much value if he let her loose. The other reason Bethany was uneasy was that the various people searching for her would consider Annabelle's family an obvious place to watch.

Although she suspected that Peter would have no trouble knowing whether he was being watched.

Bethany walked. Nervously. She felt eerily displaced, as though the city was shifting around her whenever she turned her back. She looked up and down the street, wondering whether she was quite sane. It was crazy to be here. She spoke ten words of Russian and read even less, and so would likely stand out in the Russian sections of Brighton Beach, where most of the signs were Cyrillic. These were, literally, the Caucasian people, the people of the Caucasus, and their untrusting stares as she strode among them reminded her of why their beloved Motherland, despite heroic suffering, had lost few wars in its history. Unless one counted the Cold War, a failed effort that left their proud country a shambles.

Bethany had borrowed the telephone at an Internet café to place the call. She didn't have Peter's number but she had the number of one of the other cousins, who agreed, reluctantly, to pass on a message.

And so she found herself, just before noon, standing in the spring sunshine on a noisy street of stores a block from Ocean Parkway. The restaurant was small and glass-fronted with the name in Russian but not repeated in English, although the logos for American soft drinks and American beer did duty in both. She stepped inside. The interior seemed gloomy after the brightness without. The linoleum gleamed. An identical spray of fake flowers was centered on each crimson table cloth. The lunch hour was busy and loud but everyone stopped to look when Bethany walked in, including Peter, who sat near the kitchen in his own little island of shadow with easy access to both emergency exits. It was the spot Bethany would have chosen for herself if watching the door happened to be more important than watching the street.

Peter Zhukov. Peter the Great, as Annabelle called him. Bethany had asked her once if her brother was Russian Mafia, and her running buddy had shrugged, then stretched out her hand, palm downward, tilting it delicately side to side. Maybe. Maybe not.

"But he's knows bad people," Annabelle had murmured. "I know that for a fact."

Bethany was counting on it.

———

He greeted her with rough formality, shaking her hand so abruptly that she nearly forgot he had done it. Peter was a thick-chested bullet of a man, and tended to fire off verbal shots in unexpected directions. He had wavy hair, once buttery, now touched with gray, and a Lenin-like goatee that for some reason he dyed black. His sky blue summer-weight wool-blend suit probably cost as much as her third-hand Volvo. It was cut beautifully, double breasted to conceal his heft, and never seemed to bunch or stretch. He wore gold rings on several fingers and a small diamond in his right ear. His rounded mouth, somehow prim, was the same as Annabelle's, and although his eyes were an eerily penetrating orange rather than his half sister's hazel, they burned with the same determination to best whatever the obstacle might be, untempered in his case by Annabelle's sense of fun—a virtue, unlikely as it seemed, that must have come from her West Indian side.

"I hope I'm not late," she said.

"I am always early." An explanation or a reproof? With Peter Zhukov, you could never tell.

"This place is fantastic."

"Yes. Let's eat, okay?"

Peter had ordered kebabs and pear soda for them both, and Bethany, who had hit McDonald's on the way just in case, nibbled dutifully because she did not want to be rude. He told her that the kebabs were called *liulia*, and consisted of spiced lamb and scallions.

"It's delicious, okay?" An order, not a question. His fingers played idly with the gold chain on his wrist. A small crooked plate on the end proclaimed a message: WWJD. He noticed her glance. "You are surprised, right? Annabelle gave it to me. I wear it in her memory, okay?"

"Okay. Yes."

But Peter seemed offended. "It's not cheap from on the street, okay? She took a course. She made it. It's unique, okay? The only one in existence. Like Annabelle."

Bethany swallowed, and reminded herself of his prickly pride. "I think it's a wonderful . . . gesture."

The orange glare of those peculiar eyes was too much for her, and she turned away. On the television a Russian pop star with pink hair performed a mock-Britney video with the sound turned off. From the kitchen blared what sounded like a talk show, only the arguments were in swift, virulent Russian, so perhaps it was the chef yelling at his help. Bethany knew a smattering of the language, mostly picked up from hanging around Annabelle, but this steady stream of invective defeated her. Peter hardly looked at her while speaking, preferring to leaf through the pages of *Ruskiy bazaar* to prove his disdain. He frowned at the articles, shook his head at the pictures, upset that he had missed them, no doubt, for among the many enterprises in which Peter Zhukov had his hand were two or three of Brooklyn's dozen or so Russian-language newspapers. She tried every trick she knew to charm him, but Peter refused to be drawn. Alone among the Russian side of the family, he had kept in contact with the adult Annabelle, which is why Bethany was here.

So they talked for a while about old times, and Bethany reminded herself that Peter alone among the Russian side never quite held her responsible for Annabelle's long slide into the shadow lands of addiction. She asked about his business, and he was evasive, and he asked about her business, and she was evasive. This was the only kind of conversation Peter ever had, roundabout and clever, while he made his little calculations; the fact that Bethany was on the run would not change that. And so, out of politeness, she asked after his family, but Peter shot off in a different direction. He asked her if she knew that there were blacks in Russia, and she said no, and he said his paper had done an article on them, mostly Africans, some descendants of slaves, but that those were few in number. Then he asked if she knew that in Russia they called the Chechens by a word that would translate roughly as nigger, and Bethany knew he was trying to get a rise out of her by insulting Annabelle, but did not know why. He told her that dark-skinned Russians were called black, even if they were Caucasian, as most of them were, and that "black" in Russian was derogatory. He told her how after the apartment-house bombings in Moscow in the nineties, as they did after every act of terrorism, the police had started by rounding up "the blacks"—an event missed by the Western media. Still she refused to rise. He spoke of how hard it was for the blacks to get work and, sometimes, housing. He spoke of high government officials using the derogatory words without public censure, or notice in the West. He spoke of the shame of having a child with a dark complexion, and how some Russian parents disowned their darker children. Finally she realized that Peter was still talking about the funeral, trying to explain why his half sister had never been fully accepted by the Russian side of the family. He was trying to make her understand. It is not racism, he said. It is just the way it is.

Bethany dropped her eyes to her kebab and said she understood. But another part of her burned afresh with anger at the world that had taken her beloved friend and his beloved sister; and she found herself freshened in her determination to find the culprit.

The waiter approached the table to see whether they wanted anything else, but Peter had a special stare for underlings, and the young man froze, then backed away.

"I assume you wish nothing else," Peter said, pointing to Bethany's plate, and her barely touched food.

"No, right, I'm fine," she assured him, chipper as you like.

He came at last to the trouble she was in, and she answered that it was a misunderstanding that would soon be cleared up. The pout of Peter's bow mouth, so like his sister's, told her that he doubted her forecast. But he said nothing. He only shrugged, and looked openly at his watch, which managed to be absurdly flat yet encrusted with enough diamonds to marry a dozen women.

It was time to stop messing around.

"Peter, listen. Let me tell you why I called."

He dipped his chin and lifted it again, as if to grant permission. And permission was of considerable importance just now, because she was in Peter's world, and needed his help.

"Please," he said.

"Do you remember after the funeral? Our conversation?"

"Remind me, please."

For a moment they sized each other up. Peter was a romantic, Annabelle always said. In a world in which the Russian Mafia had become just another murderous criminal gang, he was one of the handful of rising stars who nevertheless styled himself one of the *vory v zakone*, the "thieves in law" as they were once called, men who adhered to the old-fashioned code of honor that had once ruled the Russian underworld.

It was that code upon which she was about to call.

"You said, if you ever found out who killed your sister, there were people who could take care of him."

The Russian seemed to sink into deep thought, those orange eyes scrunching. "I do not recall this."

"We were on the steps of the church. I was standing with Tia Christina."

"I do not recall this."

She saw the point. "I'm not trying to entrap you, Peter. I need your help. I'm trying to find out who murdered Annabelle."

"Good luck." Peter glanced at his watch, again making a great show: a man with more important things to do.

So she said the rest: "Somebody took a shot at me."

For the first time, he seemed moderately impressed. "Look, you're alive, okay?"

"What I'm saying is, people are trying to stop me."

"I see." His gaze wandered over her face, then darted toward the door and around the room before settling on her once more. "Do you have any information for me?"

"No."

"Then a gift. You have brought me perhaps a little gift?" The severe orange eyes bounced back and forth between her face and her hands as though he expected her to present a wrapped box.

"I'm sorry," she said, momentarily thrown. "No. No gift."

"A toy for one of my children, perhaps. A game? A puzzle?"

Bethany did not understand what he was asking but could tell that he expected her to.

"Next time." She tried to look winsome. "I promise."

Peter nodded, broke off a piece of black bread, then thought better of it and, instead of eating it, pointed it in her direction. "Then you are here for a different reason? Is that why you ask about my business?"

"I'm here for Annabelle's sake. She was involved in something when she died. Doing a favor. I'd like to know what it was, and who it was for."

"And you think I know?"

"She didn't have a lot of friends, Peter. There weren't many people she would have trusted."

The eyes flared, his body tautened, as the sleeping predator awoke. This was precisely the reaction she had hoped to evoke. She didn't need the charming newspaper editor; she needed the gangster.

The tricky part now was to survive.

"Why do you ask this?" Sharply, a rebuke.

Bethany refused to retreat. "Because I need to know the answer, Peter. I can't fully explain, but I need to know. Annabelle was my friend. My best friend in the world. You know I'm on the run." A tight, reluctant nod from the other side of the flowerpot. "I believe that I'm running from the people who killed your sister. You and I have the same interest, Peter. We both want to find the killer."

She had to stop her speech just then because his cell phone burred gently. He listened without speaking for a minute or so, then said *khorosho*, and hung up. The orange eyes continued to circle and hover, angry birds looking for a place to land. And feed.

"You are on the run," he said, repeating her words.

"Yes." Her turn to pause, but there was no sugarcoating the question. "Are you going to turn me in?"

"Perhaps. We shall see." A longer interlude, while Peter gazed at her with those sober orange eyes, working out all the options the way he always did, deciding which was most profitable. "Do you know the word *krysha*?" he asked at last. "Did my sister teach you this word?"

"No. No, I don't think so."

"Then listen, please. It means, literally 'roof.' It refers to protection. If, say, a business seeks the protection of a man of influence from the neighborhood, and if this man agrees, then the business is said to be under his *krysha*, and then, if you attack the business, you make war on the man of influence. Do you see, Bethany?"

"Yes, Peter."

"Sometimes *krysha* also refers to the organization through which protection is granted. So, the man of influence might run a *krysha* and also grant *krysha*. Are you with me? Okay?"

"Yes." Peter still had not said whether he was going to turn her in. It struck her that his question about her being on the run had not come until after the phone call. She glanced out at the sunny street but saw no sign of disturbance.

"The *krysha* is a very important form of protection," Peter was saying, index finger raised in declamation, and Bethany sensed, or hoped she did, that his decision was in her favor. "It is a genuine protection. No one will want to go to war with the man of influence and his *krysha*, okay? Not unless he is a man of more influence. Okay?"

"Okay."

"In Russia, the chief of the local militia might run a *krysha*. And maybe the manager of some big sports star runs another one, okay? All it takes is influence."

"I understand," she said, folding her hands like a student.

"I have a friend of a friend whose father's brother is a man of influence. Six months ago, my sister was very worried, okay? She would call me up, she would say, 'Pyotr'—she called me that, okay? My name is Peter now but she liked Pyotr—she would say, 'Pyotr, I am frightened. Bad people are after me.' The kind of thing a woman says to get attention, you know?" Bethany kept her face stone. She might have known, she might not have known, but she was not about to interrupt now that he was telling the story. "But my sister, well, she does not usually make things up to get attention. She likes to be on her own. She never calls just because she is lonely, only when she has something to say, okay? So, when she says to me, 'Bad people are after me,' I have to take this seriously. I cannot pretend she is making this up. And I hear the fear in her voice, it is real, okay? Naturally, I ask her who is after her. She won't say. This much she tells me, that the bad people are after her because of what she is looking for. So then naturally I ask her what she is looking for. She tells me it is valuable, okay? I ask her, how valuable? She says, Very valuable. She won't say anything else. 'Help me, Pyotr,' she says. 'I can't let them stop me.'"

The powerful hands tore another piece of black bread from the loaf. Bethany wanted to ask the obvious question but dared not break the flow.

"So I go visit the brother of the father of the friend of my friend. We come to an arrangement. I give him a piece of a couple of my enterprises. Maybe he gets something from the fish market. Maybe I share the profits from a newspaper. Maybe something else, okay? It doesn't matter. Maybe I make him a promise. Maybe I owe him now a favor. Anyway, he agrees, okay? He will bring my sister under his *krysha*. He will protect her. He is a man of influence, he can spread the word in the proper places. My sister is under his roof. If anybody harms her in any way, they make war on this man, okay? He takes this obligation very seriously."

He signaled the waiter to refill his glass and bring more bread.

"So, now Annabelle is dead, okay? So now the man of influence, he has to carry out his obligation, or nobody will have any respect for his *krysha*, okay?" Peter seemed to be working himself into a frenzy, and she remembered his tears at the funeral. "You come into a man's house, you harm a guest under his roof, he has to take care of it, and he has to act swiftly, so that there is no question."

"Which means what, exactly?"

Peter's expression grew savage, and she imagined ancestors fighting to the last drop of blood on the steppes, protecting the Motherland from every invader. "The man of influence has been insulted, Bethany. This is intolerable. Naturally, he has to fulfill his obligation."

"Naturally," she echoed, voice faint.

"I loved my sister very much, okay?"

Bethany swallowed. In for a penny. "Do you love her enough to tell me who did it? Who the . . . the man of influence . . . is, um, going after?"

"This man does not tell me his business, okay?" His face had gone stony. "I do not ask."

Although she knew the stare was meant to discourage her, she refused to surrender. "Then can you at least tell me where Bethany was going? Or where she'd been?"

"My sister, she didn't tell me where she was going," he said, with finality. "I didn't ask, okay?"

"She called you six months ago. That's around the same time she visited me. Just before she disappeared." Bethany tried to work this through. "And when she called, she didn't say, 'I can't let them hurt me.' She said 'I can't let them stop me.' Is that right?"

"So what? It is the same."

But it wasn't the same. Bethany took a moment. Annabelle had been looking for something when she disappeared. Bad people wanted to kill her. And maybe Bethany was reading too much into the words, but it sounded like her running buddy's fear was less for her life than for her quest.

"And no hint of what she was looking for?"

"Look, she was my sister, okay? Who cares why she was in trouble? She needed my help. I helped her. I am her brother." He was toying with the WWJD bracelet again. "My sister was a very determined woman, okay? She had her demons, but when she wanted something she knew how to get it. And what she was doing—well, nobody was forcing her, okay? She was happy to help." The eyes smoldered. "She loved you very much, Bethany. This is why I choose to believe you, okay? This is why I don't turn you in. Because my sister loved you." The eyes flickered interrogatively. "It is possible she was planning to seek your assistance."

"She didn't. She didn't tell me anything."

"She told me she had to see the wise man. And that you would know him, too."

"The wise man? Who on earth—"

His cell phone burred softly. He raised a wide hand, fingers splayed to tell her to wait, and listened, and whispered, and listened again.

Peter put his phone down again, brows furrowed. Again she knew not to interrupt him in this pensive moment.

"My sister loved you very much," he repeated. "So I will tell you this one more thing, okay? My sister didn't tell me where she'd been or where she was going or what she was looking for. She told me only that she had to see the wise man. But you do not know who this is."

"No."

He seemed disappointed. His cell phone beeped. He glanced at it. "She told me also that an old friend of yours was very upset with her."

"A friend of mine? Did she tell you who?" She leaned forward. "Peter, please. I don't know who the wise man is. I don't know what friend was upset with her. But that's not why you met me. Please. What else did Annabelle tell you? There's something. I can see it in your eyes."

Again he studied her hands. Then he shook his head, not so much in denial as in refusal: whatever further secrets Annabelle had shared with Peter Zhukov, he was not about to betray them.

"You say you love my sister. This is good. So, I tell you what. If you find the people who did this, do not turn them in. Call. Follow me? I give you my number. You call me, I call the man of influence, your hands are clean, okay? He has been insulted, he has to fulfill his obligation."

She said, slowly, "I don't know that I can do that, Peter."

But he was not interested in her qualms. He recited the number, twice, confident that she would not forget. He finished his dessert, dabbed at his small mouth, the gesture surprisingly dainty given his large hands. "We have to be moving now," said Peter, counting out some cash to leave on the table. Bethany half expected him to use rubles. "There are some people coming this way, and they are not of this neighborhood, and they are not tourists either."

"The FBI?" she asked, as, in her mind, the cell door clanged shut, the walls her home for the next half century.

"Maybe worse," said Peter Zhukov, hopping lightly to his feet. "Come."

TWELVE

Although it had been just two days since she discovered the body of Kenneth Kirkland in her kitchen, Bethany felt as if she had been running forever. The near-constant flight had drained most of her physical and emotional reserves, and yet she knew she dared not stop.

"Where are we going?" she asked, following Peter into the boisterous kitchen, where no one remarked on their presence.

"Just follow me, okay?"

"Who are we running from?"

"I don't know." He bypassed the rear exit and led her down rickety stairs to a basement storeroom, shelves piled high with boxes and cans.

"Then why are we running?"

"Just come."

The basement was longer than the restaurant, and she guessed that several establishments shared it. They passed through a series of low arches of crumbling brick. The cases of food gave way to stacks of paper goods. There was a smell of ink. The lighting was very poor. It occurred to Bethany that Peter might well be lying about people on their tail, that she had followed him underground without a murmur of complaint, and that nobody knew where she was. But he was Annabelle's big brother, she had listened to his long-winded toasts at her running buddy's apartment, though she had been able to answer, when it was her turn, with little more than a hearty *"Za vas!"*

The basement became a tunnel and sloped downward, and Bethany, who hated low spaces, decided that this would be a good moment to start praying. Following Peter's broad shoulders as he shuffled ahead, worried as much about what lay ahead as what followed behind, she struggled to remember more of Aunt Claudia's lessons, wishing that some comforting bit of Scripture would pop into her head, unaware that she was praying already.

"Peter?" she whispered, using curiosity to kill the fear, for a question had been nagging at her ever since he told his story.

"Yes?"

"The man of influence you mentioned. The man with the *krysha*."

"Yes?"

"Has he . . . already started? Taking revenge, I mean?"

Peter spoke without slowing. The dank tunnel was wide enough only for them to travel single file, and Peter kept vanishing ahead in the shadows. Water dripped somewhere. Rats skittered in the darkness. "What this man does is not like revenge, okay?" said Peter over his shoulder. "I told you. It is more like obligation."

"And is he carrying out his obligation already?"

"He carries out his obligations always. He is a man who is very serious about his duty." He stopped, held up a hand for silence, listened. "Like I am, okay? Like you are." He listened again. So did Bethany, but she heard only the rats, and could not suppress a shudder. Rats and being buried in the earth: her two worst things. Peter said, softly, "There is somebody down here."

"You mean they followed us?"

"This is possible, okay?"

She peered back the way they had come but saw only the thin light of the intermittent bare bulbs, most of them out. She stretched out her hearing the way her father had taught her when they used to hunt, filtering each sound until she came to the next, and caught nothing.

Something.

A quiet footstep. Two. Three.

"Who is it?" she whispered.

"Come," he said, not bothering to answer. "Hurry, okay?"

They moved faster now, Peter in his fancy suit, Bethany in her slacks and flats. Twice the tunnel split, and twice he knew which was the way. Once she heard a subway rumble past very close. Another time she felt the heavy silent thunder of a water main. But mostly she heard the rats. There were no good ways to die, but being killed down here struck her as a particularly bad one.

"Do you have a gun?" Peter asked at one point.

"No. Do you?"

He slowed long enough to glare. "Of course not. I am a businessman, okay?"

"Okay," she said solemnly, ready at this point to trade a year of life for the smallest glimmer of sunlight.

They walked on. She felt all of Brooklyn pressing down above her, and she bowed instinctively from its weight. She asked what tunnel this was, for she knew the tale of a vast network of secret passageways beneath the city to be a myth.

"Just hurry," he said.

But Bethany no longer heard the footsteps, and it occurred to her that they could have been echoes. She wondered whether he was lying about the gun.

He stopped at a heavy metal door and it took them both to open it, and then, in the wake of the hideous screech as it scraped the floor, he pushed her against the wall and put a hand over her mouth. She broke free with no trouble and squared to fight despite the cramped space, but Peter was looking back the way they had come and had a finger to his lips. And it occurred to her that had there been trouble behind them, Peter had placed himself in the line of fire.

A man of honor after all.

"Come," he said, and resumed a slower pace. "Not long now."

They reached another stair and Bethany was ready to start climbing, but Peter touched her hand and told her to wait. She fidgeted as he made a brief cell phone call, and she looked around at heavy girders and loose wires and wondered whether he could possibly get any reception. Then he put the phone away and nodded, and Bethany scurried up the stair behind him. They emerged in an ornate, book-lined room with leaded windows, and stepped through a heavy wooden door into the glittering nave of a huge Russian Orthodox church, candles and icons and stained glass everywhere.

A lone priest knelt in prayer. He was in a black velvet *riasa*, and his beard as he stood seemed wider than it was long. Peter paused and whispered. The priest blessed him, and Peter kissed his ring.

Bethany stood nervously, wondering if she was supposed to follow suit, but the priest returned to his prayers, and Peter bustled her down the aisle.

"What was that?" she asked.

"I take every precaution," he said, but he looked embarrassed, as if she had caught him at sin.

They stood together outside the church, on a quiet residential street, Bethany nursing a dozen questions Peter would never answer. She cupped a hand above her eyes, but in the blinding sunlight still had to squint to make out his face.

"We have lost them. We are clean." He was speaking over his shoulder as he used his reflection in a window to adjust the line of his jacket.

"Who were they?" she asked, still suspicious.

"Maybe some bad men, okay? Maybe some very bad men."

She had her hands on her hips. "Or maybe nobody. You dragged me down there for a reason."

Peter ignored her. He straightened his tie, brushed his collar. As she tried to work him out, he pressed a button on his phone and listened without speaking. Then he slipped it back into his pocket.

"So. You will find your own way now, okay? I think you will be leaving the city."

"I guess so."

"Maybe you'll find the wise man, huh? The guy my sister was going to see." Not waiting for her answer, he waved up and down the street, possessively. "So, it wouldn't be such a good idea for you to come back to this neighborhood again, okay? Not unless you bring me a gift."

"I'm still not sure what it is you want."

"For now, until you bring my gift, all I want is for you to tell me if you find out who killed my sister." Adjusting with the bracelet again. She read the pain on his face, and knew he wore it as a reminder; and that he was dead serious about his vengeance. "You will do that for me?"

"I'll . . . think about it."

"Good. This will please the man of influence."

Peter did not say good-bye. He simply stopped talking and walked past her, down the street, on into the labyrinth of his violent world.

THIRTEEN

Edna Harrigan is in her kitchen when the telephone rings. Her thin arms are deep in the dishwater as she scrubs the cake pan, for she has been baking. She is well known in the county for her cookies and pies. Back when she was on the bench, she brought something for her law clerks at least once a month. Now she delivers the goodies to the sick and the shut-in and the recently widowed and orphaned. If the Boy Scouts or the volunteer firefighters hold a bake sale, Judge Harrigan can be counted on to contribute. Baking is therapy to her, and in her secret heart she knows that it also creates an outlet for a streak of generosity that she tries to hide from a world bound to take advantage of it.

Her desire to hide is one reason that only a dozen people have her telephone number.

The phone keeps ringing.

Stop, Edna says, but only in her mind. *Hang up. I have no desire to talk to you, whoever you are. Go bother someone else.*

She has no machine. If the call isn't worth trying a second or third time, she reasons, then it must not be important. And if it is important, somebody will track her down. But of course she is old enough to remember an era of less immediacy. Most people in her hometown didn't have telephones. If you found out about a death a week rather than an hour after it happened, you didn't feel cheated or abused.

Of course, the world was civilized then.

Edna sighs, dries her hands, and takes two painful steps across the kitchen. "Yes," she announces, which is all she ever says.

"Are you watching television, dear?"

The breezy voice of Lillian Hartshorne, Edna's closest friend now that Sylvia Kirkland is gone. Lillian lives in palatial splendor ten miles east of Flint Hill: her late husband founded one of the telecom giants.

"Hello, Lillian."

"You're not watching, are you?"

"I'm not a big television fan."

"Well, your protégé is on again. The one who killed her boyfriend."

"I'm sure she didn't do it, and he wasn't her boyfriend." Automatically. Then the kitchen with its warm baking smell goes chilly. "Lillian, did they catch her?"

"Just turn it on."

"Is she . . . is she—" But Edna cannot finish the question. *I'm afraid she's going to have to suffer a little more,* the Builder said.

"Just turn on the television."

Lillian hangs up.

The only television in the house is in the great room, and it gets little use. Edna has to remind herself which buttons to press on the remote control, and at first turns on the sound system, which she still calls a stereo. Bach's *Concerto for Two Violins* wafts from the speakers. She keeps pushing buttons and at last gets the monitor going. She switches from her favorite History Channel to the news. She catches only the tail end of the story, and therefore must sit through commercials and celebrity divorces and several minutes of mindless political screaming before the anchors circle back to "our lead story."

And, yes, there is Bethany's driver's license photograph, looking, as they all do, like a mug shot.

Another pipe bomb, the anchor intones solemnly. This one targeted an independent research laboratory near the campus of Haverford College, where the suspect was recently spotted. Like the bomb detonated in Virginia, this one was aimed at a facility that does medical research using human embryos.

Sources say the suspect may be a member of a Christian extremist group.

Carraway is in the bullpen, at his desk by the window, with its view of the Washington Monument across the Potomac River. With both the Hoover Building and the Washington Field Office bursting at the seams, special task forces like the one he helps run are typically housed in suburban office towers—in this case a tenth-floor suite in Crystal City, not far from Reagan National Airport. He is watching the rain and trying to figure out why he is so troubled by the briefing memo on his screen. His boss is on her way to a meeting at the Executive Office Building, where she will solemnly report to an interagency committee that the Bureau doesn't have any new leads. They will ask her about the press reports blaming the bombing, third now in a series, on fundamentalist Christian groups. They will ask her if it is true that the suspect, Bethany Barclay, attends a conservative Episcopal church. They will ask her unanswerable questions to fit whatever prejudices they bring to the table. But the fault lies in the lack of information.

"Agent Carraway, sir."

He looks up. One of the interns hands him two message slips. He thanks her, and even smiles, although in truth he's annoyed. Message slips are almost always kooks. Anyone who has good reason to reach him has either his direct line or one of his two cell numbers.

The messages are both from Ted Lesofsky. Great. Exactly what he doesn't need.

"If he calls again," Carraway says, "tell him I'll get back to him when I can."

The intern just stands there, wide-eyed.

"What is it, Valerie?"

"It's just that he says he used to be a special agent."

"He was."

"He says he has valuable information about your case."

"That's what he always says. He calls once a week. The reason he asks for me is that I'm pretty much the last one who'll talk to him." He saw the curiosity in her young face. "He had a nervous breakdown working on a case. He was a good man—he is a good man—but he can't stand that he's not at the center of things anymore. Okay? So just tell him I'll get back to him when I can. Tell him I'll buy him lunch."

The intern leaves. Carraway goes back to staring out the window, trying to figure out what's bothering him. The gray rain spatters the glass. He wonders whether he should—

The glass.

The *glass.*

"Pulu," he says.

His partner sits at a facing desk. He is on the telephone with the Newark field office, where agents are nearly certain that the woman who fled a cab after shots were fired at it was Bethany Barclay.

"Pulu," he says, louder.

"One minute."

"Call them back."

Pulu makes his excuses, presses the hold button, hangs up gently. Three months ago he cracked a receiver by slamming it too hard into the cradle. "What's so important it can't wait?"

Carraway is pawing at his folders. He hates the paperless office and prints out as many reports as he can. "Who shot at the cab?"

"Kids from a bridge."

"At random? That's quite a coincidence."

"The Newark guys know that, Carl. Nobody's jumping to conclusions. They just can't figure out who would, number one, want to kill her, and, number two, know where she was." He is reaching for the phone again. "Maybe it's her own people. Whoever she's working with. Maybe they're mad that she killed that guy in Virginia and blew her cover."

"Then why take two shots and run? Why not nail her when she jumped out? In a vehicle, there's glass to deflect the bullet and maybe mash its nose in. It's a lot easier to hit her once she's on foot. Why not wait?"

"Maybe they got scared."

"Or maybe they never intended to kill her."

Pulu has the receiver in his hand, but he hasn't pushed any buttons. "Okay. I'll bite. What's your theory?"

"Maybe they just wanted to scare her."

"Why?"

"To make her run."

"She was running already. It doesn't make sense."

"I don't know. We're missing something."

Pulu gestures toward the folders. "You're the deputy head of the task force, Carl. If you want to change our orders, talk to the boss. Otherwise, we've got work to do."

He goes back to his phone call. Carraway continues to gaze out the window.

"Pulu."

Down goes the hold button. "What is it this time?"

"Bethany Barclay's our bomber, right?"

"Right."

"Killed that Kirkland fellow, set off the bomb at George Mason, took off for parts unknown, right?"

"Right again." Exasperated. "Carl, I really have to—"

"We found extremist anti-government literature in her house, right?"

"Carl—"

"So how is it that none of her friends remember her reading any of it? No tirades against taxation. No late-night phone calls about how the President is the anti-Christ. Do you really believe she could keep her friends from finding out about any of her secret obsessions?"

"That's why they're called *secret* obsessions, Carl."

"Bear with me another minute. You and I have both done cases with mass murderers and bombers. And a lot of them lead ordinary lives. But once they start off on the rampage, their friends always say, 'You know, he has been acting a little weird lately'—that kind of thing. So, okay, maybe a lot of that is confirmation bias. Still. People say it. But not this time. Her friends, the folks at her church, that Judge Harrigan—none of them is saying 'I told you so.' All of them say she's the last person who'd do the things she's accused of."

Pulu sighed. "So what's the thesis here? You're saying she's innocent?"

"I don't know. Something's not right."

FOURTEEN

A light rain spattered the windows as the SEPTA train to Thorndale glided through the suburbs. Mostly the track passed commercial buildings, but here and there a house was visible. Bethany had boarded in Philadelphia, reasoning, or perhaps hoping, that nobody would expect her to return so swiftly to the very area where she had been seen the night before; or to board the same train. Getting to Philly from Brooklyn had also presented no obstacle: two subways to the Port Authority, and then the bus the rest of the way. She didn't enjoy being on the run, but she was coming to appreciate her father's wisdom: the police really couldn't watch everywhere at once. A little cleverness, a little luck, a little money: these, Everett Barclay always said, were the ingredients for a successful flight.

So far she possessed all three. She preferred not to think about what she'd do when one or two ran out.

When the train reached Haverford she held her breath, but no FBI agents hopped on. The doors whisked shut.

A friend of yours was very upset with her.

The next stop was located right at the edge of the Bryn Mawr campus, and the signs and maps helpfully guided her the rest of the way. The history department was located in a pretty building on North Merion Avenue. To her relief there was no guard. In the lobby she studied the list of offices. A couple of students passed her on the stairs, but she kept her head turned away and her hand to her ear as if talking on her cell. She knew David was in because five minutes ago she'd called his office on that very phone—a disposable purchased with cash—and hung up as soon as he answered. She'd come to Bryn Mawr on a hunch. Even though David taught only half time, he was going stir crazy in the house—Annabelle had said so many times—and, given Polly's mercurial temperament, the tension of her visit was likely to have ignited an argument. Thus human nature alone suggested that so mild-mannered a man as David would have sought the peace and quiet of his office.

And if she was wrong—or if she'd caught him on his way out the door—well, the SEPTA station was still there.

Bethany was surprised at her own calm. Imprisonment terrified her. She couldn't bear the thought of a life lived without the freedom to do as she chose. But the fear wasn't so bad, as long as she stayed in motion. She didn't know how much of Annabelle's movements she could duplicate, but she was determined to try. If she was going to get caught anyway, she'd rather go down fighting than hiding in some hole.

She found David's office without trouble, and found David, too. When she knocked and stepped in, he raised sad eyes from the galleys he was reviewing. He evinced no surprise, but Bethany suspected that he rarely did.

"Are you okay?" he asked softly, and in his eyes she saw only concern.

"I'm sorry to barge in," she said, matching his evident determination to behave as if she wasn't on the run. She closed the door behind her. "I won't take much of your time."

The office was wood paneled and cluttered in a deliciously academic way, with well-thumbed heavy books on the shelves and yellowing papers stacked on every surface: the sort of place where, in an old movie, the doddering professor would light his pipe to put you at ease. But David was anything but doddering. As he studied his guest, the manner that seemed almost sheepish in the presence of his wife was transformed, here on his home ground, into a quiet self-possession.

"I thought you might be back," he finally said. "So did Polly. If you show up, I'm supposed to call her, and about nine different federal agencies. Never mind." He lifted his chin. "Sit."

Bethany had to clear away a stack of books and papers and ancient mail to make space on a chair. "Let me say something at the outset, David. I'd rather you didn't call anyone."

"I know."

"I wouldn't be here if it wasn't important."

"I'm sure." A superior smile tugged at his thin lips. The sadness that drifted like storm clouds in his wake was inching further from weakness and closer to cynicism. It occurred to Bethany that he might not like her any more than his wife did. He was wearing a heavy cable-knit sweater. He lifted his arm, rolled back the sleeve, studied his watch. "I can give you fifteen minutes. Then I have to get back to work."

Had she described him as calm? He wasn't calm; he was cold. You either ordered a fugitive out of your presence or you decided to help or you explained that you'd have to call the police. You didn't give her a limited window of time and then go back to business as usual.

"I want to talk to you about Annabelle," she began.

"I assumed."

"I need to find out what she was doing when she died."

"Need to or want to?"

"Need to, David, believe me. I think it might be the only way to prove my innocence."

"And you think I know? How peculiar." Now the eyes were amused. "Do go on."

She swallowed. He was making her feel small, and she wasn't even sure how. "The other night—there were things Polly said—and things she didn't say"—she felt herself botching it, but she had expected to find him softer—"and, anyway, I got the impression that you and Annabelle might have had some, um, conversations, or even meetings."

"We did."

"Without your wife around, I mean."

David was entirely unembarrassed. "Three times we met. Maybe four. No, three." He was staring into the middle distance, but now focused on

Bethany again. "And get your mind out of the gutter, please. It wasn't what you think. We were working together. No. Let's be more precise. She wanted my help. I was trying to offer it."

"Help doing what?"

"Before I answer that, I want to be clear about something. You think whatever Annabelle was doing got her killed."

She swallowed. "Yes."

"Presumably there's a rationale behind this belief."

"She told a mutual friend that there were people trying to kill her, yes. Because of what she was doing."

"And this mutual friend hasn't gone to the police? Because—correct me if I'm being a simpleton here—but I'd think that would ordinarily be the sort of information that might help solve the crime."

Bethany needed to catch her breath. She felt buffeted by his wit and speed. She had a sudden vision of David Hollins as a terror to his students, and wondered whether, behind closed doors, the balance of power in his marriage was quite what it appeared to the world.

"Let me guess," he continued. "Your source won't go to the police. He's not the type. One of the Russians, I'd bet. Polly won't have anything to do with them, but Annabelle—well, she always did have a soft spot for Peter, didn't she?"

"Are you finished showing how smart you are?" She sounded rather tart, and liked it. "Because, if you are, maybe you can tell me what Annabelle was working on."

He didn't miss a beat. "She was looking for the Pilate Stone."

Bethany heard the capitalization of the two words in David's voice, and knew that he expected her to react. But she had no idea what he was talking about, and said so.

"No?" He glanced at his watch again. "How peculiar. I'd have thought that she'd have told you. Didn't she visit you in Virginia? She told me she was going down to see you."

"She did."

"And she never mentioned the Pilate Stone. How peculiar." Checking his watch. "When Polly told me what you wanted the other night—about the passport—well, I put the sequence together. The last time I saw Annabelle was just before she took the passport. Then she went to Virginia. I assumed you must be involved with her search."

And you're not the only one who assumed that, Bethany realized; but didn't say. Things were falling into place. Some things, anyway.

"What's the Pilate Stone?"

"Well, now I'm hurt." He managed a rather fetching pout. "I devoted three pages to it in my last book but one. Part of my argument for the inherent nuttiness of religion. That's why Annabelle came to me. She'd read about it in my book, and she thought I must know how to find it. I must say she was rather *intense* about the whole thing. You'd have thought the fate of the world was at hazard."

"You still haven't told me what it is."

"Why, so I haven't. My apologies. Jelly beans."

For a moment she was offended, but he was only offering her candy from a glass jar.

"No, thank you."

"Suit yourself." He grabbed a handful. "Well. We haven't much time, so I'll give you the short course. It's a myth. That's the short answer. The Pilate Stone doesn't exist."

"I'm confused."

"Yes, well, it's a confusing topic. If you look it up on Wikipedia or in some archaeological text, you'll learn that it's in a museum in Israel. It was found in 1961. It's the only contemporaneous evidence of the existence of Pontius Pilate." He saw her look. "That's right. It's almost amusing. All over the world, amateur sleuths claim that there's no evidence from the time that demonstrates the existence of Jesus Christ. Actually, there are more sources for Jesus' life than there are for the life of Alexander the Great, and the Alexander sources that have survived are from long after his death. But nobody doubts Alexander's existence."

"I thought you didn't believe in Jesus Christ."

"Christ, no. Jesus, yes." A little smirk. "I make this point in my book. You don't have to reject the whole story to reject the supernatural parts. Never mind. Point is, what they should have been screaming for all those centuries—the folks who doubt the historical accuracy of the Bible—is that there wasn't any evidence that Pontius Pilate actually existed. And there wasn't—until fifty years ago, when Italian archaeologists unearthed the Pilate Stone."

"And it proves Pilate existed?"

"Beyond a doubt. It's limestone, a good medium for carving. It's the right age. It was found in the right place. The inscription is in the correct Latin of the period. Not all of the inscription has survived, but it appears to be a dedication of some structure to the divine Emperor Tiberius, and the dedication is clearly by Pontius Pilate."

Bethany didn't hide her puzzlement. "That's what Annabelle was searching for? Some stone that's in a museum?"

"No."

"Then I'm lost."

"Let me explain. Long before the Pilate Stone was found, its existence was rumored. There were ancient tales of ancient tales. Explorers went searching for it. Some said it had been stored in a monastery but carried off to Asia during one of the invasions. Others placed it in a crypt in southern France. The point is, it was supposed to contain a message about Jesus Christ—words carved by Pilate that might confirm the biblical accounts." He grabbed more candy, chewed noisily. "The Stone in the museum merely proves that Pilate was real. Fine, but what about the other Stone? Did it ever exist? Does it still?"

"Well, does it?"

"I wouldn't have any idea. But Annabelle seemed to believe in it."

"I don't understand. Why would Annabelle go to all this trouble—breaking the law, living underground—why would she do all of that for some artifact? I appreciate that an archaeologist might risk everything to find it. But why would Annabelle?"

David's smile was disarmingly frank. She hadn't known he could be so charming. "The most obvious reason is money."

"Money?"

"A relic like that—if it's genuine—well, it would be valuable. Very valuable. Worth a small fortune. Museums, billionaires, religions, even some governments—they'd all be bidding for it. If Annabelle had the Pilate Stone, she could pretty much name her price."

"That doesn't sound like her," said Bethany. But she was arguing against her own conviction, and David's face said he knew it. *Little Miss Do-For-Me. I bet she never picked up a check when you guys went out.* "Okay. I'll bite. How much is a small fortune?"

David had the figures in his head, as she had guessed he would. "A statue of Artemis and the Stag, about the same age, sold for almost thirty million at Sotheby's a few years ago."

Bethany was staggered. "Thirty . . . *million*?"

"And that's without the attached religious controversy. The Pilate Stone would be worth a good deal more."

"I still don't see why it would be so controversial. There are plenty of ancient artifacts. Even if some of them are valuable, most people have never heard of them."

"True. Still. Imagine that the Stone contains details about the life of Christ, put down by Pilate—enough details to corroborate significant parts of the Gospel account. What would that do? On the other hand, suppose instead that it's a statement by Pilate that Jesus was some kind of hoax, a point-by-point rebuttal of the claims of his followers—see what I'm getting at? Either way, the missing Pilate Stone—the secret one—would cause a ruckus, and a big one, at the very moment when the religious world and the secular world are locked in a struggle over—well, you see my point."

She did; but still could not fathom her running buddy's role. Was it really just the money?

"Do you know if she found it?"

David shook his head. "I think I'd have heard. Oh, Annabelle thought she was close. That was clear. But I didn't know the details of what she was doing. We only met three times." A shadow passed over his face. "And after that she disappeared. Then she came back, took Polly's passport, and went . . . wherever she went."

"Presumably the search took her overseas."

"Presumably."

Something in his voice was starting to grate. "What happened at the meetings?"

Again that condescending smile. "My, my. You really are quite the lawyer, aren't you? I feel like I should have counsel of my own."

"David, believe me, I'm not trying to pry—"

He waved this away. "She came to me because I mention the search in one of my books. You know, as the sort of thing that distracts us from the here and now. I told her what I knew, which is pretty much what I've told you. She asked me for specific sources. I had a couple of old magazine pieces in my files. She asked to borrow them. I never got them back. She asked if I could get her into the college library. I got her a temporary card. She disappeared. That's it."

"Any idea what she did at the library?"

Another shake of the head. She felt his frustration. "No. I tried to find out, but none of the librarians remembered her. One of them thought she might have been looking at material on religious cults. But he wasn't sure."

The next question was obvious, but Bethany needed a moment to frame it properly. David seemed perfectly relaxed, willing to chat forever, but she planned to be out the door after his next answer.

"Do you think this Stone is why she was killed?"

"A rival treasure hunter, you mean?" The idea amused him. "It's not out of the question, but it seems a little farfetched. A lot of people have looked for this thing for ages. I can't imagine why one of them would suddenly kill off one particular competitor."

"Unless she was close and they knew it." Bethany was turning the ideas over in her head. "Or maybe she found it. Maybe she had it with her."

"The police say the car never stopped. Nobody got out to look for anything."

"I know, but the people behind this"—again she hesitated, but the warm eyes urged her on—"what I'm saying is, what if the car hits her, and somebody else steals her backpack? A confederate, standing in the crowd."

"That sounds awfully elaborate, Bethany."

"These are elaborate people." Another thought struck her. "And maybe it's not even about the money. Maybe it's a group of—I don't know—religious fanatics."

"Make them crazy archaeologists if you want. It doesn't matter. You still don't have a motive."

"Unless she had the Stone with her."

"Sure, but that's a big assumption." Again his brain leaped ahead. "And you'd think the people who put her out of the church would have said something about the extra weight. A piece like this, limestone—we're talking about a lot of pounds. And we don't know how big it is. I'm skeptical that she could easily carry it around."

"Still. It's the only clue I have."

His eyes sparkled. "So now you're going to look for it, aren't you? You're going to look for the Pilate Stone because you hope that'll tell you what happened to Annabelle."

"And why people are after me."

"Bethany, think for a minute. Say you're right. Say there's some big conspiracy. People after the Stone. They killed Annabelle, they thought they'd get the Stone, they didn't. They're after you now. That means they think you have it or they think you can find it. Either way, if you're right, these are dangerous people."

"I don't need you to tell me that, David."

He was unfazed by her defensiveness. "What I'm saying is, going off to retrace Annabelle's steps can't possibly be safer than turning yourself in." He saw her face. "Or just going underground for a while. Disappear. If you need money, I'm sure I can—"

She was already on her feet. "I can't get you any further involved in this, David. Thank you for your help."

"This is a bad idea, Bethany. A really bad idea."

"I know."

"You can't bring her back."

"I'm not trying. That's not what this is about."

He digested this. "Do you even know where to start?"

"I'll manage. David, look—"

He raised both hands, palm outward. "Hey, don't worry. There's no way I'd turn you in."

Bethany smiled, with a good deal more confidence than she felt. She believed him. He wouldn't tell the police or the FBI. But he would tell his wife. Oh, yes. It was in his defeated gaze. David wouldn't be able to live under the same roof with Polly and keep secrets from her. The truth would gnaw at him, as the truth of whatever really happened between him and Annabelle must have gnawed at him. In the end he'd confess to his wife because she was the grown-up who could make things right. It might not be tonight; it might not be tomorrow; but Bethany gave herself no more than three days before Polly called the FBI and told them that the mad bomber they were looking for was a fanatical religious nutcase, pursuing the late Annabelle's search for an ancient and possibly mythical Christian relic about which no reasonable person would care.

A perfect fit to the media's image; and there was nothing Bethany could do but keep searching.

FIFTEEN

The Church Builder was tired. He stood in the window, rubbing his temple as he glared out at the vicious Scottish rain. He was in the parlor of the Robert Louis Stevenson suite at the sumptuous Caledonian Hotel in Edinburgh. He was here to visit a client, but also to meet the man who stood uneasily behind him.

"Why the bombs?" asked the Builder, not turning.

The other man shrugged. He was tall and wiry and no more than forty. He looked prosperous and fit, both of which he was. "I'm no longer privy to their secrets."

"You know how they think."

"They do nothing without a purpose."

The Builder made an angry gesture, but didn't turn. The other man smiled to himself. His host was so small and pudgy that his occasional fits of fury often seemed comic.

"That much I could figure out on my own," said the Builder. "That's not what I'm paying you for, Hank."

The man called Hank took a scone from the table. He broke off a dainty piece, chewed for a bit. They had been sharing high tea, until the little man had stormed to the window.

"They like to deploy their resources efficiently," Hank finally said. He had been an effective operative for the opposition, until his sudden conversion three years ago from atheist to believer: a result of falling in love. "They never kill one bird when they can kill two."

"You're saying that the bombings have a purpose other than to keep Ms. Barclay in motion."

The visitor was slathering clotted cream on his scone. "I'm thinking of an operation from my time there. This was maybe six, seven years ago. There was a particular pastor, very popular, whom we very much wanted to embarrass. There was also a woman—a woman he barely knew—who, for other reasons, had to be stopped in her researches." Next came the marmalade, and plenty of it, for the tall man had a very sweet tooth. He stuffed half the scone into his mouth, and spoke while chewing. "We eliminated the woman, and arranged evidence of a relationship between the two. The pastor denied it, of course, but the media went after him. And although it was tricky to avoid defamation, they even managed to hint that he might be involved in the murder. His ministry was destroyed."

"I see," said the Builder. The rain had changed direction, swirled by the treacherous wind. "Two birds with one stone."

"Precisely." This time Hank selected a salmon sandwich. "Very likely the bombings are a different operation entirely. It happens that they need a suspect to deflect the investigation, and your Ms. Barclay is convenient because they are already using her for another purpose."

"But if they cast too much suspicion on her, she is more likely to be caught." The Builder considered. "Our working hypothesis is that they want Ms. Barclay at large, free to follow Annabelle's trail. Duplicate her research. They need to stay in the shadows. Like us. She had been gathering information to expose them. Well, you know all that. The point is, they killed Annabelle but haven't been able to find her notes or figure out who she saw during her months underground. They need Ms. Barclay for that because the women were best friends. Nobody knows as much about Annabelle. Nobody else can follow the trail."

Hank laughed. "You're describing your own motivation, too."

"But I'm asking about theirs. They obviously changed their minds. Why would they do that?"

"They might have decided that she's dangerous at large. If so, they'll want the feds to do their work for them." Hank selected another scone and reached for the marmalade. "They're probably going to kill her," he announced. "If she's arrested, so much the better. They'll find a way to get to her. They always do."

The Builder shook his head. It hadn't always been like this. For much of history, the rivalry had been almost chivalrous. There had been isolated incidents of fanaticism—not all of them, by any means, committed by the adversary—but both sides had mostly eschewed violence.

Until the past few decades.

"If the prize were great enough," he said, "would they be willing to kill large numbers of people?"

"In a heartbeat," said Hank.

SIXTEEN

Bethany stood in a gray Chicago drizzle, trying to stoke her courage as she glared up at a blandly renovated building in the Loop, not far from the grand library named for the city's long-time mayor, Harold Washington. It was Saturday afternoon. She had been a fugitive since Monday night, and five days were more than enough. She wasn't sleeping. She wasn't eating much. She wasn't doing anything but running, and the running was more than she could take. She had always been an independent soul, proudly self-reliant, but she was starting to learn the difference between being a loner and being alone. Alighting from the Greyhound this morning, she had noticed a police cruiser passing the station. Rather than turning away as had lately become her habit, she had slipped off her dark glasses and pressed her face insolently forward, half hoping to be recognized and arrested, just to put an end to the pulsing fear.

Fortunately, they ignored her.

Bethany had read somewhere about a couple of the radical students accused of crimes in the sixties who had lived underground for decades, assuming new identities, marrying, bearing children, joining the PTA. In their place, she was pretty sure she would have lost her mind by the middle of the second year.

Now she stood on the corner, shivering, marveling that she was still sane enough to form the rudiments of a plan; but it was the plan that kept her going. Since the East had become too dangerous, she had come out to

Chicago, where no doubt she was expected to go; nevertheless, she had no choice. The whole mess began when Sylvia Kirkland asked Bethany to write her new will, and the new will left eleven million dollars to the man who owned this building. Some part of the answer was therefore inside.

She was looking for the Pilate Stone.

David Hollins.

The Stone wasn't likely to turn up in Chicago. And yet Annabelle's own secret journey had passed through the city. Bethany was certain of it.

She didn't tell me where she'd been, except that an old friend of yours was very upset with her.

Peter Zhukov.

An old friend. It had to be Martin. Martin McAdams when she knew him, Martin Potus now, beneficiary of Sylvia's new will.

Bethany and Martin had been an item eight years ago, back in college. They had done prelaw. Martin was a towering man, skinny and brilliant and intense. Plenty of girls had chased him, and he was more than willing to be chased. His roving eye had led to a painful breakup, and Bethany had eventually lost track of him.

Now she could fill in the rest of the story, gleaned during a furtive visit to an Internet café two days ago. After college, he had started law school, dropped out, knocked around from one thing to another, and then, three years ago, changed his name and created the World Foundation for the Fulfillment of God's Personal Plan. His followers called themselves God's Planners, or just the Planners. There were former Planners—not many, but a few—who claimed that the foundation was little more than a cult, just as Judge Harrigan had insisted. And yet, to Bethany's surprise, no major newspaper or television station seemed to have undertaken any sort of serious investigation. The Planners did not seek publicity. They did not proselytize. They simply held services at their fortress-like headquarters, known as the Village House, and slowly gained converts.

And that was where Bethany stood now, outside the whitewashed building in the freezing rain, trying to work up the courage to go inside. She had spent her reserves just running. She was not sure how much she had left.

And yet she was here.

Bethany tended to be direct. She had left her cell phone in her car back in Virginia, not wanting to be tracked, but had purchased a disposable at the first opportunity. From Cincinnati yesterday, she had telephoned the headquarters of the Foundation—nobody ever quite called it a church—and asked for Martin's office directly, giving the name "Bets," which was what he had called her back in the old days. She had always hated to take *No* for an answer, especially from someone with a boss who could say yes—another of her Aunt Claudia's lessons—so she battled her way upward as far as Martin's personal assistant, a woman delighting in the name of Blessing Wilkes, but Ms. Wilkes was barely civil. No, Mr. Potus was not available. No, she could not estimate when he might be. No, there was really little point in calling back. On the other hand, the Planners' public relations office was pleased to be of assistance, especially because she placed the second call without troubling to mention her name. The Planners refused to put much information on the Web, which they saw as a corporatist plot, but she managed to get them to fax to a nearby Kinko's a complete schedule of the great man's seminars and sermons, from which Bethany determined, first, that Martin was indeed currently lecturing in Chicago and, second, that he would not be coming east any time in the next few weeks.

So Chicago it had to be—

"Hi!" chirped a voice at her shoulder.

Bethany turned in alarm, and found herself staring into the dark, friendly eyes of a seventyish black man, wiry and spry, who was dressed all in gray.

"Ah, hello," she said, forcing her breathing back to normal.

He waved toward the building. "There's nothing to be afraid of," he said. "Why don't you come in? We're always happy to meet searchers." Smiling broadly, he thrust out his hand. "Stafford, Daniel Stafford."

For a moment Bethany stared. A Gopo. She was talking to an actual, live Gopo. That was the term applied to the members of God's Planners by their derisive critics. Gopos, the word exuding a nicely totalitarian air, which was just what the group's detractors had in mind, for the Planners had many enemies.

She shook nevertheless, used the name she had pulled out of her hat when she registered at the seedy hotel where she was staying. "Vera Waindell."

The old man's brows knitted. Bethany had come up with the name because of her admiration for Nabokov's fiction: Waindell was the college the novelist had invented, and Vera the name of his wife. Now, as the Gopo frowned, she feared that she might have run across a fellow Nabokov fan, who would get the joke and know she was lying. But he said only, "I had an aunt named Vera," and began spinning an unlikely tale about the woman, keeping a gently insistent hand on Bethany's elbow as he led her toward the building.

Outside, behind a faded police sawhorse, a dozen or so protesters held signs, calling the Planners a cult and demanding the return of loved ones. They chanted slogans. A pudgy balding man with glasses askew shook his fist at Daniel Stafford and shouted that he wanted his son back. Bethany turned their way, but Stafford hurried her past.

"I know what you're thinking," he said. "But it's not like that. Folks are free to come and go as they please." He chuckled, sounding like everybody's kind uncle. "As far as we can tell, most of the people who stand out there and wave their signs aren't even related to any of our members. You know what it's like." He was easing her through the heavy doors. "There are folks out there who can't live without something to stand on a corner and protest. And, you know what Martin would say?"

"Um, no."

"We have to love them the most."

Daniel Stafford seemed perfectly sincere, but he didn't let go of her arm. A part of her wanted to run, but she reasoned that there was no point in being here unless she planned to go in. True, whoever was driving her no doubt wanted her here. But so what? Whatever was going on, its center was here. She was sure of it.

Once inside, however, Bethany felt her determination crumble. She had imagined somehow that she would knock on the door and ask for Martin, and they would sit down and have a chat about old times. He would explain everything, and she would return to Virginia and clear her name. A single look told her she was being silly.

The lobby was spacious and well-lighted and, given the grim exterior, surprisingly modern. At several tables, gray-clad Gopos were prepared to give out literature to seekers. The drab colors were meant to symbolize humility, but the complementary gray tones of the walls and carpet and ceiling and furniture had to have been matched by an expensive interior designer. A trickle of people filed into the auditorium, because Martin Potus would be speaking soon. Off to the side, the window of a gift shop displayed copies of the great man's best-selling advice book, *Living Rude/Living Well*.

"It's so good that you're here," said Daniel Stafford beside her, and for a mad moment she thought he knew who she was. He followed her gaze. "You've read the book?"

"No," she said. The sounds of protest outside were muted but hadn't vanished, like the distant voice of conscience when you've made up your mind to ignore it.

"You should. It'll change your life. It changed mine." Again that bashful smile. "I used to be like everybody else. I thought pleasing God meant being nice to people. I didn't understand how much God hates empty gestures. Why should I give a dollar to a beggar on the street when the chances are he'll just buy drugs? See the point? I'm just giving him the money to make myself feel better. And that's selfish."

Bethany, astonished, momentarily forgot that she was supposed to be a seeker. "It's less selfish to keep the money?"

Quite unfazed, Stafford looked around the vast space. "I don't keep it. I give it to the Foundation. That's where all this comes from."

He told her the story. The building was twelve stories high, and the Planners owned it all. Half a century ago, the building had been one of those peculiarly urban mixtures of manufacturing and marketing: blue-collar workers making widgets in the back, white-collar workers selling widgets in the front, pink-collar workers seated in the vestibule, handling the correspondence. Several years ago, looking for investors, Martin had proudly walked all through the decrepit structure with Daniel Stafford and a few others, explaining his dream. "I made a little money in real estate," the black man said now. "We met through mutual friends. And, I have to admit, I liked him at once. Never dreamed I'd sign up, but I liked him."

And in her mind's eye, Bethany could even see it, for she remembered what a spellbinder he had been: Martin McAdams, now Martin Potus, his eyes on the future, his enthusiasm infectious as he dreamed aloud, pointing to a wrecked first-floor office suite and telling them it would be a soup kitchen. Martin walking them up the shaky stairs to a large empty chamber and describing with relish the proposed chapel. Martin sketching his plans for the higher floors, which safety concerns prevented them from visiting, where his group would construct a warren of offices and apartments for the staff he imagined hiring.

All we need is money, he would have told them.

And then Martin added the best part, said Daniel Stafford, bringing her once more to the present moment: "We'd get the money back."

"What?" said Bethany, surprised again.

Stafford's grin widened. "We'd lay out hard cash in what he called his blessed cause, and, within a few years, we'd get it back. Every penny we'd put in, and more."

Her lawyer side rose, wanting to point out that it was illegal to take profits out of a not-for-profit enterprise, including a church; and, more, wanting to make the man realize that what he had described was very likely an illegal Ponzi scheme, in which earlier investors were paid by funds raised from later ones—the Sylvia Kirklands of the world. And then she thought about the Pilate Stone. If, as she was beginning to suspect, the Village House was a scam—a way to make money for Martin and his friends—then surely they'd be interested in an artifact worth tens of millions of dollars. Fortunately, before Bethany could make a fool of herself, she remembered her mission. "Really?" she gushed. "That's amazing. He must be an amazing man."

Daniel Stafford nodded. "It's hard to believe, isn't it? But it works. We give generously to the Foundation, and we're blessed in return. Look." He tapped the gold pin on his lapel. "This means I was in at the beginning. I've been with Martin a long time." Something in her studied silence seemed to bother him. "Say. You're not one of those women, are you?"

"What women?" she asked, faintly, still staring at the gold, and its embossed design in red.

"We get them sometimes. They come in off the street. They pretend they want to join, but, really, they just want to get to Martin. They think he's rich. They don't understand that he's taken a vow of poverty and a vow of chastity, although some of them find that attractive, and—" He saw her face, and the generosity of spirit that seemed natural to him came once more to the fore. "Are you okay, Vera? You look a little peaked. Maybe you should sit down. I'll get you some water."

He led her up the steps into the auditorium. He sat her on the aisle, near the front. Bethany did not resist. She'd forgotten all about the Pilate Stone.

She took a breath, trying to calm herself. Her glimpse had been very brief, but, for an instant, the design on the pin on Daniel Stafford's lapel had looked like a coiled red snake.

SEVENTEEN

The auditorium turned out to be just a large gray room, glossy paint over exposed brick, with enough gray folding chairs to hold about three hundred people, although, as Bethany sipped her water and tried to calm down, she counted perhaps fifty, many in business suits, a few probably homeless, but several wearing Gopo gray. Daniel Stafford sat beside her. He kept asking her questions, and she kept deflecting them. She did not want to be drawn into any further lies about who she was, where she was from, or what she was doing there. She kept telling herself that she was mistaken—either five days ago at home, or right here, right now. The tiny squiggle of red paint on the wall of her study and the red coil on Stafford's pin might not match at all. It was not as if she could lean in for a close look.

And yet she knew. Sick inside, she knew. None of it made sense, but the symbols were the same. Annabelle had been running from the serpents; and now Bethany sat among them.

"Have you ever met Martin?" her new friend was saying.

"Martin Potus? Um, no. I don't think so."

"He's a great man."

"I'm sure he is."

But she was remembering the Martin McAdams she had loved once upon a time: a liar, a scamp, a bit of a crook, who'd spent his uneven college years at the poker table, mostly winning, now and then taking breaks to peek into a classroom or two, where his adoring professors were always delighted to see him. During Bethany's years at Barnard, Martin, across the street at Columbia, had led the campus lefties, pronouncing radical truth at one rally after another, fiery tongue exciting the angry students, sending his confreres marching off to take over buildings while Martin himself scurried for the exit with yet another of the willing women who always surrounded the revolutionaries. Bethany remembered Martin drunk and she remembered Martin high, and she remembered his growing frustration that she refused to join him in either state of inebriation. And she remembered, once, sneaking with him through the steam tunnels beneath the campus into the registrar's office in the middle of the night to take a peek at a grade sheet and, in Martin's case, to make a secret change or two. But mostly she remembered the nights they quarreled, mainly over the fact that she was saving herself for her husband.

No real man, said Martin, would put up with that.

Three months later they were engaged.

Bethany knew at once that Martin had noticed her. He demonstrated the same lasering attention he had displayed ten years ago, eyes sweeping everywhere, spotting everything . . . and everyone. He appeared, cleverly, from behind the audience walking softly up the narrow aisle between the chairs and the left-hand wall, nodding, shaking hands here and there, never really pausing, preceded by one gray acolyte and followed by another. Nobody in the chapel was quite talking before Martin Potus slipped into the room, but as he arrived at the front of the room, his Gopo escort falling away, the group grew, if anything, quieter. Fluorescent lights dimmed jerkily and the silent crowd strained forward on the hard chairs, Martin's radiant face, sandy and freckled, drawing them like an increase in gravity.

Martin Potus made them wait.

He did not quite smile but plainly was happy; did not quite nod but plainly welcomed their adulation; did not quite frown but plainly was concentrating. He was a tall man, and Bethany had forgotten how he used his height. There were men who were tall. There were men who were very tall. And then there were men for whom tallness itself was a part of the character, and Martin was one of these. The way you had to look up to him made it difficult to criticize him or talk back to him or refuse him anything.

Very difficult: Bethany had the painful memories to prove it.

He had put on weight. The cheeks were fuller, the brows were soft and pouchy, and he no longer had the neat beard, but the wide brown eyes remained as vibrant and mischievous as they were in the old days.

Bethany glanced around. The anticipation was like a live creature in the room, sizzling from one row to the next. A well-dressed woman in the row behind was literally on the edge of her seat, fists clenched in joy. A young couple across the aisle trembled in anticipation. Only the homeless man a couple of rows in front of her seemed immune, possibly because he was asleep.

Martin began simply.

"Good afternoon. Welcome. Our subject today, my friends, is love."

From somewhere in the room came a snicker: everyone knew the title of his current bestseller. Martin ignored the sound. Or, more properly, he played to it, turning first his face and then his whole body in the direction of the laugh. The quiet lighting picked up the subtle silver-white threads in his gray uniform, matching the tangly bits of silver in his close-cropped black hair.

"Love," he repeated, using, as in his days pontificating to crowds of protesting students, no notes. All he lacked was the megaphone. "I am sure that many of you are not believers, so perhaps I should explain what I mean. For love is one of the most poorly understood duties of the believing life." A pause. "Especially by believers."

Another titter, friendlier this time. Bethany noticed that he never said *Christian*, in much the way that his followers never said *church*.

Martin went on about love, quoting not just the Bible but a variety of texts from different faiths. Bethany stopped listening to the words and studied instead the man delivering them. She had never seen any evidence back in their college days that Martin McAdams was a believer, and she doubted it still. Everything she had heard from Judge Harrigan last week, and today from Daniel Stafford, suggested to her that Martin was running a scam. It seemed so obvious. So where were the investigators? The lawsuits? Surely he could not have spent the last three years snowing the entire world.

"But, my friends," he was saying, prancing back and forth on the stage, "what God wants of us is real sacrifices. Sacrifices that matter. Sacrifices that make a difference."

There were scattered amens. Martin continued, his argument a more flowery and supple version of what Daniel Stafford had explained to her in the lobby. What it boiled down to was that money should be given not to the poor but to Martin's foundation. When she looked around, the nods were vigorous. She turned to see how Stafford was reacting, but he was hardly paying attention. He was checking messages on his Blackberry. Bethany was astonished, the more so when, with a whispered apology, the black man slipped from the pew and headed for the exit. But not before she got another look at the lapel pin. Seen closer now, it was not merely a snake, but a snake twisted around a tree. Not the same at all as what was in her house. At least she hoped not. Because running a Ponzi scheme was one thing, but committing murder—

Sharp chords of music announced the grand finale. The homeless man sat up and blinked.

"We cannot be pushovers," Martin declared, staring right at her. "We cannot be wastrels. We cannot be afraid of the world and its criticisms. And this means—I know it sounds funny, but it's true—this means that the true believer sometimes has to behave in ways that other people might consider rude. For example." His eyes moved elsewhere. He made his audience wait, still determined to draw them to him; but Bethany doubted they could move much closer than their present location, which was the palm of his hand. "Say you're just sitting down to family dinner. At that moment the telephone rings. You leap up to answer, because it might be an emergency. Only it isn't." The bright eyes swiveled mirthfully in Bethany's direction, then darted away. "Why, it's an old friend from college, maybe a friend you haven't seen in years, who has no idea that you are busy but doesn't care, because she has an agenda. She wants your attention right now. That's how old friends are." Another pause. Bethany could not miss the message. Martin definitely knew she was here. "So, do you talk to her or to your family?"

In the whirring silence, a few grumbles of *family . . . family*.

"Of course you choose your family. You get off that phone just as fast as you can, even if you have to be rude to do it. Because if you take the time to listen politely to your old friend's latest foolishness, why, you could be on the phone half the night. Wasting your precious time. Another example." Making his audience wait once more, but his cadence was perfect. "Maybe God has granted you a talent. He has made you a fine lawyer. Maybe you even practice in the little Virginia town where you grew up." Smiling at nobody in particular as Bethany stiffened. "You're representing some client, and somebody comes to you and says, *How dare you do what your client wants? It's outrageous! It's immoral!* But your duty isn't to your critics. It's to your client. It's a bit of a cliché, but it's true, my friends: you have to do what you have to do. Period. If the world thinks you're being rude, tough on the world. You're here to please God, not the world. And if you have to be rude to do it, then you have to be rude to do it, because God has called you to do a job, your calling, and you have to do it well. Period."

The intensity was infectious. The congregation was hooting. Martin could always get people to do what he wanted them to do. He had never been able to stand refusal. No means were too foul. If he couldn't charm you, he would find another way. Back in college, when Bethany had told him that she was not ready to date a man seriously, he had threatened to jump out her dormitory window unless she would go out with him.

Then he jumped, breaking his ankle.

Martin was striding again, comfortable, rolling into his finale, and the audience tensed like a bow, ready to release its energy as soon as he gave permission.

"Listen. Maybe you're a generous person. Maybe God has gifted you that way. Good for you. But if you simply give and give of your time to everybody who asks for some, even in a good cause, pretty soon you have no time left, and no energy left, and what good are you to anybody then? What good are you to God? You have to protect your treasure and your time if you are to use them for the Lord. You cannot fritter them away, for they are God's gifts. Listen. Sometimes, maybe often, the only way to protect those precious gifts, and to protect yourself, is to learn to say no. And, sometimes, learning to say no means learning to be rude."

Finally Martin Potus was where the whole group had known he was headed. Some in the audience were true believers, some were just curious, and some, like Bethany herself, did indeed have agendas; but now everyone wanted to see how the great Martin Potus intended to talk the crowd around to the famous chant.

"Remember, friends, being liked is not a sin. The sin is wanting to be liked. The sin is doing things in order to be liked. The sin is allowing the desire to be liked to cause us to squander God's bounty. The sin is refusing to be rude even when rudeness will serve God's purposes better than niceness. It is a sin that most of us commit, and all of us need to stop. Okay? My friends, it's really pretty simple. Sometimes we have to be rude. Yes, I said rude. Listen. Sometimes we have no choice. So, now, repeat after me." It was time at last for the Rudeness Chant, the little ditty that had pushed Martin's book to the top of the best-seller lists. "Repeat after me," Martin repeated after himself. "Come on. Everybody: I can be rude!"

The audience roared back: "I can be rude!"

Bethany lowered her head so nobody would see that her lips were not moving.

"Louder!" commanded their leader.

"I can be rude!"

"To protect myself!"

"To protect myself!"

"To preserve my health!"

"To preserve my health!"

"And increase my wealth!"

"And increase my wealth!"

Martin raised his hands. "Again," he murmured, and the audience repeated the chant, and this time Bethany found herself tempted to shout along with the others. For the third rendition, the congregation leaped to its feet, stomping and clapping in rhythm to the catchy verses, and Bethany was stomping and clapping too, if only to fit in. Martin Potus had the same quality back in college, the ability to hold you spellbound even when you happened to be angry at him, even when you had reason to despise him, even when you knew, absolutely knew, that he was a lying dirty dog.

A fourth time. A fifth.

At last, the sweat pouring off his brow like heavy rain, Martin Potus waved his hands above his head to call the jubilation to a halt. The entire group, Bethany included, slumped back into the folding chairs, the vortex of nervous energy dissipating like morning fog.

"I love you all," said Martin. "God bless you." Without warning, he strode through the far door, and another large Gopo materialized in front of it, lest some foolish soul try to follow the leader.

Which left Bethany in a dilemma.

She struggled to her feet, wondering how to track the great man down. Along the aisles, people were nodding and chattering happily, slipping their coats back on. An Asian woman in Gopo gray came along the aisle toward her, bearing a cardboard tray. Bethany tensed. The woman walked past her. The tray contained coffee and a bun. The Gopo crouched beside the homeless man in the second row and, smiling, handed him the tray. Then, in an excess of charity Bethany had rarely seen before, the woman sat beside him, making conversation. Soon the homeless man was smiling, too.

Maybe Bethany had misjudged the Planners. Or judged them too broadly. Even if, as she suspected, her old boyfriend was running a scam, the members surely were here because their spirits needed uplifting—

Bethany was still watching with fascination when she felt a tap on her shoulder. She turned into the unbothered stare of Daniel Stafford. A tough-looking Latino man stood unsmiling behind him. For a moment the world tilted. One of the Gopos must have been a Nabokov fan after all, she told herself wildly. The police were outside. Or Martin had decided to do to her whatever it was that Judge Harrigan had tried to warn her about.

Daniel Stafford looked her up and down.

"Mr. Potus would like to see you," he said.

EIGHTEEN

Walk me through the crime scene again," says Carl Carraway.

Detective Florio is plainly annoyed. Like so many other state law enforcement officers around the country, she sees FBI agents as interfering amateurs with fancy college degrees. But she's also no fool, which is why she's standing in Bethany Barclay's foyer on this sultry Saturday afternoon when she is supposed to be at the shore with her husband and children.

"Kenneth Kirkland's body was found in the kitchen," she says. The chalked outline, although by now well trampled, is still visible. "He was shot twice. Our best reconstruction is that the first shot struck him in the upper back. It would have caused him a great deal of pain but wasn't life threatening. He fell forward against the counter—he left prints here, a very tight grip—and then managed to turn around. The second shot was to the head, specifically entering via the right cheek. You can see the blood spatter here on the cabinet and in this corner. This time he fell all the way to the floor. We think he sagged against the cabinet for a moment and then slid the rest of the way."

Carraway is walking around the outline. So far he has seen nothing to fault her analysis. "And the gun was beside the body?"

"With Bethany Barclay's prints all over it."

"It was her gun. She went to the range regularly. She handled it all the time."

Florio gives him a look. "If someone else fired the shots and then wiped the gun clean, he'd have wiped off her prints, too."

Carraway consults the folder he is carrying under his arm. "Your lab reports say there were no prints on the trigger or the grip."

"It's almost impossible to get more than a partial from a trigger, Agent Carraway. The grip is corrugated. It's not a great surface." She mimes this with her hands. "We got good prints off the barrel and the magazine."

"How many rounds were left?"

"It's a seven-shot clip, as you well know. There was a round in the chamber and three in the clip."

"One missing bullet."

"It could have been fired earlier. At the range, as you said."

"So her prints on the magazine might not mean anything. If another shooter only needed two rounds, he'd have no reason to touch the clip."

Florio put her hands on her hips. "Do you want to look at the crime scene or play defense attorney?"

"I'm not saying she didn't do it, Detective. I'm not faulting your investigation at all. But there's something peculiar about this case. I can't put my finger on it. I'm hoping that walking the crime scene will help me see what I'm missing."

"Come on, then," she said, unmollified.

She led the way into the back bedroom, which Bethany used as a parlor and study. Reproduction Audubon prints hung on the walls, along with a fading green-on-black poster for the musical *Wicked*. There was a handwritten inscription in the corner. He leaned in close.

Which of us is which? Love, Annabelle.

For some reason the words depressed him.

"Agent Carraway?"

"Sorry." He turned. Florio was standing in front of the wall. And, sure enough, right beside the wide-open safe was that strange stylized red slash. He crouched. "What's the theory here?"

"Barclay said it looks like a serpent. I don't know that it looks like anything in particular." She inclined her chin. "The paint is from the can we found beside the shed."

"That's the shed where she built the bombs."

"The bomb thing is federal. We're just doing the murder."

An odd lilt in her tone. He looked up. "You have doubts, don't you? You're not sure she did it."

"Not my business."

"You're the lead detective."

Florio hesitated. "We like her for the murder. I'm a lot less sure about the bombing."

"Why's that?"

"Look. The murder could be passion. He's an old boyfriend, they're having arguments about Mrs. Kirkland's will, he's threatening to sue. Maybe they were seeing each other again. We don't know. But it fits. People heard them arguing. The dentist who has the space upstairs from her office says the yelling was so loud he could hear it over the drill. Kenneth Kirkland had been drinking. He'd bad-mouthed her in the hearing of several patrons of a bar just up the road. She gets home, he's waiting on the porch or maybe in his car, she lets him in, they argue—maybe he tried to take liberties, I don't know—maybe he hit her first—whatever the sequence was, she loses it. She runs into the study, she gets her gun, maybe he laughs and turns his back. A lot of domestic crimes, the wife shoots the husband in the back. The back is less intimidating, according to the experts. So she shoots him, he turns around, maybe lunges at her, and she shoots him again. Down he goes. She calls 911, but then she panics and makes up what really isn't a great story. Paints that squiggle on the wall. Why go to all that trouble? If she testifies that he was attacking her, she might even get off. She's a lawyer. She had to know that. A cute young woman, an assailant who's drunk and who has a history of abusing women. At the worst, she faces second-degree manslaughter. Class B felony. That's the most I can imagine a jury pinning on her. She'd do the time standing on her head."

Carraway smiles. "Now who's playing the defense lawyer?"

Florio blushes. "My point is, there's a narrative to support the murder charge. Juries like narratives. They like to hear a story. Okay. So, what story would the prosecutor tell about the bomb? Everybody loves her and nobody's ever seen her buy any of these materials, but after she killed her old boyfriend she had the presence of mind to clean up her little bomb lab and drive all the way to George Mason, in her own car, in full view of the security cameras, to blow up a laboratory? When nobody's ever heard her express the slightest interest in human embryos or stem cell research?" She turns to go. "I mean, I hate experiments on embryos, and I talk about it all the time. I'm not a fanatic, I just think it's wrong. But she's supposed to be a fanatic, and she's never said a word to anybody?"

They are back in the foyer. A framed photograph of a clever-eyed man hangs beside the stairs.

"Everett Barclay," says the detective, following his gaze. "A violent man. Terrible temper. He only went up once for assault, but if you talk to some of the folks who've been around the county for thirty or forty years, they'll tell you stories about the men he beat half to death over all sorts of minor disagreements." She shrugs. "Could be the violent streak lives on in his daughter. But again. That would explain Ken Kirkland. A quick and horrible moment of fury. The bombings are cold. Calculated. The work of someone who can remain calm under stress."

"She's evaded a nationwide manhunt for a week now," says Carraway. "I'd say that qualifies as calm under stress."

"You're not buying my argument?"

"I see the same holes you do. But I still think she could be our bomber. I guess when we catch her, we'll find out."

"Do you know which way she's heading?"

"West."

NINETEEN

It's been a long time," said Martin Potus, as he now styled himself. "You look good."

"Thank you," said Bethany, quite bewildered.

They were seated in his office on the second floor of the building, a smallish room, wooden shelves lined with books, the curtains closed. There was no computer, no telephone, no modern technology of any kind, save an ancient-looking intercom. The overhead light was a bare bulb. Martin sat behind his aging desk, hands folded on the blotter. A couple of folders stood in an upright file. He was drinking bottled water. She had declined.

"I understand you had a little trouble getting here," he said. A tilt of the head, and the smile of a child who knows he has been clever. "Is there anything we can do?"

"No," she said, sitting stiffly. Then she realized how silly she must sound. She tried to make herself loosen, and therefore tightened more. She recited, again from childhood memory, Galatians 16: *The fruit of the Spirit is love, joy, peace, patience, kindness, goodness, faithfulness, gentleness and self-control.* Bethany used to hate the way Aunt Claudia made her memorize these verses, but she could not deny, in her adulthood, that they came in handy. "I'm fine," she said.

Martin nodded, watching her with those dark brown eyes. He was trying to outguess her, Bethany realized, a game at which he had always excelled. She had never been able to read him, but he had never had trouble reading her.

"So, then, what can I do for you? Did you like the sermon? Hey." Leaning across the desk, dropping his voice a bit. "Don't tell me you're here to sign up?"

She shook her head. She wanted to flee, but she had come this far; besides, there was nowhere left to flee to. Nowhere to go but forward. "I'm here about a client," she said.

Martin's heavy eyebrows made a small arch. "Oh?"

"A woman by the name of Kirkland. Sylvia Kirkland. I wrote her will, Martin. She left you her money."

He said nothing. He had always been good at waiting her out. Bethany looked away. She could not bear the intensity of his gaze. On his bookshelf were Bibles and the holy books of other religions. There were texts on finance, and books about foreign policy, and government.

"I just wanted to tell you in person," said Bethany, still not able to meet his gaze. A locked glass cabinet held older books, collectibles from the look of them, none with a spine quite readable from where she sat. A couple were turned so that she could see the covers, which bore ornate designs. "That you're going to come into some money. Except, the will might be contested."

"I see."

"Her children are upset."

"I see," he repeated. His tone was too smoothly satisfied, and drew her eyes back to his face. He had opened one of the folders and was running a finger down an unseen page. "It says here that her son is dead."

Bethany swallowed. "Um. Yes."

"It says here that he was the only one contesting the will."

"I wouldn't know," she said.

The eyes came up again, frightening in their jolliness. "Take my word for it, Bethany. Everything's fine. The will's going to probate."

"Good." Bethany licked her lips. "Ah, that's good." *Peace, patience, kindness.* She was on her feet. "Now, if you'll excuse me—"

Martin, too, stood. "Wait," he said.

She went very still. She felt dizzy, and girlish, as he loomed above her.

"You're in trouble," he said, close now. If he put a hand on her shoulder she would scream. "Big trouble."

"The charges are false, Martin. I'll be fine."

"I never doubted that. You're not the murdering kind. But you can't run forever."

"I'll be fine."

"Let us help you."

"I can take care of myself."

"I don't actually think you can, Bets. Not until you get some rest." Smoothly persuasive. "Come on. Let us help. You need someplace to stay until things calm down back home. We can give you that."

Bethany turned, and met his eyes. She caught a fugitive emotion, something very like amusement, before his clever face shut down again. Now he was projecting only concern, and warmth.

"What do you know about what's going on back home?" she asked.

"Just what I hear on the news, Bets," he said gently. "That you're wanted for questioning in connection with, et cetera, et cetera."

Bethany moved away. His proximity was as frightening as his knowledge. A sudden hard rain strafed the windows.

"I have a place to stay," she finally said.

"They'll find you."

"I'll take my chances."

"You need help," he repeated, more firmly this time, and she heard the door open. A woman of about fifty walked in, a look of motherly concern on her round face. She wore jeans and a sweater, gray on gray. "This is my assistant, Blessing Wilkes. She'll get you settled on one of the guest floors. You can join us for dinner. I'm sure you'd like to learn more about our group."

"Martin, no. I can't let you take a chance like this."

"We're the Village House. We're open to all in need. And you are certainly in need." He folded his arms. "Don't worry. We won't turn you in. We're very old-fashioned. We believe in the sanctuary of the church. Let us take care of you."

About to protest, Bethany held her tongue. If she was going to find out what was going on, there was no better place than the inside.

"Thank you," she said. "That's very kind."

"Don't insult me." He laughed, and she remembered the title of his book. "I'm being selfish. Helping you makes me feel better."

"We'll send someone for your things," said Blessing.

Bethany patted her backpack. "I have what I need with me."

Actually this was not true. Following her father's advice, she had hidden most of her remaining cash elsewhere in the city.

"Why don't we get you settled then?" murmured the older woman. She stepped aside, gestured toward the hallway. Bethany took a last glance around the office, eyes lingering on the locked cabinet holding the older books. One book in particular.

"Is everything okay?" asked Blessing.

"Yes," said Bethany, not budging.

Martin, who had moved back to his desk, looked up. "She has one last question," he said. Again he anticipated her, answering the concern she had not yet decided how to phrase. "She thinks we killed that young man to get his mother's money."

Blessing was shocked. "Nobody would believe—"

"No, no, it's okay. She's entitled to an answer." The old teasing half smile. "Think about it, Bets. That's a little paranoid. We're not violent people. Even if we were, there aren't any grounds to contest the will. We're getting the money anyway. So why would we kill Mr. Kirkland?"

She managed, although it cost her, a smile in return. "I wasn't thinking anything like that, Martin."

"Yes, you were." The brown eyes measured her. "Even now, you're not sure whether to believe me. That's why you're nervous. But I'm telling you the truth." A nod to Blessing. "We'll talk later."

Somehow Bethany was out in the hall again, following Blessing Wilkes up the ramp toward the guest wing. She was thinking about the coiled snake she had seen on Daniel Stafford's pin and on the spine of the book in Martin's office. She was telling herself that it could not possibly be the same symbol the killer had left etched on the wall of her study back in Virginia. True, Annabelle had babbled about serpents, and had told her brother that a friend of Bethany's was mad at her. But, still: even if Martin was so ruthless as to have Ken Kirkland murdered, he would have to be monumentally stupid to leave so obvious a clue behind. And Martin, although many unfortunate things, was not a stupid man.

Across the street, the man in the car lifted his cell phone.

"She's in," he said.

TWENTY

Dinner was communal. Folding tables were set up in a vast space that obviously served multiple purposes. The room was rich with warmth. Nearly everyone, whether eating or serving, seemed happy. The Village House had space for twenty overnight guests, Blessing explained as she spooned overcooked eggplant from a dish in the center of the round table. Twenty-five if we push. Most of those who spent nights were members, she said, usually two or three to a room. They were free to stay when they wanted or leave when they wanted, but had to sleep here at least one night each month. Bethany had a room of her own, on an upper floor with a view of the Loop, and although everyone told her that such a space was an honor, it had already occurred to her that leaving in a hurry would be a bit of a problem.

There were four other women at the table, and Bethany had noticed that although a few of the tables were integrated, most of the thirty or so people in the room sat in single-gender groups. The serving was done by younger sisters. A corner of the room was reserved for children, and one of the others at the table, a heavy woman named Tonya, was jumping up every few minutes to make sure that her twins were okay. The others included an Asian woman about Bethany's age who did something in finance, and a nervous, pretty black girl called Janice, who looked to be eighteen or nineteen at most. The Asian woman was the one who had brought the coffee and bun to the homeless man. Blessing Wilkes presided, and, indeed, had scarcely left Bethany's side since their introduction in Martin's office. Watching out for her or watching her? Bethany didn't know; either way, she accepted fully the hint of madness in sitting comfortably at dinner in a room full of people when the police of several states, along with the Federal Bureau of Investigation, were hunting her. Yet she saw little choice. She could not keep running indefinitely, not least because she had no one to count on and no place to go.

A day, Bethany told herself. A day or two to gather her strength and make some plans; and where better to hide than in the middle of a presumed religious cult?

Under Blessing's encouragement, Tonya, the mother of the twins, was telling how the Planners had saved her life after her abusive husband finally left town. Janice, the black teenager, had a story too, and she told it with a shyly embarrassed earnestness, drooping her head in a way that hid her face behind her braids—a middle-class family, constant pressure to perform, good college, exhaustion from the pressure, a desire to find herself, dropping out, being disowned by her family—a tale that Bethany found hauntingly similar to Annabelle's.

"I wanted to take a year off before college," said Janice. "But my folks thought that meant being a slacker."

"She would be finishing her junior year," said Tonya, so proudly that the black girl might have been her own daughter. "Eighteen and a junior."

"You started when you were fifteen?" asked Bethany, interested again.

"Sixteen," Janice conceded, eyes downcast as if the truth were shameful. "The rest was just advanced placement."

But mostly Janice was distracted, and Bethany noticed a redheaded boy of about the girl's age sneaking glances their way from another table that was all teens. At first Bethany thought that she herself was the subject of his furtive looks, but then she saw that Janice kept peeking back at him whenever Blessing wasn't watching.

Bethany smiled.

Up near the front, the fierce-looking Latino man she remembered from earlier sat with Daniel Stafford and two or three others, all sporting the strange gold pin engraved with the red coil that she was quite sure by now could not possibly be a snake. Bethany supposed that these were the senior leaders present. Again, no women sat among them.

Stafford had led the uninspiring ecumenical grace.

"This is about how many we usually have for dinner," Blessing was saying in her expressionless voice. "Usually no more than five or six are overnight guests. Most are members—we encourage them to make at least one meal a week—and of course there are always some searchers, or just people with no place else to eat." She sipped her water. "We don't discriminate," she added. "We let pretty much anyone in." Bethany had the sense that this was a dig.

Janice, the teenager, was admiring Bethany's necklace.

Blessing told her sharply not to covet.

The Asian woman who worked in finance was named Cynthia. She frowned, and said that Bethany looked familiar from somewhere. Up to this point, nobody at dinner had asked Bethany's name, and Blessing had warned her not to offer it, not specifying whether this was for their guest's protection, or due to some arcane rule of Village House protocol.

"Have we met somewhere?" Cynthia asked.

"I don't think so," said Bethany, trying to sound cool, even as hot fear crept through her. She noticed Janice making eyes at the boy again.

"You don't trade commodities or anything?" Her frown deepened. "Maybe I saw you on television?"

"I'm sure you're mistaken," said Bethany. She turned automatically to Blessing for help.

"Now, Cynthia, you know better," said the older woman, right on cue.

Janice chimed in. "You're pretty enough to be on television," she said. Then she was talking about her family again, about how she would have gone under if not for her uncle, who took her under his wing and told her about Martin.

"I couldn't stop," she said. "Without Martin, I'd never have been able to stop. I'll always be grateful to him."

"Stop what?" Bethany asked.

Janice dropped her eyes and shuffled her feet. Cynthia stood, announcing that she had to prep for a meeting. Bethany was halfway to her feet before she realized that none of the others had budged. Cynthia left, not bothering with good-bye, and Bethany remembered the Rudeness Chant.

"It's fine, dear," said Blessing, patting her hand: and indeed, for a terrible moment, Bethany did wonder whether Cynthia had rushed off to call the police.

"Look," said Tonya. "There they go." Across the room, a phalanx of teens was lining up, with an adult or two to supervise.

"What are they doing?" asked Bethany.

Again it was Blessing who answered. "They're on their way out to walk the streets. They'll find people with nowhere to go. Give them food, coffee. Maybe invite them in. Maybe offer something to read."

"The Bible?"

"Possibly. It all depends."

Janice, meanwhile, was enthusing about how wonderful Martin was, how he had changed her life. "I mean, you know, Jesus Christ was great and everything, but Martin is *brilliant*."

Bethany stared, dumbstruck. She decided that she could not have heard the teenager right.

"Martin knows everything," Janice burbled on. "Everything about everybody? He can like read people? He's so warm, and so smart. And if you listen to him long enough, he can change you." She giggled. "For the better, I mean."

Tonya excused herself again, running off after her unruly twins.

Julie meanwhile was on a roll. "Like that man over there?" Nodding toward the Latino, who was now conversing animatedly with Daniel Stafford. "His name is Mr. Fuentes. They say he showed up last year, all mad and everything? Looking for like his sister or something? But she's not here anymore. So he was all mad but he talked to Martin and then he left for a while, and he came back and he talked to Martin some more, and then he calmed down, and then he joined up, and now he isn't mad anymore."

"Martin calmed him down?"

Janice nodded. Blessing watched her closely, but let her run. "I mean, he was like a Green Beret or a Navy SEAL or one of those. So he could like break Martin in half and he has a lot of anger—you can tell. But Martin taught him to control it."

"So, what does Mr. Fuentes do around here?"

The younger girl dropped her eyes. "I don't know. I think he sort of runs errands for Martin."

"Mr. Fuentes is head of security," said Blessing, with a pleasant pedagogic firmness that shut poor Janice down. "We have a lot of problems with media and other people trying to infiltrate us. Mr. Fuentes is very good at winkling them out."

Bethany looked straight at her. "Why would anybody want to infiltrate the Planners?"

Blessing's return stare was just as unblinking. "People come to us for all sorts of reasons, my dear, and it is Martin's habit to ask no questions. So it is left to others to separate the wheat from the chaff."

Bethany was about to ask whether she was wheat or chaff; but it was time for the after-dinner sing-along.

Stuart Van Der Staal was relaxing in his hotel when the call came. Relaxing in his case meant reading various Christian websites on his iPad, searching for material he could use in the classroom to skewer the believers. His method was to find the silliest or least-informed claims he could, then describe them to the students as "typical" or say that he found them on sites frequented by the faithful. He had no idea which sites the objects of his derision tended to visit, and he didn't care. Facts were for intellectual wimps. When one had a great cause to prosecute, only the end mattered, not the means. One of his subjects was Western civilization, a mandatory freshman course, and his most important goal was to wean the believers away from the lies their parents had taught them. After all, what was pedagogy for, if not to give students the tools they needed to avoid being misled? He was having so much fun studying the sites that he almost resented the intrusion of his cell phone.

Almost.

"We've found her," the voice said.

There followed a location, and a set of careful instructions. He was warned not to deviate or improvise: there were larger interests at stake.

The professor smiled. He was his own man, and would deviate as he liked. Following orders was for the lesser orders.

———

For a while, Bethany almost forgot that she was on the run; and that these people who had taken her in had been described by Judge Harrigan as a religious cult, and stood to receive eleven million dollars from the estate of the mother of Ken Kirkland, last seen reduced to a lifeless bloody mess on Bethany's kitchen floor. Daniel Stafford led the singing in a low-pitched but stentorian tone that challenged the throng to keep up. They sang "Amazing Grace" and a couple of other Gospel standards, then two or three folk tunes—"Green Cathedral" was the only one she recognized—and then swung into a series of upbeat songs about loving and trusting each other, as the whole group held crossed hands and smiled and swayed, many with their eyes closed. The singing went on for a good hour, each piece slower and more peaceful than the one before, and it occurred to Bethany in a distant way, as she rocked and swayed with the others, that there was something deliciously relaxing about the process, that she was sinking into an almost trance-like torpor, as the worries and fears of the past few days at last drained away, replaced by the unity of the voices and the swaying.

Then her eyes popped open because it occurred to her that if the Planners were indeed a cult, this would be a good moment to start handing round the Kool-Aid. She studied the dozens of blissful faces, and suspected that a good number in tonight's crowd would drink it, no questions asked. Then she caught a glimpse of the hard face of Mr. Fuentes, who was neither singing nor swaying but standing near the door, his piercing stare darting around the room, but always returning, so Bethany sensed, to her.

A chill shivered along her spine, and she shut her eyes again, trying to regain that sense of oneness with the others as she sang the words she didn't even know. Lost in the music was better than scared out of her wits. But it was too late. Even in the darkness behind her lids, Bethany could feel Mr. Fuentes's furious glare, and she wondered whether his scrutiny meant that he believed she had indeed killed Ken Kirkland, or if he had some other reason to treat her as the viper who had snuck into the nest.

Then the singing was over, and as the group blinked its way back to reality, several of the sisters began setting out dessert and coffee. Bethany found herself with Janice again, standing near a bulletin board festooned with photographs—some candid, some posed, some showing groups, some showing individuals. It was like every bulletin board in every parish hall of every church she had ever seen. There were sign-up lists for committees and Bible study and bus trips to Milwaukee and Detroit. Bright capital letters cut by children from colored paper announced how happy they were that whoever was here was here.

"So these are all members?" Bethany asked.

Janice shook her head. "Members, searchers. People who came to some of our activities. This"—pointing—"is our street fair three months ago. This"—another—"is at our soup kitchen. Don't those kids just about break your heart?"

But Bethany was staring at another photo, farther along the wall. "What's this one?" she asked woodenly.

Janice bent close, narrowed her eyes. "Um. I think it's Martin's birthday party. Right." She straightened. "That was members only, of course."

"When was this taken?"

"I told you. Martin's birthday. Last October."

"And everyone in the photo is a member?"

Janice caught a sharpening in her tone. "Uh-huh."

"You're sure? Every last person?"

"Of course, silly. I was there, too. See? I'm over by the window."

But Bethany ignored her. The circle had closed. She was staring at a black woman about her own age, standing very close to the table, handing Martin the cake knife.

Her best friend, Annabelle Seaver, who had been run down and killed in Washington two months ago.

TWENTY-ONE

There was bustle all about them, the familiar clatter of dishes being cleared away, chairs being folded, the double swinging doors at both ends of the room opening and closing as the diners, mostly in pairs and trios, drifted out. But around Bethany was the tiny island of calm she so often prayed for, and so rarely received. Once more, her fears for herself had evaporated. She was not thinking about Ken Kirkland, or her own status as a fugitive, or even the angry skeptical glare of Mr. Fuentes, who in any case had already departed.

She was thinking of Annabelle; and serpents; and the Pilate Stone; and a car in the rain, running her down her in front of a dozen witnesses.

"She left," Janice was saying. "I didn't know we were allowed to do that." She blinked in confusion at her own words. "I mean, there isn't any rule or anything. It's called disengagement. But Martin doesn't think it's a good idea, because, you know, the world pollutes us. The Internet, television, being plugged in all the time—he says all that data coming at you all the time makes it impossible to think clearly? And he's really brilliant, so he probably knows what he's talking about. So, you know, when Annabelle left? When she disengaged? I was like, 'Wow, that's so weird, she's not taking Martin's advice.' Because, you know, listening to Martin is what saved my life?"

"About Annabelle—"

"I'm *getting* to that." Testy. Once more, Bethany wondered what she had been unable to stop doing until she joined the Planners. Across the room, the last of the chairs were being racked. "Martin says we shouldn't ask questions,"

Janice continued. "I mean, we shouldn't ask each other. Because we have to respect people's God-given right to keep things to themselves. In the Gospels, there's mainly two kinds of people who ask questions. Christ asks questions, but that's for teaching. And we're not Christ, right? But the bad guys also ask questions—you know, to trap Him? And Martin says we shouldn't be trying to trap each other, and if people ask, we shouldn't answer, because the person asking just might be trying to trap us, too."

Bethany fought her way through all of this to the core: "You're saying that Annabelle asked too many questions?"

Janice nodded happily. "I think so. That's what I heard. I mean, don't get me wrong. I didn't ask. I wouldn't. I'm very dedicated to the Plan—"

"I understand."

"And, you know, Annabelle, well, she was the kind of person who didn't care all that much for other people's rules."

"She was," Bethany agreed, voice clotted.

"Martin said, you know, people like that came to us to learn self-discipline? And I guess she tried. But, you know, she didn't always do what she was supposed to. I mean, that's what I heard. And, the thing is, well"—leaning close; some instinct for gossip had evidently survived the Planners' indoctrination—"I hear that she even went in the basement."

Bethany was about to ask what was wrong with going into the basement when all at once Blessing Wilkes came bearing down upon them. "So this is where you've gotten to," she said with a brittle brightness. "Janice, your group is on its way up to bed." The teen dropped her eyes and hustled toward the far corner, where three other women waited, under the leadership of a fourth. Blessing gave Bethany a look. "Why don't we go somewhere and talk?"

"Do you believe in coincidence?" Bethany asked. She was sitting on the narrow bed in the spartan room up on the tenth floor, wrapped in a clean but threadbare robe donated for the shelter the Planners ran, entrance around the back. The plaster walls needed paint. A crack ran along the ceiling, its passage marked by the discoloration of dampness. Daniel Stafford said that he gave his money to the Foundation. Others presumably did the same. But the funds obviously didn't go into maintaining the building.

"By coincidence," murmured Blessing Wilkes from her position at the window, "you are referring to the fact that you're still with us." She was still wearing her grays; and had yet to smile. "And of course that Martin turns out to be an old friend. You may call it a coincidence if you wish. I myself have no doubt that the Lord led you here."

"I was actually thinking about Annabelle."

"Annabelle?"

Was it Bethany's imagination, or had the frost overlaying the older woman's voice thickened just a bit?

"Annabelle Seaver. I saw her photo downstairs. I had no idea that she was a"—she almost said Gopo—"a Planner."

"She wasn't. She was a hanger-on. A searcher. She'd done a dozen groups in as many months by the time we had her." Blessing's posture screamed disapproval. "She was never really serious about the work. She was here for a while, then she moved on. Is that what Janice was talking to you about? Poor Annabelle?" A motherly cluck. "I must apologize. Janice is sweet, but she's still very young, and she's not yet well versed in the rules of the Village House. We aren't idle talkers here, Bethany. We don't trade gossip, and we don't ask embarrassing questions. The people who come to us are seeking to be transformed into something new and different. We lift the weight of the past from them. It is such a burden, isn't it? But Janice is young. She'll learn."

Bethany took a moment to let all this flow past her, the way she would with any reluctant witness's effort at distraction. "About Annabelle. How long ago did she leave?"

"I'm not sure." Blessing turned, folding her arms across her broad chest. "Ah. I see. That's what you mean about coincidence. You and Annabelle must be friends."

"We were. Good friends."

"A falling out?"

"I like to think we were still friends when she died."

The older woman blinked, then sat down hard on the single metal chair. "Annabelle is dead? What happened?"

Bethany explained about the hit-and-run in Washington; and about the police suspicions, impossible to pursue, that the apparent accident had been no accident.

Blessing said nothing, but bowed her head. Bethany realized that Martin's assistant was praying: the first sign she had displayed of anything like ordinary human emotion.

"I had no idea," Blessing said after a moment. She was back on her feet, suddenly all nervous energy, striding circles into the worn rug. "We didn't always see eye to eye, but"—remembering her discipline—"never mind. That doesn't matter. What was she doing in Washington? She told me she was leaving the country. Something about India." She was rubbing her forehead as if the mother of all migraines was suddenly upon her. "I don't understand. What happened to her? This wasn't supposed to happen." She looked up. "Did you go to the funeral? Who buried her? We would have had a service."

"Her family is mostly in New York. They held the funeral in Harlem."

Only twenty or thirty people came to the service, Bethany might have added—mostly family and friends. Annabelle had not led the sort of life that generated friends of her own. Apart from Peter Zhukov, Bethany herself, and a fat old man sitting in the back whom nobody seemed to know, all the mourners were black.

"Her family? We were her family. For a while. Her own family—I seem to recall—Annabelle was estranged from them, wasn't she?" Blessing stopped pacing. "Does Martin know?" A sickly smile. "Of course he knows. He knows everything. I'll have to talk to . . ."

She trailed off, pulled a wad of crumpled papers from her pocket, pulled a pen from somewhere, wrote swiftly. "This wasn't supposed to happen," she repeated. Her face had gone gray. "This was *not* supposed to happen." Still muttering, she stuffed the unruly notes back into her pants. "I don't see how this could have happened."

Bethany was intrigued. "People do die, Blessing."

"This was not supposed to happen," she said again, grimly. "Not like this."

"How was she supposed to die?"

Blessing blinked, and seemed to remember that she was not alone. "That's not what I meant, dear. Not at all. It's just that I was very fond of Annabelle. She was a sweet girl. I was so sorry when she left us."

The lawyer in Bethany pounced. "For India."

"I'm not really sure. Someplace overseas."

"When did she leave?"

"The fall, I think. I don't really remember. She really was more Martin's project than mine." Backing toward the door. "I should leave you alone. You need your rest." A bright smile, but Bethany could see what it cost her. "I know you're not one of us, Bethany. And I don't suppose it's likely that you will be. So I was thinking that you might like to go to a traditional church service." She rushed on. "Tomorrow's Sunday. Some of us are going." She named the congregation. "It's huge, it's out in the suburbs, we'll be anonymous. You'll be safe there. Why don't you join us?"

Bethany hunted for traps, but found none. Perhaps the older woman was simply being kind. And church, Bethany realized, was exactly where she needed to go: maybe a Sunday service would chase the prickly little terrors away. "It would be my pleasure."

"Good. We're going to the second service, which is at noon. We'll leave around ten-thirty. How does that sound?"

"Just fine. Thank you. Blessing?"

"Yes, dear?"

Bethany hesitated. But she had not come this far to turn back. "Have you ever heard of the Pilate Stone?"

The eyes flickered. "Why would you ask about something like that? I've never heard of it. No." Blessing was backing toward the door. "We don't pry here, Bethany. I've tried to tell you that."

"Why is asking about the Pilate Stone prying? You just said you've never heard of it."

"You'd really have to ask Martin."

The unpersuasive denials made Bethany wonder once more what was hidden in the basement. But there was no point in asking. All she would get was another lecture about how at the Village House we neither gossip nor pry into other people's affairs. And poor Janice might wind up in trouble.

"Good night," said Bethany.

"Good night, dear."

Still wearing the plastic smile, Blessing left. Bethany sat on the bed, wondering. Then she noticed that the older woman had dropped one of the notes from her pocket. She scooped it up and hurried to the door. Then she hesitated. She heard the older woman talking, evidently on her cell, voice receding as she made her way down the hall:

"This was not supposed to happen. What do they think they're doing? Everything was going fine."

The voice disappeared. Bethany peered into the corridor, but it was empty, bare and eerie in the harsh fluorescence. More worried than ever, she looked down at the scrap of paper in her hand. It was a drawing, crudely made, of what appeared to be a rooster, beak open to caw. Next to it, scrawled in red, were the words ENOUGH IMPACT, followed by a pair of question marks.

This wasn't supposed to happen.

Was she saying the Planners had done it? Because of what Annabelle had seen in the basement?

What did Blessing know?

One way to find out. Back in her room, Bethany took off the robe and pajamas, pulled on jeans and a sweater, slipped into her shoes, and hurried out into the hall.

In her rush, she did not notice the door of the room across the way quietly snicking shut.

TWENTY-TWO

Annabelle Seaver," says Agent Carraway. "That's the connection."

Pulu is at his desk, studying the reports of interviews with Bethany's friends and classmates, looking for a clue as to which way she'd run. "We know she's the connection," he says, not looking up, "but we also know she's dead."

Carraway is at the whiteboard, drawing arrows and circles. It is the same evening, a little earlier, and the task force has gathered in the bullpen of its Crystal City offices. "Right. She's dead. A hit-and-run. Before that, she was missing for months."

"She was a drug addict," says another agent. "Maybe she was living on the street."

"Maybe so. But look at Bethany Barclay's credit card charges. Just before Annabelle disappeared, Bethany bought her a roundtrip train ticket from New York to Virginia. The two of them visited together, then Annabelle vanished, then she died. A few months later, it's Bethany who vanishes." He is erasing a line, drawing a new one. "Suppose, just for the sake of argument, that Annabelle wasn't on the street. Suppose she was up to something. Suppose she died before she could finish."

Someone whispers an unkind joke. Two or three agents snicker. Carraway lets it go. "Listen, people. Look at the sequence." Pointing. "I'd say it's pretty obvious. Whatever Annabelle was up to, it's a good bet Bethany is finishing it."

"Why?" says a voice from the back: the section chief, a spare ascetic named Vanner, who's come out to the bullpen to see what the meeting is about.

"Why, what?" says Carraway.

Vanner has her arms folded. She is standing in the shadow of a file cabinet.

"Why is it obvious that Barclay is following up on Seaver? Nobody thinks Seaver was a bomber. We know Barclay is."

Carraway is studying the blackboard. "Because of how Annabelle Seaver died."

"Not our case," Vanner cautions.

"Just bear with me. A stolen car hits her, then drives away. Okay, happens all the time. The DC police assumed that the thieves abandoned the car because they'd hit somebody with it. But what if they stole the car in order to hit somebody with it?"

"Drug dealers do that kind of thing," Pulu interjects, trying to help.

"For drive-by shootings," says someone else. "Not hit-and-runs."

Vanner addresses only her deputy. "Are you suggesting that this is about drugs, Agent Carraway?"

"I don't know what it's about. That's why I think we should try to find out what Annabelle Seaver was doing while she was underground. That might tell us what Bethany Barclay is doing now."

"No. Seaver isn't our case. She's a distraction. Our job is to find Barclay. That's all. Once we've found Barclay, we can ask her at our leisure whether she and Seaver were breaking the law together, or if this is her own thing." Vanner's tone is flat. "We're looking for a suspected bomber. She's believed to be a member of a Christian extremist group. If we find our bomber, we find the group. Three bombings so far. We don't want another. Let's keep our eyes on the ball, people."

Vanner catches Carraway's eye and tilts her head to the side just before she turns and leaves the bullpen. Her office is a glass-walled cubicle in the corner. The blinds are usually closed. They are closed now, when Carraway follows her inside.

"Close the door," she says. He does. "Sit." He does that, too.

Vanner's desk is pristine. Even the letters and memos in the outbox are so tightly cornered that they look like a package of paper fresh from the supply closet. On the credenza are several framed photographs: children here, cats there. Here in her private haven, the eyes are warmer, but no less authoritarian.

"You've been with the Bureau how long, Carl? Nine years?"

"Eleven."

"Lots of promotions. Made Special Agent in Charge early." She has his personnel file open on her monitor, turned so that he can see it. She is a small woman, bursting with surprising reserves of energy and ambition. "I imagine you'll be a section chief before long." She clicks the mouse. "A Dartmouth man, I see."

"Yes, ma'am."

"You majored in economics. I suppose you'd rather be assigned to financial crimes." Vanner's smile is smooth. "I'm sure I can arrange that if you want."

Carraway isn't sure whether this is a threatened punishment or a promised reward. He says nothing.

"You were at the crime scene today."

"The Kirkland murder. Yes, ma'am."

"And?"

"The detective in charge has some real doubts that Bethany Barclay is our bomber."

Vanner is back at her screen. "And she's an expert on bombs, is she, this detective?"

"No—"

"A profiler?"

"No, but her arguments make some sense."

His supervisor nods slowly, then rubs her temple as if to rid herself of a migraine. "Tell me the rest," she says.

"I'm sorry?"

"What you didn't want to say in front of the group. Tell me why you think Seaver's murder and Barclay's flight are connected."

Carraway takes a breath. "Why did she visit Annabelle's sister? They're not close. The sister says Bethany Barclay asked what Annabelle had been doing those months she fell off the grid."

"And the sister—this Polly Hollins—was unable to help."

"It's the questions that matter, not the answers. Bethany Barclay's following a trail. Annabelle Seaver's trail."

Vanner takes a moment. She has no nervous ticks. She never drums her fingers or fiddles with a bracelet or swivels her chair. She just shuts off now and then, eyes front as her mind whirrs through the options. She wears styleless glasses with black plastic frames.

"No," she says. "You don't have enough to go on. All you have is a hunch."

"That's why I want to investigate."

"Show me evidence of a connection between the cases, and I'll take the handcuffs off. Until then, you stick with the program. Our case is Barclay. Only Barclay. Not Seaver. Is that understood?"

"It's a legitimate lead."

"I've made my decision. You're to do nothing without my express approval. Nothing regarding Seaver. Is that clear?"

"Yes, but—"

"That will be all, Agent Carraway. Go find our bomber."

At the door, he pauses. "What if she's not?"

"Not?"

"Not our bomber."

He expects another deep think. But Vanner is ready this time. She even rediscovers the syrupy smile, perhaps to soften the blow. "You're one of my best people, Agent Carraway. You could turn out to be right. But, even if you are, we still have to find her, don't we?"

"Yes, ma'am."

"Well, then, go out and find her."

But descending the stairs to the bullpen, he wonders at his supervisory agent's strange adamance.

"Well, you sure got yourself spanked," says Agent Pulu, as the two men leave the building a few minutes later. They are on their way to a favorite Italian restaurant for a late dinner. "You might be in charge of the task force, but you should listen to your partner's advice. I keep telling you to keep these crazy hunches to yourself."

"I'm just wondering why we're not allowed to look at Seaver."

"You make it sound like a conspiracy. The way you tell the story, sounds to me like Vanner was just telling you to do your job." He claps his partner heavily on the shoulder. "You're young for a special agent in charge, Carl. Younger than I am. And, no, I'm not jealous—well, okay, maybe a little jealous—but, the thing is, you didn't get to where you are by disobeying orders. Carl? Are you listening to me?"

He isn't. He is watching a tall, slim man, flaming red hair flecked with gray, approaching them rapidly.

"Whoa," says Lupu, hand automatically going to his waist.

"It's okay. I'll handle it."

The stranger halts in front of them. He is wearing a raincoat and carrying a briefcase, thumb near the catch. He looks federal. His voice is heavy and profound: the judgment of the ages. He speaks only to Carraway, ignoring his partner. "You're been ignoring my calls."

"Sorry, Ted. I've been a little busy."

"With the bomber." The skinny man rustles closer. "That's what I'm calling you about."

"Look. Tell you what. When I have a little more time we can—"

"But there *is* no time." The eyes are very dark, and very intense. "This is what you seem not to appreciate, Carl. There is—no—time. The others won't listen. You're my last hope."

Carraway puts both hands out, palms forward, seeking peace. "Ted, look. I'll give you my card. Call me at the office, and—"

"I *have* your card. I have *five* of your cards."

"Well, I'm sorry. I'm happy to sit down with you at some point. I just can't right now."

The stranger nods. "Because you think I'm crazy. That's what they all think. I'm crazy. Well, fine. Don't say I didn't try to warn you. You're in the middle of a war, and you don't even know it. Good versus evil. That's what you're not seeing. Good versus evil. Not a war with guns. A war for souls. Which side are you on?"

He turns, not steadily, and wanders off along the sidewalk, muttering.

Pulu is about to speak, but Carraway lifts a hand in restraint.

"Don't say it. He was a good man once."

"He was FBI?"

"An analyst. This was back when you were still out West." They are walking again. "Six, seven years ago he started to come apart, muttering about good and evil, some kind of holy war being conducted on our soil. You went into his office, he had the bulletin board, the yarn, the photographs—all the things smart people produce while they're having their secret breakdowns. Every crime, every scandal, he'd fit it into his madness. We gave him medical leave, he was hospitalized for a while, got out, came back, cracked up again. Wound up with a medical discharge. I see him now and then. Coffee. Donuts. He was good once. One of our best."

"Do you know what set him off?"

"A case he was working. Blackmail. A prominent preacher." They are at the restaurant, but linger on the sidewalk. "We had a suspect in custody. There was even a trial. The case actually fell apart because Lesofsky cracked up. He'd put the pieces together, and there was no way to keep his madness from the jury. Once they heard that, it was all over."

"You said *we*. You were involved."

"I was a junior agent on the case. I spent a lot of late nights with Ted, and I saw it happening to him. We'd be talking about some piece of forensic evidence, and suddenly he'd start saying that this is exactly the kind of thing those people do, going after preachers, because their real target was the church. I asked him what he meant, and he'd start to talk about the Garden of Eden or something—about the serpent still being out there—and, well, anyway, I testified before the board of inquiry. I told them what I saw. I liked Ted, I still do, but I wasn't going to lie. He lost his job. He lost his wife. He's never forgiven me. I guess I can't blame him."

"Was there anything to it? His conspiracy theory?"

Carraway is holding the door open. "No," he says.

TWENTY-THREE

A peculiar illogic was now governing Bethany's activities, the fruit, perhaps, of the illogical situation in which she found herself. She had no reason to doubt the story that Annabelle had left the group. The timing fit. Blessing said Annabelle had left in the fall, and Annabelle had showed up on Bethany's doorstep in October.

Yet Blessing was plainly hiding something; and frightened.

It seemed implausible that Annabelle was dead because she had entered the basement of the Village House. Suppose Judge Harrigan was right in her insistence that the Planners were violent. Even so, if they meant to kill Annabelle, why drag her all the way to the District of Columbia to do it?

On the other hand, if indeed Annabelle had died because of whatever she had seen in the basement, then Bethany's own life might shortly be at risk. But her life was at risk anyway; or at least her freedom was. She knew nothing of living off the grid. Sooner or later she was bound to be caught, and then she'd likely be heading to prison. So risking her life seemed a smallish added chance.

And she had one other thing going for her—so she kept telling herself as she descended the fire stairs, having decided not to risk the elevator—she had one more point in her favor. She did not believe that Martin would do her harm. No matter who he was now, no matter what he thought he was doing, she did not believe that he would hurt her.

She prayed she was not mistaken.

The fire stairs were poorly lit, enclosed in cinder block, everything painted a dull gray. Looking down the central well, Bethany saw only darkness. The occasional scuttle of a rat in the darkness heightened the illusion that she was descending into the bowels of the earth. She hated rats, feared them, too—bad memories—and was not big on shadows either. This was why fleeing through the tunnel with Peter had driven her nearly catatonic. When she was about six, Aunt Claudia's three sons, aged five through thirteen, had shoved her in a closet, flung in a live rat, and locked the door. It was a good half hour before her aunt heard her screams and let her out. Her uncle took his belt to the boys, but they suffered their punishment almost gleefully, and for a month or more smirked whenever they passed her. Bethany's only consolation was that in her terror she had apparently kicked the rat to death.

Aunt Claudia made her clean up the mess.

Bethany missed a step, lost her balance, nearly fell.

She forced herself to slow down. She was exhausted and jittery and, she suspected, not thinking straight.

Another of the virtues Galatians celebrated was self-control. Aunt Claudia used to warn her never to let other people know what she was thinking. At the moment, Bethany decided, she would rather not know herself.

She heard a sound above, a door moving on hinges inadequately oiled, but when she looked up saw not a sliver of light.

Stop jumping at shadows.

She continued down.

The Village House was twelve stories high. Bethany's room was on the tenth floor. Not all of the floors were actually finished, Janice had told her, but Bethany had no plans to visit them all. There were no locks on any of the doors, according to Blessing, because the Village House was run on the basis of trust. And if there was a thief among them, well, Luke 6:29 remained their guide: or so Blessing said.

No locks, and, as far as Bethany could see, no security cameras in the stairwell. No guards, either; no presence of any kind, all the way down.

Very strange, if the basement was such a big secret.

But when she reached the bottom of the fire stair, she received her first surprise. The door from the stairs into the basement was locked.

You couldn't lock fire doors. They were there to let people escape in an emergency. You could set them to alarm if opened, but you couldn't keep people from using them. But all the same, there was a shiny combination lock built into the door, barring entry from the stairs.

Three floors above, leaning over the rail, Stuart Van Der Staal watched the eerie green outline of his target through a portable night vision scope. The scope picked up infrared radiation from her body, and translated it into a picture, so he was viewing, really, only a perception of a perception of a perception—a sequence that delighted him immensely.

He admired the purpose with which she had descended, and the determination with which she had overcome moments of near panic. He had studied her academic record and come away impressed. He wondered how she would have performed in one of his seminars. Her parentage left him doubtful—it wasn't as though she was from an academic or professional family, after all—and in his experience, a lot of these kids who were the first generation to go to college excelled by dint of hard work. The professor had nothing against hard work, but the intellectual in him resented the extent to which the world seemed to reward effort rather than brilliance. That didn't seem to him a terribly just way to distribute the world's resources.

She was pushing at the door now, perhaps to confirm that the lock was engaged. He wondered what she would do if she set off the alarm. Maybe she was wondering, too, because the push was a gentle one, and she had returned to her scrutiny.

Clever girl, he told her in his mind. Too bad about the way your story has to end.

Down below, Bethany was remembering a seemingly security-conscious partner at her old law firm in Washington, a man who had once sent her from a client conference to retrieve a document from his office safe. When she asked whether his secretary had the combination, he had laughed and said, no, of course not, and then confessed that the combination was actually written on a piece of paper taped to the bottom of the safe, as a protection against mortality, or fading memory.

And so she bent closer.

No numbers were taped to the lock, but there was an engraving in the metal. She studied the carving, but could make no sense of it. Yet it occurred to her, with the crystal sharpness of an intuition that she knew in her bones to be right, that for the initiated, this symbol would give the combination. If you understood the symbol, you could open the lock.

The key pad, she noted, contained letters rather than numbers; presumably the symbol stood for a word.

Bethany pinched the bridge of her nose. She was exhausted, and frightened, and nearly out of ideas. But Annabelle had made this trip before her, and she was not about to quit.

Fine. The door was locked. Presumably it was also alarmed. Breaking it down, even if she possessed the means, wouldn't do.

She wished now that she had had the foresight to bring paper and pencil on her search, but, having neither, and no longer possessing a cell phone that might enable her to take a photo, she did her best to commit the symbol to memory.

Then she headed back up.

She was not giving up on her goal of getting into the basement. She was not even postponing it. Bethany had learned the hard way never to travel without a backup plan. Like the extra money always hidden in her car. Or the way she had her laptop set to upload everything into the cloud every twelve hours.

In this case, the plan was tricky. She made her way back up to the ground floor. There, quite properly, you could exit from the fire stairs either into the lobby or into the street. But that wasn't enough. In the lobby, as she had already observed, there was a guard, and there were cameras galore, to say nothing of Gopos likely passing through, even at this late hour.

She continued climbing, the muscles of her legs singing with pain now: she had to get more exercise. Marching around the prison yard, maybe. The dining hall was on the second floor, and there had to be a way to get the refuse from the kitchen to the basement: a dumbwaiter, a freight elevator, a special stair—something.

Walking up the stairs was scarier than walking down, maybe because of another trick her boy cousins had pulled: cajoling her into climbing up into their tree house and then kicking away the ladder. Actually they had pulled this particular stunt more than once. Bethany wasn't fooled exactly the second or third or tenth time. She just wanted them to like her.

The professor was having fun. He had remained on the third-floor landing, because he had already guessed that Bethany was headed for the second. This was getting interesting. What had she figured out that these silly Gopos had missed? He shoved the scope back into his jacket and watched as she stopped on two, just as he had predicted, and reached for the door handle.

Bethany opened the fire door a tiny crack. No voices. No sounds carrying on the air. She checked her watch. Nearly midnight. By now, even whoever was charged with cleaning had to be done.

The foyer outside the dining hall was dark, but through the aging windows the street lamps provided illumination aplenty. Inside was inkier still. Bethany waited, just the way she had learned from her father on those hunting trips. There is always light, he used to say. Just take the time to let your eyes adjust. Have the patience to let the light come to you.

Aunt Claudia often said much the same about the light, although she wasn't talking about hunting.

Forms and shapes developed in the darkness, and then the darkness became gray, and then, after a fashion, she could see. She scanned the ceiling and walls but saw neither motion detectors nor cameras. True, such devices could be hidden, but since their purpose was deterrence there was rarely much point.

If the Planners were really a cult, they were a very careless one.

Or very confident.

She hurried across the room and slipped into the kitchen, and now she did risk switching on the fluorescents briefly, because the last thing she needed was to stumble over a serving trolley and bring everybody running to see what the clatter was all about.

A quick reconnaissance: again, no cameras or alarms that she could see. If they were invisible, she was already caught.

She spotted a small elevator at the other end of the narrow room, plotted her course along the floor, mapping the obstacles in her memory, then switched off the lights and waited again for her eyes to adjust.

She edged along the counters, using a faint reflection from the stainless steel refrigerator as her guide. Slowly, slowly, using her fingertips to aid remembrance of how the kitchen looked with the lights on. As the counters ended, she extended her hand in front of her, and that was when the demon, hissing and spitting, landed on her back.

Bethany screamed, lurched forward, bumped her head on the refrigerator, cried out again. The creature snarled angrily and streaked back into the darkness that had produced it.

A cat.

It was only a mangy cat, probably employed full-time in the kitchen to do battle with the rats she had encountered in the stairwell.

Bethany leaned against the refrigerator, waiting for her heart to slow, desperately frightened that the whole building must have heard her shouting. The minutes ticked by but nobody came.

"Move," she whispered in the hideous silence. "Move, or you'll quit and go back."

The elevator was the old-fashioned kind, with a sliding mesh grill. She stepped inside and pressed the button, half expecting an alarm to sound. But the car moved smoothly downward.

Stuart Van Der Staal stood in the kitchen, watching the elevator disappear. That was a cute trick. He would have to remember it. He slipped back out into the hall, walked over to a locked door, keyed in the code word. Inside was a hidden stairwell with access to all twelve floors, for the Village House was shot through with more passages than his target would ever guess.

The elevator stopped. Bethany slid open the grill and found herself in a storeroom.

She was in the basement.

And again she shivered with a complex delight at the thought that perhaps Annabelle had found this same circuitous path around the security systems the Planners had in place.

Bethany stepped out of the storeroom and found herself in a long hallway. Hanging bulbs in cages cast cones of weak yellow illumination. Pipes ran along the ceiling. Water was dripping somewhere. Between the bulbs were areas of shadow, and no doubt the shadows hid more rats, but she was not about to turn back. She just wasn't sure which way to go.

She heard footsteps and darted back into the storeroom, leaving the door open a tiny crack. Blessing walked past, striding with a swift and somehow tragic determination, like a woman late for her own funeral. Bethany suspected that the older woman didn't much like rats either.

She waited for the footsteps to fade, then slipped out of the storeroom, turning in the direction Blessing had gone. The footsteps were faint but audible. Bethany came upon a side turning, and there was Blessing, not twenty yards away.

Blessing turned suddenly, as if aware of being watched, but Bethany had spotted the twist of the hips and prudently stepped behind a pillar. The footsteps resumed. Bethany waited. A pipe dripped hot water on her neck, and she jumped, but made no sound.

When she poked her head out, Blessing had disappeared.

Bethany hurried along the corridor. By now it seemed to her they must have left the footprint of the Village House. She passed a couple of dark corridors. The basement was huge. A perfect place to hide priceless artifacts. The tunnel evidently ran underneath the building next door: a shuttered hotel, if she remembered correctly. She came to another door, this one of reinforced steel, that looked considerably heavier than the last. This door, too, required a combination; this one, too, had a symbol stenciled beneath.

A vault, Bethany realized. She was looking at a vault.

The door stood open a few inches. She took a moment to consider. Sneaking along the tunnel when she could see a good distance ahead was one thing. Slipping through a heavy iron door when she had no idea what was on the other side represented a considerable risk. She suspected that Blessing was supposed to have shut it firmly behind her, but had merely given it a shove and moved on.

She reached her decision. Maybe the Pilate Stone was hidden down here, maybe Annabelle had been sneaking around for some other reason. Either way, she would come back when Blessing was not in the basement. Now that she knew the route down, she could ignore the lock on the stairwell. The trick would be getting past this one.

This time Bethany studied the symbol more closely. It looked like an inverted horseshoe, with stars or gems or something surrounding it. But "horseshoe" was too obvious. There had to be another way to figure this out. She had the right sort of smarts to solve puzzles. She worked crosswords and acrostics; she played Sudoku and Words with Friends; she could solve—

She heard a man's voice, and spun around, but the dank corridor was empty, so the voice must have come from ahead of her.

Beyond the door.

She hesitated, then pressed as near the open end as she dared.

"Are you sure?" asked the male voice, and it just might have been Daniel Stafford's.

"She's perfect for us," said Blessing. "Just exactly what we need."

"And she just walked in."

"That's right."

Another male voice, unfamiliar: "And you are absolutely positive nobody sent her? She is not a plant?"

This question provoked general hilarity, although Bethany was at a loss to follow the joke.

Blessing again; firmly: "Martin's positive. Nobody can read people like he can."

The man who wasn't Stafford: "What about tomorrow, then? Do you plan to take her along?"

"I might as well," said Blessing. "Anyway, I already invited her. To uninvite her would be . . . rude."

More laughter.

Stafford again: "I think it's worth the risk. Two are less conspicuous than one. Besides, if we really mean to go ahead, we'll need someone like her. She really is perfect for—"

A footfall—*behind*—too late—

"Are you lost, Miss?"

A heavy hand fell on her shoulder. Bethany swung around and found herself looking up into the chilly eyes of Mr. Fuentes, head of security.

The professor by this time was back in his room. He had not pursued Bethany to the basement because he knew there were people down there, and he did not want to show himself more than necessary. Besides, he was under orders to do no violence inside the Village House. Tonight's adventure had been a reconnaissance. He had observed his target in her natural milieu of Flint Hill. Now he had studied her on the run, and learned that she could remain remarkably poised, and construct and follow a plan, then alter the plan on the fly, at a moment when a lesser woman would be gibbering helplessly in the corner.

Or a lesser man.

She was fascinating, this Bethany Barclay. As he packed his things, the professor marveled. He looked forward to meeting up with her outside the Village House. He would love to hear her view on his thesis about the Declaration of Independence. If there was time before he killed her, he would be sure to ask.

TWENTY-FOUR

I'm a little bit confused," said Martin Potus. He was sitting on the edge of his desk, but in pajamas and slippers and robe rather than the slimming suit, and she could see the beginnings of a paunch. "What were you doing in the basement?"

Bethany had already had time to work this out. Half of the truth. "I was following Blessing."

Martin's clear brow furrowed, and he looked suddenly boyish and charming. "Why?"

"First I was just lonely. I wanted to talk. Then I was curious about where she was going."

"Why?"

The repetition briefly threw her: in Bethany's experience of life, curiosity was its own reason. "I don't know," she finally said, dropping her gaze at last. More truth: "She was acting . . . furtive."

Martin stood, walked past her chair, and whispered to Fuentes, who slipped silently out the door.

"Furtive," said Martin, and laughed. She felt the release of tension, but willed herself not to relax her guard. Martin McAdams had been a devious young man, and she expected no less of the older version. "Blessing was being furtive," he said. He was at the window now, looking out at the brightly lighted Chicago night. "She's like that sometimes. She thinks we have to sneak around. She's suspicious of outsiders, I'm afraid. So's poor Mr.

Fuentes." Leaning on the glass. "Do you know how Mr. Fuentes came to us? It was, oh, last summer. June, maybe. July. He was upset. His sister had disappeared, he said, and her friends had told him that she'd joined our group."

"Had she?" asked Bethany, just to keep punching. She was sitting very straight. It occurred to her that this was the first time the two of them had been alone.

"Oh, indeed," he said, but so swiftly that she understood that he still hated interruptions as much as he had in college. "And poor Mr. Fuentes was furious. Threatening to tear the place to pieces unless we produced her at once. Well, he's big, he's trained, I suppose he could have done it. We explained to him that she'd stayed with us for a while and then disengaged. A group like ours, it happens. I believe she said something about missing traditional religion, whatever that is."

"What happened?"

"What happened was that Mr. Fuentes was indeed ready to tear the place apart. He barged into this office. He blamed me personally. He threatened me physically. I told him that we didn't keep track of former members. I didn't even know she'd disengaged. I suppose the membership committee knew, but I didn't. We're a largish organization, Bethany, and one can't just—"

He stopped himself, backed up and took another track.

"Anyway, Mr. Fuentes and I sat down, right here in this office. We talked. He had questions about his sister. I answered what I could. I told him that there would be others who would know her better. I proposed that he stay with us a few days, get to know the group. He left instead. Still angry."

"But he came back."

"He did. A month later. Six weeks, say. The two of us sat down for another chat. This time we talked about the Planners. About our beliefs and our structure. This time he agreed to stay. He met others, spent time around the place, poked his nose into various corners—your basement included, Bethany—we hid nothing from him—and, every night, we talked. Right in this office. About our philosophy. About God. About what traditional religion gets wrong. About the good Lord's plan for each of us, and how to discover it. And of course how to fulfill it. Three days later—four, maybe—he decided to join. And he's been with us ever since."

Bethany found the story quite unreasonably frightening. Suddenly she was struck by a deep awareness of her circumstance. Fleeing from arrest, worried about survival, desperate to learn whatever Annabelle learned here—but *here* was the midst of a religious cult. In her own mind she repeated the words. A religious cult. A place where the music and the swaying and Martin's own hypnotic personality could lull even a man as apparently forceful as Mr. Fuentes into a kind of docility.

She wondered, for the first time, what the place might do to her. Not the material part of her, as worried as she was about her earthly fate; the immortal part of her that Aunt Claudia had so carefully instructed and that she herself, in her young adulthood, had so poorly tended. She thought of Ephesians, and the armor of God, and wondered whether it was too late to wrap herself in it as a defense against—well, against whatever these people did to get others to join.

"You need to relax," Martin was saying, his tone gentle. "It's been a hard time for you, and I can well imagine that you're jumping at shadows. I'm truly sorry if we've done anything to heighten your fears. Our only goal, truly, is to calm that. We're very good at that, Bets, if you'll let us help. We can help you learn to calm those inner storms that pound and pound at the shores of your mind."

She said nothing, but felt her fists slowly unclench.

"You haven't been sleeping well," Martin went on, his tone now one of detached diagnosis; but when she looked up the brown eyes were so soft and sympathetic she wanted to cry. "You're worried. You're scared. That's easy to understand, Bets."

She stared, but felt the roiling within.

"But that isn't all," he continued, gently. "When you close your eyes you see him, don't you? You see the body of that poor young man who was slaughtered in your own home. You see the blood. The image haunts you. Well, so it should." Deliberately rousing her fears, even as his gentle half-smile promised that he knew her innermost secrets, and the path to peace. "It's a terrible thing to see one of God's creatures—a human being like yourself—not just dead, but butchered. It stays with us because it's unnatural. It's not the way God wants His people to live together. That's what we're about here. We're trying to build something better than all that. Do you know why we call it a Village House?"

She shook her head; she didn't trust her voice.

"'Now it happened as they went that He entered a certain village; and a certain woman named Martha welcomed Him into her house.'" A smile. "Luke 10:38. That's from the New King James Version, but the others are pretty much the same. Do you see the point? No? The Gospels speak repeatedly of Jesus and His disciples traveling from village to village to preach the Good News. The Lord was welcomed into Martha's house, and that's what we do here. We welcome people—all people—into our house, just as Martha welcomed Jesus and those who followed Him."

She was more impressed than she meant to be. She fought to find a rejoinder. "I thought you preached rudeness."

He laughed. "Oh, that's just a gimmick to get people in the door. Get their attention." Martin pushed away from the window, came and perched on the corner of the desk nearest her chair. "We preach trying to gain a correct understanding of God's Word, not some watered-down version that says 'God is nice so we should be nice.' We want to talk about the real responsibilities our Lord places on us." He had picked up the stapler and was tossing it idly from one slim hand to another. "We're hospitable people, Bethany. The Village Houses are open to anyone. We have nothing to hide." Back and forth went the stapler. Her eyes followed its every leap. "But hospitality can be abused. Snakes and vipers come into your midst."

She sat straighter; said nothing.

"All we want to do is help people." His voice was as pacific as ever. "And all the world is against us."

"I'm sure that's not true."

"It is true." Back and forth, back and forth. "Why are you so nervous, Bethany?"

"I'm not."

"Your hands are trembling."

"It's late. I'm tired."

"But you weren't resting. You were in the basement." He continued playing with the stapler. She had forgotten how long his fingers were. She felt her fight-or-flight instinct roused, and didn't know why. "Some of my advisers—Mr. Fuentes, for one—are wondering why you're here. If somebody might have sent you."

"A man was killed in my house—"

"And you got away. That's the point Mr. Fuentes makes. Police are looking for you everywhere. The FBI, because they know you've crossed state lines, and because of these bombings." His voice was hardening. "Everyone's looking for you, Bets, yet somehow you've slipped the net. And Mr. Fuentes, who has some experience in these matters, says that isn't so easy to do these days. He wonders whether it's possible that somebody *arranged* for you to slip the net."

Her fists were clenched in her lap; her entire body tightened as if for combat. "Why would somebody send me? Send me to do what?"

"Never mind. That's not the point. The point is, my advisers aren't sure whether we should have opened our doors to you."

Bethany allowed herself to bridle. "I didn't ask you to take me in, Martin. You offered. If you don't want to help me, don't."

But she remembered this side of Martin from their quarrels back in college: in this mood he could, with every appearance of sincerity, deny that the ocean was wet. "You might have guessed that I'd offer you sanctuary. The hospitality of the Planners is not exactly a state secret." He sighed, and put the stapler down. "You shouldn't have been in the basement, Bethany. We don't like people snooping in the Village House."

His prickly condescension at last brought out a touch of the old sass: "I thought you said you had no secrets."

For an instant Martin's eyes were narrow and bright with a child's fury. Then he was his old warm self again, so swiftly that she wasn't entirely sure she had seen what another part of her knew she had.

"I see your point. I'm sorry if we did anything to rouse your suspicion. If you want a tour of the basement, I'll arrange one, as soon as Blessing is free."

Bethany would not surrender so easily. "I want to know about Annabelle."

"What about her?"

"Why you took her in."

Martin was still perched on the corner of his desk, arms crossed, swinging a leg comfortably. "How many times do I have to tell you? We're the Village House. We don't turn away those in need."

"She wasn't in need. She came here looking for something."

"Most people do."

"Not something spiritual. Something material. She was looking for the Pilate Stone. Don't pretend you don't know that."

"Of course I know that."

She was stunned. She had put her weight against the door, only to have it swing wide without her help. Martin sat watching her, sadness in his eyes.

"Why do you bring up the Pilate Stone?" he asked. "It's just an old myth. I told Annabelle the same thing."

"I don't know if it's a myth, Martin. I do know, if it exists, it's worth tens of millions of dollars. And since all this"—waving her hand to encompass the office and the building—"must cost a lot of money, it wouldn't surprise me to learn that the two of you were in it together."

"You think I was helping her?"

"The thought crossed my mind."

Martin smiled. "You don't think people change, do you?"

"Not in my experience."

"Well, you've certainly changed, Bets. You didn't used to be so cynical. Time was, you gave people the benefit of the doubt. The Village House doesn't exist for my personal gain. I'm trying to help people. Why is that so hard to believe?" He sounded more disappointed than exasperated. "I didn't help her, Bets. That's why she left. I see you don't believe me, but it's true. Yes, Annabelle told me about her search. And, yes, she wanted me to help her. I refused. I told her she was welcome to stay with us as long as she liked, but I wasn't about to commit our scarce resources to the search for lost treasure. That's not what we do here. We help people find God's plan for them, and we help them stay on the path God chooses. And your friend Annabelle—well, she wasn't all that interested in finding God, or staying on His path. She was interested in money."

Bethany's uneasiness was growing. She wondered whether she had misjudged him; or if any part of this peroration was true. She clung to the idea that had sparked her search an hour ago: that a sprawling basement full of vaults and hidden rooms would be the perfect place to hide a priceless artifact.

"I felt sorry for Annabelle," Martin continued. "She was so terribly unsettled. And uncentered. For her, everything was the Stone, the Stone, the Stone. She talked to some of our other members about it. I did what I could to put a stop to that. Mr. Stafford after a while refused to sit at the table with her. That's how upset he was. But Annabelle wouldn't stop. I even made an appointment for her with a medievalist at the University of Chicago, an expert in these old stories, but Annabelle refused to go. I went in her stead, and he assured me it was just a myth, that the Pilate Stone in Israel was the only one that existed. When I shared this with Annabelle, she got pretty hot about the whole thing. Not only was the Stone real, she said, but some billionaire was offering millions of dollars for it."

"How did she know that?"

"I don't know. She wouldn't tell me. But she wouldn't stop talking about it, either. The truth is, her obsession became disruptive. Mr. Stafford wasn't the only member she upset."

"And that's why she left? Because you wouldn't help?"

"In a way. She said she'd found someone else who was interested. Someone who'd pay her a big finder's fee. And, no, I don't know who. Anyway, I wished her luck, and told her we'd still be here if she changed her mind." He stood up. "That's the whole story, Bets. Now, if there's nothing else—"

"There is." Every word of the tale was plausible, and she detected nothing on his face or in his tone to suggest that he was dissembling. And yet Martin was a practiced liar from way back. She was not about to let him take the round so cheaply. "She left here when? September? October?"

"Around then. I'd have to check."

"And she was killed in March."

"What's your point, Bets?"

"The two of you obviously spent a lot of time together when she was under your roof."

A tight nod. "We had a number of counseling sessions."

"Even better. Because I'm hoping that she might have told you something that would shed light on who killed her."

"Ah." For the first time he seemed uncomfortable. "From what I understand, it was an accident. A hit-and-run."

"But suppose it wasn't. Suppose it was murder. You must have a theory."

Martin shifted on the desk. He wouldn't meet her eyes. "I was hoping you wouldn't bring this up, Bets. As I told you, we don't pry into people's business. There are issues of confidentiality involved. And, frankly, I'm not sure you're ready to hear this."

"I was her best friend, Martin. I think I'm ready."

"Annabelle was a fine person. Hard used, and she had this shell, but once she opened up, she was quite wonderfully giving."

"Go on."

Martin sighed. "Very well. Annabelle told me over and over again that there was only one person she was worried might hurt her."

"Who was that?"

"You."

TWENTY-FIVE

Bethany blinked. "You're making that up."

"To what end?"

"I have no idea." Now she, too, was standing, as fury drove away the doubt. "But I know you, Martin *McAdams*. You always have a secret motive for whatever you do, and there's always another one hiding behind it."

Once again his tone was placid. "I'm not making this up, Bets."

"I was Annabelle's best friend in the world. Why would I want to hurt her?"

"That's what she wanted to know."

"What?"

"In our counseling sessions. It came up a lot. You still have doubts. Fine." He lifted the phone from his desk, punched a button. Blessing materialized instantly, clutching a thick folder. She handed it to Martin, vanished again. "These are my session notes. There are also tapes. Do you want to listen?" He didn't wait to be told yes or no. The folder was very thick. Martin paged through it. His voice was gentle but uncompromising, the doctor delivering the unwanted diagnosis. "I'm sorry to have to do this to you," he said. "But at the Village House we believe in facing truth, no matter how uncomfortable."

He drew out a flat chip, inserted it into the recorder on his desk. He studied the screen, scrolled to where he wanted, and pressed play.

Annabelle's disembodied voice filled the room.

" *. . . scares me sometimes. She calls me her running buddy, but she scares me.*

All those guns. Those weird friends. I don't know if she's really on my side. You know what I told my Tia? If anything ever happens to me, she's the one they should look for. Bethany. There's just something weird about her . . ."

"Turn it off," she whispered. She found to her surprise that she was seated again.

Martin paused the playback. "You should hear this next bit," he said, and, once again, was uninterested in any objection.

" *. . . the way she's always asking me questions and challenging me. I don't know. She says she's my friend, so I know you think I'm crazy. She probably thinks I'm crazy, too. She's the one who got me locked up the first time. Did you know that? When she told the judge I couldn't take care of myself? That was way back in college. She'd do it again, too. I don't trust her. I told Tia not to trust her. She's the last one I'd go to with a secret.*"

"As you see," he murmured, pressing STOP again, "I'm not making it up."

"You doctored these," she breathed.

"I repeat. To what end?"

"I loved Annabelle. Annabelle loved me. She knew I would never hurt her. She wouldn't say those things."

"And yet she did, Bets."

Bethany shook her head. She didn't know, she couldn't think. She felt a great lethargy sweeping over her. In one swift assault, Martin had turned her world upside down. The way he always used to. She had thought she was confused before, but this made no sense. She wouldn't have hurt Annabelle. Would she? Again she thought of Ken Kirkland, dead in her house, by her own gun. She hadn't hurt him, either. But the police thought she did. There were so many clues, and she was exhausted and frightened and starting to doubt her own perceptions. The text messages were real. The symbol on the wall was real. The gunshots in Newark were real. It all had to be real, because if even half of what was driving her was her imagination working overtime, there was a terrible risk that—

That you did it, said Professor Delavan, very coolly. *You don't remember, but you killed him, didn't you, Ms. Barclay? Your gun. Your house. Your prints. You killed Annabelle and then you killed Ken. All the rest is fantasy.*

"I didn't," she whispered. "Leave me alone."

"I'm afraid we can't do that," said Martin pleasantly. "You're in need. We're required to help."

"Required?" she echoed, vaguely, still staring at the recorder on his desk.

"It's what we do, Bets. It's why people come to us. We teach them how to welcome the stranger without puffing up with pride about being so welcoming. To stop spending so much time worrying about the needs of others, so that they can spend more time caring for their own needs—the needs of the body and the mind, two of God's most precious gifts to us. We help them to put aside the worries, great and small, that generate unhappiness." His voice had gone smooth and compelling. "Bets, listen. Do you know what the root of most unhappiness is? Unrealistic expectations. Of ourselves, of others, of the world. The world is a great muddle. People are a great muddle. Half the time our minds are a great muddle. The less time we waste expecting things, the less time we spend being disappointed. The less time we spend being disappointed, the more time we can spend on clarity of thought and deed. You want to see more clearly, don't you, Bets?"

"Yes, but—"

"Shhhh. Try to relax. It's going to be fine." That smooth, reassuring voice: it had worked in college, and it was working now. "You've had a terrible time. Nobody can blame you if you get things a little mixed up. After what you've been through, your mind must be exhausted. Your body must be exhausted. I don't know how you keep your eyes open. All those cares and fears you carry are such a terrible weight. You want to put them aside. I know you do. We can help you do that. You want to escape the muddle of your mind. We can help you do that, too. You want to find a space of calm. A space to relax and stop worrying. We can help you. Put yourself in our hands and we can teach you clarity."

Clarity. She half smiled. That was what she needed. More clarity. Less clutter.

"I know what it's like, Bets," he murmured. "I know how hard it is to think clearly when your thoughts are so confused and fuzzy from worry and fear. Your thoughts wander away from you. You can't trust them. You can't trust your own thoughts because the fear gets in the way. The worry gets in the way. The harder you try to think, the more confused you are. The more confused you are, the harder it is to think. It's a circle you can't get out of, Bets—not as long as your mind is muddled with worry. And it is. I know it is. Your thoughts are all jumbled up. It's so hard to think straight with your mind all muddled. You need us, Bets. You need the clarity that comes from putting aside all those worries. The clarity that comes from letting us help you learn how to think all over again. Please, Bets. Let us help you."

She sighed. She had not realized how confused she really was. How hard it was to think straight. Martin was right. Martin was—

—was—

—doing something to her—

—to her head—

—like he used to in college—

She looked up at him, fighting the cobwebs. "Stop it."

"What's the matter, Bets?" Still smooth. Friendly. "You seem so tense. So clouded with worry."

"I said to stop, Martin. I'm not here to join up."

"I know that. I would never try to get you to do something you didn't want to do. Please put that worry out of your head."

Bethany was unmollified. "I've seen your act before. You forget that. I know all your best lines."

Still she could not shake his aplomb; or his alluring half smile. "You're upset, Bets. Frightened. You need to take it out on somebody. I understand."

"Then stay out of my head." She took a deep breath. "There isn't any confusion. I don't know what Annabelle was talking about on that tape—how the issue even came up—"

"I'm not taking it out of context, if that's what you mean. You're welcome to listen to the entire thing."

Her eyes narrowed. "Why are you so insistent? Shouldn't you be keeping your counseling sessions confidential?"

"I made the judgment that you needed to hear it." But he sounded not so much confident as prickly. "I'm trying to help you, Bets."

"I didn't ask for your help." She bounced up again, two quick steps in his direction. "I don't know what you're up to, but it's not going to work. Annabelle didn't hate me and I didn't hurt her. And I didn't hurt Ken Kirkland either. I'm not imagining any of this. Don't try to make me think I'm going crazy."

"I didn't say you were crazy. I said the worry is making it hard to think straight."

"And I said to stay out of my head. I'm not here to upset your applecart, but you just keep your distance." Once more her fury was blazing. "And what in the world were they talking about in the basement anyway?"

"Who?"

"Blessing and Mr. Stafford and whoever else was down there. About how fortunate it was that I'm here and how I'm perfect for them and two are less conspicuous than one. What was that all about?"

Now it was Martin's turn to look confused. "I can't imagine what the conversation was about, assuming you heard it correctly. But it is indeed our good fortune that God has led you to us." He relaxed gain, back on familiar ground. "To have the opportunity to help is itself a blessing. As to the rest, if you want to know what they were talking about, just ask. They'll tell you if they want to. Otherwise they won't."

"You have an answer for everything, don't you?" But she backed off. "Now, if you don't mind, I'm tired. I'd like to go to bed."

His eyes flicked over her. She could not tell whether he was angry. "They found bomb-making materials, Bets. In the shed behind your house." The satisfied glow in his eyes told her that he had stored up this nugget. "They haven't released that detail publicly, but what they found matches the fragments they recovered from the bomb in Virginia."

"They were planted."

"Doesn't matter. We'd be obliged to help you either way." He spoke briskly. "We're preparing documents for you. A new identity. After all, if you're going to be spending time here, we have to call you something. Only a few of us know who you really are. Me. Blessing. Mr. Stafford. Not even Mr. Fuentes knows."

"What kind of documents?" asked the lawyer in her.

"A driver's license. Credit cards. The license will stand a computer check. We have people at the DMV." He said this matter-of-factly, as if breaking the law was a minor perquisite of his position. "You'll have a credit history, and a spotty employment history, mostly in retail. If it comes to what comes, we'll find you a position nearby." He winked. "Don't use the credit cards. They're for show. The debit card will work. It'll be linked to an actual bank account in your new name, holding three thousand dollars." He hesitated. "In case you have to move in a hurry. Don't waste it, please. We're not made of cash." He was on his feet. "Blessing will arrange things tomorrow."

She stood, too. "I don't know what to say."

"There's a class for beginners. We call it an intake. If you're with us any length of time, you'll have to join the class." He raised his hands, palm outward. "No, no, we're not trying to get you to sign up, although of course we'd be delighted if you did. It's just cover. If you stay here and don't attend an intake, people might ask questions. We train them not to, but people are people."

"A muddle."

"Exactly."

She wondered if he expected a hug. "Don't get me wrong, Martin. I'm grateful. But why are you doing all this?"

"We're the Village House. We turn nobody away."

"Do you give everybody false papers?"

"Everybody who needs them." No trace of a smile.

Blessing stepped inside, even though Martin made no obvious signal. She escorted Bethany back up to the tenth floor.

Neither spoke.

Raymond Fuentes stood in an alley across the street. He put away the earphone, and watched the light go out in Martin's office. This woman meant something to the leader of the Planners. Fuentes wasn't sure what, but he would find out: part of the job. At the moment, he saw her mainly as a distraction, and this at a time when they couldn't afford one. His disciplined mind traced the steps. Each had been worked out with meticulous care, and now, with the operation on the verge of success, a stranger comes along who could ruin what he and the others had worked so hard to attain. And Martin, unthinking, invited her in. It was so like the man. His combination of ambition and innocence was precisely what made him a useful tool for those with even more ambition; and considerably less innocence.

But this woman was an obstacle; a complication.

She would have to be removed. Usefully removed, as they used to say at Langley, but removed all the same.

Lost in his thoughts, Fuentes slipped off into the darkness.

PART TWO

POSSIBILITY

Have we the knowledge that comes when God speaks to us face to face as a man speaketh to his friend? Such knowledge is a voice in the midst of our souls.

—The Reverend J. G. H. Barry,
Meditations on the Apostles' Creed

TWENTY-SIX

Edna Harrigan's night vision was no longer reliable, and so she needed a driver for the ride to Lillian Hartshorne's palace ten miles east along what the locals still called Route 647, even though the Postal Service had forced them years ago to give the narrow, winding road a name. As the black Town Car purred through the tree-shrouded darkness, Edna caught familiar glimpses of a lighted farmhouse here, a bold McMansion there. Wealthy Washingtonians were buying up more and more property out here, and the competition to build the most sprawling and wasteful manse was considerable. Lillian complained constantly about the new houses going up, and then called in the architects to keep her own the biggest. Lillian called her estate Childhood's End, a literary reference that probably bounced off most of her guests, and she was constantly adding new wings and guest cottages and sub-basements. Edna guessed that the main house alone nowadays boasted 30,000 square feet. With its spider's web of libraries and parlors and sitting rooms, Childhood's End was perfect for tonight's activity.

Not the party. The meeting.

Edna would join the others at the party, circulating just long enough to be sociable, and then, an hour or so in, they would slip away, one by one, to a separate wing, placed at their disposal by Lillian, no questions asked, because she owed Edna everything and was of a generation that remembered its obligations. The group would meet in one of the libraries.

By tradition a fire would be blazing, just in case there was anything that needed burning.

Notes, for instance. By tradition, none were kept.

The group had a lot of traditions. At times, their meetings seemed almost genteel, a throwback to a more cultured age. If what she suspected was true, things would shortly get a good deal rougher, but for the moment it was best not to dwell on the imponderable violence of the future.

The room was not special. It was not shielded against eavesdropping because shielding drew attention. Lillian Hartshorne had posted one of her house staff outside the door to ensure that they would not be disturbed, but the best security for the people inside was their anonymity.

Tonight there were six sitting in chairs in a small circle. No objects would be held in the hand. They faced each other, as it were, defenseless.

On the rare occasions of their meeting, they addressed each other only by title: the Critic, the Judge, the Senator, the Pastor, the Mathematician, the Writer, the Builder. By tradition, each appellation had to begin with a different letter, to avoid confusion. The seven members led the organization known as the Garden, who for half a millennium had done battle with their adversary, known to the people in this room as the Wilderness.

The Church Builder ordinarily presided. It was his energy and vision that had breathed fresh life into the Garden at a moment when it had become almost moribund, a club of old men, meeting in secret, withdrawing from the world, jealously guarding their resources, and muttering ineffectually about how awful things were getting as the influence of the Wilderness spread. The Builder had ended all that when he took over the leadership two decades ago, after being recruited to succeed his late uncle, whom he regarded as a fool. He had ended the role of familial connection in selecting the members, and had forced all but one of the incumbents into retirement. He ran the rare meetings with the same determination and drive, but tonight had pressing business elsewhere and could not be present. In his stead, the Mathematician took the lead chair, because he had been part of the Garden the longest—almost forty years—the only survivor of the Builder's purge.

Edna Harrigan was the Judge.

"Let's see where we are," said the Mathematician, pearl cufflinks flashing as he lifted a brown hand. His suit, as always, draped beautifully over his long body, and cost more than Edna's pension check. In his other life, he was a Harvard professor, and in his thirties had come as close as anyone to solving the still unproved Hodge Conjecture. He often spoke of how his graduate work on irreducible prime manifolds three decades ago had led him to conclude that there must be a God. He was now close to seventy, and only the second black member the Garden had ever had. The first was widely believed by historians and the public to have been martyred in the sixties because of his activism on behalf of civil rights.

The people in this room knew otherwise.

"First," said the Mathematician, "as to the current state of the search for the Stone. The Builder's source tells him that the Wilderness believes they are closer than they have been in half a century. This is due largely to their reconstruction of the efforts of Annabelle Seaver. We are somewhat behind in our attempts to do the same, but there is an operation underway to remedy our deficit. Questions?"

There were none, not even from the Critic, who quarreled over everything.

"Second," the Mathematician continued, "as to the group known as God's Planners, and its leader, Mr. Potus, we now have available—"

The Critic could restrain himself no longer. "Are we absolutely sure that the Gopos are a front? Is it possible that they're exactly the bunch of kooks they pretend to be?"

The Writer was a thin, ascetic man of years, whose encyclopedic knowledge of the history of Judaism and Christianity made his serious literary novels into best-selling tomes. He wore a multicolored crocheted kippah, and moved with a stateliness that suggested the regal authority of age. "I would prefer that we continue to call them the Planners," he said in his slow, high voice. "Within our little group, we should speak of the religious beliefs of others, no matter how unusual, only in terms of respect."

The Critic refused to back down. He was slim and towheaded, at forty-two the youngest in the room, and famous for his attacks on religion in all its forms. He was a recent addition to their ranks. The Builder had proposed his membership just last year. Although most of the others had fiercely resisted, in the end the Builder had prevailed, on the theory that the Critic had the sort of questing, skeptical mind they valued, and hated totalitarianism and conspiracy more even than he hated religion.

"I don't see why anyone's religion is entitled to respect," the Critic said. "You're free to believe what you want, and so are they. You're Jewish, these two"—indicating the Mathematician and the Pastor—"are big Christians, on the conservative end of things. That one"—the Senator—"is more the liberal sort of Christian. And of course the Builder is a C. S. Lewis-type Christian. Now, I'm happy to live in a country where you are all free to be those things, but I'm also happy to live in a country where I can say I think your beliefs are seriously delusional. And that's why we're here, isn't it? To fight for our mutual rights to believe—or disbelieve—what we want?"

The Mathematician rapped his knuckles on the table. "If we could stick to the subject. The Critic has asked if we are sure the Planners are a front." He nodded toward the Senator, who was seated before the massive fireplace. "I believe you have information for us."

The Senator's famous face was grim. People said she had the White House in her sights next time around, and, certainly, she had staff in the field checking the numbers. But the work done in this room was of far greater importance than her political career.

"There is no longer any serious question," she said. "The Planners are fronting for the Wilderness. The problem is, we still don't know why. I had a conversation with the Builder about this before he left. He says that although the Wilderness has certainly infiltrated churches before, and used them for its own purposes, it has never, as far as is known, sponsored one. We can't quite figure out what the Wilderness means to accomplish by setting up—excuse me"—this for the Writer—"what is little more than a religious cult."

The Critic pouted. "Calling them a cult doesn't make them any different from any other religious group."

No one rose to the bait. When the Critic was in a contentious mood, ignoring his gibes was the only way to keep him under control. And yet at moments he projected a boyishness they mostly found endearing.

Mostly.

"It makes no sense," said the Writer in his slow emphatic tones. "Suppose that the Planners misbehave and get caught. I don't see how that advances the agenda of the Wilderness. Cults have misbehaved in the past, but rarely does anybody attribute their misbehavior to believers in general or Christianity in particular. I can't see the potential gain."

"But there is bound to be a gain somewhere," said the Mathematician. "If there is one thing that this battle has taught over the centuries, it is that Wilderness is controlled by thoroughgoing rationalists. They do not take foolish chances. Unlike other passionate activists, they bide their time. Their original plan anticipated centuries of struggle, and, from what we can tell, they are following it still. If they have set up a cult, they have done so in order to discredit the church. The fact that we cannot see the connection is no evidence that the connection does not exist."

The Senator had a further point to make. "Few of the Planners are probably aware of the connection. The knowledge is likely restricted to the very top."

"The leaders of the Wilderness don't strike me as particularly patient people," said the Writer. "Murdering our agent was not only vicious and immoral but also impulsive."

"We've always known they were violent," said the Mathematician.

"I believe you are making my point. Violence is intrinsic to the work of the Wilderness. Violence always attracts those who have found the one true answer, unless, like the people in this room, they've found an answer that limits the tools they're allowed to use to seek it. The Psalmist says that the Lord hates those who love violence. But we don't love violence. We abhor it." He looked around the circle. "I do not believe that we have properly mourned Annabelle. Or repented for sending her to her death."

"He's right," the Pastor announced into the general silence.

"We'll pray after the meeting," said the Mathematician, shaken.

"*You'll* pray," said the Critic. He turned toward Edna. "Any word from Bethany Barclay?"

The Judge met his gaze, and spoke for the first time. "No."

"You sent her. You assured us she could do this."

"I didn't send her."

"Sent her, tricked her, manipulated her into going—what's the difference? She's there, isn't she? On the scene?"

"She is."

"Well, what has she found out?"

"We haven't been in touch with her yet. I'm not at all sure how well she'll take to the news that her best friend was working for us at the time of her murder. Remember, too, that getting in and out of the Village House is no simple matter, as we learned from our previous agent."

The Critic was direct. "Well, I would suggest that you contact her fast, before they kill her, too."

A heavy silence greeted this sally. The people in this room were not squeamish, yet none was happy at the prospect of further blood on their hands. The leaders of the Garden shared in common a morality of means, and had spent six centuries battling an implacable foe whose only measure of success was progress toward its end.

The Senator finally spoke. "And where do we stand on the alternatives? There's still time to contact the proper authorities and leave this to the professionals."

"Vetoed," said the Mathematician at once. "We've been over this and over this. We face the same challenge as our predecessors. We simply have no way of telling who's working with the Wilderness."

The others nodded, but the Critic was unassuaged.

"You can't go through life assuming that everyone you meet is conspiring against you. Head too far down that path and we're strangling our children in their beds."

They were quarreling now, each speaking over the other, a thing nobody would have dared had the Builder been in the chair. The Builder was a businessman, accustomed to swift decisions and crisp commands, whereas the

Mathematician, a veteran of academic wars, understood how sometimes the shouting was a necessary catharsis before a meeting of intellectual equals could continue. So he let them have their fun for another five minutes before rapping the table again.

Order restored, he nodded to the Pastor, who had barely uttered a word all night. He was a masterful preacher, but also hardened by many a political battle. The organization he led had tried very hard to defeat the Senator twice, and twice she had outflanked him. On television they had called each other quite terrible names. In this room the two behaved as though there was no personal animosity between them, but Edna wondered.

"All human life is sacred," the Pastor said. "I take this to be common ground among us, even if we occasionally disagree on precisely what it is that constitutes the human. We can all agree, however, that Bethany Barclay is human. Let's please consider that for a moment. Nowhere in the Gospels does our Savior urge us to sacrifice others for our goals. We ourselves are to take risks, yes—but the innocent? Never. I have never met Miss Barclay, but from what I gather we are using her as a pawn. Nothing more. I don't say that we're wrong. I don't say that no war is ever just. But she is an involuntary recruit. I would like to urge us to follow the same route we did with Annabelle, to put the case to her directly. Allow her to know who we are and what we do and why the battle matters. If she is to risk, let her at least risk knowingly."

The Critic smiled. He and the Pastor were, improbably, friends, and occasionally appeared together on stage, debating the existence of God. "I believe those are the first words out of your mouth with which I have ever agreed, and I am including the pronouns."

The Senator was already shaking her head. "Vetoed. I'm sorry. It simply isn't possible. The Builder has considered that possibility, and rejected it. We would do well to remember that we lost Annabelle. Goodness knows where she might have shared our secrets. Or whom with."

"I'm not likely to forget," said the Critic, "seeing as how recruiting her was my idea."

Another silence, this one more awkward.

The Pastor shrugged. "Well, I know we don't take formal votes here, so

I won't ask for one. We're really only advisory, after all. The Builder makes the decisions."

"For the moment," said the Critic, his tone less combative than thoughtful.

"Any other business?" said the Mathematician. "No? Then let's summarize. The goal remains to keep the Wilderness from gaining the Stone. At the same time, we need more information about who's running things over there. That requires reconstructing Annabelle Seaver's work, and for that we need Bethany Barclay to retrace Annabelle's steps."

He glanced around the room. Nobody contradicted him.

"Let's remember what's at stake here. For the Wilderness, the Pilate Stone is the only goal. They've been trying for centuries to discover historical disproof of the Gospel accounts, and for them the Stone is another effort in that direction. But for us—well, of course we'd like to have the Stone, but the search is secondary. We didn't send Annabelle out because we wanted the Pilate Stone. We sent her out because we knew that the Wilderness wanted it. We sent her to the Village House in the hope that they'd break cover to get in touch with her, and we'd finally have a line into them. We don't know who their leaders are anymore. They know a few of ours—the Builder and myself in particular—but we don't know theirs. That disparity works to our disadvantage. We have to know who's running things over there."

"It didn't work," said the Critic. "They killed her."

"On the contrary, my young friend. It worked extremely well. I would imagine that by now Bethany Barclay believes that her friend was killed over the Stone. We know differently. Yes, we lost track of Annabelle when she went underground. And, yes, there are some among us"—a hard glance at the Senator—"who believe that we lost her, that she decided she wanted the Stone for herself, so that she could sell it. Either way, the likelihood is that the Wilderness killed her because she did her job too well. She did smoke them out. She did learn who some of their leaders were. And they killed her to keep her from telling us."

He smiled and took a sip of water.

"Now, I know what I'm going over is common ground, but the Builder asked me to review because he didn't want any of us to have any illusions about what's at stake. We recruited Bethany Barclay, on the Judge's recommendation, to retrace her friend's steps, in the hope that she'll either discover what Annabelle discovered or smoke out the Wilderness for us. That's still the mission. Our unanimous advice, I take it, is that Bethany be put in motion again, assuming that we have the means to do so. We will advise that she not be made cognizant of who is manipulating her." He waited for dissent. There was none. "Pastor?"

"Let's pray together," the Pastor said. He selected language from Ephesians, according to the traditions of the Garden, and the others bowed their heads, even Edna, the agnostic. The lone dissenter was the Critic, who remained uncompromising, sitting with arms crossed, and a look of fury on his face.

"Thy will be done," the Pastor concluded.

The Mathematician adjourned the meeting but asked Edna to stay behind.

As the others filed out, the Writer tugged the Critic by the sleeve, and drew him into an alcove. "Thank you for joining us in prayer," the old man said.

"I didn't."

"But you did. The early Christians, as a symbol of their devotion, are believed to have crossed their arms when praying. As you did just now." Smiling beatifically, he glided off.

The library was empty now, except for the Judge and the Mathematician.

"Thank you for staying behind," said the Mathematician. During Vietnam he had done something heroic that he never talked about; ever since, he had listed to one side as he walked on an artificial foot. "We need to discuss your friend Ms. Barclay."

Edna nodded, said nothing. She stood leaning on her cane.

The Mathematician was perched on the edge of a side table, bad foot swinging free. "You do realize that the others were right? That we are risking the young woman's life in a cause of which she is unaware?"

"I think I am sensitive to the issue, seeing that she's my friend and protégé, not yours."

"That's not the point I was going to make, Edna. Are you absolutely sure—one hundred percent—that she didn't kill that man in her home?"

Edna hesitated. As a judge, she knew that percentages of certainty were a fool's game; but she also knew that the Mathematician, for whom numbers were everything, wanted a serious answer.

"Ninety-eight percent," she finally said.

"So there's a one in fifty chance that Ms. Barclay is a murderer?"

"Now that you put it that way—yes. I suppose so."

He nodded as if in confirmation of a theory. "I'm glad that you didn't say you were one hundred percent sure."

"Why?"

"Because that would mean that you knew who the murderer was. That would worry me a great deal. And it would be impossible for me to tell you what I am about to tell you." He took a moment. "Tell me, Edna, have you ever heard of Pierre de Fermat?"

"I believe he was a mathematician."

"Exactly. A French mathematician of the seventeenth century. One of the greatest abstract thinkers in human history. He was a friend of Pascal. Both Roman Catholics, and very devoted to their church. Well. Fermat proposed a famous conjecture, known as his last theorem. The theorem holds that there are no positive integer solutions to the equation $a^n + b^n = c^n$ when n is larger than two. Are you following me?"

"Not a bit."

The Mathematician smiled. "Fermat proposed his theorem in 1637. It wasn't proved until the 1990s. That's more than three and a half centuries, during which half the serious science students on the planet probably spent at least a little time on it." The humor faded. "Fermat was one of us, Edna. Part of the Garden."

"I didn't know that."

"Fermat corresponded heavily with British mathematicians. They had a sort of competition going, each side trying to come up with problems that the other couldn't solve. Some historians think his last theorem was intended as part of the competition. Anyway, one of his British correspondents was known to Fermat to be a dedicated member of the Wilderness. Not that anybody called it the Wilderness back then, naturally. The point is that at this time the competition between the Wilderness and our predecessors was going through one of its phases of relative gentility. There is a letter in our archives—Fermat's historians and biographers are unaware of its existence—a letter in which Fermat told his rival of his great theorem, and that it would take hundreds of years to solve. They made a little bet. His friend said that the Wilderness would have the Stone long before the theorem was solved."

Edna felt the first chilly edge of panic. "Spell it out, George. Are you telling me—"

"I don't know what I'm telling you. Judge for yourself." He drew a sheet of paper from his jacket: a photocopy of a note written in block capitals. "The Builder gave me this before he left. He says this was mixed in with the mail at his office the week before last. Neither of his assistants knew where it came from."

The Judge was already reading:

M. FERMAT WON THE BET. BUT NOT BY MANY YEARS.

She looked up. "They have the Stone?"

"Either that, or they think they're on the verge of finding it. Or maybe they just want us to think so. The others don't really believe the Stone is important, and they might be right. The Builder on the other hand thinks that what matters is that the Wilderness is so determined to have it. Possibly the Stone has a value to them that we can't see."

"That's why you were so determined in there that we not try to pull Bethany out. That we keep her in motion."

"I'm sorry, Edna." He touched her arm. "I know how much you care about her. But we started this. We have to see it through."

The Mathematician slipped away, leaving the old woman alone with her thoughts; and her fears.

TWENTY-SEVEN

On Sunday morning, Bethany rode to church with Blessing, Janice, and a sullen fellow called Wayne. The weird conversation she had overheard in the basement almost made Bethany decide to stay; but she reasoned that she couldn't possibly be at greater risk in public than at the Village House. And playing along seemed to present the best opportunity to figure out what Blessing and the others thought she was so perfect for.

And so she went.

Their vehicle was a sparkling silver Mercedes S, and they were dressed in what Aunt Claudia would have called their Sunday best. In the fancy car, they looked rather a prosperous bunch. Blessing drove with Wayne beside her, while Janice and Bethany sat in the back. Wayne had the yellowed teeth of a long-time smoker and the unkempt hair of the spoiled brat. He spent most of the time looking out the window and drumming his fingers on the dashboard. His principal contribution to the conversation was to ask every few minutes how much longer this was going to take, although now and then he varied his routine by upbraiding Blessing for some real or imagined sin that involved driving too slowly, or too timidly, or too girlishly. If the rudeness Martin preached was ever more than a gimmick, then Wayne must surely have been his prize pupil.

Blessing did not correct him as she did most of the younger members, and Bethany began to wonder whether Wayne might be related to someone important in the group; or perhaps not a Planner at all. Instead, Blessing was chattering in the uncluttered tones of a tourist from downstate about the famous church they were about to visit, with its congregation numbering in the tens of thousands, and its parking lot the size of a dozen football fields.

"It's the perfect place," said Blessing as she entered the expressway. "It's incredible."

Although Bethany was no longer sure that the older woman was just making conversation.

"It's a brilliant idea," said Blessing. She winked at Bethany in the rear-view mirror. "I'm so glad you came with us."

As to Bethany, she had a new name: she was now Kathy Hobart, and had a wallet full of evidence to prove it, even if the credit cards were useless fakes. Unlike last night, Blessing now called her by name, impressing thereby on everyone that the woman in the car was Kathy, a down-on-her-luck Chicago native who had never in her life found a dead man in her kitchen, or fled across state lines to avoid prosecution.

They were heading north on the Kennedy Expressway, rude Wayne drumming merrily, using two hands now, and then half-singing, half audibly—"pah-pah-pah-PAH, pah-pah-pah-PAH"—and Bethany was about ready to scream when Janice, who had scarcely said a word since climbing into the car, suddenly cried out:

"Hey! Look! Hey!"

"What's wrong?" asked Blessing, slowing down just in case.

The teenager pointed at a clutch of low-rise office buildings in the Fulton River area. Just beyond, bright spring sunshine dappled off the water. "I've been there." She had her nose pressed up against the glass. "I was down there with Annabelle. You know, a couple of days before she left?"

Blessing's tone was nearly contemptuous. "That is very unlikely, dear. I'm sure you're mistaken."

"No. I remember. We were in town with Mr. Stafford, shopping at Staples? And Mr. Stafford got some kind of important call and had to go, and he sent us back to the House? So we were walking, but then Annabelle said she wanted to stop right there, and she told me to wait outside, like by the fountain? And she went inside one of those—"

"Which building was it?" asked Wayne, leering. "How long was she in there?"

Janice dropped her eyes and, on the carpeting, shuffled her feet. Then she offered the phrase used by teens all across the country when facing difficult questions: "I don't know."

"More like ten minutes? More like half an hour?"

"I don't know."

"You must know how long she was upstairs! What's the matter with you?" Leaning hard over the seat now. "Did you see what floor she went to? Which elevator she took? Anything?"

"Leave her alone," said Bethany.

"Nobody's talking to you—Kathy."

"Well, somebody's talking to you." She slipped an arm around the younger woman's shoulders. Something about Janice had engaged a maternal protectiveness Bethany had not realized she possessed. "Stop upsetting her. We're on the way to church. Let's arrive in a proper frame of mind."

"Listen," he snarled, plainly the prelude to something nasty, but Blessing intervened.

"She's right, Wayne. Sit down and hush. We have work to do." She laughed. "Besides. This is just one of Janice's stories, isn't it, dear?"

"Yes," said Janice.

"You never saw Annabelle go in any of those buildings in your life, did you, dear?"

"No."

"You have to stop making up stories, Janice dear. I know Martin is very concerned."

"I'm sorry." Eyes still downcast. "I'll try to do better."

"Good girl," said Blessing.

The rest of the drive passed in silence, except for Wayne's insistent drumming.

The church was as vast as advertised. It was all glass and whitewashed brick. The long oval building was surrounded by trees. Glistening in the May sunshine it was like a fine jewel set in silver, presented in a wooden case. Finding a parking space within a reasonable walk proved as complicated as solving a mathematical theorem, and as likely as winning the lottery, but small open-air buses, happily burning natural gas, ferried congregants to and fro.

"It's perfect," Blessing enthused as they waited.

Bethany looked at her, and wondered about Annabelle.

The bus was crowded but the trip took all of three minutes. Half the riders must have been tourists, because they were snapping photos of everything. Bethany noticed that Wayne hung onto the outside rails bordering her bench, as if to block her physically from making a run for it. She wasn't sure whether he would really try to stop her in the middle of a crowd, but escape was not her plan.

They alighted, and followed the crowd up the steps.

Bethany leaned toward Blessing and whispered: "What Janice was saying in the car about Annabelle—"

"It was just one of her stories," Blessing said. "Leave it alone, dear. This is what Janice does."

"What if it wasn't a story? Don't you want to know what Annabelle was doing there?"

Blessing took hold of her upper arm. She smiled, but her voice was steel. "If I tell you it's a story, dear, then it's a story."

But Bethany could not help remembering the older woman's pain on learning last night that Annabelle was dead; or the first words out of her mouth: *This wasn't supposed to happen.*

As they joined the throng filing into the vastness of the sanctuary, Bethany began to feel nervous. Although this was a real church and not a corrupt imitation like the Village House, she felt hemmed in by the crowd. They left the queue and settled into an empty pew at the far right rear, with a poor view of the altar: Wayne on the aisle, Blessing beside him, Janice and Bethany pressed like prisoners against the wall. Taking off her coat, Bethany happened to turn toward the aisle. She caught the intense gaze of another congregant, and wondered whether she had been recognized. But he smiled at her as he sat in the pew directly opposite: a fiftyish fellow in steel-rimmed glasses, wearing academic-style tweeds, with a shock of white down the middle of his dark hair.

"Stop fidgeting," Blessing hissed.

"I'm worried."

"You're a blonde now. You're wearing glasses. You don't look the same at all. Now, calm down, dear, you're making yourself conspicuous."

And she tried to relax. She really did. But every time she glanced across the aisle, the man in the tweeds was looking at her.

A classic hymn. A welcome. A Scriptural reading. Some more contemporary music. More Scripture. Bethany barely paid attention. A flash of warning was going off at some deep level of intuition, and she had no idea why. Not all of Blessing's whispered shushings and reassurances were able to help. Even when Janice grabbed her hand and squeezed, Bethany's unease continued to grow.

She knew why she had accepted the invitation: she hated narrow spaces, and by nature preferred to be on the move rather than sitting and waiting for her fate. That fear explained her flight itself: yes, she might indeed be acquitted, but the idea of confinement in prison was more than she could bear. Running may not have been entirely rational, but it was perfectly predictable; and so was using any excuse to get out of the Village House, for there, too, she felt trapped and immobile.

But now that she was out, she found the open spaces every bit as terrifying as the cramped upper room they had assigned her. To be on the run was to live with the sense of vulnerability that tickled against her hindbrain with every glance of every stranger she met. She was in a crowd of thousands. Only one congregant needed to marvel at her resemblance to the woman on the news and she would be lost.

What calmed her, finally, was the preacher's message. Somewhere along the way the words began to penetrate, and she began to listen.

Once more the professor was fascinated. It was like anthropological field work: exploring this primitive phenomenon, in its natural setting! A group of people—a disturbingly large one from the looks of things—who evidently believed all that religious mumbo jumbo. And yet they didn't seem bitter. They didn't seem ignorant. They didn't seem burdened by life. They seemed, for the most part, middle class. From snippets of conversations he had overheard in the foyer, many were evidently well-educated professionals. What a truly bizarre bunch. Studying them would afford a truly voluptuous pleasure.

If only there were time.

He began to wonder whether Bethany, too, might be a true believer, contrary to everything he had guessed from her dossier. If so, she would be harder to scare, but easier to kill. They were so often such fatalists, the believers. They imagined that when the brain died, some impenetrable essence was magically transported out of the natural world. One man two years ago had actually smiled at him when he saw that he could not escape. *All you're doing is getting me there sooner,* the fool had said. *If the Lord's ready for me, I'm ready for the Lord.*

Maybe there was less to Bethany Barclay than he thought. In which case maybe he wouldn't bother sharing his ideas with her before he—

His cell phone pinged.

The pastor's message comforted Bethany as she had not been comforted in a long while. The sensation entirely surprised her. Her nervousness and fear did not melt away exactly; she just felt better armed to cope with them.

The topic was Christian love, and Bethany was struck by the distinction between his interpretation and Martin's, even though they relied largely on the same texts. Love, said the pastor, is certainly an emotion, and a powerful one, but Christian love was also an activity, a discipline, a way of approaching life. The love that mattered was not the love that we professed or scribbled in greeting cards or emails or Facebook walls; the love that mattered was love in action, love that could be trusted because it could be seen. The love that mattered was the love that involved sacrifice, where we acted against our own best interests, in order to serve someone else's. That was a choice we had the opportunity to make at every waking instant, the pastor said—not an emotion but a decision.

"The Lord isn't asking us to feel," he explained. "The Lord is asking us to act." This much most serious believers in the room had heard before. But now the pastor let the other shoe drop: "And what does God promise us in return for our loving sacrifices?" A grand pause. "Nothing. Nothing whatsoever. That, my friends, is the entire point. The lack of the expectation of any return is exactly what makes love, love."

He drew an analogy to *Watership Down*, a novel about life from the point of view of rabbits. One of the rabbits in the story, it seemed, tried to make a deal with God—I'll do this if You'll do that—and was told by God, "There is no bargain." The pastor quoted the words again: "There is no bargain."

His tone grew stern. "One of the great misunderstandings of our relationship with God is that we should believe because in return He'll give us all sorts of neat stuff. Money. Good health. Friends. And of course our all-access pass to Heaven." Laughter. "But when we think of God in those terms—when we think of our relationship with Christ in those terms—we confuse cause and effect."

He spread his hands. "Our Lord commands us to love one another. I have told you already that true love entails true sacrifice. But we don't sacrifice for others in the hope that God will send by return mail all the neat stuff we're hoping for. We sacrifice for each other as a symbol of our faith in what God has done for us already, by sending His Son to die for our salvation. The sacrifices we make for each other are trivial by comparison, but they are the best we can do. We don't sacrifice in order to prevail over the forces of evil and darkness in the world. We sacrifice as a sign of our faith that those forces cannot prevail. They cannot prevail because God has already conquered them. We don't sacrifice to win His favor. We sacrifice to pay Him back."

Sacrifice. Suddenly so much about Bethany's plight made so much sense. The doubts that had plagued her fled. She still didn't know where her quest would lead her, but understood at last the importance of pursuing a higher purpose than her own freedom.

As to Blessing, she sat like a stone throughout the message, no flicker of emotion on her face. Janice, on the other hand, seemed to grow increasingly nervous as the time passed. She fidgeted constantly, and Blessing's whispered warnings did little to calm her down.

Wayne was the outlier. Halfway through the message he muttered that he'd had enough. He slipped out of the pew, hurried up the aisle, and did not return.

A moment later, the man with the shock of white in his hair did the same.

Coffee hour was as complicated as a presidential inaugural ball, and better attended. The parish hall seemed big enough to host a political convention. Bethany, still buoyed by the sermon, joined the very long line of parishioners wanting to meet the pastor—not because she thought his pride needed the flattery, but because her wounded soul needed more succor. The pastor stood on a dais at the end of the rotunda nearest the sanctuary, and there were probably three hundred people ahead of her. Bethany didn't care. She was in no hurry. Wayne had been skulking in a corner of the parish hall when they arrived, and he and Blessing had put their heads together in swift, whispered conversation, then headed off down a hallway. Janice was sitting at a table with a clutch of teenagers, laughing and carefree as she never was around the Village House, no matter what Martin had done for her. The line inched forward. Bethany shut her eyes. Love was action, not feeling. Annabelle, she realized, had always understood that. Perhaps most believers did. But Bethany had never sufficiently appreciated the way that her running buddy, despite all the demons that plagued her, would never turn away a needy friend; or a new one. In college, Bethany had gone through a serious C. S. Lewis period, and she remembered now his description, in *Surprised by Joy*, of his lifelong search for the true source of the surges of joy and longing he had felt all his life. And of course, as her Aunt Claudia used to say, it scarcely mattered if you were looking for God, as long as you stayed alert for those moments when God was looking for—

"Bethany? Bethany Barclay?"

Her eyes snapped open. Standing beside her was a tall, well-turned-out woman whom she recognized at once: a friend from college, now a thoracic surgeon. They had sat at the same table three years ago at the reunion dinner.

"Excuse me?" said Bethany, fighting to keep her teeth from chattering as she surreptitiously glanced at the others waiting on line, expecting to see cell phones at ears as they made swift, worried calls to 911. Sooner or later it was bound to happen; she was surprised that it hadn't happened sooner.

"Bethany, it's me. Paulette Thiemann. Are you okay?" Taking her unresisting arm, drawing her from the line. "What are you doing here? I saw you on television. What was that all about? It's all over with, right?"

Bethany narrowed her eyes, and stood straight. "I'm sorry, ma'am. I think you're confusing me with somebody else."

To her dismay, Paulette's smile only broadened. "Wow. You're on the lam? Seriously? I mean, this is like a movie." They were in the center of the floor again, alone in the crowd. The woman put a hand in Bethany's hair, felt around. "I mean, blond? Bethany, seriously. There are people who look blond and people who don't, and what you look like is a brunette on the lam. But you didn't do it, right? You're innocent?"

"I'm sorry, ma'am, but I'm not who you think I am. Now, would you mind taking your hand out of my—"

"Kathy! There you are!" Blessing was back, Janice with her. She sized up Paulette. "Who's your new friend?"

"This is"—Bethany hesitated—"I'm sorry, ma'am. I've forgotten your name." She smiled at Blessing. It cost her, but she smiled. "She's seems to have mistaken me for somebody she saw on television."

"Blessing," said the older woman. And when a startled Paulette said the same thing back, Blessing laughingly explained that this was her name. "But bless you, anyway," she said.

"Kathy?" said Paulette. "What's this Kathy stuff?"

Mortification, doubled: now her new name was known, too.

"We really have to get going," said Blessing, pulling her away. "The car's waiting."

All the way to the door, Bethany felt her classmate's eyes boring into her back.

Outside the day had turned brisk and drizzly, as Chicago can at a snap, even in the middle of May. Blessing conjured a folding umbrella from her bag, and the three women huddled beneath to cross the parking lot. Bethany was worried sick that Paulette would turn her in, but when she tried to express some of this, Blessing gave her a sharp look and inclined her chin toward Janice.

"It doesn't really matter," the older woman went on, having evidently decided that some sort of reassurance was needed. "There won't be long to wait now, anyway."

"Wait for what?"

Blessing ignored the question. "Besides, dear, if anything *were* to happen, they have your lovely visage on the security cameras, don't they?" She saw the look on Bethany's face. "Oh, dear. You didn't notice, did you? When you were waiting to shake the pastor's hand? The cameras got you several times. I enjoyed the message too, but you didn't see me standing there."

But Bethany was still back at the beginning. "What do you mean, if anything were to happen? What's going to happen?"

Blessing crinkled her nose in distaste. "Nothing, dear. I don't have the second sight any more than you do. I'm just saying, if something did."

Before Bethany could press her further, Wayne rejoined them, head down, reading something on his phone.

"Find a good place?" Blessing asked.

"Several," he muttered, typing a message.

"Cell phones aren't allowed," said Janice brightly. "They distract us from—"

"Hush," said Blessing.

On the ride back to the Village House, Bethany shut her eyes and tried to doze. She was still safe, she told herself. For the moment, she was still safe. For how long, she couldn't say. Even if Paulette didn't call the police, that business about the security cameras worried her. She was still new to this fugitive business, and she shuddered to think how many more mistakes lay ahead of her. And yet she was buoyed by the belief that Annabelle's words didn't mean what they'd seemed to mean.

Yes, Bethany had helped Tia and Polly have Annabelle involuntarily committed at a particularly low moment in her running buddy's constant battle with her demons. Bethany hadn't testified, though; she'd been in court for the proceeding, but mainly to support her friend. Given the shape Annabelle was in at the time, she might well have remembered that particular detail wrong. But she wouldn't have messed up the time. On the tape, Annabelle said the commitment fight had taken place while they were at Barnard. That wasn't true. Bethany had been studying at Oxford, and had flown back specially, at Polly's urgent insistence, to try to persuade her running buddy to go into treatment voluntarily. Annabelle might have been hazy on the details of her commitment, but she wasn't likely to have forgotten *when* it happened. Especially because, the instant they let her out, she had turned up on Bethany's doorstep in Oxford.

Annabelle had lied to Martin about when and how she'd been committed. The question was why.

Sitting at dinner later, Bethany continued to turn the problem over in her head, picking at the bland food while Janice described the service for several other young people who joined their table, one of them the redheaded boy, whose name turned out to be Zach. The black girl's shyness vanished around those her own age, and she even kept them laughing, as Blessing and Tonya looked on benignly. But the most interesting part was that when Janice came to the pastor's message, she was able to repeat it pretty much word for word.

"She had a perfect score on her SATs," Tonya murmured, sotto voce.

"What happened?" asked Bethany.

Blessing glared. "No idle talk, please, ladies."

Later, after the sing-along, Janice sat with a couple of the kids and a couple of adults, playing chess. They had boards in front of them but her back was turned. They called out their moves to her, and Janice shyly murmured hers in return. She won all four games, very quickly.

Who *was* this child?

Stuart Van Der Staal was still irritated. He had sat in his rented Buick, watching the Mercedes as it purred out of the parking lot. His plan had been perfect. He had worked out a way to eliminate his target as she left the church while pinning the blame on that boy with the dirty teeth. But the text message during the service changed all that.

The parameters of his assignment, as they said in the trade, had been reassessed. His revised task was not to kill her but to take her, in order to learn what she had reconstructed of Annabelle's researches. The work was not nearly as clean, but it did have one advantage: at least he would have the opportunity to assess her intellect before she died.

TWENTY-EIGHT

"So now the FBI knows she's in Chicago," said the Senator. It was Monday, and the Virginia air was warm and sultry. "One of your friend's classmates spotted her at a church service. She called the police, the police called the Bureau, and the Bureau has everything about her flagged to get in touch with my chief of staff immediately."

"Now that I find intriguing," said Edna, her cane plunging hard against the grass.

"There's nothing to worry about. I'm a close friend of the Kirkland family. It's natural that my office would track the investigation. That's what power is for, Edna."

"That isn't the intriguing part." The Judge chuckled. "I was referring to the notion that Bethany Barclay was at Sunday services. Running from the world, but she surfaces at church. What church was it?"

The Senator told her.

"Ah," said the Judge. "Not just any church. A megachurch. Thousands of congregants. In a crowd like that, how could she not be recognized?"

They were walking across the meadow behind Edna's house. The noonday sun hung close and hot. There was no breeze. They were very near the woods. Aged trees stood out sharp and green, centered in their own tiny shadows. The Senator's driver stood watch in front of the house, and a bodyguard followed, just out of earshot. The two women were able to meet together openly as often as they liked because they served as honorary co-chairs of a terribly impressive blue-ribbon committee designed to encourage young girls to consider professional careers. Official Washington took them to be friends, which they never quite were. They respected each other's talents and achievements, but Edna found that she never quite trusted the Senator; and nobody is quite as skilled as a politician at winkling out the true opinions of others.

"You're saying that if she was in a church, there was a reason," said the Senator, nobody's fool. "She wasn't there to seek consolation during her time of suffering."

"I don't know why she was in church," said Edna. "But I would be very interested to know who accompanied her."

"The Bureau is processing the security camera footage. They don't know that she's at the Village House, though, so they won't know what other faces they're looking for."

The Judge gave her a look. "I understand what you're saying, Jillian, but it's already been vetoed. We don't tell them anything. Besides." Waving her cane for emphasis. "Do you really know whom to trust over there? Can you tell me for sure that the Wilderness doesn't have people in the FBI?"

"I don't know where they have people, Judge. I'm just not as sure as you and the Builder seem to be that we can handle this on our own."

"The Garden has been working alone for six centuries, Senator."

"And losing. Don't forget that part. Since I've been a member, we've lost almost every battle we've fought." A beat. "Sometimes violently."

"True enough."

And it was true. It defined a fundamental difference between the Garden and the Wilderness: the Garden was not willing to kill just to get its way. Four Christians of various stripes, one Jew, one agnostic, one atheist, and none of them was willing to use violence as a weapon. The plan had been constructed with such care, to prod Bethany gently in the direction of her old beau in Chicago, in the hope that she would discover that Annabelle had preceded her, and so follow her footsteps. They had been prepared to wait, or even to try something else.

But the Wilderness wasn't. Whoever was running things over there wanted Bethany moving now, because now was always the only time that mattered. A simple equation. And so Ken Kirkland had been slaughtered in Bethany's house, sacrificed to the greater cause.

The adversary was militant and remorseless, determined by whatever means to break the hold of organized religion on the sheeplike minds of billions. Like so many secularists, they were impatient. The means were irrelevant, the goal was of crucial importance, but most vital was reaching their goal now: today if possible, tomorrow if necessary, waiting until next week was already a victory for the forces of reaction. And so they had inserted themselves into the operation. The reluctant manipulations of the leaders of the Garden were no longer relevant. It was time to face the possibility that Bethany Barclay belonged to the Wilderness now.

"You know, Edna," said the Senator, "Bethany had to pass through a lot of territory to get to Chicago. Western Pennsylvania, Ohio, Indiana."

"What's your point, Jillian?"

"There are plenty of colleges and universities along the way. Now that the FBI knows she's in Chicago, how much do you want to bet that one of those schools is going to have a little explosion in a lab where they work with human embryos?"

The judge made a sound. Of pain, and, maybe, fear. "They'll say it's Bethany—"

"And her band of Christian extremists," said the Senator.

They walked on.

The bombing came that very night, at the medical campus of the University of Indiana at Bloomington. Carraway and Pulu, on their way to Chicago, detoured to meet with local agents who were investigating. The preliminary results suggested the same crude thermite device that had been used at George Mason and Haverford. There were no usable prints. In fact, there was no forensic evidence of any kind, apart from the similarity of the bomb to the ones used before. Pulu suggested that their bomber was getting better. Carraway had a different theory but kept it to himself. Political leaders spoke gravely of bringing the monsters to justice. Television talk shows were crowded with talk of home-grown terror and Christian fanatics. Guests who tried to condemn both the research and the bombings were shouted down. The terrorists had to be found. One expert suggested that if this kept up, search warrants should be issued for the premises of "every so-called pro-life group in the country—now that we know their true feelings about life." Nobody had been killed yet, but there was always tomorrow. Across the country, armed guards were patrolling laboratories that worked with human embryos. And in the Village House, aware of none of this, Bethany Barclay went to Martin to ask if she could listen to the rest of Annabelle's session tapes.

He refused.

Around one in the morning, Edna Harrigan woke. Not from a nightmare, and not from a creak or footfall in her well-protected house.

No, she had been awakened by an idea. This was not an unfamiliar situation for her, but with the advancement of years it happened less frequently. When she was younger, these moments of crystal clarity in the midst of sleep had been common. While she was on the bench, during her career as a prosecutor, even back in law school a million years ago, Edna had this habit of opening her eyes from a dream and knowing, just knowing, the answer to a challenge that had been puzzling her.

As she knew the answer now.

There was no way for her to probe any more deeply into the murder of Ken Kirkland without raising eyebrows. But there was another path.

His mother. Sylvia.

The scheme had begun with Sylvia.

Prevailed upon by her old friend, the Senator, Sylvia had changed her will to leave money to the Planners. She had even agreed to have Bethany draw the will. The Senator never told her why. They had been friends forever, and when the Senator said it was a matter of national security, Sylvia had asked no questions.

"She loves it," the Senator had said.

"Are you sure we can trust her?"

"We saved each other's lives at Wellesley."

The idea was that Sylvia would have Bethany draw the new will, and then let her children know what she had done. One of them—probably Kenneth, but it didn't matter who—was bound to complain to Bethany, who was bound to come to Edna, who would point her toward Chicago.

Simple enough.

After that, Sylvia could go back to her regular lawyers down in Charlottesville and reinstate her former will, leaving her money to whomever she wished.

But Sylvia had died.

That was the event nobody had anticipated.

She had died of a heart attack, and the leaders of the Garden had put their heads together, and decided to leave the plan in place. After all, with Sylvia Kirkland dead and the will unveiled, a challenge by one of the children was an even greater likelihood.

Awfully convenient.

Too convenient.

With Sylvia Kirkland dead, the operation that was chugging placidly along all at once kicked into high gear. True, it was the murder that really revved things, but Sylvia's death provided the spark.

The sort of thing the Wilderness would do.

Edna picked up the bedside phone to call the Senator. Then her hand fell away. No. Too soon. She decided instead to wake up the sheriff. It was the middle of the night, but she was Edna Harrigan. To the county, she was an eccentric with friends in high places. That reputation had its benefits.

TWENTY-NINE

On Tuesday afternoon, Bethany stood in the Fulton River District amidst the clutch of buildings Janice had pointed out on their way to church two days before. She and Annabelle had stopped here, Janice insisted, and Annabelle had gone inside. But Blessing insisted that the whole thing had never happened, and when Bethany pressed Janice last night, the teen had stuck to her new story that the old one was a lie. Nor was there time to persuade her to tell the truth, for Janice and Zach, the redheaded boy she seemed to like, were headed off to a youth group meeting. Thus there was no way to ask which of the buildings Annabelle had visited.

Bethany had been up and down the streets, wandering amongst glistening new apartment towers and old crumbling warehouses, chic little cafés and aging pizzerias. She had no precise plan. She had put her energy into planning how to slip out of the Village House without being noticed. She had spent several hours yesterday and this morning hovering in the lobby, over near the doors to the auditorium and the tables that sold the books and shirts, chatting amiably with Janice, who seemed to have a brief to remain by her side, and keeping an eye on the front door to mark the times when the entrance was most crowded, hoping for the chance to dart off into the throng. But earnest Janice stuck with her every step, even accompanying her to the ladies' room. At last it occurred to Bethany to test the bounds of her evident confinement by simply stepping toward the door to see what happened.

Nothing.

"Where are you going?" said Janice, her tone more curious than alarmed.

"Nowhere," said Bethany.

Janice folded her hands like a child preparing to recite. "Well, if you have to leave, make sure to be back by curfew."

"What time is curfew?"

"This is Monday, so it's six."

And that was that.

Bethany was in the street, and, as far as she could tell as she made her way toward the subway, not being followed.

Nobody seemed to care.

But then why would they? she asked now, as she marched back and forth along the sidewalks, trying to work things out. Out of the shadowy confines of the Village House, Bethany found both thoughts and perceptions sharpened. Martin and his people had no incentive to keep their unexpected visitor under wraps. If anything was really going on in the Village House—anything that the Planners preferred to keep hidden—they were surely better off with Bethany out of the building than inside, snooping into dusty corners.

And yet Annabelle had gone into the basement.

The sequence seemed clear.

Annabelle, for what reason Bethany could not guess, had showed up at the Village House. Then she had gone into the basement. Then she had snuck off to one of the offices down here in Fulton River. Then she had left the group—disengaged, as Martin called it—and showed up back East, first on Peter Zhukov's doorstep, then on Bethany's own.

Then she had vanished for months; then she had died.

Suppose Martin was telling the truth. Suppose he'd rejected her effort to involve him in the search for the Pilate Stone. That didn't mean Annabelle had stopped looking.

There was an answer, and it was somewhere in front of her. If she could figure out why Annabelle had stopped here—which building she had entered—who she had come this way to see—then she would be on the way to solving her twin mysteries: why Annabelle was dead, and why she herself was being framed.

Bethany marched back and forth along the sidewalks, trying to work things out. Annabelle had gone into one of these buildings, and a few days later had disappeared. But which?

Janice said she had waited near a fountain. Well, Fulton River was full of fountains, most of them hideous decorative pieces outside the trendier apartment towers. A couple of restaurants had them; so did two or three outdoor shopping plazas. So did—

Bethany stopped.

A cul-de-sac she had missed before. Townhouses converted into office space, and, sure enough, at the entrance to the cobbled drive was a fountain.

A pedestrian gate stood wide open. She crossed the street and looked at the brass nameplates. Lawyers. A psychiatrist. A realtor. An accounting firm. Two investment advisers.

Had Annabelle wanted to make a will? Buy a condo? See a shrink? None of it made sense.

Bethany slipped through the gate. Passersby glanced at her, then glanced away. In her jeans and sweater and scuffed shoes, her hair so obviously bleached, she looked like an interloper. Felt like one, too.

She walked to the end of the plaza, where wood benches were set in a semicircle, overlooking the railroad tracks, with the river beyond. A young man in a nice blazer was eating his lunch and eying her. She turned away, began to walk along the row of townhouses, peering at the doors and windows as if they held the key to the mystery. When she reached the gate again, she crossed the cobbled drive and, walking toward the overlook once more, repeated her scrutiny at the other side.

Nothing. Not a tickle. She could hardly barge into each of the offices to ask whether Annabelle happened to have—

And then she saw him, seated on a folding chair, beneath an umbrella, over on the grass near the river. He had a sketch pad on his lap and was drawing. He was short and fussy, with thinning hair, a chubby face, and comically thick glasses.

She had spotted the same man on the day she arrived at the Village House: he was one of the protestors outside when Daniel Stafford escorted her in.

And now that she had a better look at him, she knew she had seen him earlier, too: he was the unknown white man who had been sitting in the back of the half-empty church at Annabelle's funeral.

She approached him slowly—on her cat feet, as Aunt Claudia used to say—all the while keeping a wary eye on the young man eating lunch, just in case he belonged to somebody. Being on the run had taught her to see the world that way. But the young man finished his food, hopped up, and headed off toward the gate of the cul-de-sac. He never turned and looked her way.

The chubby old man looked up as she drew near.

"I don't do portraits," he said. "This is for my own enjoyment."

He went back to his work. He was sketching the buildings across the river, she saw. The art wasn't bad, but none of the fancy galleries down the block would be giving him an exhibition any time soon.

He glanced at her again. "You're still here."

She swallowed. "I'm a friend of Annabelle's."

"Annabelle who?" His querulous tone was ready to disagree with every word out of her mouth. He was sketching again. She wondered what demons were chasing through his head. His clothes looked expensive but old. He had shaved badly. His glasses were still crooked. "I don't know any Annabelle."

"Annabelle Seaver."

"If I say I don't know any Annabelle, adding a surname won't change my mind."

She smiled and spread her hands, to show she meant no harm. "I saw you the other day. Outside the Village House." The charcoal might have wavered. "You were protesting. You said something about your son." He said nothing; kept drawing. "Please. I know you know Annabelle. You were at her funeral. In Harlem."

His head came up, and for the first time she saw his eyes: dark and brilliant and intense and, she suspected, not entirely sane.

"What do you want? I saw you going in there. I don't have any business with Gopos. Leave me alone."

"I'm not a member."

"Know how you can tell when a Gopo is lying? Her mouth is moving."

"I think that's a lawyer joke."

"Lawyers are just as bad. I've visited a couple to try to sue. Know what they told me? My son's an adult. He can join whatever sick religious cult he wants to." He dropped his eyes again. The charcoal was moving fast now, the lines hard and angry. "Leave me alone. I'm busy."

She tried again. "Annabelle was my friend."

"Your mouth is still moving, so you're still lying."

"Maybe I can help you find your son."

"Still moving."

"Please. Annabelle is dead. You know that. I saw you at the funeral. I've been trying to find out what happened to her. That's why I'm here. I know she talked to you. I just want to find out what you talked about. After that I'll leave you alone."

For another minute or so he kept sketching. Then he slowed down, sighed, shut the pad. "I'll say this for you. You're persistent. What's your name?"

"Um, Kathy. Kathy Hobart."

"Is that your real name?"

"Does it matter?"

He was packing up his things, folding his chair. "You're asking me to trust you. You're not showing much trust in return."

She swallowed. "I'm not sure what you mean."

"You're that girl on the news. The one who's planting the bombs. Did you think I wouldn't recognize you? I'm not crazy, no matter what they say."

"I—I didn't do those things."

He leaned away from her, a growing suspicion in his eyes. "And now you're going to give me six reasons not to call the police, aren't you?"

"Just one, actually."

"And what reason is that, *Kathy*?"

"Because I don't want what happened to Annabelle to happen to me."

"That's not good enough. You're a religious fanatic. They said so on the news."

"That's also not true."

"Right. You're being framed, you're not a fanatic, but you just happen to be hiding out with the Gopos? What kind of story is that? Never mind." He was holding his chair and the pad with a surprising ease. "Prove it. Prove you're Annabelle's friend. Right now. Otherwise"—pulling out a clunky old mobile with his free hand—"I'm calling 911."

Bethany hesitated. She knew a thousand facts about her running buddy's life, but had no idea which she might have shared with this mad sketch artist. Yet it was plain that they'd spoken. His fingers were still curled around the phone, and she knew his threat wasn't idle. Maybe she should run.

Then she looked at his charcoal etchings, and had the answer. So obvious.

She reached into her jacket and pulled out the drawing Annabelle had left her down in Virginia: the charcoal sketch of the two crossed arrows beneath a flat cylinder.

"She gave this to me the last time I saw her alive," she said. "You drew it for her."

The old man's response was anything but what she'd expected. His face twisted in blotchy fury. He dropped his implements and shoved her hard.

"Get away from me! Gopo! Liar! Come near me again and I'll kill you!"

THIRTY

The old man turned away from her and began to gather his things. Bethany tried, three times, to apologize for whatever she had done to offend him, but the artist was adamant. He wanted nothing to do with her. He even believed she was his enemy. She watched as he stalked off along the waterfront. She would have to come back. She would work out another approach. There was gold to be had here, and she knew it.

She turned and headed for the entrance to the cul-de-sac. One thing was certain. The old man knew Annabelle. And if Annabelle had tracked him here, then this must be a regular place for him to sit and sketch. He struck Bethany as a creature of habit. In a day, maybe two, he'd be back sitting in the same spot. She'd simply have to find a more persuasive approach.

Stuart Van Der Staal waited for her to pass. The key he had been using to pretend to lock the door of a disused office he slipped into his pocket. In his other pocket was a syringe: by far the easiest way to subdue her and ease her into his car, to take her to a place outside the city that he had already prepared for their conversation. He could hardly wait for his peek into her fascinating mind.

As Bethany hurried toward the gate, the killer matched her stride for stride, inching closer on his long legs.

Bethany was through the gate and on the sidewalk. Hooray, no large men in flak jackets awaited. She glanced in both directions, then hastened across the street, down the steps, and past the fountain. She joined the throngs in the plaza, giving thanks for her deliverance. For she absolutely could not afford to get caught, not now when she was so close; and not only because she did not want to go to prison for a murder she hadn't committed.

There was another, more basic reason.

Annabelle had met with this strange old man who'd lost his son to the Planners. An outsider who was a regular protester at the Village House. Who'd hired lawyers and tried to sue. A man like that probably had files and files full of information he'd gathered in his search. A lot of what he knew or thought he knew would likely be mad or wrong, but not all. Was it too much to imagine that he'd told Annabelle something useful?

So, yes. Bethany would definitely come back.

The professor was beside her now, as she stood waiting to cross the street. With his head covered, the poor girl had no idea who he was: perception again. His hair was his most distinctive feature, so that was what people remembered. Take away the hair, and his was simply another face in the crowd.

He eased closer, hand darting into his pocket.

Bethany, oblivious to the danger, was continuing to do her sums. Now she was firmly on Annabelle's trail. How and why her running buddy had come to the Village House, Bethany still didn't know. Given what Martin had told her, it likely was related to her search for the Pilate Stone. And the old man must have told her something useful. Bethany didn't want to let go of that idea.

Then there was the tape of the counseling session. Annabelle had told Martin she didn't like Bethany and would never trust her with a secret. She even expressed the worry that Bethany might do her harm. But Annabelle had lied about the date of her commitment. And the lie just might have been intended for Bethany's ears. Annabelle was no fool. She knew that whatever she was doing was dangerous. She had guessed that she might not survive, and that her running buddy might come looking for her.

By lying about the commitment, she was telling Bethany that the rest was a lie, too—the whole tale about not trusting her. Then why tell it? For the same reason. Annabelle was frightened. But not just for herself. She was worried that whatever might be about to happen to her would happen to Bethany, too, if anybody believed they'd made contact. And so she'd lied to Martin about whom she did and didn't trust in order to throw whoever was chasing her off Bethany's scent.

Which meant that she thought that Martin, whether or not he was helping her find the Stone, was a part of whatever was—

Suddenly there was a man very close beside her, jostling, his hand sliding up her arm. She turned to slap him—

"Miss Hobart! Wait!"

Both heads turned at the same time, and then the stranger melted into the crowd.

Behind her, panting hard at the exertion, the chubby old man was catching up.

"Are you all right?" he asked, head turned in the direction where the stranger had fled.

"Yes. I'm fine."

"Who was that?"

"Nobody I know." She focused on the old man. "I'm sorry I offended you before. I didn't mean to."

He was still out of breath. "And I'm sorry I blew up. It's just, with my son missing—the stress—maybe I overreacted. You're right. The drawing is my work. And maybe you are Annabelle's friend. We should talk."

Stuart Van Der Staal followed them at a distance. He'd been so close. The syringe was now safely capped, and in his pocket. He watched them enter a grimy little restaurant, and bought himself an iced coffee from a stand across the way. Saved in the nick of time, by that crazy old man she'd been arguing with. The mathematics of coincidence was a never-ending source of fascination to him, even though fools tried to attach great significance to the entirely explicable.

It occurred to the professor that Bethany Barclay was taking a quite considerable risk by wandering through Chicago. She was smart. Her gamble was likely calculated. That meant that little man might be an important source of information.

Stuart smiled to himself as he lapped up the coffee. Fate had thrown up two targets for him, not one. Possibly he would take them both. If not, he supposed he might have to eliminate the interloper in order to get his hands on his quarry.

He had no problem with that.

THIRTY-ONE

I'm really not crazy," said the old man. His name, he had told her, was Harry Pribyl, and he was an accountant. "I admit I go off sometimes. It's just that I want my son back. Does that seem crazy to you?"

"Of course not."

"Your friend Annabelle offered to help. She saw me outside, like you did, and we got to talking, and—well, she tried. I'll give her that. She tried to help me, and I tried to help her." They were sitting in a rear booth in a hamburger joint he knew. The wood was dark and the shadows hid most details, including, she hoped, her face. "I know all the lawyer jokes because lawyers and accountants are natural enemies. I'm retired, but I still go in from time to time. My firm is in one of the buildings out there." Craning his neck toward the window. He frowned, and the vague look came over his face again. "No, I don't think so. I was going to tell you the name of the firm, but I don't think I will. I won't tell you my real last name, either. Don't ask." He looked past her, seemed to shudder, then focused again. "I still don't know if I can trust you. You could still be a Gopo."

"If I lie to you," she said, softly, "you still have the option of turning me in."

"Sure. If I want to get run over, like poor Annabelle." Behind the crooked glasses, his eyes were wild. "I know what those people are like. Look what happened to my son."

It occurred to Bethany that Harry's retirement from his firm might not have been entirely voluntary. The episode with his son had wounded him, and now he was obsessed. She had to know what he and Annabelle had talked about, but it was plain that she'd have to get there gently.

"Tell me about your son."

"Harry Junior." He puckered his pale lips, as if having trouble with the details. "He was a good boy. Our only child. Well, my wife died years ago. Anyway, Junior was in law school at DePaul. Doing pretty well. Then all of a sudden, two years ago, he announces that he's dropping out. Joining Martin Potus's little cult. Not that he considered it a cult, naturally. He said they were helping him find the path God wanted him to walk, and the path didn't go through law school anymore."

There was bother as the waitress came back to take their orders. Harry Senior wanted a burger topped with everything. Bethany took a salad with a bit of grilled salmon on top.

"I thought it was a phase. Nobody could believe that—that claptrap. And that Martin Potus character. Come on. It's a Ponzi scheme. I know about these things. I'm an accountant. They join, they turn over their assets—not all, but a big chunk—and the guys at the top—well, anyway, you know what I'm talking about. So I wait. And Junior and I, well, we get together every couple of weeks for a bite to eat. After a while I realize this thing is serious. It isn't a phase. He's a believer. We have a couple of big arguments, and after that he won't see me anymore. I go over there to the so-called Village House. They tell me I can't talk to my own son. I'm distracting him from his path. I go back every couple of days. I leave notes. Then one day they tell me he's gone. Off on one of their missions. They won't say where. A month later, I go back. No sign of him. New people in the lobby. They've never heard of him. I make a scene, they call the police—anyway, that's what happened."

The spark has gone out of those eyes, as Bethany had hoped it would. She'd seen this before, in a deposition in a nasty divorce case, a wronged wife who arrived full of vinegar, but by the time she was through telling her story, she was too worn out to be angry.

"I'm sorry about Junior," said Bethany, voice still gentle.

"Sorry! Do you know what it's like to have your own flesh and blood disappear? Just vanish without a trace, and nobody cares?"

She thought of her father. And of Annabelle, her running buddy and, for practical purposes, her sister. "A little," she said.

"Ever lose your only child?"

"No."

"Then you don't know anything about it." But the pleading eyes signaled less umbrage than bewilderment. "There I go again. I get very emotional about Junior. After a while, I couldn't do my work. I was too upset. I'd yell at the other accountants. I guess that's why the firm—never mind. Where were we?"

"You were going to tell me how you met Annabelle. And how she came to promise she'd help find your son."

"It was the protests. At the so-called Village House." He was working on his third Diet Coke. "She saw me when I used to stand out there. One day she came over to talk to me, and I told her to go away. She was trying to be helpful, but I didn't believe her. I'm afraid I said some nasty things. But then a few days later, I ran into her again. This time I wasn't with the protesters. I was—I was over by the back door. I was hunting for a way in. The back door has this lock, with letters and numbers on it, and I didn't know the combination. Well, I was about to give up, when I noticed a kind of carving in the metal below the lock. Some kind of symbol. It looked familiar, and, well, strange symbols are a sort of hobby of mine. I was drawing a sketch of it, and that's when Annabelle came out the back door. Martin was with her, and a couple of other Gopos. They looked like they were ready to beat me up on the spot, but Martin said to let me go, and Annabelle walked me down to the end of the alley. She asked me what I was doing. I didn't lie. She looked at my drawing, and she got interested. I could tell. So she asked if we could maybe meet. Away from the Village House. I looked down the alley. Martin was pointing to his watch. The two gorillas, well, they'd gone off somewhere. I told her to meet me here—I mean, out there where I do my sketches—the next day. She was there, right on the dot. We met three more times before they killed her."

"What did you talk about?"

"Junior. I told you. She was going to help me find him. She said she might be able to get into the records of the missions and tell me where they'd sent him. At first I thought, maybe she was lying. But I didn't see any gain to the

Village House. It's not like I was giving away any secrets. She didn't want money."

"But she wanted something, didn't she? In return?"

He nodded. "This is where it got . . . well, weird. The first time, she asked if she could see my sketch. The one I was making of the symbol carved next to the door. Well, I had it with me. I still do." He reached into the box that held his charcoal, pulled out a much-folded and much-handled page. He flattened it on the table. It looked to Bethany like a drawing of a money bag—the kind robbers stole from banks in the old movies—tied at the throat, embossed with an eight-point star.

"You don't know what it is, do you?" Harry sounded proud. "Neither did Annabelle. But I'd checked my files by then. It's a picture of a purse. This was one of the images used in the medieval church to represent Saint Cyril of Alexandria. She asked me if I was sure. I said, of course I'm sure. This is my hobby. I collect these old Christian symbols. Recreationally. And Annabelle—well, for some reason, she got very excited. She said she had to go, but asked whether we could meet again tomorrow. I was amused, but I said yes."

On the subject of his hobby, Harry was remarkably lucid.

"And did she come back?"

"She did. She said, 'You were right. It works.' I don't know exactly what she meant, but she was really happy now. Bursting with joy, I'd say. She showed me some photos she'd taken with her cell phone. Must have been five or six of them. She asked if I could tell her what these symbols were, too." The animation went out of his face. "I reminded her of her promise. The quid pro quo. I'd help her but she had to help me. I recognized a couple right off, but I told her I wouldn't give her any more information unless she found out what happened to my son. She was annoyed, but she said yes, she'd do her part. We set up another meeting for—I'm not sure—four, five days later, I think."

The waitress was back with the food, and there was bother about ketchup and mustard.

"Well," said Harry when they were alone. His eyes were once more lost. "Um. Where were we?"

"The symbols on Annabelle's phone," said Bethany. She had her line drawing ready. The red squiggle from the lapel. "Was this one of them?"

"What? Oh, yes. Naturally I recognized that one." He brightened again. "The serpent, as I'm sure you can tell. It's curled around a tree. In the Middle Ages, this was the symbol for the Garden of Eden, with the serpent representing the temptations of the world. The carving is quite common all over Europe. But there's a problem with this particular exemplar." He traced the snake with his fingers. "Notice that the snake's head is the highest thing in the picture? Higher even than the tree? That's a mistake by whoever did the carving. Those medieval craftsmen would never have placed the head of the serpent above the crown of the tree. The imagery would be all wrong, because it would grant Satan a stature that no fallen angel could ever attain."

Bethany looked again at the image. Now that the architect had explained the message, it seemed so obvious.

"And this would only be done by mistake," she said.

Harry shrugged. "I suppose one could do it intentionally. Maybe to symbolize—I'm guessing here—that one values the things of the world above the things of God. Well, I figured she found it in the Village House. And I wouldn't put anything past those people. Look what they did to my son." He shivered again. "She came back. Annabelle. Three days later, four, whatever we agreed to. This time we met at my office. I asked her about Junior. She said what they all say. There wasn't any record. There wasn't any evidence he'd ever been a member. She'd looked at a file that was supposed to have information on members who'd disengaged, and Junior wasn't in it."

Bethany started to ask the obvious question, but suddenly it was a matter not of speeding Harry up but of slowing him down.

"I got mad. I admit it. I was furious. I called her names. I said she'd used me. I told her I wasn't going to help her if she didn't help me. She stuttered some nonsense about how there were some locked files that Martin kept at his house that she'd never seen, and then—well, she broke down. She got hysterical. I suppose that's the word. From the Greek, you know, meaning a suffering of the womb. Well, I don't know about her womb, but she was suffering. She started to cry. Right in my office. I mean, nobody cries in an accounting office, unless it's about the IRS." His joke fell flat. "She said she really had been in the files, she really did want to help me, but she couldn't get blood out of a stone. That's what she said, word for word. Blood out of a stone. She begged me. She said she had to know what the rest of those symbols meant, or lives would end. Her very words. Lives would end."

"You're sure she said *lives*? Plural?"

He barely heard the question. "I was still mad at her. I still thought she was a liar. But, the thing is"—he poked his tongue around again, searching for the phrase—"the thing is, Annabelle didn't seem as if she was lying for her own benefit. She didn't to have anything to gain." He gestured at the paper on the table between them. "I don't see where there's any profit in being able to interpret symbols nobody's used in five hundred years."

Bethany perked up. "What did you say?"

"I said, Annabelle seemed sincere. I don't think she was out for herself."

"No, I mean, about the symbols—"

"Oh. Nobody's used symbols like this in hundreds of years. I don't think more than twenty or thirty people in the world are even interested in them these days." His smile was grim. "It's a challenging hobby. Most of these symbols you can't even find on the Internet. You have to get down in the catacombs and up in the dusty libraries, and who wants to do that?"

Bethany's mind raced on ahead. Nobody used the symbols. Nobody could understand them. Not available online. How perfect. How utterly perfect, if you want an unbreakable means of communication.

"You said Annabelle showed you five or six photographs, but you only recognized two right off."

"That's right."

"What was the other one?"

She sensed his hesitation. His eyes had begun to wander, and she knew he was thinking of Harry Junior again. Just when she thought she had lost him, perhaps this time for good, he answered. His voice was low and solemn, as befitted the subject.

"It was a Last Judgment. The great of the world, including the great churchmen, gathered before Christ to be judged." Behind the crooked glasses, the pale eyes were troubled. "It was strange. Last Judgments are hardly ever included in church buildings anymore, at least in America and Europe. In the Middle Ages they were common, and a lot of the older European structures have them. But in America, where a lot of Christians seem to think that they can put the Gospel to majority vote, and without even consulting the text, well, let's just say that including an image of the Last Judgment is unusual. And there's something else." He shifted his gaze out the window and drummed his fingers while he took a moment to think. When Harry spoke about his hobby rather than his son, his mind was clear as crystal. "The figure who was judging in the photo she showed me—well, it wasn't a typical representation of Christ. It wasn't, say, the Dolphin or the Lion, and there wasn't the usual angel with the trumpet. Instead, the masses of men and women were kneeling before the Centaur, which in the Middle Ages was a pagan symbol. And the angel was holding a sword and an hourglass instead of a trumpet."

"What do those symbols mean?"

Harry shook his head. He admitted that he might have come across them in his long life, but pleaded, as he put it, "an inadequate memory." She sensed his dissembling but thought she understood.

"May I show you another symbol?" she asked.

"Please," Harry said, but agitation had replaced his former calm, and Bethany knew that she had little time.

She had the drawing ready: her memory of the engraving beneath the key pad on the reinforced steel door. "It looks to me like a horseshoe."

"What? Oh, no. Not at all. Not at all. It's just a poor rendering." Spoken without a hint of reproach. He opened his box again, took out a charcoal, sketched on the paper tablecloth. "Is this more what you saw?"

"I think so," said Bethany, impressed. "Yes."

"Ah. Well. Now we're getting somewhere. This is a leather girdle, the sort that knights used to wear with their armor. The three circles represent stones. The image is one of the medieval symbols representing St. Thomas, who according to tradition was stoned to death in India. Definitely a Thomas."

"A Thomas," she echoed.

"Yes." He shoved his plate aside. "And now I have to ask you the same thing I asked Annabelle. Will you help me find my son?"

"I'd like to. But I won't lie to you. I don't have any access to anything."

"You could ask around."

She calculated. "I will. Okay."

"Thank you." Drumming those fingers again. "Maybe we can meet again? Say, in two days? Thursday, around this time?"

"Out by the water again?"

"How about this restaurant. This same booth."

"If I can get here, I will."

After that, the accountant grew morose. She tried to engage him, but he was obviously mourning his son. He said he wanted to be left alone. The last Bethany saw of him, he was asking the waitress to take away the food and bring him a beer.

THIRTY-TWO

Stuart Van Der Staal hated iced coffee. But here he was on his third, because the stand he had selected sold nothing else remotely appetizing, and to wander from one vendor to the next would have made him conspicuous. This was the sort of waiting he disliked, sitting alone in the open. He preferred shadows and corners and alcoves. He liked to get close to his prey without being recognized. He knew that he had a flair for the dramatic—perhaps the melodramatic—but so far it had never harmed his work. He had been in the business for a bit over a decade now, and had fifteen eliminations to his credit, every one clean. He had never failed because he didn't care. Those he tracked were not really human—they were not really real—they were only bundles of perception, cells perceiving other cells perceiving other cells, and then imagining that they were imagining. There was no mind. There was only brain. An unthinking animal—

There she was. Leaving alone. In a rush.

The professor watched as she hurried down the block, away from the river. Her fat little companion stayed put. Bethany must have given him the brush-off. Good for her.

Stuart slipped easily into the pedestrian flow, and followed her along the sidewalk.

Bethany decided she did not want to be on a train just now, so she headed for the bus stop. She checked her watch. It was nearly four. By now, the hue and cry would be raised. Blessing would tell Martin what Janice had said, and everyone would assume that Bethany was on the trail of Annabelle's researches. What they wouldn't know—what they couldn't possibly guess—was that she was coming back. That would be the surprise, when she showed up at the front door, all smiles and apologies.

The queue at the bus was too long, so she decided to head to a hotel and grab a taxi. There was a biggish one two blocks away, and that was where Bethany headed. She turned her face up into the sun, enjoying the peculiar sense of freedom that came from having information. She had always been liberated when she had a handle on events, and now at last she thought perhaps she did.

The events fell nicely into sequence.

Annabelle's quest for the Pilate Stone brings her to the Village House. She goes down into the basement. Then she meets poor Harry in the alley. They discuss his hobby. They meet again. She shows him photographs of carvings, presumably from the Village House, some of which he interprets for her. Then she disappears.

But not immediately.

First she returned to the Village House, armed with the information the crazy old man had given her. Suddenly it was all so obvious. Symbols nobody had used for half a millennium. And Annabelle frightened, worried that lives would end. All because of what she saw in the basement. Perhaps Annabelle had found more doors, with more coded locks, and had hunted around, using the combinations the mad old man unknowingly gave her.

Fine.

Annabelle had returned to the basement. Tonight, armed with Harry Pribyl's translations of the symbol on the vault, the basement was where Bethany would go.

She had seen, so far, no reason to believe that the Planners were violent, and in any case her two conversations with Martin had persuaded her that her old beau was not prepared to do her any harm. She had no doubt that if they found her in the basement again she was in for a stern lecture about going astray, and they might decide to bar her from the building. But she planned to be contrite, and to promise to follow the rules. All she wanted was her old room back, for a single night. She had told Martin that Blessing had left the door open from the stairwell to the basement, and he had seemed to believe her. So it was unlikely that anybody had barred her actual route, through the kitchen and down the freight—

Bethany cried out and slapped her neck. Something had bitten her. Not bitten her. Stung her. But no. It felt like a needle—a burning—and her voice was sluggish and suddenly everything was so slow—

"Do you need help, Miss?" murmured the stranger beside her, very near her ear. "You'll be fine. Just relax. Don't fight." The same man as before, the one who had grabbed her, and this time he had a tight grip on her upper arm and a hand entwined in her scarf and she wanted to cry out but was far too tired, she was struggling and blinking and fading, thoughts all jumbled, and then the squeal of brakes snapped her back to consciousness for an instant. She wondered vaguely if she had stumbled into the street, but she was still on the curb. The hand on her elbow was gone. The familiar shiny Mercedes S-Class was at the curb. A tall, familiar figure stepped out of the passenger seat, and opened the back door.

"Please get in, Ms. Hobart," said an unsmiling Mr. Fuentes. "Everybody is looking for you, and—"

But Bethany had started to fold.

Fuentes caught her, and understood at once. He had noticed the well-dressed stranger leaning close to her ear, and had guessed an executive trying to pick her up. Now the man was racing back into the pedestrian stream. Fuentes shoved Bethany's unresisting body into the back seat and snapped a crisp order at Wayne, who was in the driver's seat.

The car shot into traffic.

Cursing his bad fortune, the professor watched as once again Bethany Barclay slipped from his clutches. She had the luck of the devil himself, he decided—although she would probably put things slightly differently.

Never mind. Facts were facts. What seemed on the surface a rescue would likely turn out to be anything but. Martin Potus and his merry men could hardly be happy with her latest breaking of ranks. And, unlike Stuart Van Der Staal, they were unlikely to find her interesting enough to treat gently.

His orders did not include interfering with their fun, so he would have to wait until the Gopos were through with whatever they planned to do to her. Then he could see whether there was any information to be gleaned from whatever pieces of her mind were left over.

THIRTY-THREE

That same Tuesday found Carl Carraway in the Third District police station on V Street, just a couple of short blocks from the spot where Annabelle had been run down. Earlier he had spent an hour at U Street Christian, chatting with the choir director, who was getting ready for the evening's practice. Yes, said the choir director, he'd been at Bible study the night that poor woman was run down. Yes, she was loud and disruptive, just like they said. No, he didn't think he could quite recollect exactly what she was shouting, except that it had something to do with how she needed their help to decide what to do with the book. She said she'd been all day trying to find out who God meant to help her, and she'd decided it was them. She'd known there was somebody, so would they please just listen to her—that kind of thing. And, no, he didn't know what book she meant, but from the way she was holding onto her knapsack, maybe it was inside. Sure, he remembered the pack, it was bright green and had these DayGlo orange stripes. He'd told the police—

Carraway had rechecked the inventory of property found with the decedent to be sure there was no backpack or knapsack listed. Then he'd spent time in the alley and along the street, just peeking behind trash cans and in sewer drains, on the off chance that the backpack might still be lying around two months after it was dropped.

Now it was early evening, and he was waiting impatiently for the District Three property clerk to return from dinner and open up the cage so that he could look through Annabelle's belongings. This afternoon's expedition was not only outside his brief but contrary to Vanner's unambiguous orders. Yet his every instinct told him the answer was in their suspect's past, not her present. And even a cursory examination of that past made one thing crystal clear: Bethany Barclay's life, even if eccentric and perhaps lonely, had been perfectly stable until whatever happened to Annabelle had happened.

That was why Carraway was in the Third District station, waiting.

His morning had been occupied in meetings at the Justice Department. He'd spent an endless lunch with the senior members of the task force, working out the disposition of resources as the search widened across the Midwest, in case, as seemed likely, Bethany had already fled Chicago. Afterward, he'd asked Pulu to cover for him for an hour or so.

The hour had now stretched into three and a half.

He wondered what kind of work he'd do after he got fired.

"I'd have been back sooner if they'd told me the FBI was here," said the clerk, a stout and bespectacled black sergeant named Lattimore. There was a twinkle in his pouchy eyes, and Carraway wondered whether the man was putting him on. "I hope you didn't have to wait too long."

"Not a problem."

The sergeant eyed the iPad. "Playing games on the computer?"

"Something like that."

"Which case was it you wanted?"

"Seaver. Annabelle Seaver." He showed the officer the case report, the file number prominently at the top.

"Oh, right. The hit-and-run at the church." He nodded toward the desk. "Sign the book."

Carl did.

"Come with me." The sergeant opened a gate, led the agent inside, pointed to a rickety wooden table. "Sit there. I'll bring the boxes to you. You can't take anything out of the wrappers. You can't take anything out of the cage. Got it?"

"I do, Sergeant Lattimore. Thank you."

"You want all the physical evidence?"

"Just the belongings found with the body." He was studying his file. "There's a list—"

But Lattimore had waddled into his sanctuary. Five minutes later he was back. "I was wrong. Just one box." He set it on the table, vanished once more behind the barrier.

Carraway pawed through the contents. Clothes and shoes, bagged and tagged. A wallet without identification or credit cards. A voucher for a couple of hundred dollars in cash, stored in a separate safe in accordance with the rules. A slip of paper with a number to call in case of emergency and the words *Ask for Polly*. That gave him pause. Why list the sister from whom, by all accounts, she was estranged, rather than her best friend, Bethany Barclay? He made a note to check on—

"Found something else," said Sergeant Lattimore.

Carl looked up. And couldn't suppress a gasp.

The officer was holding a big clear plastic bag. Inside was a green backpack, decorated with strips of DayGlo orange.

"This isn't in the case report," Carraway said.

"You must have an old copy. This came in two or three weeks after she died."

"Why weren't we updated?"

"There's no flag." He saw Carraway's blank look. "No note on the case file to keep the Bureau up to date. You folks have to ask for stuff like that. It's not like we have time to routinely forward everything to the feds." He was examining his log book. "Oh, besides. One of your guys already looked at it."

"At the backpack?"

"That's right." Squinting. "Says here, Special Agent, ret—that's r-e-t, period—"

"You showed evidence to a retired agent?"

"Retired, not retired, it's not my job to keep up with you people. He had an FBI identification, he said he was working on a special assignment. Who knows? Since 9/11, pretty much everybody seems to be some kind of special federal agent." No trace of humor in his voice. "Look, Agent Carraway. He signed the book, okay? Sometimes maybe we take more precautions, but it's not like this is the hottest case in town."

"What's his name?"

"Mmmm. Let's see. Looks like, um, maybe Lerosko. Something like that."

Carraway's head snapped up. "Lerosko? Could it be Lesofsky?"

"Right. That's what it says. Lesofsky. Theodore Lesofsky. Do you know him?"

"Oh, yes. I know him."

He didn't add: *He's a madman, and I helped fire him.*

"Who brought the backpack in?"

"Voucher says a couple of kids found it in the bushes in a park a block from the church. See this?" Pointing through the plastic. "Teeth marks. Officers said the dogs had been at it. Food inside, and they were trying to rip it open. Rats got in. Everything was all wet and dog-eared." He pulled on a pair of surgical gloves, then offered the box to Carraway, who did the same. The sergeant pried the bag open. "I have to verify the contents before I can let you look."

"I understand."

Lattimore had the voucher on the table. Carl read it upside down. The officer was peeking inside the backpack.

"Hey, this is funny."

"What is?"

"The voucher says there's supposed to be clothes in here, a couple of magazines, candy wrappers, a notebook."

"So?"

"Look for yourself." Opening the mouth of the bright green pack. "No notebook."

THIRTY-FOUR

Bethany had been raised in the evangelical churches of rural Virginia and North Carolina, and so had no patience with tales of Purgatory. But that was where she found herself, in that mythical place of enforced penitence that lay between earthly death and the rewards of Heaven. She had read Dante in college and knew all about how your soul lay chained to some terrible punishment for a period of cleansing from sin that lasted perhaps a century or two, nothing at all when measured against Eternity. She felt the chains when she tried to move, and felt the punishment in the pain wracking her body. Her half-open eyes caught blurry visions of angelic tormentors whispering to each other, but her hearing didn't seem to be working, which made perfect sense, given that she was already dead. At one point Annabelle came and spoke to her, while Ken Kirkland sat on the other side of the bed with half his face shot off, and Bethany marveled that he had to carry his wounds with him into the afterlife. Ken seemed to have something terribly important to tell her. What was left of his mouth kept moving but of course she couldn't hear, although she was fascinated by the way the way the blood trickled down his neck with every word. The blood dripped and dripped. Why was he bleeding if he was dead? There was so much of it, it ran everywhere, a sea of red rising on either side of the bed, faster and faster, and she had to get up, she had to swim through it, she had to flee, she had to hurry because—

—hurry because—

—because—

—because she knew—

Bethany opened her eyes. She blinked, took inventory. Not dead. Not in Purgatory. Thoughts sluggish. She was lying on an unfamiliar bed, in an unfamiliar room. Not a hospital room, although there was an IV line in her arm, and straps holding her down. She wiggled her fingers and toes. Everything worked, but she sensed a peculiar delay between the will and the act. Memory returned in jagged shards. The man on the street corner, injecting her. Fuentes shoving her into the car. After that—nothing. Her throat was dry as bone, and a metallic taste on her tongue made her slightly nauseous. Through the windows she could see that it was night. She turned her head. A woman she hadn't seen before was curled in a chair, asleep, a copy of Martin's book on her lap. The room was large but, like most of the Village House, sparsely furnished.

"Hey," Bethany said, but her voice was a gurgle. "Hey. Hey!"

The woman lifted her head, then got to her feet. She was blond and wiry. Her prematurely lined face gave her an air of a woman who had been hard-used but was tougher for it. She could have been twenty. She could have been fifty. She wore Gopo gray. Her smile came slowly, as though she had to draw on some distant recollection.

"Hey yourself," the woman said, and walked over to the bed. "How are you feeling?"

"Okay. Can you undo the straps?"

"You were flailing around a lot. They didn't want you to hurt yourself." She checked the straps but didn't loosen them. "My name is Gratitude. We spoke on the telephone."

Blessing. Gratitude. The women who advanced in the Planners had these high-sounding but somehow frivolous names, whereas the senior men, other than Martin, were all Mr. something.

"When did we speak?" Bethany croaked.

"I'm in charge of public relations. You called, remember? To see when

Martin would be preaching?" She shrugged as though she had been complimented. "I'm good with voices."

Bethany shivered. She was covered with two blankets, and she could tell from the rivulets of sweat on Gratitude's hard face that the heat was cranked up high, but still she was freezing. Bile rose in her throat but subsided. "Please take the straps off. This is very . . . uncomfortable."

"You're suffering the aftereffects of the drug, Kathy. Relax."

About to ask who Kathy was, Bethany remembered in time the fake identification Blessing had given her. Martin had said that only he, Blessing, and Daniel Stafford knew her true identity.

"I want to get loose." Trying to keep her voice steady. She felt like shrieking but doubted she had the energy. "I don't like being tied down."

"I know. I'm sorry."

"Gratitude, please. You'll have my gratitude." Bethany hadn't meant to make a pun. She felt loopy. Brain inside-out.

"Maybe I'd better call somebody."

She vanished.

Bethany moaned and shut her eyes again. The childhood fear of tight spaces seized her and she struggled uselessly. Aunt Claudia's boys had been so wicked to her, and now they all acted like best buddies, and why was she thinking about them? Still loopy. Probably she slept, because when she opened her eyes, Martin was sitting on the bed, and from the circles beneath his eyes and the rumpled look to his trademark grays, he had probably been sitting there for some while.

"We didn't want to risk a hospital," he explained as he loosened the straps. "We didn't know what they gave you, so we didn't know what you might say." A wink. "Or who you might tell them you are. No, no, don't sit up. Rest. The IV is just fluids. Here." He had water in a childproof cup with the little spout. "Drink this."

Holding her head.

"Thank you." Ignoring his advice, Bethany forced herself to a sitting position, then waited for the room to right itself. "What happened?"

"Mr. Fuentes says someone was trying to kidnap you."

"Kidnap me? Why?"

Martin shook his head. "I was hoping you could tell me, Bets." He set the cup down. "Any ideas?"

"No." Another wave of nausea. She closed her eyes briefly. "I don't understand any of this."

He touched her hand. She flinched. "Maybe it's related to what you thought you were doing out there," he said gently. "We were worried about you, Bets. We had people out looking." His gaze was sorrowful. "We can't protect you if you're going to wander around Chicago. Maybe you should stay inside the building for a while. At least until we can make arrangements to move you."

"Move me where?"

"Someplace safe."

She was still shivering. "Where are my clothes?"

"Blessing is washing them." He reached in his pocket, pulled out the line drawing she had made of the lock in the basement, the one Harry Stean had identified as a symbol of the apostle Thomas. "What's this, Bets?"

The pounding in her head was all at once a live thing, kicking and screaming and bright enough to blind her. Still, she managed a bit of pluck. "I can't believe you went through my pockets."

"What is it?"

"You know what it is," she said tiredly.

"Come on, Bets. Why are you carrying it? Why did you even make it?"

The room rocked again, but that might have been fear. The tone in Martin's voice was nothing like the smoothly cajoling induction of that first night. "You have these little images all over the place. I was wondering what they mean."

"They're none of your business."

"I thought you had no secrets."

"And I thought you'd follow the rules."

Bethany chose not to tackle this. She was still thinking about how near she had come to disaster. She didn't understand why anyone would want to kidnap her, but she was quite certain that to remain at the Village House was to remain under threat.

"I'd like my clothes," she said. "I'd like to go back to my room." More nausea. What on earth had that man given her? "And then I think it's time I moved on."

"I don't think so, Bets. It's not safe."

"That's not really your call, Martin."

"I'm afraid it is."

She looked at him, remembered his petulant anger on the night she broke off the engagement; saw the same spoiled child, but wielding a greater authority. "I'm leaving, Martin. Now."

"Not just yet, actually."

"What's that supposed to mean?"

"We need you to answer some questions, Bets. I'm sorry, but you've brought this on yourself."

Mr. Fuentes had materialized from somewhere. He loomed over the bed. She realized that he must have been in the room all along.

Panic fluttered in her chest. "What do you want to know?"

The two men looked at each other. Then Martin said, gently, "You need to go back to sleep for a while, Bets."

"I don't feel tired."

"You will." He reached toward a stopcock on the IV line.

Bethany realized that there were two bags hanging on the stand, not just one. In a panic, she grabbed for the needle where it entered her arm. But Mr. Fuentes was faster. He pinned her wrist to the bed as easily as he might a child's.

"Sleep, Bets," said Martin. He adjusted the IV flow. "Don't fight it. You'll feel better when you've had some rest."

Bethany fought as hard as she could. She resisted for fifteen seconds, maybe twenty. Then her eyes fluttered, and she slept.

The blood was back, but no Ken Kirkland. She was following Annabelle down the hallway in the basement, and blood was dripping from the pipes and running like a stream beneath their feet. It occurred to her that all this blood couldn't possibly be from one person.

That's right, honey, said Annabelle, lips not moving.

If it wasn't from one person, it had to be from more than one. Bethany congratulated herself on this deduction.

Pretty good for a chick who's drugged up, said Annabelle silently.

"You're the druggie."

Not today.

They were at the reinforced steel door. Blood was leaching up from the concrete now. The keypad was there waiting, the letters spread before her.

"Which is it?" Bethany wondered aloud. "THOMAS, or ST THOMAS, or SAINT THOMAS?" She turned to Annabelle. "You got through this door, honey. I know you did. That's why they killed you. Which one did you use?"

But Annabelle was gone. Mr. Fuentes was there, his voice coming through layers and layers of thick wavery molasses, pressing in on her, asking about something—she missed just what, but felt the memory waft past her conscious mind and out her mouth. It was fascinating to watch, and for a while she stood there staring at herself, as the questions she could not interpret slipped in, and the answers slipped out, while she just sat and observed. A feedback loop. A habit, easy to follow once they got the rhythm going, and it was so much easier to lie back and relax and listen and not worry than to fight . . .

Bethany woke sweaty and exhausted. Fuentes was sitting in the chair, adjusting the IV. Nobody else was in the room. She felt crowded and guilty, as if she had done something terrible.

"I gave you the antidote," he said. "This is just fluids now. I promise."

She opened her mouth to answer but needed a moment to remember how talking worked. "I don't believe a word you say," she finally managed.

He nodded, his expression as blank as ever. "You shouldn't have gone to see that man, Ms. Barclay. That was a very dangerous thing to do." He was still fiddling with the line. "Oh, yes. You told me a great deal, I'm afraid. Your real name. What you were doing out there. Your powers of resistance are considerable, but in the end it didn't matter. It never does."

She tried to rise but was strapped down again. Her throat felt hollow. "You gave me a truth serum?"

His laugh was harsh and unsympathetic. "There's no such thing. An invention of Hollywood and hack novelists. Truth is a metaphysical category, not a biological one. No drug can make you tell the truth. What it can do is batter at your will power, so that you become semi-conscious, and docile, and ultimately persuadable."

No answering words would come. She stopped struggling against the bonds. Never had she felt so helpless; or so violated. She knew she was crying, but she also knew she was furious; and it occurred to her that on some fitter occasion it would be a great pleasure to put ground glass in whatever this strange man drank.

Fuentes, meanwhile, was still talking as he poked around in a briefcase. "I understand now why Martin is so determined to help you. I had no idea about the details of your prior relationship." He drew out a couple of pages that she recognized as photos from the police file on the Kirkland murder. He selected one. "I now know you didn't do it, Ms. Barclay. I find it fascinating that somebody would go to all of this trouble, right down to painting Martin's symbol on the wall." Pointing to the spot in the photo. Despite fury and humiliation, she followed his finger. "Right below your wide-open safe where you couldn't miss it. Squiggly enough to be dismissed by the police, but clear enough to raise your suspicions."

She shook her head. "Don't ask me who did it. I have no idea."

"I know that. I did probe, I'm afraid. But I think it's important to figure out why whoever did it did it, and, in particular, why they wanted to point you toward the Village House. Because that was unquestionably the intention. Whoever did this wanted you here." He packed the photographs away. "That's what you need to ask yourself, Ms. Barclay. What possible purpose could be served by bringing you here? Find the answer to that, and you will know who tried to kidnap you."

Her gaze burned. "I will never in my life take advice from you. You're a sadistic coward."

But Fuentes took no more notice of her insults than he had of her entreaties. "Perhaps it's related to your friend Annabelle. You had no idea that she had been in residence here, so she isn't the reason you came. She might, however, help you decide what to do next."

Bethany was tempted to ask whether his words meant that they were letting her go, but she knew better.

The security chief, meanwhile, had more to say. "This whole business about the Pilate Stone—I can't figure it out any more than you can. I've never seen anything like that around here. I'd be the one charged with protecting it. It's a strange story."

Another wave of dizziness rippled through her head. She shut her eyes. "Why is it strange?"

"I don't understand why Annabelle would come here looking for a religious artifact. That's not exactly Martin's stock in trade." His tone had grown reflective, and he was talking as much to himself as to her. "I wonder if that's what she was really after."

"What else could she have been after?"

"I don't know. More to the point, you don't know. Believe me, Ms. Barclay, you and I did go into that subject in detail."

She thought of several choice names to call him, but she was too worn out.

Fuentes was over by the window, back turned to her. "What I'm thinking is that whoever sent you knew this might happen. That you might have to answer questions." He put a hand on the glass. "I think that's the story you were supposed to tell if you got caught."

"I don't understand."

"Neither do I, Ms. Barclay. And I've had a lot of time to think about your answers."

Bethany swallowed. "How long—how long was I—"

"A while." He looked toward her, glanced at his watch. "It's about two o'clock."

"In the morning?"

"In the afternoon, Ms. Barclay. It's Wednesday." He saw her expression. "Oh, no, no, you didn't spend all that time answering my questions. Mostly you were in a nice deep sleep, aided by pharmacology. And now I'd say you need a real sleep."

Panic again, but weak and fluttery: the aftereffect of the drugs.

"No, no. No more injections. That's all over with. I have what I need. I'm sure there are things you didn't tell me. We didn't have time to explore every nook and cranny. You're a very brave young woman, Ms. Barclay."

Somehow the praise failed to move her. "So what happens now?"

"That's not up to me." He was moving toward the door.

"The straps—"

"A couple of the sisters will be in with something to eat. Just soft food until tomorrow. The sisters will let you loose, help you to the bathroom, get you cleaned up, put on some pajamas. Please cooperate with them. I'll be outside the door, but I would rather not see you in an immodest condition."

"You don't consider what you just did—"

"I apologize, Ms. Barclay. There are things that have to be done. I did some of them. I'm not proud of it, but that's the way it is."

"Wait. Where's Martin?"

"I'm sure he'll be along." He seemed to ponder. "I know that you've had a hard time, and I am sorry to have made it harder. If you didn't kill Mr. Kirkland, I think it's safe to assume that the man who tried to kidnap you knows who did."

"Why do we assume that?"

The faintest of smiles flickered over the hard face. "You and I are insignificant people, Ms. Barclay. There are too many coincidences circling around you. For all this to happen, some person or persons must be making it happen. We need to find out who."

"Maybe it's God," she said.

Fuentes looked startled, but regained his composure swiftly. "Get your rest," he said, and left.

THIRTY-FIVE

Theodore Lesofsky has a townhouse in Olney, Maryland, forty minutes or so from the city, but Carraway makes the drive in twenty-five because he has to be on a plane to Chicago later tonight. He doesn't call to say he was coming, and he finds Ted in exercise togs, working with free weights as he leads his guest to the kitchen. The former analyst always keeps himself in tip-top shape, just as he always keeps his firearms qualification. He labors under the illusion that one of his endless appeals might eventually succeed, and Carl, during their occasional meetings over the years, has been too kind to disabuse him of this notion.

"Want a beer?"

"No, thank you."

"Some apple juice?" Ted's eyes keep flickering toward the unexpected visitor's empty hands, and it occurs to Carl that Ted is frightened. "How about a bottle of water?"

"I'm fine. Really."

Lesofsky frowns, as if to signal that this assertion was too silly to bother challenging. He is drinking one of those green teas sold by the bottle.

"What are you doing here, Carl?"

"I think you know that, Ted."

"No idea." Their eyes meet briefly. Then the tall man drops his gaze. Definitely fear.

"I believe you have something for me," Carraway presses on.

"You've made perfectly clear that there's nothing I could possibly have that you could possibly want."

"I'm referring to the notebook."

"Notebook. What notebook? Why are you asking me about some notebook?" As a liar, Ted Lesofsky rates no more than a C-minus, a failing that hurt him at his hearing. Those who are skilled in evading the truth often survive when they should go down; and vice versa.

Carraway is brisk. "You misrepresented yourself as an active federal agent to the Washington police. That's not a misdemeanor anymore, Ted. That's a felony. You removed property from their evidence room without authorization. That's another felony. And I'm willing to bet that since you've been in possession of the notebook, you've tampered with it. Given the condition it's in, even turning the pages is probably destroying evidence. That's three felonies right there."

Ted Lesofsky might be a poor liar, but he possesses courage. And pride. "If you're here to arrest me, let's get it over with."

"I don't want to arrest you. Give me the notebook, and I'll forget about everything else."

"Why?"

"I'm sorry?"

"Why do you want the notebook?" He puts down the bottle and takes up one of the weights, doing curls as he strides around the kitchen. "You're not investigating Annabelle Seaver. Not your case, right? You're not allowed to touch it, right?" Nodding in confirmation of his own thesis. "It's a cover-up, Carl, that's what it is. You're caught in the middle, just like I was. You keep this up, you'll be sitting in front of a committee of your own."

Carraway lets the protest run its course. Finally Ted stops pacing. He puts down the weight and picks up the bottle.

"I want the notebook, Ted. But this time, I want to hear your story, too." He taps his watch. "Only I need the short version. I have to get on a plane."

"Are you getting ready to arrest her?"

"I can't say."

"I'd like to be there."

"You know that's impossible."

Ted's eyes go crafty. "She's in Chicago, isn't she? She's in the Village House."

Carl is astonished. "How do you know that?"

"You have your sources. I have mine."

"So, I bet you're wondering why you're not being allowed to work the Seaver case." They are sitting in Ted's office now, and, sure enough, the place is stuffed with the same bulletin boards, bearing the same photographs, connected by the same yarn—except that after all these years there's a lot more of it. "You're not, right? Allowed to look into Seaver's murder? You're doing this on your own. Ex parte. Right?"

"You know I can't answer that, Ted."

"Well, that's an answer, maybe. So let me tell you why they've shut you down. Because they have people at the highest levels. Hands on the levers of power. That's how they got rid of me, and that's how they'll get rid of you, if you don't stop right now."

"Who has hands on the levers of power, Ted?"

"Don't keep ending every sentence with my name, okay? It's creepy. Makes you sound like one of those shrinks." But his own deep desire to tell the story overcomes his rebellion. "The Wilderness. That's what they're called. The Wilderness. Never heard of them, right? How about Roger Williams? Never heard of him, either."

"He founded Rhode Island." Carl tries tried not to look too hard at his surroundings. All these photos and clippings and yarn are giving him what his mother used to call the willies.

"That's exactly right. Founded it almost five hundred years ago, to protect religious freedom. He came up with this metaphor. The Garden and the Wilderness." His hands rotate around each other, palms facing, to illustrate. "The Garden is the people of faith. The Wilderness is the hostile world around them. There's a hedge between them—this is where the wall of separation comes from—and the hedge is there to protect the Garden from the Wilderness. Are you with me?"

"Yes, Ted, but it's getting late—"

"Right. Right. The plane. Chicago. But listen. This is important. And you have to know about it before you go. Suppose it wasn't just a metaphor. Suppose Williams was writing about an actual battle. Spiritual combat, right here on earth. There were two forces, and those were his labels for them, Garden and Wilderness. Good against evil. Light against darkness. Doing battle, all around him, and all around us—"

"Ted. *Ted.* This isn't helpful."

Once more Lesofsky is on his feet. Striding. Angry. "Right. Right. That's what everybody says. It's not helpful. It's a waste of time. Let me tell you something. That preacher who was being blackmailed? The case where you betrayed me?"

"I didn't—"

But the onetime analyst talks over him. "That was the Wilderness. It's what they do. They attack the church. Not that the church doesn't spend a lot of time shooting itself in the foot, but the Wilderness doesn't want to wait for the church to fade away on its own. They want to turn people against it. That's been their goal for centuries, and it still is. They're still out there. I found out while I was working on that case. There was a hint in an agent's notes. The hint led me to another case, and another, and I was able to put together the evidence. I talked to some people in the Bureau and they told me I was crazy. The Wilderness had obviously gotten to them, and maybe they've gotten to you, too. That would explain why you betrayed me, and why you're here." His words spill over each other. "I had to make my own way. My own investigation. My own sources. I even found an informant."

"An informant who was part of the, um, conspiracy?"

"The Wilderness. He wasn't part of it but he knew about it. I needed an informant because I couldn't rely on the government anymore. It's been infiltrated. Infested. They're listening everywhere. Probably here. I sweep my home for bugs twice a week, but maybe twice a week isn't enough. Is that why you're here? To plant a bug when I'm not looking?"

Calmly, calmly. "I'm only here for the notebook."

"Sure you are. Sure you are. Of course you'd have a story." He is standing near the credenza, inching open a sliding door. If he pulls a gun from inside,

Carl knows he'll have to shoot him. "Don't you see? The signs are all around us. Look at the Village House. That stupid cult out there. You don't think I know who they're really working for? You don't think *you* know?"

"You're saying the Planners are part of the Wilderness." He watches Ted's hands. "A front, as it were."

"Not a front. An extrusion." He gestures. "Like a piece of the other world thrust into this world. It happens from time to time. The Wilderness. It extrudes a bit of itself above the line, where it can be seen. But the evil itself is hidden."

The cabinet door is open. Carraway is careful to make no sudden move. "Tell me more about this Wilderness."

"I don't know. My informant didn't know. That's the point. I wanted to find out more, but it wasn't permitted." A sage nod as if agreeing with a particularly profound point. "That's why I was forced out. Because they couldn't let my inquiries continue."

"'They' being the Wilderness."

"And their helpers. Their fifth column. Fellow travelers. Call them what you will." He raises a finger. "But I'll tell you something, Carl. The Wilderness has a weakness. Pride. Hardest sin to purge from yourself. They should look at their own symbol. The serpent."

"The serpent," he echoes. In his mind's eye he sees Detective Florio in Bethany's parlor, pointing to the squiggle of red paint beside the safe. That, too, was supposedly a serpent. For the first time, he wonders whether there might be a grain of truth beneath the madness. Not the whole story—five hundred years or more of struggle and the rest—but if there is a group whose symbol was a red serpent, that was information the Bureau should—

Then his hand is going to his gun, because Lesofsky has spun suddenly and was reaching into the cabinet.

"Freeze!"

The tall man turns. Slowly. "What? Hey. Put that away. I'm not dangerous, no matter what the review board said. Did you know I can't even get a permit for a gun?"

And, indeed, Ted is holding not a weapon of his own, but the missing notebook, wrapped in a handkerchief.

"Most of the pages are eaten through or just turned to pulp. I tore out the ones that are left. I was trying to dry them, hoping to raise some writing. No luck."

Carraway, his gun holstered once more, holds out a plastic evidence bag. Ted shoves the mess inside. Carl seals the bag and initials it.

"I have to get moving," he says. "But I'll want to hear more about the Wilderness."

"After you raid the Village House, you mean."

"You know I can't discuss that."

"Well, just remember when you go in there. It's not a front. It's an extrusion."

"Meaning what?"

"Meaning, hardly anybody there will know anything about who its real sponsors are. That's the way the Wilderness works. It's all misdirection." True pain in those eyes now. "And arranging for other people to take the blame."

On the way to the airfield, Carraway makes a quick stop at the FBI forensic lab, located in the J. Edgar Hoover building on Pennsylvania Avenue. He seeks out his favorite technician, a motherly black woman whose cubicle is decorated with photographs of her large extended family and quotes from the New Testament. Several years ago, a complaint was filed over the quotes: another employee complained of feeling harassed. To the general surprise, rather than quietly removing the offending material, Janet Anders got herself a lawyer—recommended by Carraway—and fought the case.

She won.

Now, as she steps around her desk, her broad brown face crinkles with pleasure. "Well, well. Special Agent in Charge. Deputy head of the task force." Her voice has a lovely lilt. "Fancy meeting you here. I thought, with all your promotions and stuff, you'd forgotten us plebes. Shouldn't some intern or probationary agent be delivering evidence?"

"I need a favor, Janet."

She smiles. "I don't actually think I owe you any favors."

"Then I'll owe you one."

He is unable to match the lightness of her tone. The visit to Ted Lesofsky's madhouse has left him on edge. Very little of what the retired analyst described could possibly be true. But he knew about the Village House. And his theory that Annabelle was killed for this notebook dovetailed with Carl's own. He didn't have to buy the more outlandish aspects of Ted's claims about the Wilderness to see that something quite peculiar was going on.

Now Janet looks at his face, then glances around the room at the other techs.

"In here," she says, drawing him into her cubicle. There's no door to close, so she keeps her voice low. "What is it, hon? Tell Auntie Janet what you need."

He holds up a plastic bag. "This notebook has been out in the wind and rain for a couple of months. Rats have nibbled at what few pages are left. There isn't much here, but I need you to raise any words you can, and I need it yesterday."

The technician studies the package. "Carl."

"Yes, Janet?"

"This notebook's been handled. This wasn't all animals and rain. These pages were torn out."

"I know."

She looks at the tag. "The voucher looks clean, but there's no case number."

"That's right."

"If there's no case number, I can't log it. No chain of custody. No way to get on the machines. No way to justify computer time. No nothing." She offers it back. "You know the rules. I can't run any tests without the case number."

Carl's turn to smile. "That's the favor."

THIRTY-SIX

Friday afternoon was cold and wet. Bethany stood at the window of her room, wondering what the chances were that she would survive a drop of twelve stories, always assuming that she could break the glass. A psychiatrist listening in on her thoughts would convict her on the spot of suicidal ideation, but the last thing Bethany wanted to do was die. What she wanted was to get out of this room.

The door wasn't locked—rules of the Village House—but Wayne or some equally menacing and sullen youth was always slouched in the hallway, trying without success to get Gratitude or one of her wicked twins to flirt back. Bethany had been stuck in this room since they dragged her in on Tuesday. Her interrogation had lasted into Wednesday. After that, only the sisters for company: Not a single member of the senior leadership had set foot in the room. No Martin. No Fuentes. No Daniel Stafford. Not even Blessing Wilkes, in whose veins Bethany had foolishly imagined might run some tiny drop of the milk of human kindness. Gratitude was in and out with food or clothing or to escort her, at assigned times, to the bathroom down the hall. The only distraction, other than peering out the window and plotting impossible escapes, was reading. They had left her with the New Testament with Psalms from the pastor in New Jersey. They had given her a copy of *Living Rude/Living Well*. She had read Acts and Romans and First Corinthians, as bit by bit Aunt Claudia's patient instruction came back to her. She remembered the sermon on Sunday, and wondered whether sacrifice was demanded of her to demonstrate her love.

Once or twice, she had leafed through Martin's book, but could not bear to study it very deeply. In the parts she poked at, she found no clue to his evident insanity.

Bethany wondered how much she had told Mr. Fuentes; and how much he had thought to ask. There were corners, he said, into which he had lacked the time to poke. She would very much like to know which ones they were.

More than once, she had demanded to see someone in authority.

"You have to stay here," Gratitude answered each time.

"Then give them my message."

"I already did."

"So, what are they waiting for?"

"Stay in the room, dear."

"You know this is false imprisonment, right? A felony?"

"Back inside, please, or I'll have Wayne put you in the straps."

And he was there, leering, ready: restraining women the sort of thing he obviously enjoyed.

She went back in.

Downstairs, in the public spaces, all was sweetness and light. The smiles were welcoming, the songs were delightful, the messages were uplifting and, probably, helpful. Up here on the top floor, the monsters lived.

Sort of like the subconscious mind.

Bethany returned to her reading, and her waiting.

Every hour was the same. Confinement, which she hated. Lack of stimulation, which she hated even more. An inability to control her own destiny, which she hated most of all. Another day of this, and she might be ready to make a run for it, knocking down Gratitude and Wayne and whoever else might bar her path. The only trouble was, she didn't think she could knock down Mr. Fuentes, and as much as she feared being locked up in this awful room, she feared the straps and the chemicals even more.

And so she waited. There was no clock in the room, and they hadn't allowed her a watch, but at night she could make out the illuminated numerals on an advertising sign down the block. She checked as rarely as possible, lest the slowness of the passing of the hours drive her mad.

As the FBI Gulfstream swoops toward Chicago, Pulu asks his partner what he's been up to in these furtive hours when he sneaks away. Carraway won't say.

"Breaking ranks again, huh?" Pulu teases. "Or a new girlfriend?" He shakes his head in wonder. "You know Vanner's gonna have your badge, right, Carl? Or at least get you transferred to Kuala Lumpur."

"I'm doing what I have to do."

"I hear you went to see Lesofsky."

Carraway turns toward him. "Where'd you hear that?"

"What, you thought that man could keep a secret? You're the one who told me he's nuts." Down below, trees give way to buildings, and buildings give way to the majestic cobalt expanse of Lake Michigan. "So, what's going on, Carl? Seriously. You really think she's innocent?"

"I wouldn't go that far. But there's an awful lot of holes. This extremist group she's supposed to be a part of. We've never even heard of it before."

Pulu chuckles. "If we'd heard of it, we'd have wiped them out. It's the ones we've never heard of that always do the damage."

"I don't know. I'm starting to get an image of this Bethany Barclay. I want to be there when she's arrested."

"Why?"

"I'm not sure. Maybe to see how my image squares with the reality."

"She's a terrorist, Carl. Don't forget that. So she's got friends who like her and an aunt who loves her and a buddy who got killed. Everybody does. Doesn't change what she is."

"That's my point. We don't really know what she is." The plane jounces from turbulence over the water. "If we're wrong about her—if she's innocent—then what she's undertaking is extraordinary."

"And what's that exactly?"

"This whole business. Good and evil, fighting it out under our noses. Most of us let those questions drift away from us, because we're too busy, or because we want to fit in. But she's chosen up sides." He rubs his eyes. "No. That's too easy. Somebody chose the sides for her. Still, she's kept going. She's evaded detection. It's pretty amazing."

Pulu catches something in his partner's voice. "You like movies, right?"

"Sure."

"How about *Laura*? Ever seen that one?"

"*Laura?* No. Never heard of it."

Pulu hides a grin. "Too bad."

The first sign of a thaw came after dinner. Gratitude brought her usual meal—broiled chicken, salad, a slice of whole-grain bread, healthy but tasteless, because the Planners, borrowing unknowingly from the Nation of Islam, preached eating to live—but when the door opened an hour later, it was Janice who came to collect the dishes.

"You're a sight for sore eyes," said Bethany, her smile entirely unfeigned, but when she tried to hug, the teen stepped hastily back.

"Why did you do it?" Janice demanded, stacking the plates on a tray.

"What am I supposed to have done?"

"You betrayed us. You're trying to hurt Martin. Why would you want to hurt him? He's the most brilliant man. He's gentle and caring—"

Bethany waved this away. "I know. I know. He saved your life."

"He *did*. You don't know the mess I was in, Kathy. The messes all of us were in. The church my parents went to? With their fancy clothes and big cars and snooty airs? You think they'd welcome somebody like me?"

"I don't know anything about you, Janice."

"Exactly. You don't. So don't you go judging me."

"Wait. Honey, wait." Janice was inching toward the door. "Hold on. Talk to me. It's lonely up here."

"We're not allowed to talk to you. You've been spreading lies. Did you know the FBI's been here twice, asking about you? They talked to Mr. Stafford. They even interviewed Martin! Like he's some kind of criminal! And Mr. Fuentes says they'll be back with a warrant! All because of you!" Pointing, shouting, a witness at a show trial. "Things were fine before you came! We were happy! Then you start spreading all your lies! And you were in the basement—"

"Like Annabelle?"

At this Janice flushed; and fell silent; and looked at the floor. Bethany was sure she was on the right track. The two black women had been close, and Annabelle's disappearance had wounded the teenager.

"She's dead, Janice. I assume they've told you."

"Blessing told me."

"She tells you a lot of things, doesn't she?" Bethany was being careful, and, for the moment, all lawyer. If she said a word against Martin, the child would bolt. As long as she kept the focus on Blessing—whom Janice plainly disliked—she might be able to lead things in the proper direction.

"She's the senior sister," said Janice. "It's her job to tell the junior sisters—to tell us what we need to know." Her voice strengthened. "What Martin thinks we need to know."

The next question was pure instinct. "So I suppose it must have been Blessing who told you to come get my dishes tonight."

Janice looked up. "It was Mr. Stafford."

"Really? I would have thought, as a junior sister—"

"Blessing's on a mission. Gratitude's in a meeting, so Mr. Stafford told me to do it."

The threads were coming together. "What about Wayne?"

"I don't know. I haven't seen him around."

"Since when?"

Reluctantly. "I don't know. Yesterday, maybe."

The next part would be the trickiest. But if it worked, there might be a chance of getting out of here.

"Janice, listen to me. Listen. What do you and Blessing and Wayne have in common?"

"I don't know."

"Come on. Think. Something you did together?"

"We went to church with you—"

"Exactly. We all went to church. That's who they're sending away, honey. Don't you see? The FBI thinks I'm here, so the Village House is getting rid of everybody who went to church with me. Everybody who could tell them I'm here. Or whatever happened at that church. That includes you, Janice. Blessing's on a mission. Wayne has disappeared. And Gratitude—"

"I told you. She's meeting with Martin."

"I'm sure she is. And after that, she'll go off on some mission, too. Janice, listen to me. Annabelle Seaver was my friend. My best friend in the world."

"I told you. She disengaged."

"Think about it. She went in the basement, like I did, and now she's dead."

The teen's eyes went very wide. "You're wrong, Kathy. Mr. Stafford would never get involved in something like what you're talking about. We have rules. We welcome the stranger. We don't interfere with people's lives. And Martin—Martin is a genius. He's the kindest man I've ever met. He's helped me so much—"

Bethany wanted to shake her. "Stop it, Janice. Just stop. You're reciting your lines. Your chants. I don't know where they come from. Or did they drug you, too?"

"No. Martin doesn't believe in drugs—"

"He drugged me, Janice. Don't give me that look. Mr. Fuentes held me down and Martin put the drugs in my arm. I've been up here ever since. I'm being held against my will. I want to leave and they won't let me. Doesn't that tell you anything?" Flinging out her arms. "My name isn't Kathy Hobart. I'm Bethany Barclay, and I'm wanted for murder, and also in connection with a couple of bombings. That's right. I'm the woman on the news. And Martin is hiding me. Don't you think that proves something?"

"It proves what a good man he is," said Janice, tossing her head with the prisoner's pride. "And nobody here watches the news. We're here to work on fixing ourselves, not the world."

"Janice—"

"Don't try to turn me against him. He's warned us about people like you. False prophets, just like the Bible predicts. Martin is the kindest and most brilliant man I've ever known. He saved my life. I won't have you tearing him down."

Tears flowing, Janice fled.

Bethany sprang after her, but this time, rules or no rules, the door was locked.

Of course it was. There was nobody left to guard it.

At a quarter past eleven, the door opened again. Janice was back, crisply folded bed sheets and towels draped across her arms.

"I'm supposed to change your linen," she said. She shut the door, headed for the bed. Bethany, sitting at the desk, noticed a certain purposefulness in the girl's stride, an angry determination she had not seen before.

"My linen was changed this morning."

"Teddy doesn't know that. He's the new guy outside." Janice looked miserable. "I've been to see Mr. Stafford. He says I'm leaving on a mission in the morning."

Despite her own predicament, Bethany felt a welling pain. Janice was just a kid.

"Honey—"

"I know. Listen." Stepping close. "They're moving you tomorrow. I heard Mr. Fuentes talking to Mr. Stafford." She glanced around, leaned in to whisper. "Nobody's seen Martin since yesterday. I think he's gone."

The teen was weeping. Bethany hugged her. "Leave. Get out of here tonight."

"I don't have any place else to go."

"You can't let them send you on a mission."

"Mr. Stafford says not to worry, and I know he'd never hurt me, but you put these ideas in my head, and—I don't know who to trust." She wiped the tears. "Kathy. I mean, Bethany. Take me with you."

"With me where?"

"There's nobody guarding the door." Janice held up a key. "You're planning to escape, right? I want to go, too."

THIRTY-SEVEN

The Village House was like a city expecting invasion. The corridors were empty. There were signs everywhere of hasty leave-taking: cabinets with their doors standing open, books and papers strewn around abandoned offices. The few Planners they passed were rushing from somewhere to somewhere, too distracted to take any notice. Because they hadn't been told to, Bethany realized. Nobody had given orders to search for her, and she was therefore all but invisible.

Yet they'd been tipped off. That much was obvious. They knew the long-awaited raid was coming; possibly even tonight.

In a far corner of the dining hall, three or four people were kneeling in prayer, heads bowed, holding hands. Janice slowed. She looked young and scared, like the child she was, her expression so full of longing that for an instant it seemed she might abandon the escape plan altogether and rejoin her fellow Planners. For a moment Bethany was tempted to let her go. But there were reasons not to. Self-preservation for one: no matter how few Planners remained in the building, reuniting with them might yet move Janice to raise the alarm. More important, however, was Janice herself. Bethany was determined that some good, however small, would come from this experience. She still felt that she had somehow failed Annabelle, abandoning her to her fate. She would not do the same with Janice.

"Come on," Bethany hissed, but in the end had to take the teen by the arm to keep her moving. It wasn't prayer that was poisonous, but praying with the Gopos. At a fitter time, Bethany would explain all that. For now, what mattered was motion.

So Bethany half-cajoled, half-dragged her into the kitchen. The lights were off, but she didn't want to wait for her eyes to adjust, because Janice was still looking back over her shoulder. Quick decision. Bethany flicked the lights on, and hurried her toward the freight elevator.

"I'm not going in there," said Janice.

"Yes, you are," said Bethany, but in the end she practically had to throw her.

She hugged the cringing teen throughout their descent, sprang into the storeroom, peered into the hall, found it empty. Odd that Fuentes hadn't closed off her route to the basement. She expected to have to drag Janice again, but the girl was calling upon a reservoir of courage that Bethany had not suspected and was glad to see.

"I'm fine. Let's do this."

They hurried down the hall to the T-junction, where they turned left and ran smack into Wayne coming the other way. A moment of mutual shock. He reached toward his belt and drew out not a gun or a knife but a radio of some kind. There was nothing else to do. Bethany charged him and knocked him down. He slapped her aside, hopped up, and punched her in the stomach. She had never been hit so hard. She reeled against the wall, doubled over, trying to make the basement stop spinning. Then Janice was in front of her, helping her up, yelling to her, and Wayne was moaning on the concrete.

The teenager held up a length of pipe. "I hit him in the head. I hope he's okay. No, I don't."

Bethany did her best to stand straight. "Thank you, honey." She looked around. "Find some rope or something."

A quick search produced duct tape. Probably there was a science to using it as restraint. They did their best, taping around and between Wayne's wrists and ankles while he was still groggy, then pressing two pieces over his mouth, careful to leave his nose clear.

"It doesn't look very strong," said Janice.

"I know." Bethany backed her hand against her sweaty forehead. "We'd better hurry. Come on."

They raced along the dim corridor. As Bethany expected, the heavy steel door was locked. From the shadows behind came the sound of Wayne's noisy struggle to free himself. Bethany studied the image on the key pad. Thomas or Saint Thomas or St Thomas? The same question as in the dream.

And the same answer.

Lots of people had talked about the Bible during her week at the Village House, but nobody had mentioned any saints; not at least with a capital *S*.

"Wait," said Janice.

Bethany's fingers were poised. "What's wrong?"

"Backward. Do it backward."

"Do what?"

"I heard Mr. Stafford reminding Blessing a couple of weeks ago. At one of the doors upstairs. Whatever the code is, you have to enter it backward."

Despite the tension, Bethany smiled. "That's two I owe you."

"I know," said Janice.

Decision time. THOMAS, then, but backward: S - A - M - O - H - T.

A ping. The light turned green, something clicked, and when Bethany tugged, the door swung open freely.

Bethany had not expected anything quite so ordinary. A shrine, perhaps, with the Pilate Stone under clear glass, surrounded by candelabra. Or a crate, sealed with the best technology available against the ravages of eternity. Even another door, with another combination and another yet unseen symbol would not have been a surprise.

Instead, they were in a sort of work room: benches and tables with lathes attached, a lot of tools hanging on pegboards, and a gaggle of ancient computer monitors and clunky first-generation laptops lining the shelves like old soldiers waiting to be mustered out.

"I don't get it," said Janice. "Why do they have to keep this stuff locked up? I mean, not even homeless people would think it's worth anything."

"Look for secret doorways."

"For what?"

"Doorways. Passages. A hidden safe, maybe. See what's behind the shelves." Bethany was already tipping a cabinet. "Come on. Whatever they're hiding, it's somewhere in this room. There isn't much time before somebody comes down here. Hurry!"

The room was small. Three minutes into the search, Janice exclaimed triumphantly. Bethany hurried over. The teen had found a loose portion of wall behind one of the pegboards, but when they took it down they found only a stack of plastic parcels with some kind of pliable gray compound inside. They opened one of the bags but no Latin carving was hidden inside.

Five minutes later Bethany was sure. There was no second Pilate Stone missing for two thousand years hidden in the room. The only thing the least bit anomalous was that one of the ancient laptops, a good two and a half inches thick, stood open on a side table, held tightly between two clamps.

Maybe the Planners were teaching computer repair.

Except that the laptop was open too far.

Bethany went back and studied it. The keyboard had been removed from the casing, as if for repair. The innards were stacked on the table in an unruly heap. In their place was something thick and soft and gray-brown—the contents, she realized, from one of the hidden plastic sacks. Twin probes poked from the mess, laying flat against the casing but angled slightly apart like devil's horns. Wires connected them to a small green circuit board. The whole contraption was welded in, with wrinkled paper stuffed tightly into every crevice and corner to keep it from moving. It took Bethany another thirty seconds to understand.

She was looking at a bomb.

THIRTY-EIGHT

Edna spent the day in Charlottesville. She stopped in to say hello to a former clerk who now ran the largest law firm in the city, and dined with another, who taught torts and criminal procedure at the University of Virginia Law School, one of the very finest in the nation. These were in effect her cover stories. In between she spent two quiet hours visiting the offices of one of the town's smaller law practices, with a specialty in estate planning for a rather exclusive and rather monied clientele, a meeting which later had not taken place.

The Mathematician was also in Charlottesville, and had a similar tale to account for his movements. His principal overt purpose was to meet a former Harvard professor who now managed a substantial hedge fund and made his home in the area. The professor had long been after his colleague to join up in some advisory capacity. One of the Mathematician's favorite graduate students was now running applied mathematics down here, and he was godfather to her second child, so he dined with her and her husband, because the Builder made it an absolute rule on such occasions that two stories were better than one.

After dinner, the Mathematician happened to be passing through the lobby of the Boar's Head Inn, the most elegant in town, at the very instant that his dear old friend Edna Harrigan stepped off the elevator, and after their mutual expressions of surprise—"You're staying here, too?"—nothing would do but that they sit in the lounge and have a cup of tea. May had turned sultry along the Eastern seaboard, so the usual fire was not blazing in the high grate. They chose a cozy corner where they were unlikely to be disturbed and, between them, had good views of both entrances.

"How did things go with the lawyer?" the Mathematician asked after the pleasantries.

"It was like pulling teeth. Thank goodness for the Senator, or he'd never have agreed to see me at all."

The Mathematician smiled. Tonight the cuff links were large gold coins, no doubt pricey antiques. His shirt was a sort of pale violet with white collar and cuffs. "I think you mean, thank God."

"That's what you'd mean. I'm saying what I mean."

"My apologies." He was the senior member of the group, but he managed at such moments a boyish charm that Edna always found mildly disconcerting. "Please go on."

She recounted the facts as the Kirkland family attorney had reluctantly disgorged them. Sylvia owned to sixty-eight years, but she had never had an instant's trouble with her heart: or not that any of her doctors knew. The attack that felled her had occurred while she was out walking along a road at twilight, and nobody quite remembered her developing that habit either. So the coroner decided on an autopsy.

The waitress wanted them to order more tea, or perhaps what she called a bracer. Alas, Edna was a lifelong teetotaler, and the Mathematician was under strict orders, from both his internist and his wife, to keep to a single drink a day.

"And what did the autopsy say?" he asked when they were alone.

"Nothing extraordinary. Not in writing."

"Ah."

She knew disapproval when she heard it, even in a single syllable. "You have to understand the way things work down here, George. Old families, influence—the years pass, the world changes, but down here people still care about all that."

The Mathematician was amused. "I'll have to take your word for it, Edna."

"Meaning what?"

"Only that I seem to recall that your own people have lived in this area since before the Revolution."

Her face warmed. "My family never had money, George."

"Which is why you have such an affinity for our young Ms. Barclay. I do understand, Edna. Now, tell me."

The Judge needed a moment to calm down. She was notorious for her aplomb, but the Mathematician had a rare talent for getting under her skin. The Critic had a sharper tongue, and the Builder never thought anything was quite good enough, but this man had a way of needling to which she always rose. It occurred to Edna that he might not like her very much, and she wondered what she had done to offend him. But in the Builder's continuing absence—Latin America this time—the Mathematician was running things, so he was the one to whom she was required to report.

"This is hearsay, you understand," she said at last. "Double hearsay. Nothing admissible in court. According to the lawyer, the pathologist had some doubts. There were signs—nothing definite, or he would have had no choice—but there were some hints that maybe, just maybe, all was not as it should have been. A possible recent injection site, when Sylvia Kirkland wasn't on any medications. Some very faint narcotic traces in the tissues, but nothing prescribed for her. Under the strict reading of the law, he should have called the police. But the Kirklands are a power in the state, and if, say, there was no crime—if all that he discovered was that she had a secret drug habit—do you follow me?"

Again the Mathematician's tone betrayed a peculiar lightness, almost a joviality. "I take it that he doesn't have tenure."

"I don't know what he does or doesn't have. Maybe he just didn't want to cause the family any more suffering or embarrassment."

"And maybe next year pigs will grow wings. Come on, Edna. You and I both know what's going on here."

Somebody else came over, an attorney Edna knew she should recognize, who explained that he had argued a case before her "back when you were active"—ouch!—and that she had asked the best questions of anyone on the bench. He was presumably unaware that judges didn't care what the lawyers thought of their questions.

She thanked him until he went away.

"He's going to tell everyone that you're having an assignation," said the Mathematician in the same tone of bemusement.

"At my age? I'd be the one needing the autopsy."

"You're every bit as beautiful as you ever were."

"I believe that's known as faint praise."

They grew serious again.

"Let's sum up," said the Mathematician. "What you're telling me is that the family lawyer thinks Mrs. Kirkland was murdered."

"I believe so."

"And you think so, too."

An instant's hesitation. "Probably."

"But not by a family member—that's the real embarrassment the poor pathologist was worried about, yes? He was thinking maybe Ken did it, or one of his older sisters, to get their inheritance, what with Mom showing every sign of being indestructible. That's why the man kept his mouth shut. That was the trouble he didn't want. But you and I know better, don't we? We know who did it. We know why."

"Not quite," said the Judge.

"Do you doubt that it was the Wilderness? That they were stepping in, just as you suggested, to push Bethany Barclay into motion?"

"I'm sure that's exactly what happened, George. There's just one little problem."

"Why? Doesn't our hypothesis account for all the evidence?"

"That's the problem with being a scientist instead of a lawyer. You look at the equation and the data, and you see that everything balances. I want to know where the data comes from." She swirled her tea. "How did the Wilderness know what was in the will?"

"They obviously had somebody in the lawyer's office look in the file."

"Did they? And how did they know there was a file to be looked at? Are they familiar with every will drawn in America?" She shook her head savagely. "Come on, George. Isn't it obvious what's going on?"

"Not to me."

"We have a leak. To accelerate the plan, the Wilderness had to know there was a plan. And only seven people knew."

"You're saying one of us is a traitor? One of *us*?"

"Yes, George. I'm afraid there's a serpent in the Garden."

Edna had assumed that the Mathematician would startle, or object, or in some way evince either astonishment or irritation. But he only stirred his tea, then signaled the waitress and asked for another pot of hot water, and, no, dear, the bag I have is just fine. He was of Barbadian heritage, and loved to talk about how his frugal father could make a single bag last a week.

"I remember the first time I heard that notion," the Mathematician said when he had the tea to his liking once more. He tested it with his tongue, then took a slow sip. "This must have been—let's see—back in the 1980s. We had a fellow then called the Warrior. Actually, it was short for Cold Warrior. He'd spent time in just about every defense and intelligence agency we had. By that time he was in private industry. Aerospace. Anyway, we were in the midst of a run of defeats, much like today. The Wilderness had set up a couple of scandals that embarrassed the church greatly—not that a couple of our prominent pastors didn't make matters worse with genuine misdoings of their own—and one or two of our own plans had gone badly awry. We were meeting in California, I think. I remember palm trees." A brief frown. "Anyway, the Warrior made the same point you did. Only the seven people at the table knew enough about our operations for them to have been so badly blown. There had to be a turncoat. The Builder had just come on board. He wasn't running things yet. This was back when the Singer was in charge. Come to think of it, we were meeting at the Singer's estate in Bel Air. That's why there were palm trees. The cover was some party or other. The Singer was big out there, so when he threw a party everybody came." The dark face softened in reminiscence. "I met Tony Bennett that night, Edna. Sinatra. Jack Nicholson. I was a starry-eyed kid. The Singer knew everybody. Half a dozen Grammys, fifteen or twenty gold albums—he was richer than Midas. That wound up being important."

He was sipping again. Edna said not a word, preferring the uninterrupted narrative. The Builder had not brought her to the table until shortly before her retirement eleven years ago. He had even suggested that she step down earlier than she planned, and she had taken his advice. But only the leader and the senior member had access to the archives, so whenever she had the chance to learn the Garden's history, her philosophy was to sit still and pay attention.

"Anyway, we met in the pool house. It smelled of chlorine. The Warrior made his charges. There was fierce debate, as you might have imagined. The Warrior and another man—the Tycoon—well, they almost came to blows. One or two of the members wanted the Warrior's resignation. But the Builder supported him. I finally did, too. So did—let's see—I believe we had the Archbishop in those days. The Singer decided we should have an investigation. He actually hired an outsider to do it, a retired FBI deputy director. It was awful. We'd never had anyone poking around like that. Well, not in three hundred years, anyway. The last time was that business with Cromwell, and that one we didn't initiate, although it almost destroyed us."

He saw her face.

"Oh, yes. Oliver Cromwell was Wilderness. We had Hobbes. Not much of a contest. Never mind. A story for another day. I'll tell you that one when I tell you the one about Lincoln." The Mathematician winked, and Edna couldn't work out whether he was teasing. "Anyway, the Singer brought in this outsider, and he tore the place apart. He questioned us all, tried to catch us in lies, even wanted to administer polygraphs, but nobody would go along with that. The upshot was that we resettled the investigator in"—that boyish smile again—"let's just say, in another country. He settled down to a life of leisure. He was paid ten million for his silence, and we're talking about ten million thirty years ago. That's—let me think—around twenty-four million today. Serious money. About half came out of our treasury. Most of the rest was from the Singer and the Tycoon, although each of us was required to put something in the pot. Common sacrifice." He pondered. "The Archbishop probably told Rome. We had some worries about that for a while, let me tell you."

The Mathematician called the waitress over once more. He sent the tea back. He wanted coffee now, he said, and perhaps one of those fine croissants they serve at breakfast—oh, and from tomorrow's batch, not this morning's, please—but Edna sensed that what he really wanted was to give her time to process.

When they were alone again, she said, "Was there a traitor?"

"Oh, yes. There was. The Warrior was right."

"Who was he?"

"The Warrior."

Edna's smile was tight. She had seen the punch line coming. "Do you think I'm a traitor, George?"

"No."

"Do you think I'm wrong?"

"I can't say, Edna. I don't have enough information. Do be aware, however, that the hunt for the traitor back in the 1980s tore the Garden apart. That's why the Singer was forced to retire. It's also how the Builder was able to take charge."

That story she had heard, albeit in whispers, and in several variations: how the Builder, inheriting the mantle at the age of thirty, had put the Garden back on course in a period of low morale, but only at the cost of a general housecleaning that had all but destroyed the group's institutional memory. The Builder's grip was said to be firmer than that of any recent predecessor—although the Abolitionist, the politician who ran things for a decade and a half in the middle years of the nineteenth century, was said to have ruthlessly pruned from the Garden any member who wavered in the holy cause of destroying slavery.

"Do you understand why I'm telling you this?" the Mathematician asked. "I want you to count the cost of what you're proposing."

"I do understand, George, and I've given this a lot of thought." His eyes, she noticed, were no longer even faintly amused. Good. "I don't think it's you, because you've been here the longest. I know it's not me. And I hope it's not the Builder, because, if it is, well, we're all done."

The Mathematician nodded tightly. He didn't care for the course of the conversation. "That leaves four possibilities. The Writer, the Senator, the Critic, and the Pastor." He shook his head. "I can't see what motive any one of them would have to betray us."

"If the motive were obvious, whoever it is wouldn't be at the table."

Another hiatus as the coffee and croissants arrived.

"Have you shared any of this with the Builder?" the Mathematician asked.

"No. Not yet. I'm not sure he has the stomach for it." She rubbed a weary hand over her forehead. "I'm not sure I do."

"What are you proposing, Edna? That we take this on ourselves? An investigation to find out who's switched sides?"

"Of course not. We don't have the resources. We wouldn't have any idea where to start." She studied the dining room, wondering whether anyone was watching. "I'm just saying we should keep our eyes open."

The Mathematician stirred his coffee. "And we're looking for what exactly?"

"I wish I knew."

THIRTY-NINE

"We need a phone," said Bethany.

Janice shook her head. They were standing near the door, keeping an eye on Wayne, still tied and gagged. "You can't. Cell phones aren't allowed and anyway they're blocked or something. There's phones in some of the offices. Maybe Martin has one. I don't know."

"Then we have to get out of here."

"Good."

"We have to warn someone. Janice, listen to me." Taking the teen's chin, forcing her to lift her head. "Wherever I go—police, FBI—it doesn't matter. I'll be arrested. You don't want to be around when that happens."

The brown eyes grew very wide. "I'm not leaving you."

"Do you want to go to jail?"

"As long as you're with me."

Bethany saw that there was no point in arguing. Whatever dependence had bound Janice to the Planners had been transferred to her rescuer.

"Fine. We'll worry about that later. Let's just get out of here."

Again Janice shook her head. "You can't. There's people all over the lobby. Plus, by now they'll know you're not in the room."

"That means they'll know you're helping me." She thought fast. "We'll take the fire stairs. There has to be an exit to the street."

"We'll set off an alarm."

"That doesn't matter as long as we're outside."

"But what if—"

"No more questions, Janice. We have to get out of here." She didn't add that she was worried that the bomb might be live. "Come on."

They returned to the hall and carefully shut the door. No wonder it was reinforced steel. Wayne was awake and struggling furiously. They stepped past him and raced to the T-junction. Rounding the corner, Bethany had a choice to make. She decided not to go twice to the same well—another expression of Aunt Claudia's—and so skipped the storeroom and freight elevator and made directly for the fire stairs. They went up a single floor, and Bethany was about to shove open the exterior door, when she noticed Janice continuing upward.

"Honey, come on. This is it."

"You go," said the teen, more confident and less clingy. "There's somebody I have to—to warn."

Bethany shut her eyes briefly. Zach. Young love. Why couldn't people wait until they were grown to fall for other people? She certainly wished she'd skipped that step during her teens; but she also remembered enough about herself at that age to know that there was no possibility of changing Janice's mind. The choice was either to go with her or leave her behind.

She thought of Wayne struggling in the bonds, reckoned they had ten minutes at the most.

"Five minutes," she said, and followed Janice up to the fourth floor, where the men were sequestered, at a considerable and old-fashioned distance from the women.

The door from the fire stairs was alarmed, but this code Janice had. Bethany wondered how many of the other girls did; and how many of the boys had similar access to the women's floors. The actual operation of the Village House was evidently quite a bit different from the theory. But that was true of a lot of churches, too; and, come to think of it, of most every sort of organization Bethany had ever seen.

In the hall, two young men were on their way back from a session at the gym. They watched incuriously as the women hurried past, and it occurred to Bethany that not everyone seemed to have gotten the signal to flee. They stopped at a door off by itself quite near the elevator.

"Hurry," said Bethany.

Janice knocked, and walked right in. Bethany followed. It was an office, with what looked like an entire apartment beyond, and she could not work out why a young man who looked twenty at most would rate such relative opulence.

Janice poked her head into the bedroom. "He's not here," she said.

"We have to go, honey. I'm sure Zach will be fine."

Janice turned those ingenuous eyes her way. "Zach? What makes you bring him up?"

"Isn't this his suite?"

"No. Are you kidding? This is my uncle's, for when he stays here."

"Your uncle," Bethany began, and then realized what she had missed. The uncle Janice had talked about that first night, who had brought her to the Village House when the rest of the family turned their backs. "Oh, no. Honey, we have to get out of here. Right now, before he comes back."

"It's a little late for that," said Daniel Stafford from behind.

Janice ran into his arms, and he enfolded her, whispering softly, rubbing her back. "There's a bomb in the basement," she kept saying.

Her uncle smiled indulgently. "I'm sure there isn't."

"There is. I saw it!"

"That doesn't make any sense, darling."

Bethany hardly noticed the byplay. She was too busy staring at Mr. Fuentes, whose large frame now filled the entryway. And this time the chief of security held a gun.

"I see you were able to open the vault door," he said.

The only thing Bethany wanted was to get as far away as possible, but Fuentes announced that they were all going down to the basement. Daniel Stafford protested, but Fuentes remained politely insistent; and he held the gun.

"I'm second in command," Stafford sputtered.

"Not just now," said Fuentes, amiably.

They took the main elevator this time, and Bethany leaned against the wall, eyes shut, wondering how she could have been so stupid when she was so close. No last names. None of the junior sisters or brothers used their last names, so there was no way she could have guessed that Janice was a Stafford. But Bethany berated herself all the same.

They reached the basement. Fuentes fell behind, and told Bethany to lead the way. In between, Janice and her uncle were whispering together. Bethany heard the word "mission" a couple of times, and Stafford saying "You don't understand," followed, inevitably, by: "She's an outsider. You can't believe a word she says."

Past the T-junction, they came across Wayne, unraveling the last bits of tape from his ankles. He sprang to his feet, excuses at the ready, but Fuentes just waved the gun and told him to join the parade. The security chief made Bethany unlock the door with her code, then herded everyone inside. Daniel Stafford's handsome face was crinkled in a look of pure pain. During their forced march, his niece had disentangled herself from his embrace, and somehow was beside Bethany again, who was wondering exactly what Fuentes's plan was. Leave them here until the bomb went off?

"You did well," said Fuentes, but it wasn't clear exactly whom he was addressing. "This took a great deal of courage."

"What's the target?" Bethany asked. She had an arm around Janice, who was staring at her uncle. Stafford was staring at Wayne. Wayne was staring at Fuentes. Nobody was staring at the bomb: perhaps pretending it didn't exist would keep it inert. When nobody answered her first question, she tried another: "Why weren't the security codes changed? You knew I had them."

"Because I didn't tell anyone," said Mr. Fuentes. He was at the wall, pawing through the obsolete computer monitors. He held the gun casually, but nobody doubted who was in charge. "I'd guess one of these could hold ten, maybe fifteen pounds. Not nearly enough to bring down a building, but more than enough to blow a car to bits or kill everybody in a room." He pointed. "The laptops, I don't know, two pounds. Three. Add some shrapnel, and you have a serious weapon."

"You wanted me to get in," Bethany said. "Why?"

"Because the odd thing about my job is that I'm hardly ever alone," Fuentes said. He was examining the open laptop now, keeping his hands away. "This is pretty crude. In Afghanistan I knew children who could do a better job." He leaned closer, obviously surprised by something, then laughed. "Oh, this is rich."

"What's rich?" demanded Daniel Stafford. The smoothness was gone. He was edging toward the door. "What's so funny? What's going on? Wayne? Fuentes? What's this all about?"

Wayne shook his head. "Beats me. I was just guarding the door."

"Oh, stop it," said Fuentes. "Nobody's buying your act." He looked across at the black man who was Martin's second-in-command. "Yours either." He spun, the gun now sighted midway between Stafford and Wayne. To Stafford: "This is why I didn't have the codes for this room. Why you kept telling me I didn't need to know." To Wayne: "And why a man like you went to church on Sunday." At large: "And why Wayne and Ms. Wilkes were careful to make sure that Ms. Barclay's was the only face on the security tape."

Bethany was still catching up, so it was left to Janice to ask the obvious question: "They were going to blow up the church?"

"No. I don't think so. Not with this." He gestured contemptuously at the open laptop. "This is crude. Not so much a bomb as what we used to call a bomblet. Its purpose isn't to destroy. Its purpose is to make a point. A big bang. Some damage, a death or two, but nothing that would excite the envy of the world's more competent terrorists." He nodded to Bethany. "Take out the wadding."

"The what?"

"The paper stuffed around the edges to keep the device from shifting around. Go ahead." Impatiently. "The bomb's not live. It's not going to blow. Take out the wadding."

Janice was staring openmouthed at her uncle. Bethany hesitated, then stuck a hand in, pulled out a piece of paper. Then another. Leaflets. Leaflets and Sunday programs, all from the church they had just visited.

"I don't understand."

"This is what was going to happen, Ms. Barclay. The laptop bomb would go off somewhere—I'm betting another laboratory that does stem-cell research or the like—and the investigators would discover fragments of those leaflets from the church you visited on Sunday. It's a common misconception that bombs destroy everything, but there's always a little left. And not much would be needed. One corner of one leaflet, and the feds would be raiding the church. And they'd find whatever bits and pieces of bomb-making materials, maybe even plastic explosive, our friend Wayne here planted on Sunday. That would be enough. Within twenty-four hours, every cable outlet in the country would be screaming all over again about fanatical Christian bombers who hate technology and women and goodness knows what else, and a half a million waverers would never go to church again. Isn't that right, Mr. Stafford?"

But Daniel Stafford had decided to go missing. Permanently. He was sliding a capsule into his mouth, and by the time Fuentes was atop him, fingers in his throat to induce vomiting, the convulsions said it was too late. Wayne took off down the hall.

"Let him go," said Fuentes. "He's nothing." He stood, brushed off his pants. "You ladies go, too. I'll take care of this."

Bethany stood her ground. "You're undercover. A cop. FBI."

"It doesn't matter what I am. You have to get out of here, or you'll wind up in prison."

Janice was kneeling beside Daniel Stafford, cradling his head, sobbing. Bethany wanted to go to her, but needed another second. "Wait. If you're FBI—whatever you are—how could you do that? Pump me full of chemicals?"

Fuentes wasn't even interested. "You're wasting time, Ms. Barclay. Let's just say I'm an army of one, and leave it at that." Still she didn't budge. "I lied to you. The bomb is live. I have to disarm it. This place is likely to be raided any minute. I think it's time we parted." He yanked Janice to her feet and shoved her toward the door. "And be sure to take Ms. Stafford with you."

"I'm not going," said Janice, trying to break his grip.

"Take her with me where?" said Bethany.

"I don't know your destination, Ms. Barclay. I don't want to know. But I am certain Ms. Stafford will prove invaluable." He was shoving both women now. "Just get moving. If the feds catch you, that's bad. If the bad guys do, that might be worse."

Janice was in her arms, inconsolable, hands still stretching toward Stafford. But Bethany was not ready to drag her away. "What bad guys?" she demanded. "The Planners are done. They're about to be raided. You just said so."

"Can you really be that naive? Do you really think your old boyfriend and his bunch would have conceived an operation like this? To what end?" He shook his head. "Martin Potus is many things, but he's not a killer. He's selfish and he's a liar but a part of him is also genuine. The Village House might be part scam, but it's part real, too. He does want to help people, and he has a talent for it. But he's also being led around by the nose. That's been clear since I arrived. I want to find who's doing the leading." He kicked at the corpse. "This man was the only connection to what's really going on. That's why he killed himself. He wasn't worried about arrest. He was worried about the chemicals. Do you think people like that can't get to you in prison? Because prison is where you're headed if you don't get moving."

"But you know I'm innocent!"

"What you told me under chemical interrogation isn't going to persuade anybody. You can't afford to get caught, Ms. Barclay. Now, go. You have your own work to do, and I have to deal with the bomb." To Janice, with an unexpected gentleness: "I'm sorry about your uncle, Ms. Stafford. But he was a bad man doing a bad thing. You can mourn him another time. Right now you have yourself to think about." To Bethany: "Get her out of here. Take care of her." Parting advice: "Don't go where they'll expect you to go. But go. Let me deal with the bomb."

They went.

FORTY

A police raid is an enormously complicated task—especially when there are overlapping jurisdictional lines. The assault on the Village House, although formally a Bureau operation, would actually involve four federal agencies, two state agencies, and just about every local authority in Cook County and the City of Chicago. The lawyers had drawn up enormously complicated agreements, too, which left open to question who precisely was in charge. But Carraway had a natural if boyish authority, and gradually the others, older and more experienced in most cases, began to defer. The plan was to hit simultaneously the front and rear entrances of the Village House, along with the empty building next door, which was owned by Daniel Stafford. There was known to be a vast basement connecting the two structures, but it was largely unmapped, and nobody had come up with any official plans. Everyone recognized that there might be secret exits. So the police would cordon off two blocks in every direction—not nearly so easy a thing as it sounds in the movies, because two blocks in every direction means a four-by-four grid, sixteen blocks in total, with five possible avenues of escape on each side, for a total of twenty intersections to be guarded—always assuming the quarry didn't just bolt into a building somewhere. In Hollywood, the bad guys always shot their way through the roadblocks. In real life, they melted into crowds or snuck through an alley the police missed.

The other problem with the cordon was that it had to be thrown up before the assault began, meaning that the Planners would know the authorities were coming, but with so many people involved, they probably knew anyway.

"Most of these people are innocent," Carraway told the group. "You have to remember that. We have warrants to search the place, and we have warrants to arrest certain suspects, but other than that, the people in there are going to be frightened out of their wits. Let's not make it worse for them, people."

A DEA agent sought clarification. "But they all come out in riot cuffs, right? I mean, we can't assume they're not dangerous."

"Our informants tell us there are guns on the premises," said a Chicago police captain.

"We cuff them, we bring them out, we sit them down in this park"—using a laser pointer to show the spot on the map projected on the screen—"but we don't rough them up unnecessarily. We make sure they're not the people we're looking for. Once they're processed, we let them go."

"It's a cult," said somebody else. "I think we have to assume they'll put up a fight, whether they're the ones we're looking for or not."

"Like Waco," said another voice.

"We're trained, they're not," said Carraway. "We'll show discipline."

"Not if it gets us killed," said a sheriff's deputy.

"Our goal is zero body count on both sides," Carl answered. "But we'll do what's necessary to protect ourselves."

He nodded to an aide, who clicked a mouse. Bethany Barclay's photographs filled the huge screen: driver's license, yearbook, and one from the security camera at the church she'd visited.

"We have five arrest warrants. This is the most important one. This is our suspect in the laboratory bombings. She may have changed her appearance again. She may be carrying identification in the name 'Kathy.' That's the name she used at the church. We don't know what surname." The next part was harder to say than he had expected. "As you know, she is also wanted for murder in Virginia. The murder involved a handgun. She knows how to shoot. She's spent a lot of time at the range. She may be armed. So although we do everything we can to take her alive"—his voice actually choked up for a moment, but training and focus won out—"one way or another, we take her."

FORTY-ONE

Fresh air meant freedom. To be out of confinement—out of that room—away from whatever fate the Village House held for her—was so exhilarating that Bethany wanted to shriek from the sheer pleasure of standing on the sidewalk.

But there were more important matters to attend to.

Like getting as far away as possible.

Like deciding where to go next.

Like the fact that Janice was shivering again, clutching at Bethany's arm as if drowning. "Why did he let us go?" she kept asking.

"Shhhh. It's okay, honey. It's okay."

"No. It isn't. He had a gun, right? So why did he let us go?"

"I don't know." Bethany was hardly paying attention. She was peering into the inky shadows around them, worried that even now the next adversary might be sneaking up on them. The few pedestrians out at this hour averted their eyes. She didn't mind a bit. "Come on. We have to keep moving."

"He was my uncle—Mr. Stafford—"

"I know."

"The one who got me out of—I can't believe he'd let me—let me be involved with—"

"Later. We have to move."

Refusing to budge. "What did he mean about where you have to go next? And about the church? What's going on, Bethany?"

"Janice, please. We'll talk about it later."

"Now."

"Listen—"

Suddenly there was more going on in Janice's head than she could handle. They were scarcely a block from the Village House and she was having a tantrum. "That's what Blessing always says. 'We'll talk about it later, dear.' Which means never. My mom's the same way. 'Later.' Why can't you just tell me? I was in that room, too. I could have been blown up, too. And I got you out! Remember? Don't you owe me something? Like maybe to answer my questions and like what I think actually matters? Uncle Daniel was the only one who ever treated me like anything but a child! Ever!"

Bethany felt the space of years between them. She had never raised children but still hoped to. Now she saw the pain in the teenager's eyes, but also knew that a crisis was no time to go soft. Loving firmness was the answer: or so Aunt Claudia always said.

"We will talk, Janice. I promise we will. But not while we're standing in the middle of the sidewalk with you shouting and drawing attention to us." She slipped an arm around the girl's thin shoulders. "Come on. We have to move fast and get as far away from here as we can."

"We don't have any money." Sullenly.

"Yes, we do. We just have to go get it." More worried now, wanting to rush. The wind was coming hard off the water, and she wondered whether her sweater and Janice's thin jacket would be enough. "We'll hit an ATM, in case the Kathy Hobart account is still active. And there's more. I hid it when I got to Chicago."

"Wait."

Exasperation. "What now?"

A shy smile. "Well, we got out, right? We're safe, right?"

"For the moment."

"Then we should give thanks that we followed the right Plan. That's what Martin would say."

About to argue, Bethany held her tongue. Anything to calm the girl. She led Janice across to a small park. They sat on a stone bench, bathed in the soft glow of a pair of street lamps gussied up to look a century old. The teen prayed with her eyes shut and her palms steepled. Bethany mainly listened, certain that this act, too, was making the sort of scene people remembered later. Janice gave thanks, without quite specifying what she was thinking. Afterward, Bethany wasn't sure whether she felt any different, but it was plain that Janice did.

Sirens.

There were police cars streaking the other way, five or six of them, together with a couple of vans. The raid Fuentes had predicted was about to start.

"Come on," said Bethany.

This time Janice followed without any questions. They scurried through an alleyway between two office towers, then made a pair of right turns and emerged on West Madison. Bethany took a moment to acclimate herself in the darkness, then pointed toward the lake.

"This way."

Janice didn't argue.

The sirens fell behind. They were out of it, they realized. They had actually escaped. After another block, Bethany started laughing. She couldn't help herself. Freedom was so wonderful. Janice looked at her rescuer's half-mad eyes, and started laughing, too. A gaggle of late-night revelers, spilling out of a club, gave the crazy women a wide berth. Some were wary, some were smiling, but nobody wanted to be near them. Bethany and Janice laughed so hard in their relief that they couldn't walk. They hugged, laughing and crying, and might have stood there forever except that the world rocked and buildings shook and people started screaming, which are the sort of things that tend to happen when a bomb goes off.

It would have been a delicious irony to take them as they prayed, proving once more—to the professor's satisfaction, anyway—that there existed no Maker prepared to deliver them from evil. Either He didn't care or He wasn't there. Stuart Van Der Staal had long ago doubled down on the second option, and his only regret about his own eventual oblivion was that he would not be able to see the stunned faces of the billions of silly believers when they faced theirs. He often wished there could be a single hour of afterlife, just long enough for some official non-deity to announce with a great clap of thunder that when life ended, it just ended. For the next sixty minutes, the believers would tremble together in terror, watched in amusement by the grown-ups who had guessed the truth and lived their lives accordingly.

Oh, yes. He would have loved to take Bethany and her companion at that lovely moment. From his place of concealment twenty yards away, he could have snuck up close, put a bullet in the black girl's head, and had the needle back in Bethany's neck before she knew what had happened. But that wasn't according to orders. The black girl was not to be harmed. He didn't know the reason for the decision—he didn't even know who had made it—but it certainly complicated things.

So he was following them instead. Bethany seemed impatient with the younger girl, and the professor didn't blame her a bit. He knew from experience that the key to avoiding capture was to keep moving, and Bethany Barclay had obviously figured that out. Her companion was baggage. Look at them now, laughing and hugging when they should be running as hard as they could. *Impedimentum*, the Romans would have called the teenager, a word meaning not so much a blockade—oh, how the language had been vulgarized!—as a hindrance, a thing grabbing at your feet and holding you back. The black girl struck him that way: grabby. Sooner or later, Bethany would reach the same conclusion, and they would go their separate ways, and then he could—

The thunder of the explosion, so utterly unexpected, made him turn his head, and crouch, and halfway draw his gun. It took the professor no more than thirty seconds to decide the blast had nothing to do with him, but by the time he swung back, the women were gone.

They were a good half mile away before they slowed down. Until now, Bethany had not fully appreciated how difficult it was to learn what was happening in the world if one was not plugged in. They had no cell phones or iPads to consult for the news. To enter a restaurant or bar would cost money they didn't have, thus ruling out the easiest access to a television. Still, there were pieces she could guess at. Fuentes had said the bomb wasn't big enough to bring down a building, so the Village House was presumably still standing. He had said he could disarm it. Had he been mistaken? Or were other bombs hidden around the place, set off by the Planners in a desperate effort to stop the raid?

"What happened?" Janice asked, not for the first time, as they stood near the terminus of East Wacker Drive, in the shadow of the luxury hotels and apartments with their lake views. "Do you think they're dead back there?"

"I don't know."

"Where are we going now?"

"Give me a minute, honey."

"Where, Bethany?"

Bethany gathered her thoughts. The question had three answers: short-term, medium-term, and long-term. There was no reason to burden the teen with the last two, particularly as it wasn't clear how long their partnership, enforced by necessity, was going to last.

So she stuck with short term.

"Do you know where Martin lives?"

Janice gave her a look. "At the Village House."

"I mean, where does he count his money? Have his parties?"

"Martin isn't like that—"

"No. He's brilliant. The kindest man on the face of the earth. You know something, Janice? I believe people can change. I do. My aunt taught me never to doubt it, and I never have. But just because a person *can* change doesn't prove he *does* change, and my willingness to believe Martin McAdams has changed ended when he pumped me full of drugs."

The teenager was cringing, and Bethany realized that her own fists were clenched. She tried to slow her breathing.

"Janice, listen to me. From what Mr.—your uncle told me, the Planners collected a whole lot of money. Where is it going? The Village House isn't opulent. It's old, and it's not well maintained. And don't tell me that the money's going for mission work, because it's obvious that those missions are mostly cover. The money's for something else. Martin always liked luxury. I'm betting there's a house somewhere."

"So what? He deserves it."

"I'm sure he does. I still need to talk to him."

Janice stood there, arms across her body. She shook her head, as much in denial as in refusal. And she had a lot to deny.

"Please, honey. I have to see him. You don't, but I do. There's a lot to do, but there are some questions I have to ask before I leave town. But I can't ask if I don't know where to find him. I promise, I don't want to hurt him or get him in any kind of trouble. I just have to get some information."

At last Janice yielded, with a heartbreaking look of defeat in her eyes, and Bethany realized with a pang that the child always yielded in the end, and knew it. "There's a house out in the suburbs," the teen admitted. "We call it the Forum. It's for meetings and retreats."

"That's all it's for?"

Like many a reluctant witness, the teen answered a slightly different question. "Martin spends a lot of time there. And—and some of the other leaders do, too."

"Have you ever been there?"

A look of pure pain flitted over the lovely brown face, and Bethany sagged at this confirmation of her fears.

"Yes," Janice whispered.

"Can you tell me where it is?"

"I told you. In the suburbs."

"Which suburb?"

Carraway and Pulu were in the park across the street from the Village House, walking along the ranks of those who'd been detained. All were sitting on the ground, wrists tied behind them with plastic riot cuffs, as scheduled. There had been no shooting, but the bomb squad had yet to give the all clear after the unexpected explosion. There were thirty-three Planners in the park, and the agents studied every face at least three times.

No Bethany Barclay.

No Martin Potus, formerly Martin McAdams.

No Blessing Wilkes, formerly Shirley Wilkes.

No Raymond Fuentes.

Of the five targets of the raid, the only one found inside was Daniel Stafford, and he was found dead.

"What do you think?" asked Pulu.

"I think she's in the wind."

"All of them together?"

He shook his head. "She's a loner. She's been on her own most of her life. She wouldn't run as part of a group. The psychology isn't right. She'd feel uncomfortable."

"Oh, so now you're a profiler, too?"

"I just—"

His cell phone rang. It was Vanner, his section chief. Her voice was chilly.

"I want you in my office."

"What? When?"

"Now. There's a plane waiting for you at Midway. Special Agent Pulu can clean up the mess."

Carraway blinked in disbelief. "But she's here. She's right under our noses. If we move fast—"

"The airport, Carl. The plane. Go now."

"Can you at least tell me what's going on?"

A long pause. "You met the other day with Theodore Lesofsky."

"I was following a lead. I'm sorry if—"

"He's disappeared, Carl. And he left you a very peculiar note. I'm sending the image to your phone as we speak. Take a look, then call me from the secure phone on the plane."

All the way to the airport he pondered the message:

Carl: Think about it. She might have been crazy but she wasn't a fool. She would have made copies. Let's hope they're in the right hands, because this is way above your pay grade. Don't try to find me. Good luck. Ted

FORTY-TWO

The house was a stone affair in a pricey corner of Highland Park, a faux Gothic pile, mixed in among other gaudy mansions not a stone's throw from Michael Jordan's famous estate. They had stopped first at a public park where Bethany had buried the last of her mad money beneath a hedge set between two dying elms, then found an all-night electronics store where she bought two disposable cell phones. They took a taxi, a train, and a bus to within half a mile of their destination, and walked the rest of the way.

The property was walled, but the gate stood open. In the forecourt were a dented Ford pickup and the silver Mercedes S. There was a camera on the gatepost. By the light above the front porch, Bethany could see what appeared to be another camera mounted beside the double Dutch door.

"They'll see us," said Janice.

"There doesn't seem to be another way in."

"Then we should go."

"No. I'm doing this." She saw the misery on Janice's face. "I told you. You don't have to go in. You can wait."

The teen shook her head. "If you go in, I go in."

Holding hands, they marched boldly up the drive. Nobody stopped them. No guard shouted. No Planners leaped from concealment. The porch was brick, and slightly sagging. Close up, the mortar along the stone front of the house needed pointing. Bethany made sure the camera had a full view of her face as she rang the bell.

The sound was sepulchral. A chill ran down her spine.

She rang again.

Nothing.

She tried the door. Locked, and far too heavy to kick down. She put her hands on her hips, trying to work this out, then noticed Janice backing away. The teen lifted a finger to her lips, then whispered: "This way."

Bethany followed her along a bluestone path that curved around the side of the house. Flowers in the windows were drooping for want of water. The outdoor beds needed pruning and weeding. The kitchen door had a keyhole but also a keypad like the ones at the Village House. This one, too, was engraved with a symbol: what appeared to be a burning heart, pierced by arrows. Bethany tried to work it out, but Janice stepped lightly in front of her and began punching letters: E-N-I-T-S-U-G-U-A.

Augustine, backward.

The lock clicked, and Janice pushed the door.

"How did you—"

"Annabelle brought me here once. I watched the code she entered."

"She knew the combination?"

Janice nodded, pain and embarrassment mixed. "She was out here a lot. She and Martin . . . people said they were . . . you know."

Bethany realized that her own face must be bright red, and was grateful for the darkness within. The house was built mostly on a single sprawling floor, topped by a gabled attic. Peering past the kitchen, she could see a family room or great room, with a corridor beyond, probably leading to the bedrooms. Faint illumination, possibly candlelight, came from the hallway, but the house was as silent as a tomb, and about as welcoming.

"There's not supposed to be any . . . you know," Janice was saying as they passed gleaming granite counters surrounding expensive appliances with black glass facades. "But, you know, Martin—the rules were kind of different for him because—"

"Because he's a genius and he's wonderful and kind. I know."

The teen actually managed a snicker. "I was going to say, because he's the boss."

The great room had leather furniture, a carpet of absurdly deep pile, and a television that would have done duty as a wall. Behind the house, floodlights yellowed the night. The view was of a swimming pool, not yet opened for the season, and tennis courts beyond. Inside, Bethany poked her head into a dining room and what must have been Martin's study. In that room alone she risked flicking on a light. The elaborately designed wooden shelves were a good deal less spartan than in his throne room at the Village House. The wallpaper was a green tartan. Pale rectangles here and there suggested works of art recently removed. Either Martin was hurting for money, or he had flown the coop; possibly both.

"We should go," said Janice, so close Bethany jumped. "We should go, right now."

"It's okay, honey." Leading her back to the family room. "He can't hurt you any more."

"I'm not afraid of Martin. He would never hurt me."

"Then what?"

"Can't you feel it?" Hugging herself. "We're not wanted here."

"I think we're alone."

"He warned me. Mr. Stafford. My—my uncle. He said not to come here. He said people aren't perfect, but we don't have to help them make things worse." She covered her eyes. "I—he—he killed himself in front of me. He didn't even say good-bye."

Again Bethany felt that mysterious protectiveness, as if Janice, eleven years her junior, were blood. "I'm sorry, honey."

"Stop it. You don't have to get all huggy. I'm not going to break down again, okay? I'll be fine."

"Janice—"

"Let's do what we're here to do and get out of here. I hate this place."

The master suite was down a short hallway. Bethany hesitated. In this sad, empty space the teen's anxiety was catching, so Bethany sat her on the sofa to give them both a break. "Tell me about Annabelle and Martin."

Janice looked down at her sneakers. "I don't know. We're not supposed to gossip. But some of the junior sisters said—well, she was rising very fast, and she had a lot of—a lot of private meetings with him. They'd be gone at the same time. Things like that. And they had a lot—a lot of counseling sessions. A *lot* of counseling sessions. And just—you know—sometimes the way people act when they're together? Like they're trying to pretend they're not, but they just try too hard?"

"I know what you mean," said Bethany, her mind briefly on the Martin she had loved in college, who had behaved exactly that way with one or two of her friends. She wondered about his relationship with Annabelle; if some of it was payback. But another of Aunt Claudia's favorite lessons was that the world doesn't revolve around you. Two smart, attractive people could fall for each other without either of them giving a second thought to Bethany Barclay.

"Can we go now?" said Janice.

"I have to be sure Martin isn't here."

"Why?" They were back on their feet. "What do you have to ask him?"

Questions, questions. "You heard Mr. Fuentes. He thinks God's Planners were a front for someone else. I need to know who. That's why we're here."

"Be careful," said Janice.

"Oh, believe me—"

"I mean, don't step in the blood."

Bethany looked where the teen was pointing.

A footprint. Just one, smudged but distinct, on the floor, the toe pointing away from the bedroom wing—toward the great room, and the front door beyond.

"Wait here," said Bethany.

"No."

"I mean it this time. Don't move from that spot. Don't touch anything. We don't want your fingerprints all over the place." She turned. "Janice—"

"I'll wait," said the teen, eyes wide and near panic.

Bethany supposed her own eyes must look the same.

Three minutes later, Bethany stepped back into the great room. Her face was gray.

"We're leaving, honey," she said, tone wooden.

"What is it?" Janice, wide-eyed as before. "Who's in there?"

But Bethany was staring. "What are you doing?"

"Texting Zach. Telling him I'm okay. Who's in there?" She swallowed. "It's Martin, isn't it?"

"No. It isn't. There's no sign of him in the house. Janice, listen. About Zach. This is important. You can't—if you're—"

"I know. We're on the run. That doesn't mean I can't text my boyfriend."

"He's part of God's Planners. He'll—"

"He's not a Planner. He won't do anything." She put the phone away. "Who's in there?" she repeated.

"It's Blessing, and you don't want to see her."

"Yes, I do."

"No, honey. Not like this. Come on. We're going."

They were in the parking lot of a McDonald's in a shopping strip well south of Highland Park. They had found car keys on a hook by the kitchen door, and had chosen the battered pickup over the more conspicuous Mercedes. They had used the drive-thru lane to avoid being noticed, and now the truck cab smelled of Big Macs and fries, but Janice was doing more crying than eating. Feeling more motherly than ever, Bethany held the girl close, shushed her, rubbed her back, whispered that it was going to be all right. But Bethany was thinking about poor Blessing, and wondering whether Peter's friend—the man of influence—was already taking his revenge, even if in the wrong direction.

"Tell me about your Zach," she finally said. "You said he's not a Planner."

"He's a freshman at Northwestern. He's not really my boyfriend." She wiped her eyes and even smiled. "I know him from high school. We're the same age, but I was in twelfth grade when he was in tenth. We got to be friends in our church youth group. He's not a Planner—he thinks we're silly—they're silly—but he comes to the Village House to see me. Came. I guess nobody's going there anymore."

For they had finally caught up on the news. The police had discovered bombmaking materials and at least two bombs, one of which exploded just as the raid began, apparently to cover the escape of the group's leaders—so the reporters said. No one was injured in the blast, but the police found one apparent suicide in the basement.

It was easy to guess whose escape the bomb had covered.

"Well, to go into that place," said Bethany, trying to keep the mood light, "he must really like you a lot."

"I told you. We're just friends."

"You're the one who said he's your boyfriend. Or was that wishful thinking?"

"He's sweet," said Janice, tone intriguingly defiant. "He's a gentleman. You don't meet many of those these days."

"Tell me about it."

"My uncle was a gentleman, too." She shook her head, but the tears didn't return.

"Janice, about Zach—"

"Don't worry. I won't get us caught. I promise. If I have to stay out of touch, I will." She took out the disposable cell, opened it up, took out the battery, and slipped the sim card in her pocket. "Untraceable without power," she said. "But we should get moving. I mean, if we're going to meet him."

Alarm. "Janice—"

"I figured we can't get far in this truck. He's going to loan us his car. He'll tell his folks it was like stolen, he left the keys in it at the movies. He'll get like grounded for a month? But at least nobody will know what kind of car we're in."

Bethany already had the truck on the main road again. They drove in silence for a few minutes, then pulled into a park-and-ride lot. There was an important decision to face.

"Honey, look—"

"I want to help. I want to pull my weight."

"Yes, but this is—"

"We're going to need a car, Bethany. You know I'm right. And Zach—well, we can trust him."

Bethany drummed her fingers on the wheel. She hated when other people did it, but right now she needed the distraction. She had learned a lot about living underground over the last weeks. Few tools were more valuable than the ability to get out of town in a hurry with nobody the wiser. She hated to admit that Janice might be right. But that meant taking Janice along—

The teen interrupted her thoughts. "I still don't understand what Mr. Fuentes was trying to tell us."

"I think he meant that whoever the Planners were fronting for wants to discourage people from believing in God."

Janice snorted. "Who would blow up bombs to do that?"

"I don't know, honey. But believers from every religion have used tactics like that. So why not nonbelievers?"

The teen finally reached for her Big Mac. Bethany did the same. Both were hungrier than they had realized.

"I think you should tell me the rest of the story," said Janice between bites. "Why they had you locked up, what you meant about the chemicals they pumped into you, and what you and Mr. Fuentes think this is all about." She winked. "Don't worry. I can take it."

And so Bethany told her. An abbreviated version, to be sure, but hitting most of the highlights. The telling went on for a good fifteen minutes.

"So they killed Annabelle to stop her from finding this Stone," Janice murmured when the story was done. Her dark eyes were aglow with an unworldly light, and Bethany for the first time felt the girl's fearsome intelligence blazing. "And we're going to follow Annabelle's trail. That's the point, isn't it? If she died because of what she knew, and if that's connected to what happened in Virginia, then the only way to prove your innocence is to find out what she knew."

"Even that might not be enough to clear my name, honey, but it's the best idea I've got."

"So that means you must know where she went when she—when she left."

"I know exactly where she went, Janice."

"Where?"

Bethany shook her head. "I'm sorry, honey. You're going to have to trust me on this one."

"But—"

"It's not because you're a teenager. It's not because I don't trust you. It's because this isn't your fight. You don't have to come with me. I owe you. Big time. I'll drop you back with your parents if you want. I'll give you some money. You can go anywhere."

"I want to go with you."

"It's going to be dangerous."

"I don't care. My parents think there's something wrong with me, just because I wasn't happy being in college half my teenaged years. If I go home, they'll send me away somewhere, and I'll go nuts for real. If I go anywhere else, they'll send me to my parents anyway, or else I'll wind up just sort of wandering around, and I'll get involved in the same—the same stuff—the same people—the way I did before—before—"

"Before Martin rescued you," Bethany said quietly.

"He did. Nothing can change that."

"I know."

"That year—after I left school? Before my uncle took me to—to Martin? It was horrible, but it was wonderful, too. The things I did—the people I did them with—I can't go back, Bethany. If I get started again, I'll never be able to stop. I have to go with you."

"As long as you're sure, honey."

"I know it's not going to be easy." Janice smiled. A little. "You're saying that there's somebody out there who wants to kill you and maybe me now, and we have to stay away from them while we look for some stone that's been lost for a couple of thousand years and that nobody else can find."

"Exactly."

"And we can't tell anybody what we're doing."

"That's right."

"And you think we can do all that alone."

"Sure we can." Another hug. "We're an army of two."

PART THREE

PROBABILITY

Most of us live most of the time in forgetfulness of God and with our existence centred in ourselves.

—John Hick, *Disputed Questions*

FORTY-THREE

They're an army of three," says the Pastor. "Provided, of course, that they put on the armor of the Lord. They are about the Lord's work, and He will be with them. Of that there can be no doubt. I do not believe the forces of darkness can actually achieve victory. Things may at times appear bleak, but say not the struggle naught availeth."

"Except that the land isn't bright in the West," sneers the Critic, quoting from the opposite end of the same poem. "Unless you count the Village House being on fire, which is more of a defeat for us than a victory, seeing as how it's eliminated the evidence that might have been helpful in finding their backers. We started down this road because we don't know who's in charge of the Wilderness these days. Well, we've sent in now two spies, one witting and one not, and we still don't know, do we?" The question is rhetorical, as, with the Critic, they tend to be: a device useful in argument, not a request for information. He waggles a finger. The gesture is rude, but it's been nearly a week since Bethany vanished from the Village House, and all of them are on edge. "And don't go telling me your God will grant our side victory, either. It's a matter of history that the good guys lose as often as they win. And the losses are not as a rule particularly pretty."

The Pastor is laconic. "In the long run, the tyrants always fall. Didn't Gandhi say that?"

"Let me tell you a couple of hard truths about Gandhi—"

The Builder raps his knuckles on a side table of knotty pine, the signal for silence. "Let's stick to the point, shall we? We've lost track of Ms. Barclay. Again. Finding her is the priority. Right?" Nobody disagrees. "Second, we've lost the link we sent her there to find—the link between the Village House and the Wilderness. Correct? In other words, we're back to start."

Notwithstanding the Builder's natural tyranny, Edna finds herself more relieved than she would have expected to have him back in the chair. The little man can be a petty Napoleon, true; he is short-tempered and easily annoyed by dissent. But he brings to their meetings an undeniable order and clarity, together with a sense of urgent purpose. The Mathematician is more brilliant, but the Builder is a leader, and just now a leader is what they need.

They are meeting this afternoon in a rustic cottage overlooking the Rappahannock River, down toward the southern end where the water broadens, preparing to spill into the Chesapeake Bay. The walls are festooned with fishing tackle and period hunting prints. Beyond the window the ground slopes toward a long crumbling dock. The sky is slate and lowering, the gray water roiling against the rocks, and one needn't know the sea to sense the coming storm.

Stuart Van Der Staal ties his blackened dinghy to a mooring post. He is at an abandoned marina a mile and a half south of the cottage. A couple of battered boats float half-sunken nearby. He wades to shore, going over tonight's plan. There is more than one way to flush Bethany Barclay, he reasons; and more than one way to be sure she runs where he wants her to run, rather than into the arms of the opposition.

He takes a moment to breathe, getting his lungs used to the cloying marsh air. He reflects, but only briefly, on certain literary parallels, particularly to Beowulf, where his sympathy lies with Grendel, the thoroughgoing rationalist, who is, through his mother, a descendant of Cain, the first murderer. Stuart has always had an affinity for Cain, who in his judgment gets a bad rap in Genesis. Cain was oppressed by his popular younger brother. What was he supposed to do? He had no choice but to dispose of Abel, just as

Stuart all those years ago had no choice but to do away with the disagreeable Professor Margolis, even if all the world still believed it to have been a stroke.

Life isn't sacred, Stuart reminds himself. People no more have a right to life than they have a right to wealth. It's all just perception: choose the right angle and the right lens and anything could as easily be anything else.

Moral precepts included.

Satisfied that his boat is invisible, he checks his night-vision glasses and certain other equipment, then crouches down and scurries north along the eroding riverbank.

———

"We're not entirely back to start," says the Senator. "At least the bombings have stopped."

"The bombs were a side trip," says the Builder. "An irrelevancy."

"We might have saved lives—"

The Builder rides right over her. "From what you tell us, Senator, the feds still haven't figured out the point of the bombs. Right? It's actually more than a little irritating that they're having so much trouble following the clues."

"They just don't want to jump to conclusions," says the Senator, unfazed. "They have to analyze every possibility."

But the Builder hates interruptions. "Or they could just look at what's staring them in the face." He begins counting off on his chubby fingers. "One. They drag Bethany to the church, making sure that the camera catches her face. Two. They're building crude bombs. Three. The bombs are lined with wadding made of church bulletins. Four. Bomb-making materials are planted in the church." He balls a fist, punches the air. On cue, the first raindrops, big as pellets, strafe the windows. "Is it really too much for the feds to make the next jump?" the Builder demands. "But no. They're too busy analyzing the likely targets. They think what matters is who the bomb was intended to blow up. But we know better, don't we? We know that the real point of the bombs isn't who gets killed but who gets blamed."

"They'll figure it out in time," says the Senator, dogged in defense of bureaucracy. "You're the one who keeps saying we have to be patient. The demand for immediate results is the greatest weakness of the Wilderness. That's your slogan, Builder. They're fanatics, remember? Their fanaticism makes them rush, and in their rush they make mistakes, which we can exploit if we'll just wait—also your philosophy. Remember?"

Edna smiles. "I'm afraid she has you there."

The Builder glares, but the women refuse to drop their eyes. The expression on his pudgy face softens. "Well, maybe you're right. The feds will figure it out. Eventually." Drawing the word out, just to make his point. Outside, the thunder rolls in slow, almost lyrical counterpoint to the argument raging in the cottage. Somebody laughs. "In any event," the Builder continues, "we still need to track down Ms. Barclay. As I've said all along, it does no good to have her following Annabelle's path if we can't follow hers. And at this point I see no other way to pull together the threads."

"I'll be notified the instant the feds get a hint," says the Senator.

"I'm frankly more worried about the other side getting a hint. By now they might have decided that they're better off letting her run, at least if they know where she's running. For all we know, this kid she escaped with is a plant."

The Writer clucks his tongue. "She's just a child."

"She's a teenager," says the Pastor. "And the Wilderness is not above recruiting on college campuses."

The Critic intervenes. "Which doesn't differentiate them from you."

Again the Builder raps on the table. "This isn't productive. Plainly, the first order of business is to track down Bethany Barclay. I have a plan. It will take a little work, and I will have to call in a few favors, but I believe that the plan stands a good chance of bearing fruit." Nobody questions him, or even demands an explanation; they have experience enough of what he is able to do. "Second. As far as the bombings are concerned, let's assume that the Wilderness will abandon that strategy for the time being. They will have to wait to see how far the government gets in the investigation, just as we will. The Wilderness may be fanatics, but they aren't idiots. I assume this to be our shared view." Again, no murmur of question or dissent. Edna looks out at the storm. This is the Builder at his best, but also at his worst. His commitment to the cause is absolute and unshakeable. Yet he is burdened by pride, for her money is always the most dangerous of sins.

Edna tenses, and leans toward the rear bay window. In the brief jagged glare of the lightning she has detected movement out at the end of the dock. She squints. Another flash. A tall man, bending low as he creeps toward the house. Probably one of the Senator's bodyguards, she decides, although the last time Edna noticed them they were both around front, watching the road. One of the other drivers, then—the Builder's man is said to carry a gun—although why any of them would risk the crumbling dock in this foul wind she cannot imagine. A fisherman, then, seeking any port in the storm. Edna scolds herself. She is far too old to start jumping at shadows. She turns her attention back toward the room, where the Builder has moved to the next item on his agenda.

But within seconds, much against her will, her eyes stray to the window once more. The man is gone.

"Now let's talk about the Pilate Stone," the Builder is saying. "Let's remember, please, that finding the Stone is a priority of the Wilderness. But it's not a priority of ours. The only purpose of our search is to flush them out. We can't fight them effectively unless we know who they are."

"I hope you're not suggesting that we should abandon our own search," says the Pastor, sitting very straight. His blond hair is trimmed with a military precision. "The adversary"—he never says Wilderness—"cannot be permitted, under any circumstances, to gain possession of the Stone."

"I'm not suggesting that we abandon the search," says the Builder. "I'm reminding us that it isn't a priority."

Edna is half-listening to the old argument. She is trying to decide whether to mention the man she may have seen. The others would likely laugh, and being an object of fun is what the Judge hates above all things: she, too, is burdened by pride.

"We dare not widen the circle of knowledge," warns the Mathematician. "That's been considered and vetoed over and over."

The Builder seems annoyed. "I'm making a different point. We recruited Annabelle Seaver. We sent her into the Village House because we knew of the affiliation between the Wilderness and the Planners. Her mission was to talk about the Pilate Stone until she got some kind of response. We knew the Wilderness wanted it. We knew they'd have to take her seriously, even if they thought she was working for us. What we don't know is what went wrong. I'm not talking about her murder. I'm talking about before the murder. When she disappeared. She hit upon something—some kind of clue—someone she spoke to, probably—that led her in a particular direction. We don't know what the clue was because she refused to tell us. It's not as if we had the facilities to require it out of her. Nor would rougher tactics have matched our commitment to morality of method. For us, unlike our adversary, *jus in bello* is every bit as important as *jus ad bellum*."

Again he waits for a contradiction; again none comes. Outside the window the sloping lawn has gone silvery. The storm has brought with it that peculiar dark light that often presages tornadoes. But there is no further movement behind the cottage.

"So Annabelle went off on her own. I take full responsibility for that." The Builder taps his chest. "Recruiting her was the Critic's idea, and a good one. The plan, however, was mine, and I was the one who debriefed her. Or tried to. The point is, she went her own way. She disappeared, then showed up in Washington, and was killed. We have no way of knowing whether she found the Pilate Stone or even got close. We have reason to think that she identified one or more leaders of the Wilderness, but even that we're not sure of. We have no way to tell what progress she made. Neither does the Wilderness."

"Unless she was with them all that time," says the Writer. "The Wilderness would not cavil at method. They might have drained her of every fact she unearthed."

"And then released her to wander the streets," says the Builder with his devastating sarcasm. "I think not. They didn't have her. They need to know what she was doing as badly as we do." Behind the thick lenses, the Builder's glare brooked no disagreement. His fist strikes the arm of his chair. "We were so close."

Outside the cottage there is a shout. The Builder's driver materializes in the doorway. "We may have a problem," he says.

Stuart Van Der Staal is in the woods north of the house. He is at once amazed and disappointed that he was able to approach with such ease. He does not understand how the people who are likely inside can manage with so little security.

Finding the fools was child's play. His masters are somehow able to track Bethany's mentor, that judge, even though she has switched to a disposable cell. Stuart promises himself that on a fitter occasion he will figure out how the trick is done.

In his work it would surely prove useful.

Now, at his post on the hill, he stands very still, watching as a pair of armed men approach the woods, guns out. He intentionally allowed them to see him dart across the lawn, but of course he is nowhere near the spot on which they are converging. He pats his pockets. He has all the tools he needs. He is wearing fatigues impregnated with the latest pixilated threads, a technology that makes ordinary visual detection all but impossible across long distances. True, he was at risk running along the dock due to the way the lightning caused rapid changes in the background. But only for an instant.

He studies the two remaining guards. Trained, but not experienced. Basically high-end rent-a-cops. The professionals have already left, their first charge being the safety of their employers. He has seen two women hustled into a limousine by a pair of serious-looking crushers, and two men driven off together with another entirely competent bodyguard. By Stuart's count, that leaves three in the cottage, guarded by the two men now tangled in the trees. Two town cars stand in the forecourt, engines running, drivers behind the wheels.

Stuart draws a pistol from his holster. The next part is going to be fun.

FORTY-FOUR

Why aren't we leaving?" says the Critic, palm cupped above his brow as he peers into the storm. "I thought that in an emergency we're supposed to disperse."

The Mathematician is at the buffet, refreshing his coffee. He seems amused by life's sudden twists. "Well, some of us have gone and some of us have stayed. That's a dispersal, isn't it?"

The Pastor is over by the bookshelf, where he has discovered, with unfeigned delight, a first edition of J. G. H. Barry's *Meditations on the Apostles' Creed*. "Don't tease him," he says, carefully turning pages. "Tell him."

"Tell me what?"

The Mathematician has joined the Critic at the window. "You haven't been with us long enough to know that we have these scares every year or two. It's not unusual. It rarely amounts to anything. The Wilderness hasn't resorted to violence against our physical persons since the 1960s."

"Then why did the others go?"

"The Senator's bodyguards are ex-Secret Service. Their training is to get the protectee away from the threat, and check the credibility later. The Judge went with her because they arrived together. The Builder's driver has similar training. If he invited the Writer along, I suspect it is because they have something to talk about." He sips his coffee. "One thing you'll learn about the Builder is that he likes to keep things compartmentalized. He never lets any one of us know everything that's in his head."

"He's a bit of a tyrant," says the Critic.

The Pastor meanwhile has decided to read Barry aloud: "'In the heart of Christianity is not a great idea, but a loving person.'" He looks up, shoves his spectacles onto his forehead. "That's why it doesn't matter in the end whether the Wilderness finds the Pilate Stone. Christianity isn't an idea. Our faith involves a communion, with an actual person named Jesus."

The Critic groans and covers his eyes. "Please. Don't torture us. It's bad enough we have to wait for the all clear. Can we maybe avoid the details of your superstition in the meantime?"

The Pastor smiles and goes back to his book. But the Mathematician refuses to let the point go. "The search matters immensely," he says, tone still bemused. "Now my faith or the Pastor's might not be affected by what is or isn't written on some ancient artifact, but many people believe a truth simply because the truth is old and crumbling, as if it is axiomatic that our fathers' fathers' fathers knew better than we. Nations have gone to war over much less."

The Critic remains unpersuaded. "The Stone says whatever it says. Whether we find it or the other side does, its significance will doubtless be debated by scholars for all of a month, then promptly forgotten."

"I don't think so," says the Mathematician. "Just consider. If the Stone is helpful to the Christian cause—or to the cause of belief more generally—I wouldn't put it past the Wilderness to chip off key pieces in order to leave the message vague, or even to change the meaning entirely." He glances at the window, where the thunder has stopped. The rain is letting up. The guards who went into the woods have not returned. "The Wilderness has a long history of going after relics. Quite ruthlessly, I might add. They'll find an old bit of papyrus, say. They'll size it up, and either publicize it or conceal it—maybe destroy it—depending on whether it's hurtful or helpful to the cause of religion in general and Christianity in particular."

"Example," snaps the Critic, quite unpersuaded.

The Mathematician considers. "Suppose the Stone is found, and its inscription reads—excuse me, my Latin is a bit rusty—but suppose a line reads *Iesus fecit miracula*, and the Wilderness knocks off the last word, so that *Jesus did miracles* becomes just *Jesus did* . . . and the rest is up for debate.

See the danger? That could mean anything. Or *Iesus resurrexit* could easily become—"

He is interrupted by the sound of gunshots.

"You might as well hear the rest," says the Senator as the limousine ticks through the countryside, heading for the Interstate. The driver has twice been on the radio, and the other guard has a mobile phone glued to his ear. "Bethany is your protégé after all."

"The rest of what?" says Edna, wondering whether this is another of the Builder's drills, or whether there might be reason to worry. She keeps looking over her shoulder, but spotting pursuit is impossible in the rainswept gloom.

"Don't worry," says the Senator, sensing her mood. "My guys know what they're doing."

"What about the people we left behind?"

"They have cars. They have guards. They can leave any time they want."

"Suppose they're in trouble?"

The Senator is exasperated. "What do you want me to do, Edna? Go back and offer them a ride?"

About to respond in kind, Edna manages to calm her anger. She reminds herself that the woman beside her has had a life by no means easy, and may well be the toughest of them all. At the same time, she remembers her conversation with the Mathematician, and their shared suspicion that there is a traitor in their midst.

She is on the verge of apologizing when her disposable phone rings.

The Builder.

"Sorry about the unpleasantness," he says. "There was indeed a situation, but it's my understanding that it's being handled."

"What kind of situation?"

"Our people are fine, if that's what you mean. I'll call you at the usual time."

The Builder hangs up, leaving Edna to ponder. The Senator leans close, and as her face creases with worry, she suddenly looks her age. "What did he say?"

A beat. "He says everything is under control."

"What's that supposed to mean?"

Edna watches the rain-heavy trees tick by. "That it isn't."

Stuart has moved to higher ground, a further hilltop overlooking the one on which he previously roosted. He crouches low, enjoying the patter of rain spilling from the branches above onto his wide-brimmed hat. His night-vision glasses pierce the storm-sodden darkness. He is watching the panic below, but also wondering why they have posted lookouts so carelessly. He should not have been able to approach the cottage so easily. His sprint to the woods should have been spotted earlier, and the entire coterie should have been abandoned at once. Had his assignment involved assassination, he could have caused at least two leaders of the superstitious opposition to cease being perceived. He almost did it anyway, just for the thrill.

Even now, squatting on his hilltop as they tend to their wounded rent-a-cop, Stuart is tempted. He hasn't brought a rifle, but from this height he could probably bring down at least one by pistol shot. He even draws his Beretta Px4 Storm .45 and sights down the barrel. So easy. It would be so easy. But discipline holds. The point tonight is not to take them but to let them know that they can be taken. And Stuart even sees the reason. They are all people of prominence. Their killings would bring out more forces of law enforcement and technological detection than his employers are prepared to cope with.

Wound a guard, however, and the police will assume that a hunter did it by accident. Nobody in the Garden will contradict them. And still the message will have been sent.

A favorite verse of Hesse comes to mind, paraphrased: as long as I create my own individuality, my life has worth. Thus the determination of Stuart Van Der Staal not to travel the path urged by conventional morality. Even his pleasure in killing distinguishes further his individuality. Why be like the great mass of people when one can go out on one's own?

Time to move. Stuart rises easily to his feet, barely disturbing the foliage.

Now that the message has been sent, his next task is to reacquire Bethany. To do this means guessing where she will head.

He has a good idea.

A final look down the hill. Then, satisfied with tonight's artistry, he slips away into the brooding Virginia night.

"I'm not staying here," says the Critic, striding toward the door.

The Pastor grabs him by the arm. "You can't go out there. You could get shot."

The Critic's face is sardonic. "Are you afraid for your life?"

"Right now, I'm afraid for yours."

"That's very Christian of you, I'm sure, but I'm not the sort of man who sits around waiting for the axe to fall. If somebody's after us, maybe we should go after him first."

"That's what the guards are for."

"Do you notice they haven't come out of the woods?"

The Pastor's tone is indulgent. "Maybe they've caught him."

"And maybe he's caught them."

He plunges through the door.

"Let him go," commands the Mathematician.

"I can't do that," says the Pastor, and steps out into the night rain.

"What were you going to tell me before?" Edna coughs again. This is getting serious. "You said you had something to say about Bethany."

The Senator is watching her closely. "Not about Bethany precisely, but it does pertain to her. If the meeting hadn't ended so, ah, abruptly, I would have shared my findings with the group." She consults a small card on which she has scribbled a few notes. Ordinarily it would have been destined for the fire once the meeting ended. "It's about Janice Stafford. The young woman your Bethany is on the run with." She glances at the Judge. "I'm sure some of this is repetitious, but do bear with me. There's a point to it all. Actually the main point of the meeting."

"Please," says Edna, mystified.

"Janice is from a well-to-do African-American family. Doctors and lawyers and so forth for several generations. Mother's a professor at U Chicago, a historian. Father's a cardiologist. They live in Evanston. Janice is the youngest. An older sister in law school, an older brother working for a civil rights group in Washington."

Edna's head pops up: could this be Bethany's destination?

"The Bureau doesn't think so," says the Senator, reading her friend's mind. "They've talked to the brother several times. He says he hasn't heard from Janice in six or eight months. His phones are tapped. If they get in touch, the Bureau will know about it. So they won't try." She resumes her narrative. "Okay. Janice has a genius IQ. She started Northwestern when she was 16, and brought along a year's worth of advance placement. Declared a major in physics. A's in math and science, B's in the rest. Dropped out a year later. Knocked around for six or eight months, wound up at the Village House, apparently through her uncle." The Senator flips the card over. "Janice is a pretty strong chess master, I'm told. Finished second at the national women's championship at age 14. Won it at age 15. Profile in the *New York Times*. The American chess federation had high hopes for her, but when she quit school she apparently quit chess, too." She lifts her eyes again. "The Mathematician knows some members of the family. Not Janice or her parents, I gather, but a couple of cousins. He's checking with them. Subtly, no doubt."

"No doubt," Edna echoes, and the two women smile, although not at each other.

"It's my understanding," the Senator resumes, "that these teenaged math prodigies are actually a dime a dozen, and most of them don't amount to any more than the smart kid who never picks up a calculus book until junior year of college. So I wouldn't attach too much significance to the IQ test and the chess and so forth."

Edna is thoughtful. "That's part of the problem, isn't it? From what I understand, it's not unusual for children who have academic success earlier than their peers to have trouble coping with adversity. Some of them can't take the pressure. This may be what happened to Janice at school. Why she quit."

"Possibly." But her reluctance is almost palpable, and Edna knows they are at the heart of the matter.

"Tell me the rest," she says, gently.

The Senator's squarish jaw is set. "Janice Stafford has an FBI file. I don't know what's in it—they won't even give my people a hint—but the file was opened during her freshman year of college, and it's flagged for a very high level of clearance." She hesitates. "All inquiries go to the Bureau's counter-terrorist division."

Stuart Van Der Staal is halfway to the dock when he realizes that the sounds are not wildlife. Somebody is following his trail, somebody trained to move silently in the woods. A hunter, perhaps. A fisherman. Or a man much like himself.

He wishes that his employers had more information about the leaders of the Garden. It is possible that one or two of them might have seen military service. Certainly someone is being brave.

The professor draws his Beretta and takes several steps backward the way he came, then settles into the brush to wait. Waiting ranks among his finest skills. He has crouched motionless for hours at a time in order to spring a trap. This time he is confident that the wait will be only minutes.

Ninety seconds later, a tall, slim figure passes his position. Not a rent-a-cop. One of the leaders. His orders are to leave them alone, but this opportunity is too good to pass up.

He steps from concealment, making noise, waiting for the other man to turn.

Both of them stare in astonishment.

"You!" says the Critic.

"And you," says Stuart. "I would never have guessed. And may I say that I am a great admirer of your work. A pity you're on the wrong side in this thing."

"But you can't just—"

Already tired of the conversation, the professor fires twice, center mass.

He hears a gasp from behind, spins, squeezes the trigger twice. He recognizes this one, too. A big political preacher. And not dead yet. The man is on his back, hands flailing, struggling for breath.

Stuart crouches beside him. "Do you expect your God to save you?"

The Pastor's eyes swivel his way. "Not . . . the way . . . you mean it."

"I suppose not," says Stuart, and fires again.

FORTY-FIVE

I don't cook out of no can," said Tia Christina, and Bethany believed her. Soup was simmering in a shuddering stock pot on a back burner on the gas stove, and, as Bethany and Janice watched, the old woman sliced another onion into it, tasted the concoction with a wooden spoon, which she immediately dipped back in to stir, not rinsing it first—Aunt Claudia would have fainted on the spot—and added a few chunks of ham that had been waiting on the cutting board for the suitable moment. "This is the only way to cook."

"I know," said Bethany, straddling a kitchen stool turned around backward as her mouth watered.

"You like plantains?"

This to Janice, who sat at the dining room table jammed beneath the windows, turning the pages of the *New York Post* with a wide-eyed reverence suggesting that the print version of a newspaper was a fresh discovery.

"Yes, thank you," said the teen.

"Good." Working on the fryer. Soup, plantains, rice, and chicken: that would be dinner tonight, and the best one either of the younger women had tasted in quite a while: an improvement, by several orders of magnitude, on the fare offered by both the Village House and the fast food that had sustained them in their flight across the country.

"Annabelle, she hated to cook."

"I know," said Bethany, stomach rumbling with pleasure. The multiple mentions of Tia on the session tapes could only be a clue to Annabelle's intended path from the Village House; but Bethany was under no illusion that she alone could see the connection. Therefore she had planned a quick visit to Tia's apartment, in and out with her questions answered before anybody could guess they were even in Manhattan; but Tia was never hurried, and would never let you leave without a meal.

"I taught her everything else, but she always cooked out of those cans."

"I know."

"But she was a good girl."

"Yes, she was."

A long pause like an uneasy groom at the altar. "Most of the time," added Tia, but whether she was talking about running around with too many men or infiltrating a religious cult, Bethany was unable to guess.

"Yes, she was."

The old woman turned toward her, whole solid body at once, like a swiveling statue. Her yellowy eyes were very small behind her glasses. She pointed at Bethany with the dripping spoon. "Why are the police looking for you?"

"It's kind of a misunderstanding."

"You were on television."

"I'm trying to fix it," said Bethany, confident that Tia would never turn on her. Half-confident. She wrapped herself more tightly around the stool, and felt Janice's alertness tauten behind her. "It'll work out."

"They've been here talking to me, child"—what Tia had called her during her many delightful visits with Annabelle: nowadays a quaint, buried, warm yet moderately sad memory, like a summer love.

"I'm sorry, Tia."

"They've been here twice. Three times. I'm supposed to call them if I see you." A nod toward Janice. "Her, too."

"I hope you're not going to do that, Tia."

"Did you hurt my Annabelle?" Her tone was suddenly hard, and Bethany knew that if the old woman did not like the answer, she would try her best to throw her niece's best friend through her fifth-floor window onto 101st Street. For the first time, Bethany saw not the grandmotherly woman who watched game shows and fried plantains and whose feet ached constantly, but the rock-hard survivor who had built Annabelle a life from the ruins her parents had left. Yet the question struck her as peculiar, a suggestion nobody had yet made.

Unless the FBI had invented it to get Tia to talk to them.

The FBI or . . . somebody.

Somebody, for instance, who might have heard the tapes of Annabelle's counseling sessions.

"No, Tia. I would never have hurt her. I loved her. I still do," she added, to her own surprise.

"Do you know who did it?"

"I'm trying to find out." A beat, as she exchanged a glance with Janice. "That's sort of why I'm in trouble."

Tia Christina grunted, face rocky. She turned back to the stove, said over her shoulder: "Set the table."

"Okay."

"She was such a good girl," Tia said again, and Bethany sensed without turning that she woman was crying. Setting out cutlery for three as this tough old woman sobbed soundlessly, Bethany remembered how she and Annabelle had both been raised by aunts, and how that formed a bond between them. She glanced at Janice, still at her newspaper. The teen had grown up in the midst of plenty, but had been raised, in her own telling, by nobody at all, apart from those she met over the chess board or over the Internet. And it occurred to her, not for the first time, that despite Janice Stafford's bursts of childish dependence, there was a depth to her, a distance, something held in reserve. You saw it in her watchful gray eyes and her way of puffing out those lips in thought, as if that powerful brain was constantly twisting things around, plotting for contingencies and planning four moves ahead. For the first time she saw Janice not as a child she had saved from the Village House but as an adult who had survived the better part of a year in the midst of that madness. And Bethany remembered their departure, too—not the teenager's tears at her uncle's suicide, but the unbothered confidence with which she had smashed Wayne over the head with a lead pipe.

Bethany made a mental note not to provoke her.

"Time to eat," said Tia Christina.

How many times had she visited this apartment, smelled the grease, laid out the cutlery, sat on the sofa, and watched television while Annabelle rubbed her aunt's gnarled feet? There had been periods in Bethany's life, and many of them, when Tia Christina's place felt more like home than Virginia, where the spider's web of social and racial expectations had trapped far too many of the kids she had grown up with into a helpless yet fiercely defended immobility in which lack of initiative was taken as respect for authority, and lack of curiosity as adherence to tradition.

Sitting here tonight at Tia's table, Bethany could almost imagine that the last couple of years had never happened, that the dark, slight, nervous girl sitting across, stuffing herself with the most wondrous chicken on the face of the earth, was not a teenager she had rescued from the Village House, but her old running buddy Annabelle, healthy and happy and tossing off thrilling, improbable ideas for fixing politics, or the economy, or just New York City; and that after dinner, as Tia slept, the two of them would wash the dishes, after which Annabelle would beg Bethany to go clubbing with her, and the evening would end with Bethany rejecting some young investment banker and heading back to Tia's place while her running buddy did quite the opposite. In the morning, in Annabelle's absence, Bethany and Tia would have a strained breakfast together, the old woman silently reproaching the younger for not protecting her wild niece.

As she hadn't protected her from Martin; and whoever else was out there.

Dinner was noisy. They sat at the far end of the table so that they could see the television in the crowded, overly ornate living room, plush furniture burdened with the custom-made plastic slipcovers that every immigrant of a certain age seemed to buy. The first verse of the Twenty-third Psalm, King James Version, hung in a gilt frame. Photographs of Annabelle at various ages hung nearby. None showed her in Gopo gray. *Jeopardy* was on, the sound turned way up in order to compete with the useless air conditioner that rumbled and blatted in the window. The sash was also open, because nothing could persuade Tia Christina that she should not leave the hot air a way to escape. From down in the street came the constant rumble of traffic, the endless cry of recognition or fury or threat from one human being to the next, and the intermittent yowl of sirens as police cars and fire trucks hurried toward the latest disaster.

Bethany, working on her second helping, proved to be a poor companion for watching *Jeopardy*. She was appalled at how much knowledge she lacked about vice presidents and film actors whose first and last names begin with the same letter. Janice, on the other hand, seemed to know every fact ever unearthed in the history of man. Tia could scarcely conceal her delight, and by the time dinner was over and they had moved along the L-shaped room to the living area, turning the television around on its swivel to watch *Wheel of Fortune*, the teen was on the sofa, snuggled into Tia's encompassing warmth, and the clasp of the old woman's powerful arms around her slight frame seemed, for a precious moment, to free them both from their grief. And Bethany, who would have expected to feel a pang of jealousy, was infused instead with an almost luxuriant relief.

Love was still possible amidst the ruins.

While Janice dozed, Bethany rubbed Tia Christina's feet the way Annabelle used to, and finally backed into the true purpose of her visit.

"We haven't really spoken since the funeral," said Bethany. "It was a beautiful service."

"Very beautiful," Tia murmured. Her eyes were closed but Bethany could feel her attention tauten like a vortex.

"I thought the eulogy was wonderful."

"Mmmm-hmmm."

"So many people loved Annabelle so much."

Tia grimaced, her small, dark face remarkably unlined, as though, like Merlin, she youthened instead of aging. Her chin was knobby. "God always seems to take them early. The ones we love best."

Bethany licked her lips, for the proposition was empirical and, she thought, in principle falsifiable. Had this been, say, Annabelle, she would have argued. For the sheer fun of it. But it was Tia, who inhabited a different plane of existence. "Yes, He does," she murmured.

"Not the potter but the potter's clay," Tia murmured.

"True."

"Do the other one."

"Sure." Eight decades on the earth had left Tia's feet leathery and twisted and cool. Bethany felt the urgent need to warm them, as though their low temperature presaged impending death. "You know, Tia, somebody told me that Annabelle found a new man a few months ago."

Tia made a very West Indian sound, a cross between a laugh and a sniffle, a sliding of tongue over teeth in disapproval. "That girl always had a new man."

Bethany glanced at Janice. "This one's name was Martin."

"She never mentioned no Martin to me."

"I think he lives in Chicago."

That snort again. "Is that where she was all that time? All that girl ever told me was that she had to go away for a while. As a *favor.* For a *friend.*"

Bethany took a long chance. "Maybe this Martin asked her to come see him?"

"No, child. That was the favor. To go talk to some man. She said it might take awhile."

Bethany knew she had pressed as far as she dared. She still believed that Annabelle had wanted her to come here. She just wasn't sure why. Still, she did not want to rouse Tia's suspicion. Tia possessed no education to speak of but she was no fool, and if Annabelle's best friend asked too many questions about Martin and Chicago, the time would come when Tia would ask questions back. So, still rubbing the old woman's feet, she covered the card with others from the deck, sharing the old stories about the old days. She asked about Annabelle's vanished mother, and about her father, the Russian, Vassily, who had fled. Tia retold a funny story about the two of them together, Dolores so tiny, Vassily so tall, trying to dance a slow number.

Then Tia said, "My Annabelle told me you have a new man, too, child."

"Me?"

"Some kind of African prince or something. She said you won the lottery, too."

Bethany shook her head, unable to make anything of this, wondering whether Tia was talking in her sleep.

And then she noticed. "What's that?"

Tia's eyes were half shut. "What's what, child?"

Janice's head popped up. "What's what?" she echoed sleepily.

Bethany nodded toward the side table. Several pieces of jewelry were lying in a clump.

"Janice," Bethany said, still rubbing Tia's feet, "would you mind handing me that bracelet?"

The teen did. Gold. Handmade. WWJD.

Tia smiled. "She made it for me. Annabelle made it. She was in a class. Therapy. I don't even think it's real gold."

"It's very pretty," said Janice.

"It is," said Bethany, remembering its mate. "Tia?"

"Yes, child?"

"Could I maybe borrow it for a few days?"

Soon after, Tia fell asleep, breathing so softly that Bethany had to lean in close to make sure. She and Janice lifted the old woman, more feathery than she expected, carried her to the back bedroom, and tucked her gently in. Bethany expected Tia to open her eyes and impart some final bit of wisdom, but Tia slumbered on. Unaccountably depressed, Bethany led the teen back to the kitchen.

"Why do you need the bracelet?" asked Janice as they washed dishes. "Wait. Let me guess. You can't tell me."

"Sorry."

"I'm used to it." A theatrical sigh. "Anyway, she's really sweet. I wish she was my aunt."

"She's wonderful," Bethany agreed.

"And she's the one who raised Annabelle?"

"Pretty much. She and her husband—he's dead now—took her in after her mother went back to Panama."

"I wish she was my aunt," Janice repeated as they finished up the kitchen.

"I know, honey," said Bethany, distractedly. Most of her mind was engaged in doing her sums. The story Tia told plus Bethany's own knowledge added up to a simple fact: Annabelle hadn't stumbled into the Village House by accident. She had gone to Chicago in search of Martin and the Planners. She had done it as a favor, Tia said—meaning someone had sent her.

That meant that there must be, somewhere, a human being who had recruited Annabelle, briefed her, dispatched her on her mission. And who might that be? She remembered what Fuentes had said after her interrogation: *What possible purpose could be served by bringing you here? Find the answer to that, and you will know who tried to kidnap you.*

Bethany had been manipulated at every turn. Was it too much to imagine that whoever was doing the manipulating had also sent Annabelle?

The Pilate Stone, she reminded herself. Find the Pilate Stone, and she'd have the answer.

"What do we do now?" Janice asked.

Bethany dried the roasting pan and crouched to put it away beneath the counter. Tia always slid the pots in smoothly, but Bethany, as usual, made an enormous clatter. She took down the address book that Tia kept in a cubby beside the refrigerator and leafed through to find the number she wanted.

"Where are we going next?" Janice persisted. "We can't stay here. We could get Tia in trouble."

"We're not staying here," said Bethany. "We're going to find a motel over in New Jersey and get some sleep."

"What are we doing tomorrow?"

"You're spending the afternoon at the library."

Janice stiffened. "Why?"

That was when the telephone started ringing.

Bethany stared at the instrument, a bit stupidly, not sure what to do.

"Maybe we should answer it," said Janice.

"If somebody's listening—"

"If it keeps ringing, it'll wake Tia."

The ringing stopped.

"I guess it already did," said Bethany.

"Why do I have to go to the library?" Janice asked again.

"There's some research to do. Somebody I have to find."

"Oh. I shouldn't." Voice suddenly small. "Do research, I mean. I mean, I'm not really allowed."

Bethany took this to be a holdover of some weird bit of Village House protocol. "You'll be fine, honey." Scrubbing the counters. "His name is Sam DeMarco. He won't be living under that name. He's in Ohio. Most likely in or near Ashland. It's supposed to be hush-hush, but when he moved it was kind of an open secret in Flint Hill that he was going to Ashland."

"I can't. I'm not supposed to."

"It's fine. You'll be fine." She didn't say the rest: that there was no way Janice would ever find a protected witness by searching on line, but the assignment would give her something to do, and in a safe place.

Janice's slim brown face was close to tears. "Please. I'm not supposed to. I'm really not." Turning her hands out as if warding off some danger. "Can't you do it?"

"I can't, honey. I'm going to be busy. This is how you can help."

The teen digested this. "Busy doing what?"

Before she could answer, Tia Christina was shouting for Bethany.

By name.

Bethany was in the bedroom in two seconds.

"What is it? What's wrong?"

Tia was sitting up in bed, shaking her head, holding out the receiver.

"It's Polly. She's upset. You talk to her."

"What?"

"I can't understand what she's saying. You talk."

"Tia, I can't—"

"Talk," she ordered, and handed over the phone.

"Polly?" said Bethany, voice tentative, terrified that half the world was listening in even though she knew it was unlikely: she had given nobody probable cause for a warrant on either Tia's phone or Polly's.

"You!" Polly snarled, and then was weeping again, weeping and crying, cursing and accusing. From the torrent of abuse, Bethany was able at last to distill the basic facts; and what she learned chilled her to the bone.

Polly's husband David was dead.

He had been shot, apparently by a robber, while on a fishing trip. His body was found near a cabin in Virginia. A famous conservative pastor, a friend of many years standing, was found beside him.

FORTY-SIX

This doesn't make any sense," says Carl Carraway, standing on the promontory looking out over the dark flat water. Behind him is the frenetic activity of a crime scene where the victims matter to people of power: bright lights and loud generators, orders shouted, forensic teams trampling this way and that. "There's no reason for it."

Pulu has his arms crossed. "David Hollins rented the place. We know Bethany Barclay snuck over to the campus last week to see him. So far as we know, he's the last person who saw her before she took off for the Village House. Stands to reason he'd be the first person she'd look up when she left."

"They were having an affair?" asks Carraway.

"I'm thinking more like coconspirators."

Carl shakes his head. Since the failed raid in Chicago, he is still, formally, deputy head of the task force, but two other special agents have been made, in effect, co-deputies. Vanner told him that a formal reprimand would go in his record for his unauthorized visit to Ted Lesofsky. She didn't ask him what they had talked about. When Carraway offered to share part of what he'd learned, Vanner shut him down. It was outside the rules, and so, in her bureaucratic mind, irrelevant.

But he hasn't been fired and he isn't headed for Kuala Lumpur.

Pulu isn't finished. "The other victim. This Norval Jamison. He's a big Christian activist. Very conservative. We're thinking she's part of a group of extremists, right? Well, his group sure fits the bill."

"Jamison's people do politics. They wouldn't do something like this."

"You're the one who doesn't like coincidences."

"He'll be in surgery all night. If he pulls through, we can ask him."

Pulu's laugh is gruff. "One in the chest and one in the head. The chances that he'll pull through are pretty slim."

Another agent comes over. Pulu excuses himself, walks a few feet away, listens. Then he is back.

"There's evidence that somebody came up from the water," he says. "Maybe left that way, too. And tracks from at least three, maybe four cars other than the one still in the driveway."

Carl doesn't answer. He is thinking about conspiracies, and Ted Lesofsky's parting note. Annabelle would have made copies of whatever was in her backpack, in case she went under a bus. That was Ted's point. Annabelle would have made copies and—

And left them for Bethany to find.

He turns to Pulu. "I think we need to talk to the grieving widow."

Bethany Barclay and Peter Zhukov met at the same Russian Orthodox Church they had used for their escape last time, and it occurred to her as she stepped into the drafty nave that he might have dragged her through it for this very reason: so that when one of his people told her that he would meet her "at the church," she would know what church he meant.

The interior was largely in shadow. The overhead lights were mostly off. Candles flickered in front of the icons. In the gloom, an immense bearded man intercepted her. He put a hand up, signaling stop, and for a bad moment she thought he meant to frisk her. But he only glanced over her shoulder, and when she turned, she saw a woman of indeterminate age shaking her head: the same woman, come to think of it, who had been behind her for the last two blocks.

"You are not followed," the giant said.

"Glad to hear it."

He led her to a pew and told her to wait, then vanished into the sacristy. Orthodox churches in the Eastern Rite frowned on pews, she knew, and she understood the argument: if the Savior could hang on a cross for a whole day for us, can we not stand for an hour or two for Him? But a growing number were installing at least a little seating for parishioners unprepared or unable to remain on their feet, and this one had a few benches, well off to the side. As her eyes became accustomed to the darkness, she was able to make out another man, more fat than muscular, across the aisle.

She shook her head and dropped her eyes. David was dead. Who on earth would kill David? It couldn't possibly be a coincidence. Annabelle, then her brother-in-law, confidant, and maybe more.

Poor Polly. Small wonder she blamed—

"I wondered if you would come back," said Peter from behind.

She turned wearily, less impressed than he probably meant her to be. "Just if? Not when?"

He looked her up and down. "Listen, I am happy you have survived, okay?"

Bethany no longer felt the need to fence with him. A week on the run had changed her, and Peter's orange eyes said he knew it, for they seemed to reflect a genuine respect. And so she was direct. "I've been to see Tia Christina. This is the bracelet Annabelle gave her. It matches the one you're wearing."

"So you saw Tia, huh? Look, she's one tough lady. You tell her I said hello. Tell her, anything she needs, okay?"

Bethany refused to be sidetracked. "You said Annabelle only made one of these. Turns out she made two. This is the gift you were expecting me to bring last time."

Peter's smile was rueful. "You understand I had no choice but to refuse you. I made a promise to my sister. Promises are sacred. Promises to family, more so."

"I've given you the bracelet. You're supposed to give me whatever she gave you to hold for her."

Peter seemed to take a very long time answering, although in actual fact it could not have been more than a minute or two. "How did you know Tia Christina had it?" he finally said.

"Annabelle left me a message. Indirectly. On a tape that I—never mind. Just tell me what she left."

"Duplicates. She said the papers were duplicates."

"Of what?"

"Of the originals she kept with her." He nodded to the fat man across the aisle, who retrieved a heavy package from somewhere, walked across the aisle, handed it to Peter, then returned to his post. Peter's pudgy fingers gripped the package. He studied the duct tape wrapped around the paper, then handed it over. "I have not looked. You'll have to take my word for it."

"I believe you."

"You were a good friend to her. She loved you."

"She loved you, too. You were a good brother."

He escorted her out to the street. "Maybe I have one of my people drive you back to Manhattan, okay?"

"No, thank you."

"This way he'll know if anybody is following you."

"I'll be fine."

"Tia's well? You had a good visit?"

She didn't answer; but a man like Peter Zhukov could read the mute self-horror in her face.

"And these papers will help you to avenge my sister?" Peter asked.

"They'll help me track down the people who killed her and . . . and framed me."

"And then you will contact me? So that I can speak to the man of influence, and punish the insult to his honor?"

Again Bethany had no answer to offer. They shook hands.

"Peter, wait."

His eyes played over her face as though searching for clues. "Yes?"

"May I ask you one more thing?"

"Please." Peter stroked his goatee as if he had just discovered it. "Ask me one more thing."

Careful, Bethany. Careful. "There was a . . . a killing in Chicago." Peter said nothing. A curt nod as the afternoon sun glistened from his buttery hair, now flecked with gray. "It would have required several men to do it." Another pause but still he waited for her to come to him. She felt the suspicious stares of Russians passing on either side. "The woman who was killed . . . I was wondering if you think she might have had something to do with your sister? Is that why she's dead?"

"If you are asking me about the activities of the man of influence, he does not confide in me." Raising a hand to forestall her protest. "If you are asking me if the man of influence could have done this thing? If you are asking if his reach extends so far?" Peter lifted his hand, palm down, the same familiar gesture Annabelle had made so many times. Slowly he tilted it, this way, that way, sunlight glinting from his rings. "I would not be able to say, okay? Not for sure."

"You could make an educated guess."

"So could you, okay?"

"What I'm trying to say is, the people Annabelle was with in Chicago—they weren't great people, but I don't think they meant her any harm. If you are in touch with the man of influence, please let him know that he's going after the wrong people."

"He doesn't ask my opinion, okay? Or yours."

Peter didn't bother with a second good-bye.

FORTY-SEVEN

The motel was in New Jersey, near the Delaware Water Gap. They stayed away from chains, where their insistence on paying cash might raise flags, but looked for places that were at least half full, so that they wouldn't stand out. This particular motel was tumbledown and nearly deserted, a good four miles off the Interstate, and therefore didn't fit the profile. On the other hand, the place catered to the sort of customers who preferred to park their cars around back where passing friends or spouses wouldn't see them from the street. Besides, Bethany and Janice were exhausted and not a little frightened, and the package from Peter Zhukov could wait no longer.

"Can't I look, too?" Janice grumbled. The teen lay in one of the lumpy twin beds. Bethany sat beside her.

"No, honey."

"Come on. I went on the computer all day for you."

"And I'm grateful. But I need to read this myself. And you need to catch up on your rest."

"Don't you want to hear what I found out?"

"Tomorrow, honey. You sleep."

To their mutual surprise, she did, shutting her eyes and dropping off immediately. Bethany seated herself at the unsteady desk. Her view was of the parking lot, and that was the view she wanted, because if police cruisers showed up, they would have a few extra seconds of warning to rush out the back.

The package was thick, and sealed, and taped over at various crazy angles. Annabelle had signed her name three times in three different directions, sloping across the paper onto the tape and back again. Slitting the envelope felt like a slur on her memory.

Inside Bethany found several magazines and photocopies and printouts of Web pages. A quick glance told her that these were about the real or imaginary Pilate Stone. She leafed through. Speculations and guesswork. Not a hard fact to be found, other than the facts she'd heard from poor David Hollins when she visited him at Bryn Mawr. Claims that the Stone had been "moved secretly from one monastery to the next during the Dark Ages" or "smuggled out of Europe, at enormous risk, during the Second World War" evoked colorful images, but gave no actual clue as to its whereabouts—or even whether it existed. An advertisement Annabelle had downloaded from some obscure corner of the Web promised, for a fee, to send an actual piece of the Stone, guaranteed to cure your illness. Did her running buddy, she wondered, actually believe any of this stuff, or did she squirrel these nuggets away for cover? Annabelle wasn't well at the end, the newspapers had suggested. Who knew what horrors life on the run had perpetrated?

Bethany put the articles aside and delved further. She found three legal-sized white envelopes, helpfully if oddly labeled in her running buddy's hand: *Open me first*. Okay. *Open me second, but not the same day*. Hmmm. *Open me only in an emergency.*

"Sorry, honey," Bethany murmured to the air. "But this counts as an emergency."

Nevertheless, she opened the first envelope first. It was thick and heavy as a brick. She reached in and pulled out money: hundred dollar bills, and lots of them. A quick count told her that she was holding twenty thousand dollars. *And the thesis, Ms. Barclay, is what?* asked Delavan, in her head. The thesis, she answered, was that Annabelle had learned from Bethany herself the importance of stashing mad money everywhere. Although it was a little strange that she would hide it with Peter, who would gladly have given his sister ten times that for the asking.

In the middle of the bills was a handwritten note: *If you're reading this, I guess I'm dead, huh?*

Bethany gasped. Maybe it was the surprise that did it; maybe the teasing tone; maybe the playful *huh?* Whatever the reason, the energy and adrenalin drained out of her, and for the first time since fleeing her home on the night Ken Kirkland was butchered, she put her head down on her arms and, quite helplessly, wept.

And slept.

The Church Builder's face was ashen. He sat in his favorite seat in the archives, but the familiar dusty bookish surroundings failed to rouse within him the energy or confidence of years past.

"I don't understand," he said for the fifth or fiftieth time. "Why would they do it? Why break the truce like this?"

The Mathematician sat across from him. On the table between them were the records of the Builder's luckless predecessor, the Singer, and, before him, the Poet. The head of the Garden was expected to make journal entries no less often than weekly. The records were kept in the traditional manner, cardboard folders tied with ribbon. Again, there were no digitized copies anywhere. They had divided up the pages, to be sure they'd missed no act of violence against the leadership. But the Mathematician's memory proved correct. The last time the Wilderness killed a leader of the Garden was nearly forty years ago.

"It doesn't make any sense," the Builder was saying. "They have nothing to gain. Absolutely nothing."

"You've said it yourself," said the Mathematician. "We don't know who's in charge over there. The generations change. So do the methods. For whatever reason, they've grown less patient. That might make them careless in the long run, but in the short run it makes them dangerous. Not to the church. To us, to our physical selves." Trying, and failing, to get a rise out of his friend. "That makes it even more vital that we see the operation to its conclusion."

All through the conversation the Builder's head had been buried in the journal as he continues to turn the pages. Now he looked up. "What? Don't be ridiculous. We have to stand down."

"We can't do that."

"There are six of us left, George. I'll risk my own life but not the lives of you and the others. The Garden must stand down, and the Wilderness must see us stand down. Let them see us regroup, take time to reflect. They have to believe that we're frightened. That we're no danger to them."

The Mathematician was astonished. "This isn't you talking."

"It's exactly me talking. I approved this operation. But look at the cost. Annabelle Seaver gone. The Critic gone. The Pastor and Bethany Barclay as good as gone. Put it all on my account. But count the cost. How many bodies is it worth to us to find out the identities of the leaders of the Wilderness?"

"We have to know who's in charge over there. We have to know whom we're fighting."

"And we will."

"How? If we stand down?"

The Builder's fingers slipped along the volumes they had been reading together. "The rest of you are to stand down. The operation will become my sole responsibility."

"That's a terrible idea. The others would agree."

"Nevertheless, it is what we are going to do. This is not a question for the group. This is my prerogative. I will use my own resources and connections to locate Bethany Barclay. I owe her that."

"We owe her that."

"No. The decision was mine, George. As is the responsibility. I will find her, and I will allow her the option. I know that's what the group wants. I shall lay the choices before her. She can come out now if she wants, and we'll do what we can to restore her life. Or she can stay in and help find whatever Annabelle Seaver left for us." Slowly, slowly, the color and vigor were returning to his face. "The rest of you will stand down. The Garden must be preserved. Go back underground if you need to. The resources are there. I alone will take the risk."

The Mathematician managed a sad smile. "You're a little old to be playing hero."

The Builder's voice was deadly serious. "This isn't heroics, George. It's duty."

"There's too much for one man. Too much we don't know. Where Annabelle went. Who killed her. Why they killed David and tried to kill Norval. For that matter, why Janice Stafford's FBI file is so tightly sealed that not even the Senator can get in. You can't possibly think you can answer all those questions on your own?"

"I'm surprised at you, George. Isn't it written that with God all things are possible?"

"It's also written that you shall not put your God to the test."

The Builder was on his feet. Age and health notwithstanding, the aura of combat was in the air. Then his shoulders sagged. "Look around us, George. Look at the archives. Yes, there are chunks missing, but we have eight hundred years of history in this room. The Garden has survived a long time. If I'm making a mistake, it will surely survive my leadership." He straightened. "In any case, I'm not changing my mind. I expect you and the others to accept my decision."

Carl Carraway is in the bullpen, the sparkling lights of Washington across the river. In the morning, he and Pulu will head up to Philadelphia to interview Polly Hollins. He should be home catching up on his sleep. The rest of the task force has quit for the night. But not Carl. Home has been a dangerous place for him of late. He would never admit even to himself how loneliness chases him back to the office. So here he is, back at his desk, still hard at work.

He has left a message for Janet Anders, in the hope that the lab might have recovered something from the notebook, and now sits in front of his monitor, wearing earphones, listening to the tapes that were captured when the Village House was raided. He finds the spot he's looking for, clicks on the PLAY arrow.

"Why are you so nervous, Bethany?"

"I'm not."

"Your hands are trembling."

"It's late. I'm tired."

"But you weren't resting. You were in the basement. Some of my advisers—Mr. Fuentes, for one—are wondering why you're here. If somebody might have sent you."

He stops the playback. The analysts are divided on the significance of this part of the session. Some think it shows that Bethany had no knowledge of the basement. Others argue that she knew perfectly well that there were bombs, and that Martin was chastising her for going *back* into the basement. And then there are those—Vanner prominent among them—who contend that the tapes themselves are fakes, evidence of Bethany's innocence to be found by the government in the event of a raid, so that she can continue her rampage undisturbed.

Carl makes a note, presses PLAY.

"A man was killed in my house—"

"And you got away. That's the point Mr. Fuentes makes. Police are looking for you everywhere. The FBI, because they know you've crossed state lines, and because of these bombings. Everyone's looking for you, Bets, yet somehow you've slipped the net. And Mr. Fuentes, who has some experience in these matters, says that isn't so easy to do these days. He wonders whether it's possible that somebody arranged for you to slip the net."

Again he stops the recording. Rewinds. Plays that last line.

"He wonders whether it's possible that somebody arranged for you to slip the net."

Of course. Say the tapes are genuine. Then Martin wasn't covering for her. He was suspicious of her. He genuinely thought she was working for the Bureau; or for whomever he feared more than the Bureau.

Carraway leans back in the chair, folds his hands behind his head, gazes up at the drop ceiling. Whoever put her in motion planned beautifully. Nobody will trust her. The government thinks that she's a conspirator, the conspirators think she's with the government. The goal has to be to keep her in motion. That means this isn't about the bombing: that's secondary. She's an unwilling agent, on a quest she herself doesn't understand, but forced at every turn to stay on the path.

And if whoever is manipulating her wants her to keep moving, it only makes sense that there has to be—

Somebody watching her.

Alert again, reaches for the telephone. He could bring up the interrogation transcripts and do a keyword search, but he isn't sure how he'd phrase it; besides, there were times when the old ways were just better.

"You're kidding," says Jake Pulu. "You're calling me now?"

"Bad time?"

"My wife and I are out together to dinner for the first time in over a month, so I'm going to go with yes."

"I'm sorry," says Carl.

"You have a way of forgetting that some of us have lives."

"Never mind. It'll keep until tomorrow."

A beat.

"Fine," says Pulu. "She's already mad at me for stepping outside to take the call. Might as well tell me what you want."

"You've studied the transcripts of the interrogations of the detainees from the Village House. You know them better than anybody."

"Go on."

"I'm just wondering. The day Bethany Barclay showed up. Were there any other new arrivals? People nobody knew?"

"No."

"The day after?"

"No. There was one guy who showed up two days before she did. He got VIP treatment. His own room, never hung out with the group. Nobody knows what happened to him, or even if he was there when the raid went down. He showed up, then he disappeared. One woman said she'd heard he was a cousin of some big donor, hiding out from the debt collectors."

"Is that consistent?"

"Sure. Even before Bethany Barclay, people would show up there from time to time to hide out, and Martin would take them in. He always talked about his obligation, but from our examination of the books, it looks like the hiding out occasionally involved major contributions to the coffers."

"Do we have a name? A description?"

"Nobody paid close enough attention. Caucasian. Tall. Intelligent. Dark hair with a streak of white. Kind of distant. Not unpleasant, but kept to himself. Oh, there was one other thing. He had a nickname. Somebody heard Daniel Stafford use it, and it just stuck."

"What was the nickname?"

"The Professor."

"Is that what he was? A professor?"

"No way to know, Carl. Can I go back to dinner now?"

"Maybe we should work up a sketch."

"I doubt we have enough of the detainees still in custody, but I'll see what I can do. Tomorrow." Emphasizing the last word.

"Thanks, Jake. Go back to dinner."

Alone with his thoughts, Carraway rubs tired eyes, then leans back and looks out at the familiar view that never fails to exhilarate: the Washington Monument with its blinking red lights, the Capitol dome in the distance.

The Professor.

"I'll find you." Carl is unaware that he is speaking aloud. "I'll find you before you find her. That's a promise."

FORTY-EIGHT

Fear was a new experience for Stuart Van Der Staal. He found the sensation fascinating. He was sitting in a rented car on the third level of the short-term parking garage at Bradley International Airport in Hartford, Connecticut. Both of his mobile phones were on the dashboard. Both of his hands were on the wheel, in plain sight. The car was in the first row, facing the terminal, and therefore away from traffic in the garage, and he was required to keep his eyes to the front. Still, using the mirror, he had already spotted the dark sports utility vehicle as it pulled into a space two rows back. He knew it was the one he was waiting for because the one person who had so far emerged had immediately melted into the shadows of the garage, as Stuart himself would have done were the roles reversed. Whoever was still inside was the contact, but he—or she—wouldn't climb out until assured that the meeting was unobserved.

Stuart watched the lights of a plane clawing swiftly upward into the darkness. It was almost nine, and outgoing flights would soon be shutting down for the night. The garage was open twenty-four hours, but it was unlikely that a security patrol would stumble upon—

Well, upon whatever was about to happen.

His hands were trembling. That was new, too. Of course the professor well understood that the response resulted from a chemical imbalance as his body tried to dump the right substances into the bloodstream to allow him to flee or put up a fight. It irritated him that the possibility that he rather than others might suddenly cease to perceive and be perceived would cause him quite so much terror. Still, the knowledge of how those he held under his gun might feel could be useful. He focused on that: Use these emotions to improve your own work.

The door of the SUV opened, and Stuart went very still. Not one but two men stepped out, and he knew that if he was to be executed, they were his executioners. They walked toward his car, staying very wide of each other, so that even should he change his mind and shoot one, the other would kill him before he could shift his aim. And even if he were to get them both, there was still the other man out there, invisible in the shadows.

The men arrived at opposite sides of the car. One of them leaned over and rapped on the driver's side window.

Stuart lifted a hand from the dash, very slowly, and pushed the button to lower the glass. When he looked up, he was staring at the barrel of a gun.

"Keep your eyes on me," the man said. The gun was in the folds of his coat. Anybody who drove past would think they were chatting. "If you turn your head or look in the mirror, I'll kill you."

The professor said nothing. He nodded.

"Don't say anything unless asked a direct question."

He nodded again.

The back door opened. Stuart sat very still. Someone climbed in. The car shifted. The back door closed.

A moment of silence, the gun never wavering.

"We're very disappointed," said the man behind him. The voice was aged yet powerful, the tone belonging to a man accustomed to public speaking and plenty of applause. It was a low, rounded voice, belonging to a heavy man. "You didn't follow your instructions, Professor Van Der Staal. Such impudence disturbs me. I wanted to meet you personally to see for myself what sort of fool decides to upset centuries of planning on a whim. Or is it just that you're so in love with the killing that you don't understand what we mean when we tell you that particular people are not to be harmed?"

Stuart realized that he had been asked a direct question. No longer worried about dying, he was now fascinated by the logistics. The gun in his face was a clever touch. He'd have to borrow the method sometime.

"They saw my face," he said.

The man behind him was unimpressed. "We're reasonable people," he said. "We're at war with irrationality, but we ourselves are reasonable. People do die sometimes. We wish that could be helped, but it can't. We harm as few as possible, but we are doing battle against the far larger harm, to the society and to the world, that comes about when the minds of millions of the ignorant are poisoned by delusions of supernatural beings, the afterlife, and all the rest of that nonsense that you presumably reject every bit as firmly as we do. Your fate is a triviality when compared with the larger battlefield. Do you understand?"

"I do, but—"

"'I do' will suffice, Professor. This is not an argument or a negotiation. It is a statement of our position. You are an impatient man. Often unpredictable. That makes you dangerous to such an organization as ours. You count the days of your life, but we count the centuries of our struggle against the Enemy." The professor noted the capitalization in the tone of voice. "Naturally you take a certain risk, but that is irrelevant. You are well compensated, and the degree of your risk is priced into the contract. Therefore you cannot cite the risk of exposure as an excuse for violating our instructions. That is not a reasonable position to hold. Do you understand me?"

"I do," he said, itching to turn but staring at the gun.

"We hired you for two reasons, Professor. First, because you have an unparalleled record of success. Second, because of our common beliefs. But neither one will matter if we are unable to rely on you to do as you're told. We work out our plans with enormous care. Your impulsiveness cannot be allowed to destroy the work of centuries. If you will not follow our instructions, Professor, then you are worse than useless to us. You actually make our task harder. When you do not do as you are told, you, you yourself, actually advance the Enemy's cause. If you worked in my firm, you would already have been dismissed. But the unique combination of your skills and your beliefs is not easily obtainable in the market. Do you understand me?"

"I do."

It occurred to Stuart that the man behind him was from very high up in the councils of his client—possibly the very top. It was plain from his cadences, from the proprietary way he spoke of his unnamed organization, and from the elaborate precautions they had taken. Until now, he had dealt only with intermediaries, several times removed from his actual clients. It was about time they sent an emissary of genuine worth.

"The Enemy is clever. Don't ever make the mistake of thinking otherwise. The fact that their beliefs are irrational doesn't mean that they themselves are stupid. Over the past few decades, we have avoided direct confrontation, and thereby lulled them into complacency. They seem less and less concerned about hiding their physical identities from us. Do you begin to see the point? Our recent history of not threatening them directly arose from a conscious choice on our part. We now know several of those who run the Enemy's operations. They know nobody who runs ours. But once they decide that their lives are at risk, they will retreat from their relatively high prominence. They will assemble a new board, unknown to us, and we will lose what we have gained. Do you understand me?"

"I do."

"I am going to share with you information of which you are not aware. Annabelle Seaver was sent out as part of a plan of the Enemy's. She was pretending to search for a relic that is of interest to us, but in actual fact her purpose was to draw us out, so that the Enemy might learn some of our identities. We realized too late what she was doing. We took certain measures to protect ourselves, but she had already succeeded in part. And then of course she died. That complicated matters considerably. Unfortunately, we have not managed to recover whatever records she compiled of her investigations. From here on, no goal is more important. Do you understand?"

"I do."

"Do you wish to continue in our employ?"

The professor stared at the gun barrel. "I do."

"Then you will finish this project, but without remuneration. Do you understand me?"

"I do."

"Listen carefully. I have new instructions for you. You will reacquire your quarry and follow the instructions precisely. No deviation of any kind will be tolerated. Do you understand me?"

"I do."

"This is difficult for me. Getting away from my responsibilities for a meeting like this. You have caused us a good deal of trouble. Consider yourself on probation. Do you understand me?"

"I do."

The instructions took ten minutes. When he was done, the man in the backseat simply climbed out and shut the door. Stuart continued to stare into the gun, because the man at the window didn't budge. For another two minutes, they remained in the same positions. Then the black SUV pulled up beside his car. The gunman stepped back, his weapon still trained on the professor. The door was pushed open from inside. The gunman climbed in, and the car sped away.

The professor immediately pulled out a notebook and wrote down his impressions. The make and model of the car, the green sticker on the rear window, the tiny scrape in the rear passenger-side fender. The type of gun and the face of the gunman. The cadences of the man who sat in the back. The fact that he sounded over seventy but active and busy. That he had responsibilities from which it was difficult to get away. That he ran some sort of firm. That he was heavyset: Stuart could tell from the way the car settled when he sat. Most of all, that Annabelle had squirreled away the records of the identities of at least a part of the leadership of the group that employed him. And they had no idea where those records were.

It wasn't much, but it was a start. Professor Stuart Van Der Staal did not like being threatened. As far as Stuart was concerned, his client was on probation, too.

And there was something else.

Speaking of Annabelle, the man sitting behind him had said: *And then she died.* Said it with disappointment. Annabelle had died, and therefore Stuart's client had been unable to make her tell them where she had hidden her records. That meant that his client hadn't killed her.

There was another player in the game; a very brutal one.

FORTY-NINE

The second of Annabelle's envelopes lay on the rickety table. *Open me second, but not the same day.*

Bethany's nap was over. It was past midnight but she had no intention of turning in. She hefted the envelope in her hand. Squeezed. Two sheets of folded paper. Maybe three. She glanced at Janice. Still asleep. She crossed to the minibar, removed a bottle of lukewarm water, and returned to the desk. She hesitated, then took up the scissors. Under the circumstances, she reasoned, waking from her nap counted the same as waiting until tomorrow.

She slit open the envelope.

And struck gold.

Okay, so you couldn't wait. I guess if I'm dead I can't be offended, huh? Have you figured it out yet? Are they after you? Or maybe you haven't even found this yet. It's so so so so dangerous out here. It's hard to sort out which part is the truth and which part is the lie and which part my head is making up for me. My head is making up a lot. I might be using again. I'm not sure. I don't remember. I've been out of the country. Now I'm back. Maybe you haven't figured it out. Maybe you're not even looking. Too bad, because I'm going to tell Pyotr to burn it if you don't show up by the Fourth of July. And now you're wondering why I picked that date. What does it signify? Is it a clue? Sort of. I guess so. I'll come back to that. I have to get moving now because they

The first page just ended like that. Bethany took up the second. It turned out to be a two-page letter, apparently intended for her, one long paragraph with Annabelle's customary paucity of punctuation.

Okay. This is the story. I started out trying to save the world. I'm caught in between the good guys and the bad guys. I know how your mind works. You don't think there are good guys and bad guys. You think that people are a little bit of one thing and a little bit of another. You think it's all one big muddle. Well, it's not. I've seen both sides face-to-face. The good guys aren't necessarily the great guys, but the bad guys are really really really really bad. David came to me. Yes, that David, my sister's David, perfect David, David the genius, David the brilliant, David who Tia always adored and always asked me when I was going to find somebody like him and settle down. That David. He's one of the good guys. You can trust him. I know he seems kind of soft but he's only like that around my sister. Get him alone and you'll be surprised. Or at least I was surprised. But here's the thing. If something happens to me and you read this you need to go talk to David. You need to go now now now now. I don't care what time it is. There's a bunch of them and they're working together but David is the only one I know, so you have to call him . . .

Bethany wiped her eyes. This was getting ridiculous. If she was going to keep crying she'd never finish. So David had lied to her. All that talk about Annabelle telling him about the Pilate Stone: evidently the telling had gone the other way. Whatever her running buddy had been involved in, poor David had been up to his neck in it. But if Annabelle's master plan was for

Bethany to get in touch with David, then there was a rather serious glitch. Annabelle had planned carefully for her own death, but had made no provision for the murder of David Hollins.

But there were others, she said. David was part of a group. Maybe she could track down the rest.

> *. . . David is the only one I know, so you have to call him. You need to talk to David and you need to tell him so he can tell the rest of them. You need to tell him how far I got and you need to tell him that I didn't really betray them like betray. I just got myself into kind of a mess and I didn't know any other way out. Tell them I have two names. One of them for sure and one of them for not so sure. David said they don't have any names so two is a big improvement, huh? And one of the names is really going to surprise everybody. So I did my job. But then I got in trouble. They sent me out to attract the attention of the right people but I also attracted the attention of the wrong people. Tell them they messed up picking me. We all messed up. We forgot that there are other people who believe that the Stone is real and who'd like to have it for themselves. Not just the Wilderness but other people. I went to Chicago like they told me and I talked about it like they told me and I said I had leads and Martin wasn't interested in it but a couple of his people were and that's how I got started. You understand that, right? Martin wasn't interested. He's not part of the Wilderness. I mention this just in case you still want to ride off into the sunset with him or something. I'm sorry I won't be there to be maid of honor. Not that I'm a maid. And come to think of it I don't know if you know what the Wilderness is. I don't really know either except that they're the bad guys. David can tell you a lot more. He's really not so bad once you get him away from my sister. And she's not so bad either by the way. She'd do*

anything for me so I know she'd do anything for you too. You should go see her. I bet she can help you. She sure helped me. Because it wasn't just the Wilderness. Once I started talking about how I had a lead to the Stone other people tracked me down too. They wanted the Stone too. I had to give them something. I did what I had to do. The thing is I think they think maybe I cheated them. They're a little bit mad at me. Tell David I'm so so so so sorry. But I have two names. I guess I should say I had two names, since I'm not alive any more. Tell David. That's the most important thing of all. Two names. And if you're wondering why I don't mention them here it's because I don't know for sure if you're the one reading this. You could be Pyotr. That wouldn't be completely terrible. But you could also be the bad guys. And the two names aren't for them they're for David. David and the people he works for. But, honey, if it is you then look out for the Wilderness and look out for the other people who want that Stone. Maybe you heard that I met the wise man. He's a good man. But watch out for the Dread Serpent. You can't trust his best friend. You know what? Neither can he. But his best friend is one of them. And maybe you heard by now that you and your new boyfriend won the lottery. For a minute I thought I did too. I went out of the country and I went back to the beginning. I saw the wise man. I sent you the rest. I love you!

There Annabelle's note ended. No hint of where she might have hidden the names, or even who it was who'd contacted her and frightened her into doing a deal. But at least now Bethany knew, sort of, what her running buddy was up to. And she knew something else. She flipped back to the first page and reread what Annabelle had written about her sister:

And she's not so bad either by the way. She'd do anything

for me so I know she'd do anything for you too. You should go see her. I bet she can help you. She sure helped me.

This the sister who supposedly couldn't stand her. The sister who'd been so derisive toward Annabelle when Bethany visited the night after Ken Kirkland's murder. Pondering what this might mean, she took up the third envelope—

Bright blue-red flashers outside the window.

A police car was pulling up.

They never unpacked their bags and they always slept in their clothes. She roused Janice, who had only to slip into her shoes and grab her backpack. Sixty seconds from the moment Bethany spotted the police car they were out the door.

Too late.

There were two cruisers in the parking lot, and one was playing its searchlight along the motel's lower porch. Bethany grabbed Janice and pulled her behind a pillar as the beam passed. Their car was right there, directly in front of them, she had the keys in hand, and they dared not budge. Janice's slight form trembled against her. Bethany begged her silently not to whimper.

The light reached the far end of the platform and didn't circle back.

Bethany calculated the odds. The beam was so bright and sharp that it left everything else in gloom. This was their chance to run for the car, before the searchlight swung back their way.

The alternative was to sit where they were and wait to be arrested. Being arrested meant being returned to Virginia to face murder charges, with a federal bombing trial along the way. Annabelle's letters were in an inner pocket, pressing against her side. She would not fail her running buddy again.

"Get ready," she whispered, and felt more than saw Janice's answering nod. She shut her eyes briefly, but it was several seconds before she realized that she was praying. "Let's go," she said.

Bethany started to move, and that was when the hand snaked out of the darkness and grabbed her arm.

Instinct.

She responded just the way she had practiced on the self-defense course Sam DeMarco had made her take, turning into the hold and smacking the side of her hand against her assailant's ear. Only the blow never landed, because he blocked her wrist with the butt of a shotgun.

A state trooper.

In full riot gear.

"Hold still," he said. "Stop it. We're the good guys." He released her as she stood, staring, not sure what to say. "I think you ladies should get back in your room," he added.

"What?" Bethany blinked. "What did you say?"

"Let's go back in," said Janice, calmly, as the officer moved past them. "They're not here for us," she whispered.

As Janice tugged Bethany back toward their door, the police converged on the room outlined by the searchlight. A helmeted officer smashed the door with a battering ram. The others poured inside. There were shouts and commands and cries.

Minutes later, the police emerged, leading a couple of skinny, hapless, trembling kids in cuffs.

"Drug raid," said Janice, with the expert's authority.

"We should go anyway," murmured Bethany as the cuffed teenagers were thrust into the back seats of separate cruisers.

Janice gave a tight nod. "I'll say."

They got into the car, waited for the police to clear the lot; and, a few minutes later, followed.

FIFTY

That was close," says Bethany, still not sure nobody was following.

"Close?" The teen's laugh is unexpected, and warmly alive. "I've been in a lot worse. That was *fun*."

They are on Interstate 80 in Pennsylvania. Farmland and small night-washed towns roll past. The motel is a good ninety minutes behind them. They are headed for Ohio, and Sam DeMarco, her old shooting buddy, the only person she can think of who might be able to help her with the next and hardest step of her mad flight in Annabelle's wake. They are still driving Zach's Jetta. Bethany would prefer to abandon it, but trains and buses mean conductors and crowds, plenty of people who might have seen her picture on television. Besides, Janice says nobody knows yet whose car they have.

Her confidence is unnerving.

"What was in the package?" asks Janice.

"I'm still trying to figure it out. There's another envelope yet."

"What was in the first two?"

Bethany hesitates. She is not yet ready to open the third, because she has realized that Annabelle might have had good reason to warn her not to open it except in an emergency.

Like the possibility of chemical interrogation, say. She can't disclose what she doesn't know.

"We'll talk about it later, honey."

"But—"

"Later."

Janice scoots over to the window, rolls it down, rests her head on the sill. This is how she sulks. Bethany sighs. The teen has been behaving oddly since her jaunt to the library. Although it is difficult to know what normal behavior is supposed to be when you're on the run.

On the run. At least now Bethany is fairly clear that she is running toward, not running away.

Maybe you heard by now that you and your new boyfriend won the lottery. For a minute I thought I did too. I went out of the country and I went back to the beginning. I saw the wise man. I sent you the rest.

But she doesn't have a boyfriend and she's never played the lottery.

My Annabelle told me you have a new man, said Tia Christina. *Some kind of African prince or something. She said you won the lottery, too.*

Forget the intermediate part. Whether Annabelle won the lottery, and where she went on her sister's passport.

I sent you the rest.

Is that the clue? Sent it how?

A new man. An African prince. Winning the lottery. Put it together, and it almost sounds like—like the junk that you get—

"I have to check my email," said Bethany, mostly to herself.

She thought Janice was dozing, but the teen yawns and stretches and nods. "Okay."

"I think Annabelle sent me a message before she died. She disguised it as one of those junk emails about how you won the lottery or how some African prince needs your help to get his fortune back, but she sent it. It's in my email trash, probably."

"Okay. Let's go look."

Bethany smiled. "Well, it's not actually that easy, honey. The FBI will be monitoring my account. They'll know if I log on."

"Okay."

"They'll be monitoring it."

"I can help."

She gave the teen a look. "I'm sure they're monitoring yours, too. And it doesn't matter. I need to find an old email that was sent to me months ago."

"Okay."

Bethany suppressed her irritation. Janice had been first needy, then a delight, but now she was getting to be a burden. She wondered, by no means for the first time, whether she should arrange to send her home and continue on alone. She might have done it, except that she had made a promise not to; and she had been raised to honor her commitments.

And besides: the memory of turning her back on Annabelle was still too strong. So she would keep Janice with her.

For a while.

"I think you should turn around," Janice said after a bit.

"I'm sorry?"

"We shouldn't be going west."

"Ohio is west."

"We shouldn't be going to Ohio."

About to tell her passenger to hush, Bethany caught something in the teenager's tone: the steel she had noticed from time to time, at moments when Janice was absolutely confident.

"What are you saying? Did you find him?"

"Uh-huh."

"Seriously. You tracked down Sam DeMarco."

"Uh-huh."

"You did?" Sudden excitement. Bethany had planned the library assignment mainly to keep the teen busy and off the streets and safe while she went off to meet Peter Zhukov. Aunt Claudia used to do the same: use the library as a babysitter. "But he's a protected witness."

"I don't know. Maybe."

"This is Sam DeMarco in Ashland?"

"Uh-huh."

"You confirmed that he lives there?"

"Uh-huh. I don't know his address or what name he's using, but he's definitely there."

"I don't believe it. Honey, you're amazing."

Janice was shaking her head. She had her shoes off and her feet up on the seat. Skinny arms were wrapped around denim-clad knees. "I shouldn't have done it. I'm trying to stop. Martin was helping me. So was—my uncle. Oh, Bethany. I tried so hard. I prayed and prayed. I just couldn't stop. I couldn't."

"It's okay—"

"You don't understand. It's not okay. I have to stay away from computers. Have to. Have to. Or I can't fight it." Shuddering now. "You have to turn around."

"This is the quickest way to Ohio—"

"He's not in Ohio."

"You said you found him in Ashland!"

"Not Ashland, Ohio. Ashland, New Hampshire."

"What? How do you know?"

A long moment. When Bethany had decided no answer would be forthcoming, the words whirred out, as dry and technical as an answer in class.

"I found his niece. Tara. She lives in Florida. I hacked her email."

The car swerved. "Janice, come on."

"What, like it's hard?" The rest came out in a great rush. "I used the library computer to open an app I wrote last year—it's hidden on one of those political blogs—we like political because nobody blocks them, and it's like this really clever app, it's disguised to look like a packet manager, so there's no way their webmaster will find it—and, so, anyway, I used my app to find an unprotected laptop hooked to the U of Texas system. College students are best. They never run proper security software. I turned the laptop into a proxy server, and I used a remote Linux OS—not quite as good as using a disc but not too bad—along with a nice little program from a friend of mine to get into his niece's computer and hack her password. Linux is really good for hacking into Windows computers. You install the Linux operating system and then when you run the computer on the new OS the old hard drive is just data, right? You scan the Windows architecture for password files, and if they save their passwords on the computer—which is totally the wrong thing to do, you should type them in every time—anyway, if the passwords are on the computer, I can usually get them. I mean, there are security updates to make this harder, but college students never download them, and so—anyway, the point is, they've been emailing back and forth. Tara and Uncle Sam. He wasn't supposed to but he did. I mean, that's not how you hide, right? Emailing old friends. Family.

Visiting loved ones." A sidelong look as they both thought about Tia. "I don't know what name he's using, but I know what town he's in. Or at least what town he's in when he logs on."

Bethany stopped the car. Just pulled over to the side of the road. Janice's face was obscured by the braids, but she wasn't moaning anymore. She didn't sound dispirited. She sounded . . .

. . . *proud of herself* . . .

. . . happy.

"Who *are* you?" Bethany breathed.

A parting of the braids. A gray eye, then a pixie smile. "I shouldn't do it. I'm trying to stop. But you wanted to know, right?"

"Yes, but—"

"So, let's go."

"Honey, what you did—you know it's against the law, right?"

"Uh-huh. Like stealing Kathy Hobart's identity."

"That was different. I didn't have a choice."

"You also didn't have a choice if you wanted to know where to find Mr. DeMarco." She straightened. "We better hurry. If I could do it, the bad guys can do it, too."

"I'm not so sure."

"Well, I am pretty good. But I'm trying to stop." She looked around. "I wish this thing had GPS. I'm hungry. Let's find McDonald's."

"It's the middle of the night."

"Look behind us. The sun's almost up."

And indeed the clouds in the rearview mirror were turning a faint lazy orange. A fresh new morning, and still Bethany was in flight. But now the teen who was her companion was starting to scare her.

FIFTY-ONE

I don't know why you're so sure she can't be the Lab Bomber," says Lillian Hartshorne. The women are breakfasting together on one of the many terraces of Lillian's palace. The maid who is serving is actually in uniform. "I know she's your protégé, darling, but at some point you have to look at the facts."

"What facts are those?" asks Edna, fork midway to her mouth. The chef has prepared shirred eggs, with ham on the bottom and a lovely variety of garnishes sprinkled on top. Edna, to her embarrassment, is on her second helping. The appetite that slumbers when she is alone always comes wide awake at Lillian's.

The telecom widow has a practiced, just-so smile that Edna would find condescending had they not known each other for three decades. "She's a loner. That's number one. Don't look at me that way, darling. You're her only friend, and, evidently, there's a lot about her that you don't know, isn't there?" Folding a finger as she counts off her points. "Number two, she attends one of those really right-wing Episcopal churches, doesn't she?"

"Right wing?"

"Goodness me, Edna, you're not actually defending them, are you? They're always dissenting from the national church about one thing or the other. And, my goodness, don't they use the Prayer Book from 1928 or something? They're positively primitive. If any Episcopal church would provide a fanatical bomber, it would be one like that."

"Just because they give the Bible a traditional reading—"

"And number three." Riding right over her. "Number three, she's one of those gun nuts. Well, she is. Don't look at me that way. A woman who goes to the shooting range? Goodness, darling. She sounds like she has a good deal of violence to work out."

Edna shakes her head and takes another bite. Beyond the terrace are broad stone steps, and at the foot of the steps the neatly manicured lawn stretches off toward eternity. In the distance horses canter. It occurs to Edna that if she didn't happen to know Bethany, she would likely share Lillian's casual certainties. It is so easy to disdain those who are different; to assume them guilty of the most monstrous crimes simply because they fit a media stereotype. Poor Bethany. She wonders whether there is anyone, outside of the Garden and the Wilderness, who truly doubts her guilt.

"But that's not why I wanted to see you," says Lillian. She is holding a slice of toast at eye level, frowning. Edna wonders whether it might be buttered wrong side up. Lillian shakes her head, signaling, perhaps, the impossibility of getting good help these days, and took a delicate bite. "I wanted to talk to you about a problem your friend Bethany might have if she does happen to be innocent."

Edna contrives to smile. "Doesn't she have problems enough?"

"Evidently not. Tell me, darling, have you ever heard of bllnet? No? Well, not too many people have. They're pretty anonymous. A group of hackers. International."

"I don't think so. Wait. Yes. Didn't they do something to an investment bank last year?"

The maid is refilling their coffee cups. Lillian takes two lumps of sugar, Edna none.

"They did," says Lillian when they are alone once more. "They got into one of their secure servers and posted confidential client data on a website. The bank's been settling lawsuits ever since." The blue eyes seem almost impressed. "They've been a mischievous bunch. Most of these groups are annoying, but bllnet are very good. They've broken into corporate systems and government systems galore. Politicians. Even software companies. They took down a university website to protest the expulsion of a student who did—something or other. I don't recall. That's not the point." She leans forward. "The reason I know all this, darling, is that we have to keep track of people like that. If they ever get into a telecom network, we could lose our customers' confidence in two days. You see that, don't you, darling?"

"What does this have to do with Bethany?"

"It's that black girl she's supposed to be on the run with. That Janice Stafford. They say she's some kind of genius." Lillian nibbles at the shirred eggs, sighs with pleasure: something has turned out right. "A computer genius," she clarifies. "The FBI and Homeland Security haven't had much success in tracking down the members of bllnet. An arrest here and there, but only around the fringes. Some suspicions, I'm told, a couple of hints, but not enough to get a warrant for the inner core. This Janice Stafford, on the other hand—well, that's why she dropped out of college, they say. To work full time on bllnet projects. Not only is she a member, but she's believed to be one of their top people."

"Wait—are you saying—"

"What I'm saying, darling, is that your friend Bethany is on the run in the company of one of the most dangerous computer hackers in the world."

"You know what this means," says the Mathematician, when he has heard his friend's summary of the Judge's disturbing report.

The Builder's tone is mournful. "That we may have misjudged matters rather seriously."

"Exactly. Daniel Stafford was Wilderness. Why not his beloved niece? The niece he brought into the Village House?" He twirls his water goblet. They are once more in their favorite restaurant, in the usual shadowed corner on the mezzanine. The buzz of talkative diners rises from below. "It's perfect. Bethany is running away from the Wilderness, but it turns out that they've planted an agent on her. Janice isn't a child. Not really. She's eighteen, and if Lillian Hartshorne's information is correct, she has experience living underground, and has little respect for authority. I wouldn't be a bit surprised if she maneuvers Bethany into a meeting with her people. We remain invisible, but they get a human face. When you're underground, stretched, frightened, unsure—well, humanity makes a big difference when the time comes to choose up sides."

"I know," says the Builder. "That's why I'm leaving the country."

"Where are you going?"

"You know where, George. If Bethany survives, her destination is a near certainty. I have to be there waiting. It's our best chance to make contact."

The Mathematician takes a sip of his lobster bisque. He savors it for a moment, gathering his thoughts. "Bad idea, Harry. You already made contact in Chicago, remember? Against my advice, you pretended to be a mad old man who'd lost his son to the Planners."

"It was a risk. I know that. But Bethany needed the information on how to defeat the locks. The same information I gave Annabelle."

"My point is that somewhere along the line she is bound to have realized that your son was never in the Village House. If Martin didn't tell her—or if she didn't believe him—then I'm sure Janice has."

"So?"

"So, Bethany has already seen your human face, and she has no reason to trust you. You lied to her, Harry, remember? She doesn't know who you really are, and if you told her I don't think she'd care. If she spots you, she'll run as fast as she can the other way." The Mathematician's dark finger stabbed the air. "And why on earth did you give her your real first name?"

"It's an old habit. Always use your own first name in your alias, because you never know what long-forgotten friend is going to happen along at the key moment and call out, 'Hey, Harry, how's the wife?' That's why."

"Well, in this case, it was a terrible idea. You think it'll never occur to her to check? To go on-line and find a photo of Harry Pribyl?" He ran an exasperated hand over his eyes. "And there's another factor. There's a killer out there, in case you've forgotten. These aren't the old days. They're targeting us now. That's why you told the rest of us to stand down."

"The Wilderness knows who I am, George. They don't know the rest of you, but they know me. If they want me dead, they can get to me at any time of their choosing."

"An African prince," said Bethany, leaning over Janice's shoulder as the teen scrolled through the email discards. "Annabelle said she sent me a message. She told both Tia and Peter that I had a new boyfriend, a prince, and that I'd won the lottery. She had to assume that at least one of them would tell me. So her message is hidden in the kind of junk nobody reads."

"And the kind the FBI would ignore," added Janice, sounding impressed. "We never thought of that one. That is so cool."

They were using a public pay-as-you-go Internet terminal in the lobby of the train station in Newark. Janice assured her that the government would think they had logged on from Cleveland, and, upon breaking through her proxies, would think they were in Washington, D.C. True, sooner or later the trace would get through, but they planned to be long gone by then—so Janice insisted, and she sounded like she knew what she was talking about.

But they'll know which deleted emails we recovered from the trash, Janice warned. There's no way to avoid that.

As cover, they decided to open several dozen.

It took a good forty-five minutes to eventually find the one from Annabelle—that is, the only one that mentioned both an African prince and a lottery win. They could have done it faster by a word search, but Janice ruled it out: the email service provider might save the searches.

"Helps them sell ads," Janet explained.

The email began "My dear and respected friend," and related the usual tale of woe—millions of dollars locked away, the fruits not only of the sender's personal inheritance but of a lottery win, and twenty percent could be hers if she would only provide her bank information—because the poor prince who had sent the note had, alas, been exiled, and so—

Nothing special about it. No clues of any kind.

Except for a single line in his description of himself:

. . . fortunate enough to have been educated at the finest college within the finest university in the world . . .

Bethany stared at the screen. Up until now she had been guessing. Now she was sure.

"Time's up," said Janice.

"Wait." Paging over to Google, typing in a search. "I need to check one thing."

"No. We have to go now."

"Let me print this."

"No time." Tugging at her arm. "It's been too long. They'll know where we are." Their eyes met. "Trust me."

They were around the corner, heading for the parked Jetta, when the first patrol cars went screaming by.

FIFTY-TWO

Not much was salvageable," says Janet Anders. "And when I say not much, I mean that literally. Just a couple of pages yielded any data, and on those, well, nearly everything was destroyed or missing or illegible. This is what I have."

She hands him a printout.

`Page one: No data`

`Page two: No data.`

`Page three: Recoverable data`

think it's all one big muddle.

Yes, that David, my sister's David, perfect David, David the genius, David the brilliant, David who Tia always [adored?] [abhorred?]

they're working together but David is the only

you have to call him

`Page four: Recoverable data`

just got myself into kind of a mess

have two names. One of them for sure and one of them for not so sure. David said they don't have any

messed up

just the Wilderness but other people. I went

wanted the Stone too. I had to give them something. I did what I

important thing of all. Two names. And if you're wondering why I don't mention them here

Carl looks up, an expression of disappointment on his boyish face. "That's it?"

"That's it." She hands over the original package. "Now, I have a favor to ask of you."

"Anything."

"Give this a case number. Put it where it belongs."

Back in his car, he considers heading back to his office, then changes his mind and turns north, toward his condo near the National Zoo. He needs to sleep before he and Pulu head up to Philadelphia tomorrow to talk to Polly Hollins.

Janet is a wiz. She found what he needed, even though he dared not tell her. From the little she was able to recover, he gleaned three facts: first, that Annabelle Seaver was indeed working with David Hollins; second, that she at least advertised herself as knowing the location of the Pilate Stone; and, third, that she had uncovered two names. And although he won't mention his theory even to Pulu, it was a reasonable guess that the names were of two leaders of the Wilderness.

Meaning it was all true.

"I'm not a hacker," said Janice, forehead tipped against the window. "Real hackers are just way serious computer people. I used to be one, I guess. But now the real hackers would call me a cracker."

"Because you break into people's systems."

The teen had her legs drawn up and seemed to be folding into herself. "I don't do that anymore. I'm trying to stop." A long breath. "And we didn't hurt anybody. We didn't steal money. We didn't crash the power grid. We were just sending a message. How fragile the systems are. And the whole thing. The world—everything—it's so fragile." Shaking her head. "I was trying to stop. Why did you make me do that? I'm trying to stop."

"I didn't know. I'm sorry."

"I can't do it anymore. It's an addiction. If I start again I can't stop. Please don't ask me."

Bethany was gentle. "And that's what Martin did for you, isn't it? He was trying to help you stop."

"And Uncle Daniel."

"That was kind of them." But Bethany was remembering a visiting pastor at church from when she was maybe ten or eleven, a hugely fat man named Cawley, preaching on Romans 7. Cawley told them that what appears to be good, if not done for the sake of Our Lord, will turn out to have evil hidden in it somewhere. At the time the message had perplexed and infuriated her, but now she could see at least the edges of his point. Martin might have helped Janice, but for his own ends, or those of whoever was holding his strings. After all, Janice went to the church with them on the day that Wayne planted the bomb-making materials, and Bethany was willing to bet the teen's face was on the security camera footage. That would have been quite a haul for the feds after the evidence pointed them back at the church: a wanted murderer suspected in a series of bombings, and a known computer hacker affiliated with the group that broke into those bank servers last year.

Cracker, not hacker.

"You know, Janice," said Bethany after a bit, "a real pastor might be able to help you, too."

They passed a construction crew, working by floodlights behind orange cones. A police car guarded the closed lane, blue-white flashers piercing the dark. Both women turned their faces away instinctively.

"So, let's see," said Janice. "Your friend Sam's in witness protection. Peter's a gangster. And Martin—well, I guess he was a fraud, right? You have some interesting friends, Bethany."

"I guess I do."

The roadwork slipped behind them, and night closed in once more. Heavy trucks barreled past. They were in Connecticut, heading north.

"I mean, you don't think it's weird?" Janice persisted. "You try to follow Annabelle, who was looking for this missing Stone, and you just happen to have the right set of acquaintances? I mean, that's some coincidence, right?"

"Or God arranged it that way," said Bethany, much to her own surprise.

"So, you believe in God?"

"I do." She felt crowded by the younger woman's penetrating curiosity, made to talk about things she usually kept to herself. "Maybe it's my raising, but God—well, God explains so much. Annabelle and I used to argue about it when we were students. Aquinas and his case for God. Hume's case against. Buber on atheism. Polkinghorne on scientists and faith. All that."

Janice was twirling a braid. "I don't know. I mean, we went to church and all, but it was just the kind of church where people go. It didn't mean that much to them. Nobody ever talked about if God existed or what He wanted us to do or anything." She leaned back and shut her eyes. "But, I'll tell you one thing. If what we're doing is God's will? I wish He'd arrange for us to do it without anybody else having to get killed."

"Sleep, honey," said Bethany, softly; not knowing how prescient the teen's prayer would be.

FIFTY-THREE

They opened fifty-seven emails in fifty-one minutes," the agent from technical services is saying. She is standing at the front of the bullpen in the position usually occupied by Carraway. Rather than using his bulletin board, she has lowered the screen from the ceiling. "That's not an unusually high rate of speed. In fact, it's a little low. The average time to read an email is between ten and thirty seconds." She sips from her water bottle. "What slowed them down was that they lingered on some of them. It's not possible to tell which they lingered over, however, because they kept them open in batches of eight to ten at a time. We know which eight to ten were in which batch, but we have no way to tell which windows they clicked on. The emails they opened, however, overwhelmingly share a single characteristic. They're junk."

She clicks the mouse. The screen changes. She is explaining the algorithm the analysts are using to sort the junk email into different categories. Carl tunes her out. The work of the analysts matters, but they are searching for the right tree in a big forest. The deeper question is why Bethany chose this particular moment to log onto the email account that has sat untouched since the night of Ken Kirkland's murder. Carraway doubts that she simply yielded to the temptation and so left digital traces that the Bureau will eventually figure out. No. She took a calculated risk. The reward must be large—but it also must be one she has only just discovered.

They know from the tap on Polly Hollins's telephone that Bethany was at Annabelle's aunt's apartment three nights ago, but the old woman insists that she has no idea where the young women went when they left, and the interviewing agents report that they believe her. She gave them dinner, they watched television, Polly Hollins called, and their fugitives fled.

The Bureau's working assumption is that the phone call and the decision to check the email are related. Carraway is skeptical: he doesn't see Mrs. Hollins as a conspirator. But of course by now he and the Bureau are looking into quite different conspiracies.

Either way, today's trip to Philadelphia to interview Polly Hollins has been cancelled: she and her lawyer now want full immunity before she says another word.

"Then they checked one other thing," the analyst is saying. "They went to Google and looked up this man. Harry Pribyl. Former corporate accountant at a prominent firm in Chicago."

"Did Mr. Pribyl have any connection with the Village House?" somebody asks.

"His son lived there for a few months."

Carraway looks up from his doodling. "Was Barclay in touch with him while she was in the Village House?"

"Unlikely," says the analyst. "Mr. Pribyl died of cancer a year and a half ago."

"And the son?"

"Alive and well, waiting tables in Evanston. We've sent people to talk to him."

"What about—"

Before Carl can complete his inquiry, the lights come up. The technical analyst yields the floor. Section Chief Vanner steps to the front of the room. Her clever eyes dart around the bullpen.

"I am pleased to announce that Martin McAdams, a.k.a. Martin Potus, has been arrested trying to cross into Canada from Detroit." Not quite a cheer from the group, but, certainly, sounds of relief. Carraway, freed from the need to head to Philadelphia, is already gathering his papers. Vanner's gaze seeks him out. She smiles. "Agents Bolgren and Ramirez will be heading to Detroit to conduct the interrogation."

Marching back to her office, she passes Carl's desk without a glance.

"Hey, it's not so bad," says Pulu, strong hand on his partner's arm. "I hear Kuala Lumpur is beautiful this time of year."

Janice was reading *USA Today* and devouring pancakes. Lots of pancakes. They had found a motel near Stockbridge, Massachusetts, checking in at four in the morning and rising again at eight. Then Bethany, to Janice's great amusement, had insisted on driving for two hours in a great circle, mostly on back roads, before deciding that nobody was behind them. Now they were enjoying a late breakfast in Greenfield, not far from the New Hampshire border. Bethany had chosen one of the larger chain restaurants, because already they knew that anonymity lay in crowds: a waitress serving a hundred people was far less likely to remember them. The special was all the pancakes you can eat, and Janice was taking it seriously. If the teen ordered a third helping, Bethany would have to make her stop, lest they make too obvious an impression. It was almost eleven, and they had to get moving soon anyway.

Bethany was paging through the little notebook where she had taken to writing down the clues, lest she leave any out. Today's project was straightforward, although perhaps not simple. They had to get to Ashland, New Hampshire, to find Sam DeMarco. Bethany had no doubt that Sam would know how she could get a passport. Maybe even two passports: she hadn't yet decided. The email that purported to be from the African prince mentioned *the finest college within the finest university in the world*, and that had been their private joke years ago, when Bethany was at Oxford, and Annabelle showed up on her doorstep uninvited. That night in a pub they overheard another student referring to his own college that way, and the line had been a standing joke between them ever since. Annabelle had gone to Oxford. What she had done there, whom she had seen, Bethany had no way to tell. But if she could get to Oxford, she had little doubt that she could pick up the trail of—

"Look. You're in the paper again. But now you're all the way back on page five."

Bethany hardly glanced up. "I don't want to see it. I don't know how you can keep reading these stories."

"Maybe I'm hoping to be famous."

"This isn't the right kind of fame, honey. Besides, you're a minor. They won't mention your name."

"They found some of your college friends. They all say you weren't such a right-wing crazy back then." She giggled. "Oh, and it says here that according to experts, bombers are usually loners—"

"Will you please just stop?"

Janice read on, brown face creased in seriousness. Bethany returned to her calculations. She wondered how long false passports took. Suppose she needed a day and a half to locate Sam. Tomorrow was Wednesday. If she saw him Friday, maybe she'd have the passports by Monday. Was that time enough? Or would there even—

"Wait," said Janice. "They have the facts all wrong."

"I told you not to read this stuff."

"No, look. They also found prominent people with connections to some of the Planners. And look down here—"

"Thanks, honey, but no."

"Come on, Bethany. Seriously. They make it sound like they hardly knew each other. That's not true."

A line tugged at the back of Bethany's consciousness.

"What did you say, honey?"

"They quote this media guy? Elliott St. John?"

"The billionaire?"

"Uh-huh. The one who owns all the TV stations and newspapers and everything? And he says he used to know Uncle Daniel in the old days, like in college, but hadn't seen him recently. That's not true."

"Really." Suddenly she was interested. Janice had the paper folded back to an interior page. Bethany slid it closer. "He knew your uncle?"

"They used to hang out all the time. I even used to call him Uncle Elliott." A sigh of reminiscence. "They were like best friends."

Bethany stared at the printed page, but in her mind's eye she was seeing her running buddy's crazed testament.

Watch out for the Dread Serpent. You can't trust his best friend. Neither can he. But his best friend is one of them.

Dread **S**erpent.

Daniel **S**tafford.

Elliott St. John, his best friend.

She had found one of Annabelle's names.

"Change of plans," Bethany said. "Different destination."

"We're not going to Ashland?"

"We are, honey. Just not yet." She tapped the page. "About your Uncle Elliott. Do you have a way to get in touch with him?"

As a consolation prize for missing out on the chance to interview Martin Potus, Vanner hands Carraway the heavily redacted file finally handed over by the Central Intelligence Agency on its ex-employee Raymond Fuentes. There is only one copy in the office, and apart from Vanner nobody but Carl and his partner will be permitted a look. No notes may be taken. An Agency security officer with a metal briefcase follows the file from room to room, and will return it to Langley after three hours, whether they are done reading or not.

"I tried to argue," says Vanner, quite embarrassed, "but they told me to call my boss. I did, and he called his boss, and the attorney general told him to tell us to be happy we have this much."

The file fascinates him.

Raymond Fuentes is the child of Christian missionaries who, in the course of his childhood and adolescence, planted churches in six different countries. During his time at a small Christian college in the Midwest, an unnamed professor noticed his gift for languages and pointed him in the direction of the armed forces. He did three years as an intelligence officer in the Army, followed by a language course at Middlebury and additional graduate work at Georgetown, before shifting over to what is now known as the National Clandestine Service. Both his expertise and his exploits have been removed from the file. So have his overseas postings. But Fuentes is listed as speaking reasonable Pashto and passable Dari, so he almost certainly served in Afghanistan. He left the Agency eleven months ago. He is thirty-one years old, and as unlikely a candidate for recruitment to a religious cult as Carl could imagine.

On the other hand, the Planners could have had no finer bomb maker.

Carraway closes the file. His partner has already studied it.

"Pulu."

"Hmmm?"

"You were in Afghanistan, right? When you were doing counter-terrorism? You worked the Kandahar bombing in 2009."

"Mmm-hmm." Pulu is resting, his solid body against the back of the chair, his hands folded across his stomach. The front legs of the chair are off the ground.

"What's the difference between Pashto and Dari?"

Pulu yawns and opens his eyes. But he smiles, perhaps because for once he is the one being didactic. "The majority speaks Dari. Pashto is the language of the south and the east. Where the Taliban come from. Most Afghans nowadays hate Pashto, and a lot of them pretend not to understand it. Under the Taliban, the Dari-speaking majority was suppressed. Even the schoolbooks and street signs were Pashto. Now Dari is the whole ballgame."

"So a Pashto-speaking Agency officer—"

"He'd be next to useless in Kabul. They'd send him to bad country. No question. They have teams who live with the tribes for weeks or months at a time and try to wean them away from the Taliban. Dangerous work. Make a mistake and you could lose your head. Literally."

"A man would have to be very stable to live like that."

"The Agency shrinks make those guys sit through so many psychological tests before they go out, you'd think Langley was getting royalties."

"Doesn't sound like a man who'd join a religious cult."

"He was looking for his sister. Fell under Martin's spell."

"I don't know." He is pulling something from a drawer. "According to the field reports, Fuentes is very devout. Reads the Bible, prays a lot. Credits his faith with keeping him sane during the war." He has found what he's searching for. "Look here. The parents are dead. His sister's all he has. From what we've put together, she was in college in Iowa, she started going up to Chicago with a friend, and then dropped out of school. Her brother comes back and announces that she's joined this cult. He goes to look for her."

"So?"

"So, nobody else knew she'd joined. None of her friends have any idea what happened to her, except what Fuentes told them. And another thing." He opens the CIA file again. "Notice what's missing?"

"About 90 percent of the words."

"Not what I mean. Not the classified part." He flips through the pages. "The file is blank on what Fuentes has been doing since he left the Agency."

"Maybe they don't keep track."

"You know they do."

"Fine. But you know what he's been doing. He's been in Chicago with Martin Potus and his merry men."

"Not the whole time." Paging through his notebook. "According to interrogations at the Village House, he showed up eight months ago, asking what happened to his sister. He left for two months, then came back. And not only did he join. He very quickly worked his way to the top."

"So?"

"So, two anomalies. By all accounts Martin Potus is a suspicious sort. How could Fuentes rise so high so fast? And why would he go back and join the people he thought had somehow misplaced his sister? And where was he for those missing two months?"

"That's three questions, not two."

"And why doesn't the Agency have any reports on his activities? Even the fact that he'd joined the Planners?"

Pulu opens his eyes very wide. The front legs of his chair come back down to the floor. "Are you saying he's an Agency asset? They had a guy inside the Village House? Wouldn't that violate about six different federal laws? They can't operate domestically."

"I know. Still. Something's not right."

"You've said that before."

"I'm going to talk to Vanner."

"Why?"

"She's a bureaucrat. If there's a chance the Agency's playing on our turf, she'll want to find out so she can hand them their heads." He points to the phone. "Do me a favor, Jake. Call the team that's interrogating Mr. Potus. Make sure they cover Fuentes's role early and get back to us fast."

"You know, Carl, they don't work for me."

"They don't work for me, either. Not anymore. And they like you a lot more than they like me."

"Everybody does," grumbles Pulu, picking up the phone.

FIFTY-FOUR

She stood amidst the trees on a grassy rise a few hundred yards from the small colorful carousel on the Boston Common. A wedding party was riding round and round, two photographers and a videographer busily recording the event. Bethany watched the crowd through a pair of expensive binoculars, purchased for cash at an outlet mall. She was wearing a couple of devices carefully selected by Janice at an electronics boutique near Boston College. What they were undertaking constituted a considerable risk, and so they had done their best to guard against unpleasant consequences.

It was six minutes past three. The meeting had been set for three o'clock sharp, and the fact that Elliott St. John had been waiting since five minutes of told Bethany that he probably needed the meeting as much as she did.

She wondered why.

Bethany had been on the knoll since quarter past two, and although she was no expert, she detected no signs of surveillance. The media magnate had come alone, as she instructed. That fact, too, yielded information. She studied him. He was a diminutive man, but there was nothing comic about him. People made room as he walked; there were people who simply oozed power, whose every lazy gesture suggested minions waiting in the wings and billions waiting in the banks. He projected the aura that the Martin McAdamses of the world dreamed of. Thirty-odd years ago St. John had been a college dropout, making ends meet by stringing for a couple of small papers. A decade later he owned the chain. Now he controlled one of the largest media empires in the world.

And he was waiting for her. For Bethany Barclay.

Pride goeth, Aunt Claudia warned in her mind, and Professor Delavan chuckled along: *Rational actors maximize their own welfare, Ms. Barclay—not yours.*

How true.

She put the binoculars away and circled through the trees, so that she could approach the carousel from a different direction. Emerging onto the pavement, easing her way past darting children, she waited for the bullet or the handcuffs that would take her choices away for good.

But nothing like that happened.

She simply walked up to Elliott St. John, who was licking contentedly at a chocolate ice cream cone, watching incuriously as she approached.

For a moment they sized each other up, and Bethany, determined to retain the advantage, waited for the mogul to speak first.

"It's a pleasure to meet you at last," he finally said, his funereal tone suggesting that they had survived a great disaster together. "I don't know how things got so far out of control. We made some mistakes. I'm sorry about that. But I'm hoping we can put the past into the past and, from here on, work together."

Still Bethany made herself remain still, wanting to stretch his nerves. Worried, he opened his mouth to continue—and she immediately spoke over him.

"Before we start, Mr. St. John, let me make something clear. I am transmitting a signal. Our conversation is being monitored. I don't have to tell you by whom. I'm sure you know her capabilities. If the signal is interrupted, or if anything should happen in the course of the conversation that the person listening in doesn't like, your dealings with Annabelle Seaver will go public."

He seemed saddened by her words, but his confidence was unshakeable. "Why should anything happen that the person listening doesn't like?"

"Because it occurs to me that you might be planning to have me taken."

"You mean arrested? Pah. I'm in the media business. Maybe I'd want an exclusive interview first, but that's all." He squinted and pinched the bridge of his nose, and although the world might read this as evidence that he was fighting a migraine, the edgy perception Bethany had developed on the run suggested that he was making a signal to some unseen crushers, maybe to seize her, maybe to leave her alone—she would know momentarily.

"There's something else," she said. "If anyone tries to prevent me from leaving this park—if I'm harmed or detained by your people in the course of the things I have to do over the next few weeks—that same information on your dealings with Annabelle will go public, in too many places for even a man of your influence to stop. Is that clear?"

He tilted his head to the side. He wore rimless glasses, and his hair was thin on the tiny head. But there was power in those small eyes. This was a man who did not lose.

"What dealings have I had with Annabelle Seaver?" he finally asked, his tone one of disappointment, as if Bethany had let him down. "And what difference would it make if they were to go public?"

She fought the urge to drop her eyes. He was succeeding in sowing doubt, and she must not let him know. "Please, Mr. St. John. You're in media. You know what happens. You get identified as being close to a young woman who died under mysterious circumstances, and just the words together alarm investors. It doesn't matter what the facts are. It doesn't matter what denials you issue. Your stock tanks, the SEC wonders why and opens an investigation, a bunch of local prosecutors who want to make a name for themselves open investigations, a bunch of members of Congress see free television time and open investigations—you can't buy off everybody."

"I suppose not." He looked more mournful than ever. "It would be cheaper to buy you."

"You don't have anything that I want."

"Which means that the reason for this meeting is that you have something that I want."

"I might."

"You do." He studied her with wide unhappy eyes. His ears were floppy and his face too jowly for a man of just fifty. But nobody would ever dare laugh. "You have Annabelle's research. It's obvious. That's how you found me. You're following her lead, right? Good. Then we're after the same thing."

"Maybe not for the same reasons."

"The question, then, is how much it will cost for you to trade your reasons for mine." They were circling the carousel now. The wedding party was packing up. Squealing children waited their turn. The billionaire had turned the cone sideways, but the ice cream didn't dare drip on his suit. "I want the Pilate Stone, Bethany. It's really that simple. Annabelle was supposed to find it for me. I paid her good money and she cheated me."

Bethany felt a coldness come over her. "Is that why you killed her?"

"What? Me?" His surprise seemed genuine. "Why would I kill her? She might have cheated me, but she had the information I needed. She just was going to charge more for it than we'd agreed." He finished his snack and tossed the napkin in a can. "The thing you have to understand, Bethany, is that I wasn't fooled. Not for a moment. I knew from the start that Annabelle was a plant. She was sent to the Village House to smoke us out."

"Sent by whom?"

He eyed her. "You really don't know, do you? She'd fallen in with a dangerous bunch. Religious fanatics. Call themselves the Garden. Dangerous people," he repeated. His words were quick, his sentences simple, not unlike the chyron summaries that ran along the bottom of the screen of every one of the many news stations he owned around the world. "Fanatics, as I say. They've been around a long time, and they have been responsible for a good deal of evil. We don't have time for a history lesson. Suffice to say that the group of which I am a member was formed some years ago to oppose their plans." He sighed. His unhappiness seemed to be growing, as if the weight of it all was too much for him. "They call us the Wilderness. Silly notion. If there's a wilderness for humankind, they're the fools who are still trying to lead us into it."

"Do you prefer another name?"

"It doesn't matter. The point is, it was obvious to me. And, over time, to my colleagues. She'd been sent. It doesn't matter by whom. The point is, she talked about the Pilate Stone to get our attention. And, believe me, she got our attention. Through our intermediary at the Village House. He reported that a young woman claimed to be on the track of the Pilate Stone and wanted money. We knew it was too good to be true, but we had to check. After two meetings, it was clear that Annabelle wasn't even sure if the Stone existed. She had used publicly available sources, some of them quite obscure, to cobble together the story and some persuasive hints and rumors, but that was all. She had nothing to add to the general storehouse of information. Nothing except a single nugget she didn't know she possessed. I'll get to that in a moment."

On the grassy verge, two racing children had collided and tumbled. Neither was hurt, but both screamed for their mothers. Bethany's head was whirling. David had told her that the Pilate Stone didn't exist, and the few serious mentions she had found on the Internet said the same. Now Elliott St. John was insisting that it was real; and that her running buddy had unearthed a clue to its whereabouts.

"I went to Chicago and met Annabelle myself," he was saying. His tone was wistful, almost despondent. "We made a deal. She would locate the Stone, and I would give her a finder's fee. A minimum of two million dollars." His eyes shifted her way. "Yes. You heard me right. That's how much I wanted the Stone. If the Stone was in a private collection, she would get the fee anyway, and if I had to negotiate, and the purchase price was more than twenty million, she would get ten percent of the difference."

"You said *I* this time. Not *we*."

"Did I?"

"This is some sort of private enterprise of yours, isn't it? It's not related to your . . . your organization. That's why . . ." She trailed off, not willing to say *That's why Annabelle said your friend Daniel Stafford shouldn't trust you*. "You want the Stone for yourself," she said.

"I'm a collector of artifacts. That's no secret. Someday, when this is all over, I'll show you my collection. My curators conservatively estimate its value at nearly half a billion dollars. That's half a billion if I could sell it in the market, of course. Obviously, I can't, because many of the pieces are not supposed to be in private hands."

She looked at him, trudging sadly along beside her. "Why are you telling me this? I could turn you in. Trade with the FBI for my freedom."

"You could try, certainly. In that case, I suppose I might have to put aside my own hatred of violence and risk the wrath of little Janice." He shrugged. "But that isn't the point, Bethany. I'm telling you this because I want you to trust me. I'm telling you things the world would give a great deal to know, because it seems only fair, given what I want you to do."

"Which is what?"

"Find the Pilate Stone for me."

"You're not serious."

"But I am. I would like you to finish Annabelle's work. Follow the bread-crumbs she scattered. Nobody else seems to be able to figure it all out. But you knew her best."

"I don't understand. You had her at the end. You interrogated her. Anything she knew, you know."

The magnate seemed uneasy. "You're wrong. We didn't have her."

"Then who did?"

"We assumed it was her own people."

"What?"

"She was sent out as a lure, and fell for her own line. She was supposed to *pretend* to want the money. But she really did want it. She betrayed them, Bethany. She betrayed them, they snatched her up, they pumped her dry, and when they were done, they shot her full of drugs and shoved her out on the street. At least that's what my informants tell me."

But that was impossible. It fit none of the facts. And that meant—

—that meant—

Annabelle did it to herself.

Everything Bethany had assumed about her running buddy was wrong.

She *had been* using again at the end. She *had* been hallucinating or worse when she showed up at U Street Christian. Chalk it up to the stress of life underground, the terror of the triple cross, a life of abusing brain and body, or simply her inherent weakness of character, just as Polly always insisted. The point was, Annabelle was nobody's prisoner in the weeks before she died. Nobody's but her own.

And yet . . .

"Then who killed her?" Bethany asked.

"Her own people, one assumes. They are ruthless, as I have been trying to tell you. Our side is reasonable. Theirs is fanatical." They had crossed to the Public Garden and were on the grand bridge, looking down on the swan boats. "They're paranoid. They see conspiracies everywhere. They believe the church is under threat. Systematic, conspiratorial assault. Every time a monsignor pleads guilty to child abuse, every time a Muslim cab driver is forced against his faith to carry a man with a seeing eye dog, every time some store-front church is denied a zoning variance to expand, the Garden sees not the inexorable evolution of the culture in the direction of reason but the sinister conspiracy at work. That Reverend Jamison was one of their leaders. You know what kind of man he was. And yet that's the group Annabelle was representing." He seemed to sense something in her stiffness. "You're thinking about David Hollins. The famous atheist activist. How could he be a part of such a group? We don't know the answer to that, Bethany. We didn't know he was involved. But, in all honesty, our best guess is that he was one of them all along. His atheism was a pose. A public posturing. His militant, aggressive anti-Christian stance might actually have helped the churches retain old members and gain new ones. It wouldn't be the first time that skulking, paranoid conspirators have sent out an agent provocateur."

Bethany's head was spinning. It all seemed so reasonable. And yet—and yet—

"It's very simple," Elliott St. John continued. "I'll make the same deal with you that I made with Annabelle. The same money. More if you'd prefer. Name your price. I'll also use my considerable influence to see that no charges are brought against you for your supposed crimes. Believe me when I tell you, once a media empire like mine takes up a cause, those who think they hold the power tend to cave." A broad smile. "By the time I'm done cleaning up your reputation, half of Congress will want the FBI director's head on a platter for ever thinking that the sainted Bethany Barclay could ever be involved in anything so nefarious."

"That's why you did it," she said softly, wonderingly.

"Why I did what, Bethany?"

"Why you framed me. To get me moving, yes. But also so that I'd need you in the end to get the charges dropped. I'll bet one or two of your reporters even have evidence that it's a frame."

For the first time, a ghost of a smile danced on those disapproving lips. "I wouldn't be a bit surprised."

"And the evidence will be made public just as soon as you have the Pilate Stone."

"I'm glad you're coming to see how the world works. I was worried for a moment there, frankly, that you were too naive to do me any good."

"You said that Annabelle had uncovered one nugget of gold."

"Annabelle went to Europe in December. I saw her when she returned. She had traveled extensively. She wouldn't tell me where. All she would say was that along the way she'd met someone she called the Wise Man, who claimed to know where the Stone is hidden. The Wise Man told her that the Stone was part of the Theatre at Caesarea, where it sat opposite the famous one, but was removed centuries before the famous one was found."

"So?"

"So, Annabelle couldn't have found that fact in any public source. It is mentioned only in a medieval scroll that I have in my possession. If her Wise Man knew that much, he might know a lot more. The trouble is, she disappeared without ever telling us who he is. But you knew her best, Bethany. You can go where she went, see the people she saw, figure out which one of them was the Wise Man."

"I don't know where she went. I don't know whom she saw."

"We assume she left records for you somewhere."

"But you shouldn't assume those records are complete."

"Then you'll have to reconstruct her travels as best you can. She left traces somewhere. If anybody can follow her breadcrumbs, Bethany, it's you." He pulled out a business card, scribbled a number on the back. "Here. You can reach me at this number any time of day or night. I have a lot of mobile phones, but this number only my wife and my children and my mistresses possess. Nobody should answer but me. If anybody else does, act like you're one of my other women. Call yourself—Anna. That fits. Say it's Anna calling, and that you'll call back later. I'll know it's you."

She played with the card, turning it this way and that. "And what about my companion?"

"Little Janice? Goodness. You're not planning to take her along, are you, Bethany? She's not at all well, I'm afraid. You've been with her. It has to be obvious to you that Janice needs help. Legal and psychiatric both. She shouldn't be mixed up in this."

"She already is."

"Well, fine. If she can help you, let her help you. If she can't, she's dead weight, and you should dump her. Don't give me that look. We're not barbarians. The fanatics are on the other side. Send her back to her family is all I meant." He hunched forward again. "The point is, the Garden is dangerous. You'll be in danger the whole time. They'll stop at nothing to keep the Pilate Stone from seeing the light of day. You may not want to put Janice through that."

"I may not want to put myself through it."

"You're welcome to take your chances on your own. Drop out of sight again. People do it. You might survive for a while. But sooner or later, you'll make a mistake. The FBI will catch you, or the Garden will. And if I were you? I'd root for the FBI."

"I'll think about it."

"Don't think too long, Bethany. Time is short, as you know. Oh, I almost forgot."

She doubted that Elliott St. John had ever forgotten a single thing in his life.

Meanwhile he was reaching into his jacket once more. He pulled out a thick envelope. "More cash. You might need it."

"No, thank you."

"You have Annabelle's cash, do you? Was there some left over?"

"I have to go now."

"I understand. But you have my number. Call if you need anything. Money, transportation—it doesn't matter. And, in particular, call if you think the Garden is closing in on you. We have our people. We can get you out."

"I understand."

His earlier depression had lifted entirely. He was positively beaming. "I know you doubt me, Bethany. I know you'll spend hours and hours trying to figure out which parts of my story hold together and which parts have holes. But do consider one undeniable fact."

"What's that?"

"The Garden has hidden itself from you at every turn. Lying to you, manipulating you, concealing itself in the shadows. I've given you information that can send me to prison and a phone number where you can reach me night and day. So if you're trying to figure out which side you can trust, ask yourself this: which side trusts you?"

As she hurried off into the trees, Elliott St. John was still smiling.

The billionaire continued to stroll around the park. He had told Bethany the truth. None of his people would follow her. There was no need. If she decided to help him get the Stone, she'd be back in touch anyway. If not—well, there were ways to exact guarantees.

His phone rang: not his personal cell or his business cell, but the special prototype given him by the head of the council, known since Cromwell's day as the Protector; at formal moments, the Lord Protector. He stepped off the path and onto the grass, then settled between two boulders where nobody was close enough to overhear. The Protector had assured them that decrypting calls made on this device was impossible, even for the masterminds of the National Security Agency; and on such matters, the Protector was always right.

"Did she bite?" The Protector, as always, came straight to the point. As a fellow executive, Elliott appreciated the habit, if not the tone.

"Who?"

"Bethany Barclay. Have you heard from her yet? The story in the paper should have brought her to you by now."

"Sorry," he lied. "Not a word."

"But that's absurd. Janice knows you were Daniel's best friend. I hardly think she'd keep that knowledge from Bethany."

"Maybe they haven't seen the papers."

"Maybe."

"I'll let you know if she calls."

"I'm sure you will, Elliott."

The Protector hung up without saying good-bye.

Elliott hurried toward the carousel. One of his bodyguards was waiting around the other side. St. John was worried. The Protector was always brusque, but today had been almost rude. He wondered whether the Council suspected that he had struck a side deal with Annabelle and was now trying to do the same with Bethany. No. He had been careful. They couldn't know. They weren't clairvoyant.

And besides: were the Council aware of his double-dealing, there would have been no querying phone call from the Protector. A drug-induced heart attack was more their style.

Very likely they'd have used his own hired gun to do it.

FIFTY-FIVE

They reached the town at first light. Ashland, New Hampshire, was like something out of a Currier and Ives print, right down to the covered bridge and Victorian inns along Main Street. All that was lacking was an advertisement for an ice cream social and little boys in knickers and they could film the opening scene of *The Music Man*. The lake shimmered down below, and misty green hills rose triumphantly beyond.

"Your friend picked a nice town," said Janice as they sat in a diner munching sausage and eggs. "I'd love to live someplace like this."

"I don't think he picked it. I think it was picked for him."

"By the Marshals Service."

"Yes."

Janice was smearing marmalade all over her toast. "But if they know where he is, they'll be watching the house, right?" She looked around. "I don't see anybody my color. People are watching us. We must be pretty conspicuous."

"I'm counting on it." She saw the teen's face; hunched closer; explained. "You don't know small towns. I do. People will talk. They'll say a black girl's in town. They won't talk to the feds, because the feds are outsiders. The feds will just be watching. They won't be asking around because they can't ask every day without getting people all upset. So they're in a bubble. But people will talk to Sam. He lives here. They'll gossip, and he'll hear about us." A smile of reminiscence. "When I used to visit him, he could tell me about every stranger who'd stopped in Flint Hill for the past week. He told me once that the basic rule of survival is to always make friends with the owner of the local diner."

"That's why we came to the diner?"

"It'll be Sam's early-warning system. He'll know we're here."

"And then what will he do?"

"He'll find us."

"What if he's on vacation or something?"

"Then we're in trouble," Bethany admitted. She fingered the still unopened third envelope in her inside pocket, hoping not to need it.

Morning briefing. Special Agent Ramirez stands at the front of the bullpen. She has just returned from Detroit, where her partner Bolgren continues to lead the interrogation of the man the Bureau is now calling Martin McAdams. Ramirez is using the screen and the laser pointer. Vanner is at the back of the room, beaming. Everyone knows that Ramirez is on the fast track, one of the section chief's protégés.

Carraway is a face in the crowd.

"McAdams insists that he has nothing to do with the bombings," Ramirez is saying. "At this point Agent Bolgren and I are inclined to believe him. The more we learn about the Village House, the clearer it is that McAdams was a figurehead. A part of him believed in what he was doing. A part of him was in it for the money. The place was actually run by the late Daniel Stafford."

A photo appears on the screen.

"Stafford raised the money. He identified the targets for scamming. All the signs suggest that he was also intimately involved in the bombing campaign." She looks around the room. "At this point, we can find no evidence that any mainstream church or religious organization was involved. But the investigation of Norval Jamison's organization is continuing. They're resisting subpoenas on First Amendment grounds, so that fight is likely to go on for a while. The Justice Department is confident that we'll win in the end."

And every minute that the churches stand on their rights, Carraway is thinking, their reputation is further shattered. Strange world.

"McAdams insists that Bethany Barclay could not have been involved in whatever was going on, because she never showed up until the week before the raid. Again, we believe that he believes it. But since he didn't know about bombs being built in his own basement, it's not hard to imagine that the conspirators kept her involvement from him too. We still think the balance of evidence is that she is part of the bombing campaign. Too much still points that way." She ticks the points off on her fingers. "She attends a conservative church. She arranged for Sylvia Kirkland to leave eleven million dollars to God's Planners. She is the principal suspect in the murder of Mrs. Kirkland's son, who was challenging the will, and now there's some evidence that Mrs. Kirkland's death—which enabled the transfer of the funds—might have been a murder."

Carraway sits up straight. He hasn't heard this. Pulu slides a report his way: a signed statement from the pathologist in Richmond, including his suspicions about the manner of Mrs. Kirkland's death, as well as the fact that he had shared his worries with the family lawyer. The lawyer in turn had refused to be interviewed, citing attorney-client privilege.

"How long have we had this?" Carl whispers. But the date is staring him in the face: last week, when he was in Chicago.

Ramirez is back to her list. "After she kills Kirkland, she stops at the home of David Hollins, now dead, and then heads straight for the Village House. A very odd place to hide unless she knew in advance that they would take her in." She looks around. "Questions?"

Someone asks about witness statements that the target left with Janice Stafford. Ramirez says the working assumption is that they are or were traveling together. Someone else wants to know how they are moving around. Ramirez says that Janice's boyfriend has reported his Volkswagen stolen. He won't back off his story, but the working assumption is that this is, or was, their mode of transportation.

Carl is on his feet. "What about Raymond Fuentes?"

Ramirez exchanges a look. Not with Carraway. With Vanner. "We're frankly not sure about the extent of his involvement," Ramirez says. "Martin McAdams seems not to have trusted him. He thought Fuentes was a plant. It's possible that the conspirators thought so too. It's also possible that he's one of them. We're still working on it."

From the back of the room, Vanner claps her hands once. "Okay, people. That's it. Back to work."

After breakfast, they drove through the picturesque town, gawking like the tourists they hoped to be taken for. They passed the elementary school and headed north, toward the mountain. They took their time, stopping often. As they climbed Riverside Drive toward the southwest corner of Squam Lake, they watched for cars that happened to follow their circuitous route, or seemed to keep popping up ahead. A young man on a bicycle overtook them as they sat on the shoulder chatting. He slowed to look them over, and vanished over the hill an instant later.

"He's the waiter," said Janice. "He messed up my order."

"The waiter was older."

"Everybody looks young on a bicycle."

Bethany glanced at her. "Your imagination's working too hard."

Nevertheless she started the car and took a side turn before the cyclist could come back for a closer study. Stout red maples made a canopy across the narrow road.

"This is a really bad plan," said Janice.

"The only way I know to find Sam is to let him find us."

"We could drive all around town until we spot him walking his dog or something."

"He doesn't have a dog. He doesn't walk. He's in a wheelchair. Besides, honey. Driving all over town is a lot more conspicuous than stopping in for breakfast and then leaving again. We'll spend two or three hours in the hills, then double back."

But every day away from the Village House was lessening Janice's dependence and submission. By now she was arguing about everything. "Why do you have to see this Mr. DeMarco anyway? He didn't even know Annabelle. That's what you said."

"As far as I know, they never met."

"Then why? This is such a big risk!"

Bethany was exasperated. "Do you have a better plan? Someplace to go?"

"I thought we were following Annabelle!"

"Believe me, honey, we are."

They burst from the trees. The ground fell away beside them, sloping to the shining gold of the lake.

"I think we should head back," said Bethany.

"To the diner, right? In case God arranged to leave us a note from Mr. DeMarco."

Bethany resisted the urge to snap at the girl. She backed across the narrow lane and turned the car around. "Just keep watching the mirrors, honey, okay? In case that cyclist comes back."

"Sure. And you stop trying to change the subject. What's the big secret? You've told me everything else about Mr. DeMarco. Why won't you tell me why it's so important to see him?"

No choice. "I need to see Sam because he's the only person I know who might be able to get us what we need to keep following the trail."

"Which is what?" asked Janice.

"Passports."

Stuart Van Der Staal considered his options. He stood in the bedroom window of his second-floor suite at a lovely Victorian bed and breakfast on a busy Main Street corner. He had been in Ashland for three days, waiting. He had a team this time, a development he hated, for he was at heart a loner. But he bowed to necessity. He could hardly surveil an entire town on his own, twenty-four hours a day, even a town as small as Ashland. Alas, the three men assisting him were rubbish: not an advanced degree among them, nobody who would be able to appreciate his theories, or even those of a poseur like Margolis. Stuart did not understand how America could have grown so mighty, awarding the franchise to so many who were manifestly unqualified to exercise the privilege. He was largely in agreement with the notion, floated now and then among academics and various intellectuals, that the best way to determine right policy was to ask the smartest people. It made perfect sense to him that those with the highest IQs should get the most votes. Otherwise your politics was polluted by all sorts of creepy ideas—religion, patriotism, tradition, that sort of thing—the irrational biases that the brilliant for the most part were able to resist.

He hadn't yet decided whether Bethany Barclay was really up to the challenge of citizenship in that refined sense. This Janice Stafford, on the other hand—she might well have the brain for it, but would need proper direction. He grinned, reflecting on his new instructions. His masters now believed that Bethany, with the right incentive, would be able to—

His cell phone was burring, and his reflexes had it at his ear almost before he noticed.

He said nothing, just listened. A possible sighting on Riverside Drive, and were there any orders?

"No," he said, and ended the call.

His plans were already in place. There was no point in chasing after every phantom, especially when the FBI was also in town, and might notice his people rushing hither and yon. No. He would stick to the schedule for the operation. After all, there was only one place they could be going. Stuart would have to be there waiting.

True, the Bureau would have the same idea, and they were not exactly amateurs. But they would be no match for Stuart Van Der Staal.

FIFTY-SIX

"Why don't you believe in God?"

Janice lifted her head, braids twirling. She had foregone her usual burger for a grilled cheese sandwich. They were in a booth near the front window, with a view of Main Street, but nobody was paying them inordinate attention.

"I didn't say I don't believe in God," the teen mumbled as she chewed. "I said you can explain the world without God."

"Then where did all this come from?" Bethany did not know why she had become so insistent on the point. It was as though she had never spent all those years letting the question drift away unanswered; but running for your life has a remarkable power to concentrate the mind. All at once she wanted to know the answer; and so pressed on. "The Big Bang, right? So, who made that happen?"

"Can we not talk about this?"

"I'm serious, honey. Humor me a minute." Glancing around. The restaurant was full, but nobody was paying them any special attention. "If there was a Big Bang, who made it happen?"

"Nobody. It happened."

"At random, right? Out of nothingness, somethingness?"

Janice stuffed fries into her mouth. Bethany tried to remember whether she had gobbled carbs so enthusiastically at eighteen. She thought not—but perhaps that extraordinary brain burned up the calories.

"Not at random," the teen allowed. "No. First there was nothing. The quantum vacuum. So, what's nothing like? Without the equations, it's hard to describe, but you can prove that nothingness is lumpy."

"Excuse me?"

"It's lumpy. Because, you know, nothingness can't be perfectly featureless. Know why? Because featurelessness is a feature. Being perfectly smooth isn't nothingness. It's smoothness. So there have to be irregularities. Clumps of thicker nothingness, floating in the thinner nothingness. Before the Big Bang, there isn't any time—"

The waitress sashayed over. Bethany looked up hopefully, expecting the awaited message from Sam DeMarco, but the redhead wanted only to debate the vital issues of who needed a refill. The name tag on her pink smock read *Mickee.*

"Time doesn't exist before the Big Bang," Janice resumed when they were alone. "But there are still quantum fluctuations. The vacuum twists itself around. It's hard to explain without the equations, but as long as the laws of physics hold, the vacuum will twist and curve and even sort of shiver and then bam! Something out of nothing."

Bethany shook her head. "And you really think that's a simpler explanation than God made it?"

"It's more scientific. Maybe not simpler."

"It doesn't sound very scientific. It sounds like guesswork."

"Well, it's not. A lot of smart people have spent a lot of time figuring out how it's possible to get something out of nothing if you don't assume a Creator—"

"But that's the point. You're assuming away a possibility."

"Because there isn't any evidence for it."

"Is there evidence for the proposition that nothingness is lumpy? Or is that just an assumption to make the equations work?"

"Nothingness has to be lumpy. If it was formless, and there was a Big Bang anyway, there wouldn't be any galaxies, or even any stars. Everything would have been moving apart at too high a rate of speed. Some of the material from the Bang had to collide with other material. It had to go off in other directions, propelled by gravity and maybe other forces we haven't discovered yet—"

"Like God's will?"

"Or other forces," said Janice, doggedly.

Janice said nothing. Her face was turned to the window. Bethany followed her gaze but saw only a truck unloading bread at the supermarket across the road.

"What's the matter, honey?"

"Your friend is in a wheelchair, right?"

Mickee, the waitress, was pouring extra coffee they hadn't ordered. Bethany shooed her away.

"Yes," she said. "He's in a wheelchair."

"He can't walk."

"No."

"Then I think we might have a problem, because some guy in a baseball cap has walked past the window twice in the past five minutes. He keeps peeking at us through the glass."

"I've got a positive ID."

"Both of them?"

"Affirmative."

The professor actually took the phone away from his ear and glared at it. Where did they pick this stuff up? Television? Never mind. Focus. If Bethany and Janice were still in town, they hadn't made contact yet. Probably they would wait until night. Fine. The dark had always been his friend.

The next problem was the idiot at the other end of the call, patiently awaiting instructions. Stuart thought it through. No choice, really. He had survived this long by working alone. Never a witness to anything.

"Okay. Back off."

"Want me to follow them?"

"No."

"But—"

"Leave it alone," he said. "I don't want them spooked." Which the idiot was sure to do if he hadn't already. Ending him would actually be a relief. "Walk away. Far away. We'll meet in two hours."

He hung up. Then he went to his briefcase and, after a moment's thought, chose the Glock, and a fast-draw hip holster from Tactical. It was important that the holster be seen. Camouflage. Today everything was camouflage.

After almost a week together on the run, the duo had the drill down pat. Whenever they ate, they carefully added up the tab as they ordered, and asked for their check with the food. Now Bethany threw bills on the table while Janice took a careful look to make sure they were leaving behind nothing they needed. Once, at a truck stop in Indiana, Bethany's little notebook had tumbled from her jacket, and would have been lost but for Janice. Another time she had recovered their money clip. There was no point, they had decided back on day two, in worrying about fingerprints or DNA: if the authorities were close enough to retrieve them, the party was over anyway.

Now they scurried out the side door, over by the rest rooms, which they had marked down this morning. The door led into the alley between the diner and the hardware store, and the alley spilled out a block away. But a woman's voice was shouting, "Hey, you! *Hey!*" long before they reached School Street, where they had left the car. Bethany would have kept going if not for Janice, who reacted automatically to the tones of authority. The teen stopped dead and turned. Bethany turned with her, to find redheaded Mickee bearing down on them.

"You forgot your change."

"That's for you," said Bethany, tugging at Janice's sleeve.

"Hey, thanks," said the waitress. She pocketed the change, tore the receipt from her pad and handed it over, then flounced back up the alley.

"Let's go," said Janice.

But Bethany ignored her. She was staring at the scribbled words on the back of the receipt:

> You're an idiot. I'm embarrassed for you. Gray saltbox out Winona Road. Wait until dark. Usual route.

"How do you know it's real?" asked Janice. They were in a motel thirty miles up Route 3, resting until the sun went down. "It could be a trap."

"It's his style, honey. That 'idiot' part is pure Sam DeMarco. And anybody who wanted to trap us could have taken us in the alley."

"You don't know that, Bethany. This could be dangerous."

"That's why you're staying here."

Those sparkling eyes widened. "By myself?"

"I'm leaving at seven. If I'm not back by ten, you take the money and run."

"Run where?"

"Don't tell me." Bethany shivered with memory. "If this is a trap, you don't want me to know."

Janice's calm was unearthly. "Make sure your cell is charged."

"Got it."

FIFTY-SEVEN

Winona Road turned out to be mostly thick trees screening low houses built half a century ago and set well back from the winding lane. She wasn't sure how she was supposed to recognize Sam's, especially at night. He hadn't even told her which side of the road he lived on. Worse, she figured that she dared not make a second reconnaissance. There was no other traffic, and doubling back for another look was a good way to make herself conspicuous to whoever was watching the—

Then she saw it: a gray saltbox a good two hundred yards from the road but set amidst its own little theater of floodlights, and therefore perfectly visible. And that was very much like Sam, to keep his property brightly illuminated, so that nobody could approach unseen. In the crisp white radiance, she could see the house and two outbuildings, and the dark sedan parked quite openly across the street. But she was wearing a baseball cap and glasses, and although her heart had become a trip-hammer, she was careful to slow down and peer at the car and the two men in it rather than speed up suspiciously and turn her head away.

Then the lights were behind her. She took a moment to regain her aplomb; and her nerve; and to get all the synapses firing together. The road had been running northeast but was now curving due east. That was bad. Sam had said to take the usual route, and her usual route, back in Flint Hill, had been to drive down an abandoned farming road into the woods behind his house, then scramble down the grass slope to his back door. She had asked him once why he insisted that she take so circuitous a path on her visits.

"Training," Sam had said and laughed. Laughing along with him, Bethany never asked what he might be training her for.

Now she knew.

She reached a fork, and took the road to the left, then another, unmarked, to the left again, and now the dashboard compass told her she was heading due west. She passed more houses, a couple of them fairly new colonials. She breasted a rise, and the little subdivision was behind her. The road took a sharp right, and a dirt path kept going in the same direction, and Bethany drove into the dirt, swiftly, dousing all but her parking beams, so that anyone following would come down the hill, see no lights, and assume she had stayed on the main road.

The path swiftly became overgrown, and she had to get out and walk. She had the flashlight they had taken from Martin's house in Highland Park, but decided to use moonlight instead, the way Everett Barclay had taught her on those hunting trips. She already knew where she was going. She had identified the glow from Sam's floodlights, down beneath the ridge where she now stood.

How Sam knew whoever was watching the house had missed this route was a mystery: but knowing such things had kept him alive for all those years he had been retired from . . . whatever he had retired from.

Bethany could pick out no path, so she scrambled down the slope, just the way Sam had trained her in Flint Hill. The brambles scratched her and low-hanging branches nearly blinded her, and she suspected that not even her jeans and sweater would protect her from a fearsome case of poison ivy.

But she made it, and found herself in a well-tended garden. The smell of fresh mulch greeted her, an aroma she had loved since childhood. A bluestone walkway awaited. She moved with purpose but not too fast, because a disturbance might draw the attention of whoever was in front of the house.

The back door stood ajar, the screen shut but not latched.

Just like in Flint Hill.

And just like in Flint Hill she stepped through into the kitchen, with the difference that this time she was remembering what she'd found in Highland Park, and so steeled herself for the worst.

"You're fine, sweetie pie," called a voice from the next room, making her jump, but it was only Sam, ageless and wiry, smiling as he put away the book on his lap.

"Nobody saw you," he added, confidently, turning his chair her way. "Nobody followed you. The FBI guys out front didn't get a whiff. You're as clean as you can be. Now why don't you pour yourself some coffee, pull up a chair, and tell me what's going on."

Evening.

Carraway is in Vanner's office, facing yet another scolding. She never raises her voice, and sometimes you have to strain to hear her rake you over the coals.

"There's no trace of Ted Lesofsky," she says. "I'm told that it looks like he's been planning his departure for years. You must have really spooked him."

"I offered to tell you everything he told me."

"And I reminded you that he was forcibly retired because of mental instability. I was on the board that made that decision, as I'm sure you remember."

"I remember, ma'am."

"Good. Because I wouldn't want to lose you to the same obsession that claimed him." She flicks at the air as if driving away a distracting insect. "The point is, if you're going to remain deputy head of the task force, I have to know that you'll do as you're told. You think Bethany Barclay is innocent. For all I know, you're right. We still have to find her. That's the job. Not going on these side trips to investigate some other crime." She's still smiling, but her tone grows colder. "I like you, Carl. I always have. But you can't go around pursuing every hunch—"

A knock on the door. Pulu steps in without waiting to be told.

"Sorry to interrupt, guys. There's a possible sighting. Greenfield, Massachusetts."

"When?" ask Carraway and Vanner, at the same time.

"Yesterday morning." Pulu wears a sheepish expression, as if the fault is his. "Guy served two women answering their description at IHOP. Didn't think anything until he saw the news today."

"She's on her way to visit DeMarco." Carraway is on his feet. "Alert the team covering his house."

"Already done," says Pulu.

Carraway turns to his boss. "Ma'am—"

"Go," Vanner says, flicking those slim fingers again. "I'll call them to get the plane ready. Oh, and this time, gentlemen, do remember to keep me posted."

But she is speaking to empty air.

Substitute father to substitute daughter: they both understood the nature of their relationship. In Virginia they had gone shooting together, both at ranges and in the woods, Sam rolling along merrily in his powered wheelchair, barking advice and criticism and commands. In return she had done a bit of legal work for him gratis—nothing complicated, but, as Everett Barclay used to say, a dollar is a dollar.

"It's good to see you," said Sam. "Even if you are a little fool."

"What have I done wrong now?"

He slapped his knee. "Do you really want a list?"

She colored. "I think I've done pretty well. The FBI is looking for me, plus some maniac who shot at me, and another one who tried to kidnap me, and I escaped—"

"Maybe you better start at the beginning. But get me the comforter first, from the bed. Just in case."

"In case what?"

"In case it gets cold."

The bedroom was behind her, easily visible from where she sat. The room they were in was the entire house, she realized. All the walls had been cut to waist height. Those that were load-bearing had been replaced by pillars. Sam wanted to be able to see everything. The only exceptions were the bathroom—which had no windows—and the kitchen, where she had come through the back door. The kitchen had folding panels above the counter, complete with louvered blinds. She saw no reason for this exception from the rule that governed the rest of the house, but she also knew that Sam had a reason for everything.

"For when I entertain," he said, following her eye. "So my guests don't see the mess."

"You never entertained back home."

"I don't here either. But I might one day." She tucked the blanket around him. He shooed her away and finished the job himself. "So, what happened to your little friend? Gone home?"

She didn't bother to ask how he knew she wasn't traveling alone. She was the one who'd made sure to be seen around town. "She's fine."

"Ah. You've got her in hiding. Good plan. Now tell me everything."

She did. Unlike with the pastor in Newark, she left out very little. She spoke for a good forty minutes, and Sam never interrupted once.

"We'll be on the ground in ten minutes."

"Raise the agents on the scene," says Carraway. The adrenaline is pumping hard. He can hardly stay in his seat as the Gulfstream sweeps across low night mountains. "Tell them we're on the way and to stay put."

Pulu hides a smile. The communications officer looks affronted. "We just checked in with them ten minutes ago. We gave them the same message ten minutes before that."

"Humor me."

Carraway rubs his eyes. He reviews his arithmetic. Bethany has to be heading for Ashland. No other reason to be in Greenfield. But she must know that the Bureau will have DeMarco's house staked out. He wonders how she thinks she can sneak in unnoticed.

But of course Sam DeMarco will have thought of that. A man dodging as many enemies as he has to be constantly thinking about—

The communications officer is back. "Sir, we can't reach the agents on the scene. They're not responding to either phone or radio."

"Maybe they've gone inside," another agent says. "Bad reception."

Carraway shakes his head. "We can't take chances. Call the locals. Have them get a couple of cars over there."

"They won't like it," says Pulu.

"Ask nicely."

When she was done, Sam adjusted the blanket, then drew a thick cigar from somewhere. "Want one? No, I see you don't. Well, that's fine." He took his time over the lighting, puffed thoughtfully. "Filthy habit. I took it up after—well, after." A grimace of memory. "Anyway, you've certainly had a time of it. I thought I'd had an adventure or two, but you—well, never mind. You didn't drop in to hear me ramble, and I imagine you won't want to stay very long. You took quite a risk to get here, so why don't you tell me what you want?"

"I need to get out of the country, Sam."

"Spoken like a true fugitive."

"I'm serious."

"Then you'll be needing a passport," said Sam, all business now. "It's been awhile since I had to do this, but I should be able to help with that."

"I hoped you would."

"I have a source who used to be the best. One guaranteed single-use passport. It won't be American, but if you present it at the border, you'll have no trouble getting out of the country. What happens next is up to you." He was at the side table, reaching for a sheet of paper and a pen. "Of course, my source might not be in the business any longer. People who work both sides of the street often retire." A wink. "Now and then even voluntarily."

"I appreciate it."

He wrote the name and the address because, he said, she was in no shape to remember. But she noticed that he wrote on a single sheet of paper against the gleaming glass table, to avoid leaving an impression.

She coughed—the smoke was getting quite heavy—and then tucked the paper away. "How can he possibly guarantee the passport? With the technology these days?"

"There's a way. Pretty obvious, too, and not much the authorities can do to stop it. He'll tell you if he wants to."

"Thank you, Sam."

He smiled sadly. "A word of advice, my dear. When you're on the run, get as much sleep as you can. Rest is a weapon, too."

"I'll remember."

"Are you sure you want to go through with this, Bethany? You can still turn yourself in. The longer you spend running, the less inclined they'll be to believe you when they catch you."

"I know."

"And they will catch you, my dear. Sooner or later, either the good guys will catch you or the bad guys will."

She tried not to think about that. "How much will the passport cost me?"

"Nothing. I'm owed a few favors."

"So now I owe you a favor."

"The only favor I ask is that you never contact me again." He made no effort to hide the sadness. "Not that I have much time left."

Her smile faded. "Sam, I—I don't know what to say."

"I have to suffer, Bethany. I'm not saying it's God's will. I'm saying it's well earned." He leaned back, and she saw now, in addition to the beads of sweat on his forehead, the way he kept his body rigid in what must be a constant battle against the pain. "But I also know that I've been forgiven. I'm ready to face my Maker." He straightened. "Never mind. Look. There's a lot of advice you need, but we don't have time. So let me tell you two things, and two only. One, they'll be watching everyone they can think of who might help you."

"I know—"

"Hush. Listen. The other thing is, they're not ten feet tall. They'll make mistakes, same as you will. Somewhere in your past are people nobody's dug up. Those are the only people you can go to."

"I understand."

He took another long drag, then hunched forward. "Bethany, listen. That fellow you spoke to yesterday. Elliott St. John. You don't think it's odd that he let you go?"

"I told him that I was being monitored."

"That shouldn't have slowed him down for an instant. Not with what seems to be at stake. I think you should consider the possibility that he might not be speaking on behalf of his—group. He might be engaged in a bit of private enterprise, to get his own hands on the Pilate Stone."

"That was my thinking."

"Well, then, I'd be careful. Sounds to me like this Wilderness is divided. I know you think you have him over a barrel, but you don't want to be caught in the crossfire. Excuse my mixed metaphor. On the other hand, dissension in the ranks of the one's opposition always presents certain opportunities, at least if handled carefully."

"I'm not entirely sure anymore which side is the opposition. I can't even say with confidence which side Annabelle was on."

"Sounds like she was on a side of her own. And that's the curious part. If St. John's people didn't kill her, and if you're sure that David's side didn't kill her, then who on earth—"

The doorbell rang.

DeMarco rolled smoothly over to the console. Over his shoulder she could see two men already holding up their credentials for the camera.

"FBI," he said, tonelessly.

Bethany was halfway to her feet. In her mind, whirling images: handcuffs, the cell door slamming, maybe even the needle, because the murder took place in Virginia—

"Calm down," said DeMarco. "Of course they'd want to talk to me. They're just a little earlier than expected, that's all." He pondered. "I have to let them in, Bethany. Now, relax. They're not serving a warrant, so they can't search my house. They don't think you're here or they'd have SWAT with them. This is routine." He nodded toward the kitchen. "Go in there, close the slats. You can listen if you want, or sneak out the back. It's up to you."

"They might be watching the back!"

"Calm down, sweetie." He actually smiled. "I told you. It's routine. I have experience. If they were covering the back door, they'd be breaking down the front door."

"Yes, but—"

"Go on. Shoo." Something in his eyes was deadly serious again. "And be quiet." A wink so grim she felt a chill. "And pray."

Bethany prayed. Hard. Then she stood in the small kitchen, peering through the louvers as DeMarco's wheelchair backed into the family room. She had already opened the back door a crack so that if she decided to run they would not hear the latch.

She saw the two agents follow him in. She couldn't make out the words. DeMarco inspected their credentials, then rolled back to put some distance between himself and his visitors, and waved toward a couple of chairs. One of the agents sat; the other remained on his feet, over near the shelves, hands never straying far from his coat. He also never removed his hat, which struck her as odd, even provocative.

She noticed that Sam kept glancing his way.

It occurred to her that they were treating him like a very dangerous man; and she wondered, as she used to when she watched him at the shooting range, what exactly he had retired from.

"I don't know where she is," Bethany heard Sam saying. She realized that he had raised his voice for just that reason, hoping, no doubt, that the agents would raise theirs, too. "I haven't seen her."

"She's in town," said the agent who was sitting.

"What town? This town?"

"Don't fence with us, Mr. DeMarco. As I'm sure you realize, sir, abetting a fugitive will void the provisions of the Witness Protection Program." He turned a page of the notebook. "I wonder whether Ms. Barclay is even aware of your crimes."

The old man smiled. "When you catch her, let me know. I'll be happy to fill her in."

"Let me guess. She thinks you're Mafia or something, doesn't she? She has no idea what you really did. Or for whom."

"I don't know what she thinks or doesn't think, Agent Fiedler. She's never asked."

"Nevertheless, she's in town. And I very much doubt that it's the covered bridge, lovely though it is, that has brought her to Ashland. So either she's been here or she's on her way here."

Sam shrugged. "Well, either way, I don't know where she is. Sorry I can't be of help."

The agent in the chair seemed satisfied. The taller man near the bookshelf frowned. He took off his hat and held it in to the side. His dark hair was parted with a streak of white. Bethany had seen him before; she was certain of it.

"I'm sorry, Mr. DeMarco," the taller man said. "I don't think I believe you."

"I'm telling you the truth. I don't know where she is."

"Oh, I believe that part. I'm sure she didn't tell you where she'd be hiding out. She might have tried, but you would never have allowed it. Nevertheless, she's been here, in this house, and you've spoken to her."

Sam still seemed relaxed, hands in his lap. "What makes you say that?"

"I'm good at reading people."

"So am I."

"Good. Then you know we're not leaving here until you tell us what we want to know."

Sam DeMarco looked from one visitor to the other, then backed his wheelchair off slightly. "May I see those credentials again, please, gentlemen?"

The nearer of the two visitors made a mistake. He glanced at his partner first, and only then slipped his hand into his jacket. But long before he could draw his firearm, DeMarco had shot him twice, center mass, with the gun he had pulled from the folds of the blanket.

The taller of the two was more clever, and more watchful. He had his gun out and trained before DeMarco could shift his aim. He fired a single shot through the old man's forehead.

Her fingernails were digging into the Formica. Waves of nausea made her vision go gray, but still she had the presence of mind to make no sound.

The man with the streak in his hair was kneeling beside his fallen comrade. He leaned in close. The wounded man was whispering something. The killer tried to get him on his feet. When it became apparent that the wounded man could not stand, his partner picked up DeMarco's gun and shot him a third time, then held him while he died.

By this time Bethany was already out the door, stumbling up the rocky slope behind the house. She remembered now. The killer with the white streak in his hair, the man who had just murdered Sam, was the same man who had tried to kidnap her on the streets of Chicago.

FIFTY-EIGHT

Stuart Van Der Staal crossed the covered bridge and climbed into the hills. Ten minutes along, he reached forest land that was deep enough for his purpose. He turned in at a dirt track, cut his lights, and waited. Satisfied that nobody was following, he dragged his associate's body from the car and into the trees. He stripped the corpse of identification, including wallet and watch and a gold cross on a chain that he found around the neck. No doubt the remains would be found within a day, but a day was all he needed to get clear.

He should have known better than to take on baggage. But he had been wary of visiting Sam DeMarco alone. The man might have been in a wheelchair, but in his time had been a formidable figure. Had Stuart gone in by himself, he might never have come out.

No matter.

The professor stood, brushed off his hands, turned away. Then he stopped. A prickle on the back of his neck. Something he had forgotten. Overlooked. He patted his pockets. He had the CDs that recorded the footage from the security system, and from the backup drive he'd found in the bedroom. Yet there was something scratching at his mind, some detail to which he should have attended.

Then he knew.

He pulled the gold cross out of his jacket. Odd decoration for a man who killed for a living. Did he really expect to go to Heaven with the lives he had taken still on his ledger?

And where on earth had that thought come from?

Stuart shivered. The dying man had been whispering, trying to tell him something. The professor wondered whether he might have been repenting the evil he had done.

Then he shook off the mood. Repentance, evil, Heaven, Hell—the stress of the chase was starting to get to him. After he caught up with Bethany and squeezed her dry, he would have to take a vacation.

Only as he left the woods and climbed back into his car did Stuart realize that he no longer had the cross. Without really thinking about it, he had fastened the gold chain back around the dead man's neck.

Bethany raced the borrowed Jetta through the darkness, no longer worried about being caught speeding. She had no choice but to take her chances. The address Sam had given her was in Baltimore. All she wanted now was to grab Janice, get the passports, and get out of the country.

She tried Janice's cell, twice, but the call went straight to voicemail. Maybe she was talking to Zach. Maybe she was asleep. Either way, she was breaking the rules. She was always to answer. Always. The second time, Bethany left her a message: get up, get dressed, get packed.

She screeched into the motel parking lot, flew to the room—

And found it empty.

Not just empty.

The room had been cleaned, top to bottom. The carpet had been vacuumed, the bathroom sparkled. The room might never been stayed in. Bethany's overnight bag was neatly packed, standing by the door. There was no sign of Janice, or any of her things.

Where had she gone?

Then she saw the printed note in the middle of the crisply made bed.

When you have everything, call. Not before. You have two weeks.

Clipped to the page, just below a telephone number, was a photograph of Janice. She was blindfolded, and looked terrified: not surprising, given the gun pointed at her head.

FIFTY-NINE

She had no choice. She rushed back to the car and plunged into the darkness. She drove into Vermont, then south, going hard for a full ninety minutes before she felt safely outside whatever cordon the FBI by now had set up. She pulled over into a deserted strip mall and tore open the final envelope—the one reserved for emergencies.

> *Guess you're in trouble, too, huh? Text this number the details. Don't call, just text. Don't say who you are. Do what you're told. They can get you out of whatever mess you're in. But it'll cost.*

Bethany took a long breath, then pulled out her phone. She watched the road for a bit, but the few cars that passed took no interest. Feeling a fool, but having no choice, she texted:

in trouble

Nothing happened. She put her face in her hands, ready to surrender, but shook off the mood an instant later. One of Aunt Claudia's favorite sayings popped into her head: *He hasn't brought you this far to drop you now.*

Her phone beeped.

are you injured?

She texted back:

no

She waited. Caught herself almost smiling. Wished Janice were here to argue that the message arriving just as she was thinking about God was just coincidence. Wishing Janice were here.

The phone beeped.

are you mobile?

i have a car.

are you in the united states?

yes.

what state are you in?

connecticut, she lied.

Long pause.

can you get to newburgh new york in three hours?

yes.

route 9w, north from the bridge 8 miles, elaine's grill. order cheesecake. go now.

Another beep.

and don't lie about your location next time. i'm a friend.

She went.

"The carnage is inexcusable," the Protector says. "They'll never stop now. You have to know that."

"I know," says Elliott St. John. He is standing in the master suite of his Manhattan triplex, the lights of the city glittering far below. Once again he wonders how this phone can possibly be as safe as the Protector insists; but the last thing he wants to do is argue the point. "He's out of control."

"I smell a 'but.'"

"He has a plan to reacquire the target."

"I'm sure he does, Elliott. He always has a plan for something. He just isn't as talented as we thought."

"Or God's on their side."

The magnate means this as a joke, but the Protector's tone betrays not the slightest amusement. "He's become a liability."

"I agree."

"You know what that means."

"I do, Protector, but consider the possibility that he's hidden information about us. Guarantees for his own survival."

"Do you think he has?"

"I would."

A chilly silence on the line. "Point taken, Elliott, but you needn't worry. We're reasonable people here, not fanatics. We don't treat each other that way." Another pause, to let this sink in. "Now, listen to me. If our Professor does manage to reacquire the target, so much the better. She's most likely planning to leave the country. I assume that he can follow her if need be. But, to be on the safe side, we've taken out some insurance."

"Insurance?"

"Just to make sure she knows who's in charge."

As usual, the Protector hangs up without saying good-bye, the way important people do these days: Elliott himself has the same habit. He tiptoes back into the bedroom to make sure his wife is asleep, then goes up to the top level of the three-story apartment. His private sanctuary. He uses a key card and a code to open the door, and steps into his large office. A bodyguard who doubles as an assistant is dozing in the corner but leaps to his feet.

"Relax, Ben. I'm just going into the vault."

The vault is on the two-man system, and both he and Ben turn their separate keys. Inside the air is pressurized and dust-free. The artificial light is dim. The temperature is a chilly fifty-five degrees. Elliott keeps only a few of his baubles here. He walks along a row of display cases until he finds the cabinet he wants. Already sized, just waiting for its prize. Underneath is a plaque, blank except for the title, because until he has something to place in the box, the curators won't know what the inscription should say.

The Pilate Stone, the title reads.

Elliott braces himself against the case, bowing his head, although not in prayer. "They won't keep you from me," he hisses. "I don't care how much insurance they take out."

Elaine's Grill turned out to be a burned-out shell, the sign askew, the windows bashed in or boarded up, the once-shiny surface defaced by years of graffiti. Whoever was on the other end of the phone either hadn't been here in a while or had a bizarre sense of humor.

She drove on past, turned around, passed again. The parking lot was closed off with a rusty chain. Weeds had sprung through the asphalt. No cars were parked and waiting; nobody lurked in the shadows.

A quarter mile to the south was a dead-end street of small but well-kept homes. She turned in, pulled to the side, tried to work out what she was supposed to do now. She had the name and address of Sam DeMarco's passport man in her pocket, but he lived in Baltimore, and she had serious doubts about her ability to make it that far undetected. She knew she needed help, but hanging around a boarded-up diner was the sort of tactic likely to attract the attention of the local police.

Wait.

The phone.

She picked it up, sent another text:

i'm here. where are you?

No answer.

As Bethany pondered her next move, headlights swept through her windows. She stiffened, but the passing car continued down the street. She waited, sitting very still, until its taillights vanished around a corner. Bethany let out the breath she didn't realize she had been holding. From her jacket she pulled the photograph of Janice, eyes wild and frightened, the gun tapping her temple. She had to—

Headlights again, coming the other way, very fast.

A car pulled up beside her, a dark sedan, blocking her in.

The window rolled down, and a familiar head poked out.

"Nobody's following you," said Raymond Fuentes. "Grab what you need and get in."

They drove for a while in silence, heading south. He hadn't asked her where she wanted to go. She was waiting to see where he would take her. The green mileposts ticked past in the glow of the headlights. Probably she dozed.

"You were working together," she said when she could stand the silence no longer. "You and Annabelle. You were working together."

A moment as he thought this through. She had a vision of a list in his head, questions and permitted responses side by side.

"We were working together," he finally agreed.

"For how long?"

"A while."

Well, thanks. She tried again: "Working for whom?"

Another age before he answered. "All that matters is whom we were working against." The muscles of his face described something very near a smile. "I told you, Bethany. I'm an army of one."

Her turn to ponder. "Where are we going?"

"Wherever you need to."

"I don't know yet," she said, and this was true: for she had no idea whether to trust him. What had sent her scrambling into his car wasn't the certainty that he was there to rescue her, but the sheer bone-weariness of running alone.

His nod was tight and precise. "That makes sense. You shouldn't give me your ultimate destination. Not unless there's no alternative. My plan is simply to drive you past what I consider the danger zone, then to let you make your own way." A sidelong glance. "I gather you're good at that."

"What's the danger zone?"

"Wherever that man can reach you."

"What man?"

"The man who killed Sam DeMarco and the two federal agents. I'm glad you got out. In the worst case, I was prepared to go in after you."

"You were *there*?"

He chose to answer a slightly different question. "The man who did the shooting is a professional assassin. His name is Stuart Van Der Staal. He's also the man who tried to kidnap you from the Village House."

Bethany rubbed her arm, remembering the IV line. "Somehow I'm not surprised that the two of you are acquainted."

"We're not. I used various sources to check him out. I suspect that the Bureau will have his name by tomorrow. If they don't, I'll make sure they get it."

She gave him a hard look. "Who exactly *are* you?"

But Raymond Fuentes had his own agenda.

"I don't know precisely what Van Der Staal wants you for, but I am certain that he'll try to reacquire you. I don't plan to let that happen."

"You know how he's going to do it?"

"I know how I'd do it."

The steadiness in his dark gaze warned her not to ask. A sign said they were entering New Jersey.

"If you were in Ashland," she said suddenly, "why did you make me go all the way to Newburgh?"

"So I could follow you. There's not a surveillance detail in the world that I wouldn't notice during a three-hour drive."

Another silence; and again she was the one to break it.

"They said your sister was part of Martin's group."

"Meg. She was."

"What happened?"

She had the sense that she had offended him, and did not expect an answer. But he was only gathering his thoughts. "Meg and I used to be close. Very close. Then I went off to war, and Meg—well, she was antiwar. Our parents were missionaries. Traveled the world planting churches. That's what I thought I'd be doing now, too. And Meg—well, she's very serious about her faith. And very into Christian nonviolence. For her, well, war, self-defense, abortion, killing animals—they're all violent, and all sinful. I understand her. I did my honors thesis in college on Augustine and just war theory. I suppose the difference between Meg and me was the same difference that distinguishes theologians who write about war. Some of them think peace is God's intended condition for man, so that every act of violence is an aberration, to be allowed only in the most extreme cases. That was Meg's view." He sped up to pass a weaving pickup. "The others believe that justice is God's intended condition for man, and that injustice is the aberration, to be allowed only in the most extreme cases. That's closer to my view. War is sometimes a tragic necessity, a period of destruction to avoid a greater injustice. We should always hate the war and we should never hate our enemy, but there are times when you have to fight."

She was surprised to find him so forthcoming; and even more so that he could calmly discuss theology while driving her away from a hired killer and toward an uncertain destiny abroad.

"So, the two of you had a falling out over just war?"

"I was in Afghanistan. Meg thought the war was wrong. She thought I was wrong. She was in college. We kept in touch. Email. Skype. Then she stopped."

"When she joined up with Martin."

He had skipped ahead in the story. "I took early discharge after—well, things happened in Afghanistan, and I was offered the option, and I took it. I went looking for Meg. I found Martin. He told me she'd been there for two months, maybe three. Then she'd gone off to follow some guru in San Francisco. I didn't know people still did that."

A brief shared smile.

"I went to California. Found the guru, but no Meg. I tracked her for weeks. I finally found her at a vegan commune outside Seattle. Perfectly nice people, but she wasn't particularly happy to see me. Martin teaches that government is a threat." A sidelong glance. "You don't get that until you've been there a few weeks, but he does. Did. A lot of these cult leaders are the same. Once you're hooked on the joy and the mantras, they tell you to stay away from the outside. The authorities mean you ill, don't trust them, and so forth. Poor Meg was running from one cult to the next. They had different ways of finding salvation, but all of them agreed that government was out to get them. Anyway, she had it in her head that I was the enemy now."

"What did you do?"

"Hung around for a few days, trying to get past her barriers. I think I did, a little. But then she asked me to go away and not come back. If she wanted to talk to me, she said, she knew where to reach me."

"So you left."

"I did."

"But why did you go back to Martin?"

"Because the vegan commune was harmless and the guru was merely offensive, but Martin was actually dangerous. I wanted to get the goods. Put him out of business."

"An army of one," she said, remembering.

"That's right."

But it wasn't right.

"If you and Annabelle were working together, did you know what she was doing? Did you know—the people who sent her—did she tell you who?"

"We're not going to have that conversation. I'll get you where you have to be, and then I have to go cover your tracks."

"But why? Why are you helping me?"

He was pulling onto the off ramp. They were at a rest stop. The top of the New Jersey Turnpike. It was well past two in the morning. A couple of long-haul truck drivers dozed in their cabs. Other than that the parking lot was nearly empty.

"This is how it works, Bethany. I can leave you here to make your own way. I can take you into Newark or Philadelphia, and you can get a bus or a train to wherever you need to be."

She hesitated. "The young woman I was traveling with. Janice. You haven't asked me about her."

"I assumed you'd tell me if you wanted me to know."

"I do." She swallowed. "They took her. I don't know where she is."

"I see."

"Can you—is there any way—I mean, you obviously have some kind of connections—"

His hand came up and, with surprising gentleness, touched her cheek. "It's unlikely that I can help, but I'll see what I can do."

She smiled: first time in a while. "Then can you do one more thing for me? Can you drive me a little farther?"

"How much farther?"

"Baltimore."

SIXTY

Professor Stuart Van Der Staal is at a shopping mall in Stamford, Connecticut, because the mazes of stores and endless escalators that fill these vast indoor spaces provide excellent conditions for detecting surveillance. Shoppers are constantly pausing, peering in windows, changing their minds, darting out of one store and into another. To the uninitiated, Stuart's is another face in the mindless consumerist horde. The natural cover allows him plenty of opportunities to watch for the unfortunate tail who is wrong-footed by his antics and has to match him, dart for dart.

After an hour's wandering, he decides that there is nobody.

Good. Now he gives himself over to thinking. It is the morning after the mess in Ashland, and he has a decision to make. The instructions he received in Hartford were crystal clear: take Bethany Barclay and discover what she knows. The plan failed. It might have worked, except that his fool partner forced Stuart to kill Sam DeMarco before they could question him; but Stuart's employer will be uninterested in his excuses.

Therefore he must conceive a plan to reacquire her.

Everyone in the trade understands the trick: to find a target when you don't know where to start looking, you have to make the target come to you. This in turn requires both decisive action and a way of ensuring that your target learns of your action.

Stuart is in Brooks Brothers, trying on a two-thousand-dollar tweed blazer, when the solution comes to him. Perception is everything, yes, but no two people see the same event the same way. He needs an event whose import Bethany alone will perceive.

A kidnapping.

A spectacular one. A kidnapping that will make the news wherever Bethany may be in the world, along with a message that she alone will understand.

Stuart pays for his jacket and hurries to his car. On the road again, heading south, he feels a wash of relief. Smiling to himself, he tunes in a religious broadcaster, hunting as always for topics for his blog. Some fool is preaching on the problems of today's teenagers, viewed through the lens of the Bible. The sermon puts him in mind of Janice Stafford. The two women were in Ashland together, but the black girl is baggage. Sooner or later, he suspects, Bethany will perceive this truth, and dump her.

"This time we know it wasn't Bethany Barclay," says Carl Carraway. "The video feed from Sam DeMarco's front door camera is clear. The two men held up badges, they went inside. Fifteen minutes later, one of them carried the other out. The discs had been removed from DeMarco's surveillance system and the backups, but the killer didn't know there were backups to the backups. That's where the images are from."

It is the morning after the shootings. Carraway and Pulu are once more in their superior's office. Nobody reads the winds like Vanner. Ramirez and her partner have been packed off to Philadelphia to interview Polly Hollins. It is very much Carl's task force once more.

"We found Bethany's prints on the kitchen counter," he continues. "Our best reconstruction is that she hid there while DeMarco held the killers off. It's the only scenario that makes sense of the evidence."

Pulu chimes in. "Norval Jamison is awake. A couple of agents are on the way down to the hospital with a print from the video camera. If his assailant is one of the men from DeMarco's house, that puts her off the hook for the shootings in Virginia too."

Carraway again: "A state trooper already has made a tentative ID of the man who exited DeMarco's house as the driver of a car that passed him, very fast, while he was on the way to the scene at our request."

Vanner goes into one of her distant reflections. Her two subordinates wait.

"Good work," she finally says. "We'll get the information out about this shooter. He sounds like a professional, so he should turn up in a database somewhere. Probably he gets his own task force." She brushes her hands as if to put the unpleasantness behind her. "Now let's talk about Barclay."

Carraway is agitated. "It's obvious now, isn't it? She didn't do this shooting. She didn't kill David Hollins or shoot Norval Jamison. Martin Potus says she wasn't involved in the bombings. With her name attached to so many crimes she didn't commit, the chances are we'll find out she didn't kill Ken Kirkland either. I think we're chasing an innocent woman."

"That's not our call. That's up to the Justice Department."

"But—"

"Our job remains the same. Find her and bring her in. If she's innocent, I'm sure she'll point that out."

A prickly pause.

"We've processed the motel room where she and Janice Stafford stayed," says Carl. "No prints at all. People in town saw them together, but two witnesses saw Bethany leave alone in the car."

"It's a motel. Not the White House. The witnesses can't know for sure that Barclay left alone. The Stafford girl could have been hiding in the backseat of the car. She could have been down the block at Burger King. She could have been anywhere."

"But suppose the witnesses are right," Carraway persists. "Just for a moment. Suppose Bethany did leave alone. Why would she do that? From what witnesses tell us, the two of them seemed very close. Her attitude toward Janice has been described as maternal. Bethany calls her 'honey.' The way you would a child. I don't think she'd drop her voluntarily."

Vanner steeples her fingers. "Ah. I take it that we're back to Ted Lesofsky's conspiracy theories again."

"Don't dismiss it out of hand. Ted's note said there would be duplicates of whatever records Annabelle left behind. Suppose Bethany has those copies. Then she'll be following the trail. And if I'm worried about what she might find—if I want first look, say—then what better way than snatching Janice?"

"It's a reasonable theory," says Pulu.

Vanner's tone is brisk. "Makes no difference. We can do theoreticals all week, but they won't bring us any closer to finding Barclay. Try to remember who the target is." She lifts a warning finger to forestall his interruption. "And if you're right, Agent Carraway—if Seaver left behind notes that point to a conspiracy—then surely those notes are better off in our hands than in Bethany Barclay's."

Carl is unable to hide his surprise. "You're saying you want us to find Annabelle's notes and—and just turn them over?"

"To the Bureau. Not to me personally." Vanner seems amused. "Don't be like Ted Lesofsky. Not everybody's a conspirator."

"Pastor Jamison has given us another tentative identification of your gunman," says Vanner. It is three hours later, and she has summoned them back to her office. "And I'm told that three of the Village House survivors have also picked out his photo as the man they call the Professor. Congratulations, Carl. It appears that you may have been right."

Carraway and Pulu exchange a look. This was the most fulsome praise they had ever heard their superior bestow.

"Meanwhile," she continues, "you'll be astonished to hear that no amount of pressure will persuade our friends at Langley to say anything other than that Raymond Fuentes has had no connection with the Agency for nearly a year. I'm almost ready to believe them."

"Almost?" asks Carl.

"Let me put it this way. He wouldn't be the first retired officer to sell his services to a less seemly bidder." She clicks to another screen on her laptop. "There's something else," she says, scrolling. "Agent Ramirez just called from Pennsylvania with a preliminary report on the interrogation of Mrs. Hollins." Vanner flashes her most clever smile. She is fully aware of the drama of the moment. As a rule she does not like being on stage, but just now she seems to be enjoying herself. "We now know why Mrs. Hollins was so determined to get immunity. Last fall, she let her sister borrow her passport."

She lets this sink in.

"Obviously, Annabelle Seaver wanted to leave the country without being detected. Evidently there is considerable physical resemblance between the two sisters. Nevertheless, loaning a passport is of course a felony. And we're not sure that's the only thing she did. Mrs. Hollins continues to hedge, but Agent Ramirez believes that the sisters may have been in touch several times during those missing months."

"Do we know where Annabelle went?" asks Carl.

"A report is being compiled. It should be in your digital mailbox shortly. Because, Carl, if your theory is correct, then wherever Annabelle went, that's where Bethany plans on going, too. It also explains why she went to see Sam DeMarco. She needs a fake passport, and he's the only one she knows—knew—who could tell her where to get one." The smile fades. "Well, don't just stand there. Go find her."

Pulu is out the door. Carraway lingers.

"Yes, Carl?"

"About this Professor—"

"What else do you want me to say? You were right. And he killed two of ours. We have hundreds of people looking for him. On the off chance that he really is a professor, we have facial matching software checking his photograph against images of every college faculty member here and in Canada. We'll get him. Don't worry."

"Yes, ma'am. But having his name and having him aren't the same thing."

Her eyes narrow. "Go on."

"You remember the other part of my theory? That whoever's behind this would be following Bethany?"

"I remember."

"Well, I think the shooting in Ashland may not have been the original plan. It's possible that she's slipped the Professor's net as well as ours."

"So?"

"So, he'll have to pick up her trail again."

"Let me guess. You have a theory on how he might do that."

"I do. And if I'm right, we'll catch him in the act."

As Carl Carraway descends the short flight of stairs to the bullpen, his partner leaps to his feet, smiling broadly. "We have the report on the passport. She went to Europe."

"You don't say."

Pulu is still smiling. "Annabelle Seaver took possession of her sister's passport in October or November. In December she flew from Dulles airport to London. No passport controls in the EU, but over the next month, she used the passport to register at hotels all over the continent—Amsterdam, Paris, Rome, and a whole lot of smaller places. She also traveled as far east as Istanbul, and as far south as Cairo."

"We didn't see any of this on her credit cards?"

"Paid cash everywhere."

"For a month? That would have been tens of thousands of dollars. She'd have set off alarms somewhere."

"She did. Or rather, her sister did. That's why we got the information so fast. It's already in the system. Financial Crimes picked up the pattern of cash transactions linked to the passport and was looking into the movements of Polly Hollins, seeing whether there might be any illegal activity." He grins. "It never occurred to them to check and see whether she'd actually left the country." He has laid all the reports on his partner's desk. "Anyway, now we know where Annabelle Seaver was."

Carl considers. "Right. Now, back to Sam DeMarco. It's possible that he was killed before he and Bethany met. But let's assume otherwise. Let's assume she somehow got out before the shooting, with the information about where to get a false passport. She'll be using it to follow Annabelle to Europe."

"So all we have to do is figure out what name she's using and watch every border crossing and airport in the United States."

Carraway is reaching for his jacket. "Maybe there's an easier way."

SIXTY-ONE

Judge Edna Harrigan is unhappy to find the FBI men back at her door, not least because she is reciprocating the brunch Lillian Hartshorne gave her the other day. The morning is rainy, so they are eating in the glass-walled dining nook rather than on the terrace, and the food was prepared by the hostess herself rather than by a staff. But Lillian professes to be enjoying the meal anyway, and Edna supposes that she might be. Lillian has spent most of the hour trying to persuade her friend to join the board of some charity, but toward the end Edna manages to turn the conversation back to bllnet.

"What about them, darling?"

"Have they done any actual damage? As opposed to getting into people's systems? They haven't attacked the power grid or air traffic control or anything like that?"

"Not that I'm aware of. No." Pursing transparent lips. "You never know with young people today. But I think I would have heard."

"What I'm wondering is why Janice Stafford left them."

The painstakingly plucked eyebrows levitate. "Edna. Dear, darling Edna. Whoever said she's left them?"

It is at that moment that the doorbell rings.

"I'm terribly sorry," she tells Carraway and Pulu as they stand in the foyer. "This isn't a good time. I'm entertaining."

"Nonsense," says Lillian, who has come padding up behind. "This is official business, Edna. You have to cooperate."

Edna shuts her eyes briefly. Her friend's view of the world has been largely formed by the movies in which she herself once acted, before she married her late billionaire. Her great Hollywood claim to fame is that she was the girl who died at the seven-minute mark of one of the more forgettable Bond films.

"I really think the agents should come back at a more convenient time," says Edna.

"We didn't mean to interrupt," says boyish Carraway. "We only need five minutes."

Lillian is already reaching for her coat. "Nonsense. I was just leaving anyway. Edna, thank you for a lovely meal."

She does kissy things in the air near Edna's cheeks, then glides out onto the porch, where her driver waits.

"Bethany may be trying to leave the country," says Carraway.

Edna sniffs. "I shouldn't be a bit surprised, with you people hounding her for crimes she didn't commit."

"Yes, ma'am. But let's say you're right." He hunches forward. "Suppose she didn't do those things. We still have to find her. She's in trouble. She needs help."

"They teach you that on the course, I believe. Pretending that you're in this for the good of your suspect."

"They do, ma'am. But in this case it's true." He opens a folder, passes a photograph to her. "Have you ever seen this man?"

She studies the print, shakes her head. "Not that I can recall."

"We believe that he's trying to find her. He killed two federal agents and a protected witness."

Edna's face goes gray. "When?"

"Two nights ago. The shooting in New Hampshire."

"I saw it on the news. They said it was an organized crime hit."

"We don't think so. The man who was killed was Sam DeMarco. You remember. He used to live around here? Took Bethany shooting? Her surrogate father. I seem to recall we discussed him the last time we were here."

Edna continues to hold the photograph.

"We believe that the killer went to DeMarco's house hoping to trap Bethany. She'd been there—we have her prints—and there's some reason to think she might have witnessed the shooting. No, no"—she is about to object—"we don't think she was involved. We think she was hiding in the kitchen. We know she got away. We found the car she'd been using. It was abandoned on a side street in Newburgh, New York."

"If you're asking me why she would be in Newburgh, I have no earthly idea." She hands the photograph back. "Why exactly is this man after Bethany?"

"That's what we'd like to find out. We were hoping you might be able to shed some light."

"I'm sorry, Agent Carraway. As I said, I don't know him."

"Yes, ma'am." He glances at his partner. "But you still might be able to help."

"How?"

"Judge Harrigan, our working theory is that Bethany is being manipulated by someone—some group—to follow the path of her friend Annabelle. We don't know why. We do think that this, um, this group's intentions may have been benign. But matters have spun out of their control."

Edna says nothing. Her eyes are wide behind the rimless glasses, but the energy has gone out of the small body.

"Ma'am, our thinking is, if there were some way to get in touch with this group—with, say, some friend of hers who got her into this—we might stand a better chance of tracking her down." He taps the photograph. "Of finding her before this man does." He watches her closely. "This man, or perhaps others we haven't yet been introduced to. We don't really know how many people may be interested in her movements."

Edna moistens her lips. "I'm not sure what you expect me to say, Agent Carraway."

"Do you know where Bethany is?"

"No."

"Do you know where she's going?"

"No."

He never breaks eye contact. "Ma'am, we believe the reason that Bethany is trying to leave the country is that she is following Annabelle Seaver's trail. It's possible that Annabelle was recruited by the same people who recruited Bethany."

The judge shakes her head. Her hands are trembling. "I wouldn't know anything about that, Agent Carraway."

"But you do know that Bethany and Annabelle were close."

"Of course."

"Here's why I ask. We have reason to believe that Bethany is familiar with Annabelle's itinerary. She knows that Annabelle left the country. She knows when and how and where. So far, she's followed Annabelle's path precisely. Annabelle visited her sister. So did Bethany. Annabelle visited her aunt. So did Bethany. Annabelle visited her half brother. So did Bethany. Annabelle went to Chicago, to the Village House. So did Bethany. She isn't just going to the same places. She's following a design. I think she's trying to get inside Annabelle's head at the same time that she's following Annabelle's path."

Edna's eyes narrow. Her faculties are working again. "I think I see what you're leading up to, Agent Carraway. You're going to ask if she would also follow Annabelle's precise itinerary around Europe."

"Yes, ma'am. Exactly."

"You're thinking she might even try to use the same airports. If she's trying to get inside Annabelle's head. Go to Europe by the same route, to be sure she's not missing anything. You'll excuse me, Agent Carraway, but I find that rather farfetched."

"Come on, Judge. She's counted up the risks and decided to keep going. Still, in her mind, this may well be the last trip she'll ever make. Doesn't it stand to reason that she'll take into account Annabelle's itinerary?"

Edna purses her lips. "If what you mean, Agent Carraway, is that she will most likely visit the same places Annabelle did, trying, as you put it, to pick up the scent, of course you're right. But if you're suggesting that she'd depart from the same airport—well, she's much too clever for that."

"It's not cleverness I'm thinking about. It's sentimentality. Bethany is honoring her best friend, and she doesn't want to miss a thing. That's why I'd expect her to follow exactly the same route, beginning with that flight to London."

"If you're right, Agent Carraway, I'm afraid you have it backward. The psychology works the other way around. Annabelle's effort, if your explanation is correct, ended in disaster. If Bethany knows which airport Annabelle left from, that is the one airport you can be sure she'll avoid."

"So if I were to tell you that Annabelle left from Dulles Airport . . ."

"I would advise you that Dulles is the last airport you should be worried about."

At the door, Carraway said gently, "With Annabelle gone, you're probably Bethany's closest friend in the world, aren't you? She adores you."

"I really wouldn't know, Agent Carraway. Certainly I admire her."

"Do you like her?"

The question took Edna by surprise. "Of course I do."

"That's why you're worried about what she's gotten herself into, then. Because you're close to her."

"I believe I have made that point from your first visit."

"So I suppose you must have regrets, then." He kept his tone mild. "About getting her into this mess to begin with, I mean."

Her answering glare chased them to the car.

"So, where do we go?" says Pulu.

"Where do you think?"

"Let me guess. Dulles."

Carraway nods. He is driving very fast along back roads. "Judge Harrigan knew I was right. All that talk about Dulles being the last place Bethany would go—that was just to throw us off."

"But wouldn't Bethany assume we'd be watching that airport in particular?"

"Maybe not. She knows we're after her, but she doesn't know we know she's following Annabelle. And what I said to Judge Harrigan was true—Bethany can't afford to miss a clue. There might be something about that airport, or that flight, that fills in a crucial detail."

Pulu is reaching for his cell, but Carraway touches his wrist. "Let's keep this to ourselves for now. We're circulating the information. Every customs and immigration official in the country will have her photo. We'll have people at every international airport in the country. But Dulles—that's just between us."

"You know what the difference is between you and me, Carl? I've actually been to Kuala Lumpur. You on the other hand seem aching to go."

"I hear the Petronas Towers are breathtaking."

Pulu never cracks a smile. "What were you trying to say at the end? About Judge Harrigan getting her into this?"

"Just sending her a message. If she's part of this Garden—and you'll notice she never denied it—well, maybe if they know we're on to them, they'll keep their heads down."

"But that's not the only reason. You wanted to confirm that she's Bethany's best friend. Why?"

"Because, just now, Bethany Barclay's best friend is one of the worst things you can be." He sighs. "We'll have to send a team out here."

"I know, Carl."

"You noticed?"

Pulu nods. "You never told her Annabelle went to Europe."

SIXTY-TWO

Has it been worth it?" the Mathematician asks.

The Church Builder shakes his head, not in denial but in refusal. He refuses to weigh the damage against the goal. He fully accepts Augustine's teaching that it is licit to use force to achieve the positive good of justice, but he finds the practice daunting. His gaze roams the stolid, dusty shelves of the library, but somehow the usual reassurance doesn't come.

The Mathematician seems not to notice his old friend's difficulty. "When do you leave for Europe?" he asks.

"Hmmm? Oh, tomorrow. Tomorrow evening."

"And you're still sure you don't want any company?"

"You're supposed to be keeping your head down."

"I was asking if it's been worth it," the Mathematician resumes. He begins counting on his fingers. "Annabelle dead. David Hollins dead. Norval Jamison in critical condition. Two federal agents dead. One of our own bodyguards wounded. Janice Stafford missing. Her uncle dead. And of course Bethany Barclay still on the run. Can we justify all of this?"

"It's not our doing."

"But all of it was foreseeable, Harry. We knew this could happen."

"True." The Builder's fingers play with the folder. "And if it were simply a question of the Stone, we would have backed down. But I refuse to believe that Annabelle was simply duplicitous. Maybe she did take their money. That doesn't mean she sold us out."

"You still think she had names? The leaders of the Wilderness?"

"I suspect that's who was trying to buy the Stone. That's the point, George. She attracted their attention, and somebody over there made her a better offer. We have to find out who that somebody was."

"And that's worth it? All those deaths in exchange for that information?"

Harry Stean takes a long breath. "No, George. It's not worth it. Of course not. Not even close." He slumps, exhausted, and shuts his eyes. "Our Savior admonished His disciples to be as cunning as serpents. But I worry sometimes that I've become so cunning that I'm starting to forget why we're here." He sits straight again. "We have to live our faith. Even while we fight this battle, we have to live our faith."

The Mathematician's voice is gentle. "You need to rest, Harry."

"I have duties first, old friend. As to rest—well, it will come for me soon enough."

Night.

Stuart Van Der Staal is standing in the woods on the hill above Edna Harrigan's house. He has been here for over an hour, studying the landscape with the night vision glasses that render everything a shifting, sparkly green. Last month he gave a paper at the American Philosophical Association on research by neuroscientists into the possibility that the "green" or other colors that we see are not identical from one person to the next: if I saw the world through your eyes, I'd be frightened, because all the shades would be wrong. The experiments, he argued, lent weight to his view that there was no reality but only perception.

Yet tonight, as he has to admit to himself, there is a reality. He must reacquire Bethany swiftly, and snatching the prominent Edna Harrigan seems the most direct way to get her attention. He earlier considered taking Annabelle's sister or even her aunt, but there was no guarantee those stories would make the national news.

This one is sure to.

Time. The only movement he has detected over the past two hours is in the house, and only one small, stooped figure.

They are not waiting for him. They have not predicted this move.

He straps his rifle to his shoulder and begins to clamber down the slope—

And suddenly he can't see. All the world is blinding green. A light is shining directly into his face. Half blind, he tugs off the goggles and drops to a crouch, but there are shouts all around, harsh orders to drop his bag and get down on the ground, and, within, the steady, hated drumbeat he has always feared: "FBI! FBI."

Then it gets worse. He hears his name:

"Stuart Van Der Staal! On the ground!"

He backs toward the trees, although there have to be more agents behind him. Later, there will be considerable debate over the sequence of events. Several agents claim that their target began to unstrap his rifle. Others insist that he was removing his backpack, as ordered. In either case, the volley is swift and effective, most of the bullets striking his torso, driving him to the ground.

He is fascinated.

Even as the agents stream out of the woods to surround his shredded body, the professor is performing one last act of perception. For death, as Stuart has preached to generations of students, is the final event of existence, and so should be observed with detachment, and care.

He would have expected more pain. And more fear. He lifts a hand, or thinks he does. As the helmeted men approach and kick his gun away and flip him over and cuff his strengthless wrists, he wants to signal that his perception is as keen as ever, that he has always intended to meet his end fully aware of . . . of the . . . the pointlessness of life . . .

But what if there is a God?

A moment's panic at the thought that this might not after all be the end. Then Stuart Van Der Staal's eyes close for the final time, and he has the chance to find out.

SIXTY-THREE

Bethany Barclay sits in the international departure lounge, astonished that her passport has carried her this far. She is squeezed between a morbidly obese man and a woman who needs plenty of elbow room to work on her laptop. Bethany is watching CNN on the overhead monitor, the screen showing the driveway of Judge Harrigan's property, where last night federal agents killed a deranged ex-litigant, angry about an old case that went against him, who was there to kidnap or perhaps murder the judge. Only whenever they flash the dead man's face on the screen, Bethany can see only the horrific events three nights ago in Sam DeMarco's house, and her own near-miss when he tried to grab her off a Chicago street corner.

And she remembers Raymond Fuentes in the car, warning her that the killer will do what is necessary to reacquire her.

Reacquire. So clinical.

She had known they might take Janice. Somehow she had always known. That's why she never told Janice, or Tia, or Peter, or Elliott St. John that she perfectly well does know the identity of the Wise Man whom Annabelle kept talking about. Wise Man was Bethany's private nickname for her moral philosophy tutor from Oxford, a pompous, brilliant tyrant whose given surname was Wisdom. She never shared the nickname with anybody but Annabelle. The trouble is that Wisdom is dead. He's been dead for years. There is no way that Annabelle could have seen him; and no way she could have been referring to anybody else.

Nevertheless, it is in Oxford that she will find, if not the answer, at least the question.

"Excuse me, Miss."

She looks up. Two men stand before her, one in uniform with a gun on his belt, the other wearing a suit and carrying a walkie-talkie. He is doing the talking.

"Would you mind coming with us?"

Bethany rises. "Come with you where?"

"Please," he said.

"My flight—"

"Please don't make a scene," says the man in the suit. And takes a firm grip on her arm just in case.

Harry Stean is alone in the archives, ambling among the shelves. His mood is valedictory. He does not expect to pass this way again. He runs his fingers through the dust, and it is like hugging a friend. In a few hours he will be boarding his flight. He has left instructions for the succession; and for bringing the plan to fruition.

He ends his tour standing beside the Jonathan Edwards Bible once more, thinking back to the day, two weeks ago, when the attendant barged in to tell him that Bethany Barclay had gone off in an unexpected direction. At the time the information frightened and even depressed him, but now he is glad for it.

A remarkable young woman.

She escaped the traps laid for her in Virginia. She chose to run toward the solution to the mystery rather than run away to save her own skin. She evaded capture in Pennsylvania and New Jersey. She survived the Village House, and even helped bring it down. She survived Ashland. She was wanted by the authorities, but by all accounts was not even slowing down.

A formidable young woman.

Now she is preparing to leave the country, and he is doing the same. Very likely the Wilderness will send people after her as well. And so will the government.

And Bethany, knowing all of that, will keep going.

She has motives aplenty: saving Janice, avenging Annabelle, proving her own innocence. Yet Harry suspects that what drives her even more strongly is a determination to defeat the Wilderness. She might not know her adversary's name or history but she can surely sense its evil.

He opens the Bible, turning to the story of David and Goliath, reminding himself of what popular accounts so often miss. It is not David's confidence but his faith that leads him forward against the taunting giant. Harry recalls the words of Sarah Pierpont Edwards, Jonathan Edwards's wife: "I should be willing to die in darkness and horror, if it was most for the glory of God."

At this moment, he suspects Bethany Barclay capable of uttering the same sentiment, and meaning every word.

They take Bethany through a door marked Authorized Personnel Only, up a short flight of stairs, and along a narrow cinderblock hallway. A code opens another locked door, and she is in a small room furnished with an aging table and rickety chairs. A coffeemaker bubbles away on a faded credenza. A wide window gives a view of the airfield.

"Wait here, please," says the man in the suit.

Bethany sits.

This is it, she tells herself. You've known it was coming, so smile and accept whatever happens next. You've done what you can do, and the rest is out of your control. Nevertheless, she is already looking for a way out. The photograph of Janice is never far away. She remembers the pocket New Testament in her carryall. She pulls it out, but before she can even open to her bookmark, the door opens.

A slim man not much older than Bethany herself smiles his way into the room. His charm has her wary before he opens his mouth.

"My name is Carl Carraway," he says, pulling up a chair. He is holding a manila folder, quite thick, which he puts on the table, unopened. "I'm a Special Agent with the Federal Bureau of Investigation. I'm also co-chair of the task force assigned to the laboratory bombings."

Bethany nods; says nothing. Her chair has a short leg and won't keep still.

She's read in the past about interrogation gimmicks, and she can imagine situations in which this one might be effective. At the moment, however, the artifice merely annoys her.

The agent, meanwhile, is flipping through her passport. "Elaine McMullen. That's your name."

She is careful to look puzzled rather than defiant. "Yes. That's my name."

"Born in Ireland."

"Scotland."

"My apologies." He closes the passport, sets it carefully beside the folder. "You don't have an accent."

"I've lived here since I was a little girl, Agent Carraway."

"But you retain Scottish citizenship."

"Dual citizenship. May I ask what this is all about?"

He taps the passport. "This isn't a fake. It's genuine."

Bethany allows herself to flare. "Why would it be fake? Can you please hurry? I have a plane to catch."

"Why aren't you carrying your American passport, too?"

"I don't need it for Scotland, and, frankly"—she manages a confiding smile—"I'll be traveling on the Continent, and there are times when it's better if people don't think you're an American."

"When you return to the States, you won't be able to go through the green with your Scottish passport."

"I know the procedure, Agent Carraway."

"You really should carry both passports."

The sweat is gathering at the small of her back. She fights the urge to squirm. "I appreciate the advice."

"I imagine you're on the way to London for something important."

"Yes."

"Mind telling me what?"

"Yes."

"Yes, you'll tell me?"

"Yes, I mind. It's personal business."

"Family business?" He has taken up the folder and is leafing through whatever is inside, holding it at an angle where she can't see.

"Yes."

"Because I thought you might be flying off to right enormous wrongs. Catch the bad guys. The sort of thing, Ms. McMullen, that my Bureau exists for."

"No."

The eyes soften, taking her by surprise. "You're not in the middle of some huge battle? Good versus evil?"

"I—I'm not sure what you mean."

"I thought you might be on some sort of mission. Maybe a friend talked you into it. Maybe you've seen enough, Ms. McMullen. Maybe people have gotten hurt. Maybe you're starting to feel it's too much to handle alone." He has what he wants from the folder, but holds the page facedown. "If that's what's happening, maybe it's time to seek the help of someone like me. It can't be easy to battle secret enemies all by yourself."

Bethany's hold on the moment wavers. Only for a second, and then she has her control back, but she knows that his pale, clever eyes have spotted her brief instinct to yield to the desperate lonely desire to share her burden. She is caught, and she knows it. And cannot afford it. She forces her thoughts around to Janice; and fights her way through the temptation.

"If I ever meet any secret enemies," she says, in an awful stab at lightness, "I'll be sure to let you know."

"You should do exactly that, Ms. McMullen."

"I'll bear your advice in mind."

He turns back to the first page of the passport. "It says here that you're married."

"That's a typographical error."

"You should get it fixed."

"I know. But then I have to send in the whole passport, and I can't travel. Besides, when I'm abroad, the mistake can protect me."

"From what?"

"Men."

Carraway offers only half a smile. His pale eyes flick across her face. "Then you should get yourself one of those fake wedding bands. If you're going to live a cover story, you should live it to the full."

"I'll remember that," she says, looking at him very straight. Carl is impressed that she never hesitates, never seems to be guessing the answers, even when they sound wrong.

"This personal business of yours. I don't suppose it would involve tracking down what a good friend of yours was up to?"

"That's why I used the word 'personal,' Agent Carraway. To indicate that I would not be happy to discuss the details with a stranger."

"I only mention this because sometimes you can track people better with official help." When this offer elicits no response, Carl selects another approach. "Are you aware that it's a federal crime to lie to a federal officer in the course of an official investigation?"

"It should also be a federal crime to detain an innocent citizen and make her miss her flight."

He ignores the gibe. He flips over the page he has pulled from the file, sliding it across the table.

"Do you recognize this man?"

Bethany shakes her head. "No." But her voice is a distant croak. "No," she repeats, more strongly, if no less shakily. "Should I?"

"He killed a couple of federal agents three nights ago in Ashland, New Hampshire."

"I'm afraid I've never been there."

"I didn't ask if you had."

She slides the photograph back. "I have no idea who this man is."

"That's what I thought." The agent is smiling again. She isn't sure why. "You understand that I had to ask."

"I don't understand any of this, Agent Carraway."

"We're almost done. But I now need you to deny, for the record, that you are Bethany Barclay."

"Who?"

"The lawyer wanted in the bombings."

She throws a look of confusion onto her face. She has never been better. "You need me to deny it? I'm not her." She waves her fingers. "Want to take my prints?"

"That won't be necessary." He slides the passport back across the table. "Have a pleasant flight, Ms. McMullen. I apologize for the inconvenience."

"Thank you."

"Oh, one more thing, Ms. McMullen. If there's anything we can do for you while you're abroad—a friend who needs protecting, say—or maybe somebody who's missing and needs to be found—you shouldn't hesitate to call."

She drops her eyes. She can't help it. There is too much decency in his straight gaze; too much truth; too much sympathy; too much of what Aunt Claudia would have called honor. He is the man parents wish their daughters would bring home; and for that reason, extremely dangerous.

"I have to go, Agent Carraway. My flight will be boarding."

She leaves the room, expecting somebody to stop her.

Nobody does.

From his spot at the bar, Raymond Fuentes watches as Bethany emerges from the secure area, escorted back to her seat this time by the uniformed guard rather than the man in plainclothes. Good. That they questioned her at all worried him. That they let her go is exactly what he predicted.

So far, everything is according to plan.

"It wasn't her."

Pulu is beside himself. "What do you mean, it wasn't her? It was obviously her."

Carraway is standing at the window, watching a long line of planes waiting on the taxiway for the moment to take to the air. His hands are clasped behind his back, and he is rocking back and forth on the balls of his feet like a nervous child. "I'm telling you. Officially. For the record. That wasn't Bethany Barclay."

"Then who was it?"

"According to her passport, Elaine McMullen."

Pulu has been plundering the refrigerator. Now he takes his stance beside his partner, small orange juice carton almost invisible in his massive hand. "Elaine McMullen."

"That's right."

"You're taking a big chance, Carl." Pulu takes a sip, pulls a face. "Bethany got to you, didn't she? Vanner was right."

Carraway is laconic. "Let's say I'm pursuing a theory."

"What theory is that?"

"That Annabelle's notes are better off in Bethany's hands than ours."

Pulu chuckles. "Oh, so now you're with Ted Lesofsky? You think the Wilderness is secretly running the government?"

"Not at all." Through the window they watch Bethany's plane on the taxiway. "I just think there are times when a dedicated individual can do what a bureaucracy can't."

"And there's the Stafford girl to think about, I guess." Pulu takes another sip. "So, what now? Do we call British liaison? Arrange for somebody to watch her?"

"No."

"Carl—"

"If they watch her, they'll spook whoever else is watching her. If you want to catch the shark, you leave the small fish in the pond." He turns away from the window, rubs his exhausted eyes. "We solved the bombings. That's a big deal. We killed a maniac who murdered two of our agents and old Sam DeMarco, and probably David Hollins and a number of other people besides. That's a big deal. If we happen to miss one fish? If she stays in the sea?" He shrugs. "Sooner or later, the shark will come for her."

"And eat her up."

Carraway shakes his head. "She's done fine so far on her own. A very impressive young woman, Jake. Very impressive."

They are walking down the corridor now, heading back toward the airport security office. "Carl?"

"Hmmm?"

"What exactly do you plan to put in your report?"

"The same thing I told you. We made a mistake. That wasn't Bethany Barclay."

From her window seat near the rear of the massive plane, Bethany watches the jetway retracting, each boxy white section withdrawing into the next. The plane bucks and shudders as it is pushed backward out of the bay. Even as the aircraft begins moving under its own power, taxiing toward the runway, Bethany waits for the command from the tower to return to the terminal, or perhaps to park at some remote corner of the field while a suspected terrorist is taken into custody.

"Nervous?" The smooth young executive seated beside her has been trying to get her to talk to him from the moment they sat down. "Don't fly much?"

"I'm fine," she says, gruffly, wondering which side employs him, or if he is an army of one. Then she turns to him and makes herself smile. "Sorry. I'm just tired."

Now that he has her attention, he begins his patter, insinuating that nobody knows London's best night spots like he does, offering her half a dozen reasons to, as he puts it, hang out together once they arrive. Bethany ignores him. He's too boorish to be a threat.

She puts her head back, and once more does her sums. She has read the message right, she's sure she has. She'll find out why Annabelle said she'd seen the Wise Man when the Wise Man is dead. She'll track down whatever clues Annabelle stashed abroad, whether in England or elsewhere, to find the Pilate Stone or the leaders of the Wilderness or whatever Annabelle was hiding.

And she'll use what she finds to get Janice back.

Still, one thing puzzles her: she can't figure out why Agent Carraway let her go. Her best guess is that he was following orders. Raymond Fuentes told her there was no way to guess how high this thing goes, and she is inclined to believe him.

The plane is at the end of the runway. The captain tells them they are next for takeoff. The executive is still burbling in her ear, but Bethany shuts him out. She leans back and closes her eyes and prays to God to please keep Janice safe, whatever happens.

When she looks out the window again, the jumbo jet is clawing its way toward the clouds.

"Stay strong, honey," she whispers. "I'll find you."

EPILOGUE

Do we stop the bombings now?" asks the admiring young man, standing before the massive desk.

"We do," says the Protector of the organization sometimes known as the Wilderness. "We won half a victory only, but half is enough. Pretty soon the FBI will figure out that the churches had nothing to do with the bombs—and, certainly, that Bethany Barclay is innocent—but the damage we sought to inflict will mostly be done. Not perhaps as thorough as we hoped, but progress has been made in our struggle. And the news that no churches are suspected will be buried in the back of the papers. It won't make the evening news at all." Aged but brilliant blue eyes take the young aide's measure. "The bombings were a clever idea, no question, but were we to continue, the FBI would keep looking for the bombers. So let the buck stop at the Village House, as planned, and leave it to the bloggers to puzzle out the motive. As for us, we have a more pressing matter to discuss."

"Elliott St. John."

"Precisely," says the Protector. "I've known from the start what Elliott was up to. He can't help seeking his own advantage. He sees things his own way. He wants what he wants. He'd betray our great cause for an ancient relic that he'll never display for anyone's pleasure but his own. What do we do with a man like that?"

"We get rid of him," says the aide. He fights the urge to glance around the paneled office. He reminds himself that the room is as protected against eavesdropping as a room can be: for the Wilderness invests, always, in the most advanced available technology. "He's a liability."

"You're mistaken. We do nothing of the kind."

"Then tell me, please." His voice is stiff.

"Don't be hurt." A twinkle in the ancient blue eyes. "I was young once. I joined the Council when I was scarcely older than you are. I once shared the dream that problems should be dealt with decisively. Even violently." A chuckle. "But we are people of reason. You haven't forgotten that, surely. It's the Enemy, not we, who are the fanatics. We're the seculars. We're guided by reason. We make rational decisions. And it isn't rational to sacrifice a man like Elliott St. James, merely because he's greedy."

"I still don't understand."

"For one thing, he's rich. Very rich. His resources are useful to us."

"You're richer."

"Maybe so. You'd have to ask my accountants. After a certain point, I stopped paying attention. In any event, I am no longer what I was. My contacts have thinned. Elliott, on the other hand, knows everyone, and has enough nasty information stored up in those files of his to bring pressure when we need it brought." Now the laugh is full and throaty. "And the best part is that because he's a journalist, he can compile his files without seeming to do anything wrong. I'll bet two dozen of his highest paid reporters mostly pour blackmail fodder into his files."

"I didn't know that."

"You do now. And I'll tell you another thing. Elliott is smart. Very smart. Fine, so he kicks at the traces a bit. Show me a thoroughbred who doesn't."

The aide attempts another sally. "Having Bethany Barclay in his clutches and letting her go isn't just kicking at the traces. It's interference with basic policy."

"Interference we can live with, as long as we can watch it happen—and, when necessary, run a little interference of our own. That's why we sacrificed Annabelle. Because of that side deal she'd made. And because she was drugged out and useless. We knew that little would be lost. The Garden was bound to put Bethany in motion. They'd been nibbling around her since Annabelle vanished. Naturally, I was aware of their thinking. And it made sense. Bethany is the smarter of the two, organized, disciplined. She'd easily pick up her best friend's trail, and all we had to do was follow."

"It was a risk, though, keeping the Council in the dark about your intentions. Especially about Annabelle."

The blue eyes darken. The Protector can change moods in a snap, and woe to those who lose track. "I suppose we all have our secrets, don't we, dear boy?" Then she laughs, the sound light and trilling once more. "To be one of us you have to love victory. Not simply want it. Crave it. You have to see winning as an end in itself. Means are trivial, you see. Victors write the history books." The eyes sparkle with excitement. "And winning is so easy when you have the technology we do. Those poor fools over in the Garden have never been able to grasp that. This whole thing started because they were able to send messages to Bethany's cell phone. But who provided the technology? We did. Technology that we could control, and turn to our own purposes when necessary. We knew the right moment to sacrifice Ken Kirkland and leave the clues that would send Bethany to Chicago when the Enemy couldn't get her moving. We were able to monitor activity inside the Village House when the Enemy couldn't. We found Bethany in Ashland when they couldn't. We tracked her and Janice Stafford to that motel when even the FBI was baffled. We snatched Janice—and now Bethany, wherever she may travel, will be working for us, as she should, rather than for the Enemy, or for poor Elliott." Again the admonitory finger comes up. "Which is not to say that Elliott's idea is a bad one. Always be willing to listen to new ideas, no matter how attached you are to the old ones. In this case, letting Bethany continue to run is better than taking her and finding out what she knows. That's why I felt free to sacrifice our friend the Professor. His usefulness in any event was at an end. The FBI had his picture. He was done."

The Protector has swiveled the chair around. Outside the window the vast emerald lawn rolls in smooth perfection toward distant hills where trees stand in serried ranks.

"Ours are the plans of centuries. We are patient people. We are rational. That's the other reason we'll defeat the Enemy. Not just because of our superior technology. But because we have no God to constrain our choice of methods. We are willing to do whatever is necessary. They allow what they call morality to hold them back. But it's not morality. It's fanaticism. And that fanaticism—their belief in the supernatural, in the afterlife, in this God of theirs—this foolishness, ironically, is the very force that makes proper battle impossible for them. The weight of its own contradictions means that the Enemy cannot possibly prevail. Our final victory is simply a matter of time."

"I agree, Protector."

"I know you do. Agreeing with me is your job." She stands up, surprisingly spry for her years. "I'm hungry. Have the steward bring me shirred eggs and toast."

"Yes, ma'am," says the aide.

Alone again, the Protector allows her smile to fade. There are challenges yet ahead. Big ones. Nevertheless, the Wilderness is winning. That is what matters. They have Janice, and therefore they have Bethany. They have their hands on the levers of the investigation. The loose ends are few. She sees no obvious route by which the Enemy might prevail. Not without the help of the God in whom she entirely disbelieves. There have been bad moments along the way, especially when Bethany dropped out of sight, but now they have her under proper control. Everything is proceeding according to plan. Slowly, slowly, the good humor returns to the deeply lined face of Lillian Hartshorne, Lord Protector.

AUTHOR'S NOTE

No "second" Pilate Stone exists or has ever been rumored. There is also no town of Pennville, Virginia. Both are myths I invented for this novel. Please don't go hunting for either one.

A. L. Shields

June, 2013